# RACIALIZING OBJECTIVITY

A VOLUME IN THE SERIES
## Journalism and Democracy
EDITED BY
*Kathy Roberts Forde and Sid Bedingfield*

# RACIALIZING OBJECTIVITY

HOW
THE WHITE
SOUTHERN PRESS
USED JOURNALISM
STANDARDS
TO DEFEND
JIM CROW

**GWYNETH MELLINGER**

University of Massachusetts Press
*Amherst and Boston*

Copyright © 2024 by University of Massachusetts Press
All rights reserved
Printed in the United States of America

ISBN 978-1-62534-810-4 (paper); 811-1 (hardcover)

Designed by Sally Nichols
Set in Adobe Minion Pro
Printed and bound by Books International, Inc.

Cover design by adam b. bohannon
Cover art by donatas1205 and Olga, *abstract background*, #37638563 and *newspaper background* #427481493, adobestock.com.

Library of Congress Cataloging-in-Publication Data

Names: Mellinger, Gwyneth, author.
Title: Racializing objectivity : how the white Southern press used journalism standards to defend Jim Crow / Gwyneth Mellinger.
Description: Amherst : University of Massachusetts Press, 2024. | Series: Journalism and democracy | Includes bibliographical references and index. |
Identifiers: LCCN 2024033350 (print) | LCCN 2024033351 (ebook) | ISBN 9781625348104 (paperback) | ISBN 9781625348111 (hardcover) | ISBN 9781685750817 (ebook) | ISBN 9781685750824 (epub)
Subjects: LCSH: Journalism—Southern States—History—20th century. | African Americans—Segregation—History—Press coverage. | Racism in the press—Southern States. | African Americans—Southern States—History—20th century. | American newspapers—Southern States—History—20th century. | African American newspapers—History—20th century. | Press and politics—Southern States. | BISAC: HISTORY / African American & Black | HISTORY / United States / State & Local / South (AL, AR, FL, GA, KY, LA, MS, NC, SC, TN, VA, WV)
Classification: LCC PN4893 .M45 2024 (print) | LCC PN4893 (ebook) | DDC 071.375—dc23/eng/20240814
LC record available at https://lccn.loc.gov/2024033350
LC ebook record available at https://lccn.loc.gov/2024033351

British Library Cataloguing-in-Publication Data
A catalog record for this book is available from the British Library.

Part of chapter 1 was previously published as
"An Idea before Its Time: Charles S. Johnson, Negro Columnist,"
*Journal of Human and Civil Rights* 4, no. 2 (Fall 2018): 62–89.

For Mike and Cassady, as always

# CONTENTS

*Preface and Acknowledgments* ix

INTRODUCTION
1

CHAPTER 1
**INDICTING (AND OTHERING) THE BLACK PRESS**
RESECURING RACIAL BOUNDARIES DURING
THE WAR DECADE
28

CHAPTER 2
**THE AP AND THE NEGRO IDENTIFIER**
AN IDEOLOGICAL BATTLE FOR
JOURNALISM STANDARDS
64

CHAPTER 3
**THE POLITICS OF MEANING**
HARRY ASHMORE AND THE GRADUALIST
NEWS NARRATIVE
93

CHAPTER 4
**SOUTH VERSUS NORTH**
THE MASON-DIXON LINE IN
JOURNALISM STANDARDS
126

CHAPTER 5
**OBJECTIVITY THROUGH A DIXIE PRISM**
WHITENESS AND THE SOUTHERN EDUCATION
REPORTING SERVICE
161

AFTERWORD
**"THE BIRTH OF A NOTION"**
204

*Notes* 217
*Index* 269

# PREFACE AND ACKNOWLEDGMENTS

*Racializing Objectivity* is the story of white southern journalism's defensive reaction to the ethical mandate for social justice that propelled the freedom struggle during the 1940s and 1950s. A full telling of twentieth-century press history must reckon with white southern positions on racial (in)equality and white editors' distortion of professional norms as they constructed self-serving narratives about Black Americans, northern whites, and racial democracy. As such, this book shows that white southern editors used objectivity and other journalism standards as a professional rationalization for white supremacy and a political strategy to resist desegregation. This book argues that white skin privilege gave white Americans a stake in the racial status quo and was, therefore, a conflict of interest for white journalists and editors who defended Jim Crow. By claiming journalistic objectivity and neutrality, white southern editors attempted to conceal their ideology and reframed their objection to desegregation as a debate over professional standards. Within the Associated Press (AP) news service, for example, white southern editors advocated, with some success, that stereotypical representations of Black Americans were accurate reporting. Their agitation altered the news values in the AP's daily wire report.

Standpoint is a theoretical consideration throughout the book, and this white scholar, a former journalist transplanted from the North to a southern university, must acknowledge her own vantage and its implications for the historical project. I grew up in Kansas where a "Brown paradox" helped mold my thinking on race and whiteness. In the years after World War II, Topeka's residential segregation generated the racial grievance that culminated in the landmark *Brown v. Board of Education* decision and outlawed segregated schools.[1] That ruling immortalized Kansas into legal history as a bastion of Jim Crow, but the state's preferred self-image, a white perspective, foregrounded a nineteenth-century "Bleeding Kansas" narrative that placed Kansas on the right side of America's central moral question about race. That version ignored the Indigenous residents and valorized the Kansas Territory's white settlers as Free Staters and Jayhawkers, antislavery militants who defeated the proslavery terrorists who slipped over the border from Missouri to murder and plunder in the years before Kansas's 1861 statehood. Whether to allow or reject slavery was, in the historical frame taught in the Kansas public schools I entered in the 1960s, a moral choice that defined the character of white Kansans.

This history also was inscribed into the state's public culture, and its double standards and contradictions were difficult to ignore by the mid-twentieth century. Across town from where young Linda Brown had to attend segregated Monroe School, prompting her father to sue the Topeka School Board, the white-virtue narrative was documented on the walls of the Kansas Statehouse. There, "Tragic Prelude," a thirty-foot mural by John Steuart Curry, featured the other Topeka Brown, the white abolitionist John Brown—wild-eyed, larger than life, and ready to die for a principle, a Bible in one hand and a rifle in the other. Painted in the early 1940s at the behest of newspaper editor William Allen White, the scene presents "Bleeding Kansas" as a harbinger of an avoidable Civil War and the white South as having made the tragically wrong choice to defend slavery.[2]

I was among the thousands of schoolchildren who have filed past the mural on field trips to the State Capitol, and at some point I heard about *Brown v. Board*, which was framed as a solved historical problem, irrelevant to those of us in all-white grade schools.[3] Eventually, the gaps in the official history on race begged for attention, and I became concerned about America's broader democratic contradiction, that racial inequity could endure in a country governed by our Constitution and its amendments, particularly the Thirteenth through Fifteenth. In the 1980s, when I was a journalist in Topeka, the American Civil Liberties Union reopened *Brown v. Board of Education* because the public schools, reflecting neighborhood attendance districts, remained de facto segregated.[4] The irony of Topeka's two Browns was impossible to ignore.

Over time I became curious about another democratic paradox, the segregated American press and the role of white newspaper editors in maintaining racial barriers despite their self-image as defenders of freedom who gave voice to the voiceless. As I read white editors' own words, published and private, I realized that the white southern press—based on circulation and regional economics—had outsized influence over American journalism at midcentury, just when the nation was deciding its racial future. Yet white southern editors, who were defending a racial status quo that placed them on the wrong side of the American moral question, routinely manipulated journalism standards to protect and advance their racial narrative. And because they claimed to be defending professional integrity, the newspaper industry in the North entertained their objections to integration. I began traveling to the South for this research when the Confederate flag still flew over the State House in South Carolina and Confederate heroes towered above Monument Avenue in Richmond. I had become a Virginia resident by 2017, when racism and antisemitism brought violence to Charlottesville.

That more recent event arose on the same continuum with the white supremacy in this book's history of the 1940s and 1950s. The white southern editors we meet in *Racializing Objectivity* show us that our current struggles over the racial narrative feed contemporary identity politics, just as they did for previous generations. A powerful white backlash now demonizes antiracism, whiteness theory, critical race theory, and social construction in studying and discussing race. The message: white people should not be made to feel uncomfortable about America's racist past. At this writing, public school (K–12) curricula are the primary targets of the new defenders of white culture, but censoring university teaching and scholarship is also on the far-right agenda. I finished this book knowing that my academic freedom could be challenged, but I also documented my intellectual debts so anyone wanting to audit my work for ideological clues can find me. No one who cares about social justice and intellectual honesty should shrink from this fight; I do indeed theorize race—and everything else—critically. Writing this book is no less a political act than the advocacy of white southern editors who defended the racial status quo after *Brown* or their ideological descendants who have declared war on wokeness; however, by acknowledging my own stake in the American racial binary and my antiracist aspirations, I strive to write transparent history.

Given the attention paid to racial identifiers by our historical subjects in the 1940s and 1950s, usage in the book becomes important for both theory and archival accuracy. As a white scholar mindful of power differentials embedded in text, I choose to use "white" without capitalization.[5] This book intentionally uses the term "Black," not "African American," because not all Black Americans have African descent. Racial designations change over time as common usage and social understanding evolve, and this is reflected in direct quotations that appear in the narrative. In addition, concrete newspaper style rules were still being negotiated after World War II. This book quotes references to "negro" and "colored" directly from historical sources, preserving racial identifiers that varied depending on the author or publisher and time period. Capitalization of the racial tag was an unsettled matter in the 1940s and 1950s, and sometimes an archived source wavered on style even within the same document. Therefore, readers may consider inconsistent racial references in direct quotations to be accurate. The narrative also includes direct quotations from private correspondence in which white southern editors used a racial slur that they likely would not have used in public.

Since moving to Virginia, I have been reminded of the two Topeka Browns and how place and perspective shift the racial narrative. Here, the NAACP's Prince Edward County litigation, one of the four other cases incorporated into the Supreme Court's *Brown v. Board of Education* ruling, is more historically significant, as is *Loving v. Virginia*, the 1967 ruling that legalized interracial marriage—the white supremacist fear that energized the defense of Jim Crow a decade earlier.[6] This is also where the abolitionist Brown, more zealot than tactician, met his predictable end. John Brown's hanging took place at Harpers Ferry, now just over the border in West Virginia, and a national historical park memorializes the failed slave insurrection that sent him to the gallows. Although the two Browns in Topeka show that a racial narrative is inherently self-interested and incomplete, they also teach us that antiracism is a choice, even if we execute it imperfectly. In pursuit of social justice, we must continuously struggle against the undertow of our white supremacist history.

The research and writing of this book spanned more than a decade, as I applied theory to history in papers and panel presentations at perhaps sixteen conferences and symposia. I am therefore indebted to a community of scholars far larger than I could possible identify here—colleagues who offered blind review, comments from an audience, or insights in passing. Most important were the American Journalism Historians Association (AJHA), the History Division of the Association for Education in Journalism and Mass Communication (AEJMC), the International Communication Association, the Media and Civil Rights History Symposium at the University of South Carolina, and the H-Net monthly online JHistory Salon.

This work benefited from scholarly generosity that exceeded my imagination. In 2011 Doug Cumming, who had decided not to write a book from his dissertation on the Southern Education Reporting Service, gave me extensive notes on the literature and archives I would need to pursue that scholarship. Kathy Roberts Forde and Sid Bedingfield were mentors and friends before they became my series editors. Michael Fuhlhage read the entire manuscript; Ryan Alessi and A. J. Bauer commented on chapters. I received extraordinary guidance from knowledgeable and diligent blind reviewers whose insightful critiques improved the book. This was just one bonus of working with Matt Becker and the University of Massachusetts Press.

I also am indebted to media historians who supported my work and made this solo author feel that she was not really working alone: Kenneth Campbell, Erin Coyle, David Davies, Aimee Edmondson, John Ferré, Dolores Flamiano, Melita Garza, Alex Leidholdt, Terry Lueck, Kim Mangun, Randy Patnode, Mike Sweeney, Ashley Walter, and Pat Washburn. At specific junctures Fred Blevens, David Katzman, Carolyn Kitch, Anamik Saha, Henry Suggs, and Sherrie Tucker offered important validation. Special thanks to Elliot King, David Mindich, and the JHistory denizens.

Three universities supported this work with internal grants and leaves: James Madison, Xavier, and Baker. The research and writing also were funded by a Rockefeller Foundation Archives Grant-in-Aid; the AJHA Joseph McKerns Research Grant (twice); and, from the University of South Carolina, the W. J. B. Dorn Research Grant and the Ronald T. and Gayla D. Farrar Award in Media and Civil Rights History.

The research entailed extensive work in several archives, where I received assistance from dozens of colleagues over the years. Special thanks go to Francesca Pitaro and Valerie Komor and their team at the Associated Press Corporate Archive; Mary Ann Quinn, who assisted me at the Rockefeller and Ford Foundation archives in Sleepy Hollow, New York; and Herb Hartsook at the University of South Carolina Political Collection. Kathy Elliott, Ryssa Kemper, John Gruver, and Sherry Brooks provided invaluable help processing documents from my research.

Part of chapter 1 was previously published as "An Idea before Its Time: Charles S. Johnson, Negro Columnist," *Journal of Human and Civil Rights* 4, no. 2 (Fall 2018): 62–89. Thanks to editor Michael Ezra for permission to incorporate that scholarship here.

My husband, Mike Auchard, has patiently lived with this book since its inception, reading all the drafts and providing unconditional support for my labor of love. I could not have asked for a more generous partner.

My parents, Eisenhower Republicans who epitomized the white, postwar middle class, have been on my mind during this project. This was their time, and I deeply missed being able to gauge their perspectives on my research. During my childhood three newspapers were delivered to our doorstep each day, five when the Kansas Legislature was in session. The Associated Press narrated most of the national and regional news in those papers, and as this book shows, molded news about race on orders of the segregationists in the southern press. As I remember my father in his reading chair, the target audience for the campaign to racialize objectivity is not theoretical.

# RACIALIZING OBJECTIVITY

# INTRODUCTION

When the *Brown v. Board of Education* rulings effectively outlawed Jim Crow segregation, Don Shoemaker, the white former editor of a North Carolina newspaper, became an apostle for journalistic objectivity.[1] As director of the Southern Education Reporting Service (SERS), whose mission was nonpartisan journalism about the unfolding school desegregation story, Shoemaker traveled the country in the mid-1950s to advance the SERS's claim to be an impartial source of news about the southern response to *Brown* and the racial upheaval it portended. In speeches to local clubs and other organizations, Shoemaker hoped to expand the SERS's readership—school administrators, government officials, and citizens who closely followed the desegregation issue—and persuade them that the constraints of journalistic objectivity ensured that SERS reporting on racial conflict was free of ideology and served no political agenda. According to this logic, any reader, regardless of sentiment about racial law and custom, should consider information in *Southern School News*, the SERS's monthly publication, to be accurate, truthful, and unbiased because the SERS's white reporting staff, all of them southerners, had pledged faithfulness to objectivity. As evidence of the news service's impartiality, SERS leaders noted that members of both the National Association for the Advancement of Colored People (NAACP) and White Citizens' Councils were among readers of *Southern School News*. Subscription orders from Georgia governor Herman Talmadge, a segregationist, and writer Lillian Smith, an antilynching advocate, had arrived in the same day's mail.[2] With this claim, Shoemaker struck a pose of neutrality, presenting himself and the SERS as dispassionate referees whose objectivity could be taken for granted.

In arguing that the professional standard of objectivity made journalism credible to readers with divergent views on segregation, Shoemaker attempted an unlikely maneuver, namely positing objectivity as an ethical absolute at the same time that he embraced ethical relativism. While noting that "one man's facts may be another man's prejudices," Shoemaker insisted to an audience in Kinston, North Carolina, that *Southern School News* reported the desegregation story "right down the middle and bereft of personal opinion."[3] In the mid-1950s the methodology for objective journalism was fairly rudimentary: censuring use of adjectives and other signals of opinion and requiring a nonjudgmental balancing of opposing views within a story. Under this rubric, the two sides in the separate-but-equal debate were made morally and ethically equivalent; in theory, ideology was erased if both perspectives were given equal voice. "From our standpoint," Shoemaker said, "the word 'segregation' without the prefix is as important as the word with it—that is, 'desegregation.' For we are reporters, not advocates. We are gatherers and dispensers of facts." This, Shoemaker told a New York audience, was a "necessary declaration of faith. . . . It is faith in the words 'factual' and 'objective,' which we have nailed to our masthead."[4]

Shoemaker was just one white southern advocate for objectivity and other journalism values after World War II, when Black demands for civil rights collided with the racial status quo. As the legal framework of Jim Crow began to wobble, many in the white southern press felt their control of the news narrative slipping away and clung to professional standards to ensure that the rough draft of history presented in white newspapers validated the norm of a segregated society. As such, the SERS's claim to be all things to all people after the *Brown* decisions was anything but a stand for political neutrality on the twentieth century's defining controversy over social (in)justice. Under the banner of objectivity, Shoemaker and his white southern peers hoped to make both tacit and overt approval of racism appear to be ethical choices on a plane with support of integration. An objective news story, they argued, would portray segregation as a social preference, not an institution that was now illegal; whites who opposed "racial mixing" as one of two sides in a developing news story; and Black Americans as unfit for integrated society. In this way, the southern white press continually weaponized journalism standards to discredit reporting that challenged the assumptions of white supremacy.[5]

For the Southern Education Reporting Service, a project ostensibly committed to the ideal of objectivity as well as to balance and accuracy, the vibrant Black press would have been a logical source of journalists to cover the unfolding civil rights story. On the contrary, Black voices were pointedly excluded from the SERS reporting staff, just as they were excluded from most newsrooms of the white daily press. On this point, Shoemaker's comments on the lecture circuit pertained to the practice of journalism in the mid-twentieth century, when the profession was segregated into a white press and a Black press—each staffed, with few exceptions, by unintegrated newsrooms; each supported by racially defined news services and professional associations; and each prioritizing the interests of their respective monoracial communities.[6] The Black press, which developed organically in the nineteenth century in opposition to racial exclusion by the white press, is a case study in institutional racism within the public sphere and profession of journalism. As historian Kathy Roberts Forde noted, "To understand the role of the Black press and print culture in resisting white supremacy, we must also understand the role of the white press in constituting it."[7] In the twentieth century, the white press systematically employed journalism standards as a purportedly colorblind strategy to prevent integration of its newsrooms and claimed a news value in racial distinctions that continually reasserted white superiority in news content. For example, many white southern editors insisted that Black Americans be designated as "Negro" in news stories distributed by the Associated Press (AP) wire service, claiming it was necessary for accuracy and objectivity even as white news subjects went unlabeled. Similarly, through their unrelenting activism during the 1950s, white southern members of the AP elevated the news value of stories that made Black Americans seem deviant, antisocial, and unqualified for citizenship as both a justification for segregation and a response to unflattering northern reporting on white southern animosity toward them. Journalism standards provided the ideological cover.

Because power historically accrued to whiteness in American politics and culture, no white journalists, even those who recognized the fundamental injustice of segregation, could be truly disinterested in the outcome of the freedom struggle. For all white journalists and editors, but most particularly white southerners, the personal stakes entailed in the racial caste system constituted an unavoidable and perhaps irreconcilable conflict of interest, an ethical quandary that undergirds this historical analysis. As such, this book offers a counternarrative to much civil rights history that assumes Black Americans alone were invested in the movement's outcome. Although many white people, mostly situated in the North, were sincere in supporting the Black quest for civil rights, good intention could not resolve racial inequity that was structured into an institution like American journalism.[8] Even the most egalitarian whites benefited from the status quo, which was predicated on the value of white identity in opposition to a devalued, nonwhite "other."[9] The segregated American press is therefore a racial project in which, according to the theory of Michael Omi and Howard Winant, "race becomes 'common sense,' a way of comprehending, explaining, and acting in the world."[10] Moreover, the ideological work of the racial project relies on essentialized definitions of race, such as those that marginalized the Black press and Black news subjects, and also requires the project itself to continually resecure racial distinctions and racial domination.[11]

In addition to the inherent legal, political, economic, and social advantages of their racial classification, white southerners of this era shared a history grounded in the legacy of the Civil War, the Lost Cause narrative, and the myth of separate-but-equal. Even for southerners who were born generations after emancipation, narratives about the meaning and significance of white southern-ness were passed down within white families; however, these shared understandings also permeated the broader white community, where they were enshrined in collective memory—for example, in statues, parks, holidays, and other public commemorations of the Confederacy—and were taken for granted as fact.[12] So present was the southern past, David Goldfield noted, that "southerners growing up in the first half of the twentieth century found dating the [Civil] war difficult because their elders often discussed the conflict as if it had happened yesterday or was still in progress."[13] Media products—including newspapers, magazines, books, and films—also validated and normalized popular constructions of white superiority and Black inferiority, embedding Black subjugation and Negrophobia into the American psyche as common sense.[14] With its counternarrative, the twentieth-century civil rights movement challenged the orthodoxy of white supremacy that kept Black people in their place. As Jason Sokol observed of white reaction, "The freedom struggle forced sudden cataclysms and gradual transformations in southern race relations—the kinds of changes that had been felt only one other time in the life of the South: After the Civil War."[15]

Shoemaker's embrace of journalistic objectivity affirms how politically fraught this historical juncture appeared to the white journalists and editors who navigated it. In the late 1940s and 1950s white southerners who edited newspapers for white southern readers and reported on *Brown* and other challenges to Jim Crow segregation were chronicling a historic repudiation of a way of life that depended on white-skin privilege. As the federal courts rewrote the rules of southern society, the defense of journalism standards offered segregationists in the southern press a professionally expedient response that obfuscated their actual objection to integration. By restating their position not as racism but as a stand for journalistic integrity, white southern editors presented themselves as professionally noble and forced racial liberals in the North to engage their arguments, even though the racial politics of segregation were odious to many outside the white South. Ultimately, through agitation within the profession, the white southern press altered the midcentury conversation about race and journalism by normalizing the segregationist perspective in the national news narrative.

## Racial and Regional Divides

A foundational curiosity of this book is how professional journalism standards, a normative template fashioned by the white press, functioned as a racial mechanism, valorizing white news workers and their news narratives while delegitimizing racial "others" based on assumptions about disparities in white and Black aptitude for journalism. This included the capacity for meeting the professional expectation of objectivity and its defining components, among them accuracy, balance, and fairness. At stake were questions of how Black Americans would be portrayed in their quest for social justice, who was allowed to tell the story of southern whiteness before and after *Brown,* and how the civil rights story could be framed. Within white racial discourse both North and South, the Black press, the primary advocate for Black equality, was largely invisible unless the white press held it up to ridicule or used examples of its content to warn white readers of the danger of integration. This was the case during World War II, for example, when Virginius Dabney, editor of the *Richmond Times-Dispatch,* and conservative syndicated columnist Westbrook Pegler, both writing for national audiences, accused the Black press of being unpatriotic by promoting a Double V campaign to secure civil rights at home as well as freedom abroad.[16]

Although southern whites were usually unaware of what Black newspapers were saying about civil rights and would have dismissed those concerns had they read them, the disapproving fascination of northern whites was another matter entirely. The scornful northern press, enthralled by undemocratic and sometimes violent segregationist reaction to *Brown,* fueled defensive outrage by white southerners who believed the federal courts had overreached and were trampling regional customs that outsiders simply did not understand. Moreover, southern whites believed their regional history and the large Black population in the South gave them greater insight into the true nature of Black people, making the white southern press more qualified to tell the story of civil rights than either Black newspapers or the northern white press.[17]

On this point, the Mason-Dixon line supplied a second ideological fault line for the segregationist press. During the first half of the twentieth century, the northern white press's relentless and pointed scrutiny of southern social norms had exacerbated historical tensions between the victors of the Civil War and the vanquished in what historian George Tindall termed the "benighted South."[18] Most notoriously, columnist H. L. Mencken, writing for the *New York Evening Mail* in 1917, took aim at the region's culture—its *beaux arts*—in a column titled "The Sahara of the Bozart."[19] There, Mencken complained of the artistic and political barrenness of the South and charged "that the civil war actually finished off nearly all the civilized folk in the South and thus left the country to the poor white trash, whose descendants now run it."[20] Mencken continued his assault on the South throughout much of his career, most prominently at the *Baltimore Evening Sun* and as editor of the magazine *American Mercury.* The northern media, led by Mencken, descended on Dayton, Tennessee, in 1925 to document and mock the southern religious conservatism on display in the Scopes "monkey trial," which criminalized the teaching of evolution in the public schools.[21] This sustained critique of southern culture, coming from a prominent columnist with a national audience, intensified the regional self-consciousness of the white southern editors considered in this book and contributed to what Angie Maxwell described as a southern inferiority complex. "For many white southerners, the denunciation of southern culture throughout the twentieth century resulted in an intensified clinging to the power and privilege associated with their whiteness," she wrote and noted that "southern whiteness is unique in the sense that it is constructed by oppressing a black 'other,' while serving paradoxically as the 'other' in the larger construct of American identity."[22]

Mencken's second important contribution to the North-South divide was his mentorship of W. J. Cash, the North Carolina journalist whose iconoclastic *The Mind of the South* remains a leading explication of white southern cultural history. A book with broad and enduring influence in both North and South but for very different reasons, *The Mind of the South* offers a historically contextualized analysis of the white southern legacy and white lived experience. That Cash was a white journalist adds to his book's relevance to this project; that he died by suicide just months after its publication in 1941, amid concerns about how the book would be received in his homeland, enhances its reputation and intrigue.[23] Cash wrote that the mandatory defense of slavery in southern society had "set up a ban on all analysis and inquiry, a terrified truculence toward every new idea, a disposition to reject every innovation out of hand and hug to the whole of the *status quo* with fanatical resolution." In the early twentieth century, Cash worried about "certain rising fears and hates" that evoked the white southern past, "the first were the resurgent fear and hate of the Negro."[24] For white editors in the midcentury South, many of whom had known Cash, *The Mind of the South* acknowledged racism's constitutive role in white southern-ness and deepened both the region's stigma and their own sense of alienation from the national American identity.

Cash's book appeared three years before Gunnar Myrdal's two-volume treatise, *An American Dilemma: The Negro Problem and Modern Democracy*, which explained the racial caste system in the United States and paid particular attention to the South. Myrdal made multiple references to Cash and betrayed Cash's influence when he wrote, "The South is intensely conscious of its history, and there is a high level of historical knowledge among the educated classes. But history is not used, as in the North, to show how society is continuously changing, but rather, on the contrary, to justify the status quo and to emphasize society's inertia." Although Myrdal was optimistic that "the material and spiritual changes under way are so momentous that they cut through these barriers," he could not anticipate the political siege that would paralyze much of the South after *Brown* mandated integrated schools a decade later.²⁵

In many accounts of the renewed animosity between the northern and southern white presses following World War II, the defining moment is pegged in 1955, when wire services, metropolitan and international newspapers, and magazines set up camp in Mississippi for the trial and exoneration of the murderers of Emmett Till, a fourteen-year-old Black lynching victim. As Gene Roberts and Hank Klibanoff noted, the Till trial was "the first massive move by the northern press" to cover civil rights in the South, and the northern audience, forced to reckon with the unspeakable cruelty of lynching and the white psychosis that enabled and excused it, was "shocked and shakened by what they read."²⁶ The South's response to *Brown* was thus ensconced as a white news beat, and the northern press routinely chronicled the defensive excesses of a region whose racial culture had been delegitimized by the U.S. Supreme Court. The white mothers who were photographed screaming racial epithets at Black children trying to enter southern schools affirmed a stereotype exploited by Mencken but reinvigorated by northern news coverage of the Till trial and white southern candor about the prospect of integration after *Brown*. The vilification and stigmatization of the South by the northern press in the 1950s merely extended an established narrative.

Many white southern editors believed such media portrayals of civil rights resisters were unfair, that their neighbors' opposition to integration was justified within the context of southern history but the reasons for their defiance were ignored by a biased northern press uninterested in the objective reporting of facts. Writing in *Harper's* in 1956, Thomas R. Waring, editor of the *News and Courier* in Charleston, South Carolina, asserted that "few white Southerners are able to accept the prospect of mingling white and Negro pupils." This, he alleged, was understandable because Black Americans lacked white, middle-class values and had slower intellectual development as well as higher rates of venereal disease, divorce, and crime. Waring lambasted "the almost unanimous attitude of the national press—daily and weekly—toward the subject of race," which had dismissed the southern commitment to racial purity. "The testimony these publications print is almost entirely one-sided," Waring wrote. "While less violent than the Negro press—which understandably presents only the militant anti-segregation case—the metropolitan press almost without exception has abandoned fair and objective reporting of the race story. For facts it frequently substitutes propaganda."[27] Waring and other white southern editors described this presumed censorship of the segregationist perspective as a "paper curtain" separating North and South.[28]

In this vein, many white southern editors sought to deflect attention from the South's racism by charging that the northern press's criticism of de jure segregation and racial injustice in the Jim Crow South was disingenuous, given the de facto segregation throughout much of the North. Indeed, as Black Americans migrated from South to North, fleeing poverty and terrorism, white southern editors were pleased to note that northern cities experienced increased racial "strife" and "friction" when their Black populations increased. This the southern editors blamed on the arrival of Black people, not white reaction to their presence. Several southern editors, including Waring and Grover Hall Jr. of the *Montgomery [AL] Advertiser*, responded to northern critiques of southern racism by charging the northern press with journalistic hypocrisy. Hall's paper even reported on housing segregation and other racial ills in northern cities with large Black populations.[29] Editors' agitation on behalf of the conservative white South also entailed protests within the Associated Press news service cooperative, where they used their status as member-owners to lobby for journalism that affirmed the segregationist perspective and emphasized racial unrest and Black crime, particularly Black-on-white crime, in the North. Anything else, they argued, was not objective or accurate.

## The Ideology of Segregation

This analysis brackets for emphasis the period beginning with World War II, when a new conversation about civil rights seemed genuinely possible because the United States was fighting racism and fascism abroad, to 1957, when the confrontation over the forced integration of Central High School in Little Rock, Arkansas, concluded the first wave of southern resistance to *Brown*. By declaring segregated public schools to be unconstitutional, the *Brown* decision in 1954 and the implementation ruling in 1955 signaled changes in daily life that were unthinkable for many segregationists, including some white newspaper editors and journalists. After the United

States and its allies won a global war to save democracy, defense of Jim Crow at home became less tenable. Segregationists had watched for more than a decade, many with apprehension and dismay, as an invigorated civil rights movement chipped away at institutionalized segregation.[30] In the years leading up to *Brown*, white supremacists lamented such gains for Black Americans as President Franklin Roosevelt's implementation of the Fair Employment Practices Committee in 1941; President Harry Truman's integration of the U.S. military in 1948; and a series of U.S. Supreme Court rulings that, among other things, began the integration of graduate schools, outlawed the white primary, banned segregation on interstate transportation, and found race-based real estate covenants to be unconstitutional.[31] As Numan V. Bartley observed, "For the first time since Reconstruction, the federal government was launching a serious and sustained attack on southern racial practices."[32]

Even so, many white southerners initially hoped the *Brown* decisions would prove as toothless as the 1896 ruling in *Plessy v. Ferguson,* which had not compelled southern states to provide the separate-but-equal accommodations and public schools that the ruling designated as constitutional. Mississippian Hodding Carter Jr., one of the few white southern editors who sometimes editorialized on behalf of racial fairness, wrote in 1954 following the first *Brown* ruling: "If ever a region asked for such a decree, the South did through its shocking, calculated, cynical disobedience to its own state constitutions, which specify that separate school systems must be equal. For 75 years, we sent Negro kids to school in hovels and pig pens."[33] Carter's was a voice in the wilderness, however. Less controversial in the white South of the mid-1950s was the states'-rights embrace of James J. Kilpatrick of the *Richmond [VA] News Leader*, who editorialized that the *Brown* decision was "a rape of the Constitution."[34] Because flagrant defiance of the legal and ethical mandate in *Plessy* had brought no obvious repercussions for their parents and grandparents, many white southerners initially expected the racial status quo to remain intact after *Brown*, that local defiance ultimately would prevail over federal intervention.

What may seem like magical thinking in presentist retrospect, as we consider this period from a remove of many decades and knowing how the whole thing turned out, is actually a measure of the disconnect between the ingrained white supremacist beliefs of many white southerners and a growing, though certainly not universal, acceptance of integration as fundamental fairness by the white population in the North and West. Until President Dwight Eisenhower federalized the Arkansas National Guard in 1957 and sent the 101st Airborne Division to Little Rock to ensure the integration of Central High School, the desegregation mandate was, for many racially conservative white southerners, merely theoretical. As Elizabeth Gillespie McRae wrote, "For segregationists who were counting on avoiding *Brown*, the two years following the decision sent some hopeful signs." A segregationist counteroffensive was in place in local school districts, stalling integration plans in many communities throughout the South, and the NAACP, whose litigation secured legal mandates for racial change, had been hamstrung by laws in most southern states that limited or outlawed its activism.[35] Indeed, until 1958 it also seemed plausible to optimistic southern whites that implementation of *Brown* could be thwarted by massive resistance to forced school integration, led by editor Kilpatrick in Richmond and founded on a shaky constitutional premise.[36] After Little Rock, however, the rhetoric about race sharply intensified as segregationists shifted from a defensive pose of watchful waiting to the offensive stance of intractable resistance to an existential threat. After Little Rock, McRae wrote, "Invasion and occupation became the rallying cries for anyone who wanted to invoke the image of a behemoth federal government, unresponsive to the wishes of its white citizens."[37]

Many histories of the civil rights movement and the press emphasize the eventful decade after Little Rock when the visual, public drama of lunch-counter sit-ins and police assaults on freedom riders and peaceful marchers drew the attention of television news networks and made white southern defiance a national story.[38] Instead, this analysis focuses intentionally on wartime rhetoric and the postwar years leading up to Little Rock in order to observe the ideological maneuverings that took place before white resistance to desegregation hardened.[39] Before the confrontation at Central High School in 1957, arguments over racial equity could still be nuanced as southern white editors and journalists, as well as many of their readers, responded with varying degrees of stridency and acquiescence to the specter of the *Brown* decision and more openly discussed their assumptions about the southern past, present, and future. Before Little Rock, many white editors and journalists still rationalized segregation, within the context of southern history, as social control that benefited Black people as well as whites or as an antiquated custom that would eventually disappear if the South were left alone, or both.

In their professional debates over the journalistic standards of objectivity, accuracy, and fairness, and in their squabbles with the northern press over negative—and biased, in their view—coverage of the South, many white southern editors manipulated journalism standards in an effort to control the news narrative about Black Americans and civil rights and, in the most extreme cases, to frame racism as normal and necessary. Moderate editors, in contrast, tended to accept the inevitability of desegregation and support gradualism, delaying integration as either a strategy to thwart *Brown* or a means to preserve the peace, because violent white supremacists might offer less resistance to slow and incremental change.[40] According to the racial logic that replaced Jim Crow in the post-*Brown* South, Black Americans, who were assumed to have been happy with segregation until they were manipulated and agitated by northern interest groups with communist ties, an accusation often lodged at the NAACP, were not the oppressed; rather, the once-again-invaded white South was the victim whose rights had been violated.[41] As Sokol noted, "A peculiar conception of individual freedom animated many white southerners—the freedom to segregate oneself by race, regardless of what others desired." In this construct, demands for black equality "looked like villainous attempts to challenge whites' freedom."[42]

As they met these challenges to the southern way of life, white southern editors did not keep their own counsel. Instead, they wrestled with the poignancy of the moment in private correspondence and publicly on their editorial pages—but also in speeches, books, and magazine articles targeted to audiences inside and outside the region, documenting their thinking as it evolved or calcified. In the process, these editors joined a long tradition of white southern writers who felt compelled to defend their homeland to disapproving outsiders, what literary historian Fred C. Hobson Jr. called "the southern rage to explain."[43] Southern white editors and journalists sought to rationalize and, in some cases, justify the South's racial traditions to a national audience, even though they had criticized their northern and Black counterparts for similar engagement on behalf of civil rights. Even white southern editors who were less convinced that the segregationists should or would prevail made it their mission to explain and defend their region to northern audiences. And magazine and book publishers, aware of northern readers' insatiable demand for content about the South and civil rights, offered white southern editors plenty of venues for publication. As such, the archive for this history is broad and deep.

The professional community of journalism also provides an important framework for this discussion. The southern editors who debated the objectivity of reporting on race worked for newspapers that were members of the Associated Press news cooperative, the leading U.S. wire service for regional, national, and international news. The AP was already a century old at the end of World War II, having reported to the nation and the world on significant news events since before the Civil War, but dissension within the membership over race in the mid-twentieth century challenged the shared journalistic mission of the AP.[44] During the 1940s and 1950s, segregationist editors, a minority of the AP membership, were relentless in their complaints about AP content that portrayed Black Americans as worthy of full citizenship. In response, AP leadership and staff acquiesced to their demands and, when selecting stories for distribution on the wire, elevated the news value of reporting about racial disturbances and antisocial Black behavior. As a result, the southern faction forced the entire AP membership to receive news stories that stereotyped Black Americans and disqualified them, in the minds of segregationists, from equitable participation in American life.[45] Here again the archive is plentiful as the perspectives of editors in the South and North, as well as AP staff and leadership, are documented in extensive correspondence.

The experience of school desegregation and leading their communities through a period of historic change affected individual white editors differently. Some of the more racially conservative, like Waring of the Charleston *News and Courier* and Kilpatrick of the *Richmond News Leader*, became more fervent in their support of segregation during the 1950s. Racial moderates who were rewarded for their relative open-mindedness with Pulitzer Prizes also were changed by the experience of *Brown*: Virginius Dabney of the *Richmond Times-Dispatch* became more conservative; Ralph McGill of the *Atlanta Constitution* became more liberal; Harry Ashmore of the *Arkansas Democrat* in Little Rock left journalism and the South two years after the forced integration of Central High School; and Mississippian Hodding Carter Jr. of the *Delta Democrat-Times* in Greenville, a gradualist defender of basic racial fairness, won praise from the northern press, prompting Waring's newspaper to accuse him of communist sympathies.[46] As white southerners, these editors represented a philosophical spectrum on race but none of them supported *Brown*'s mandate to desegregate the schools, most believing, despite the high optimism entailed in the end of World War II, that a Supreme Court order was counterproductive federal intervention, that the South should have been allowed to manage its own racial affairs. None of them welcomed *Brown* as an opportunity to advance democracy. These are the white southerners of whom historian John Egerton asked, "Why did it take a virtual revolution in the courts and in the streets, and another generation of time, to bring us to a point that was almost within our reach when America . . . won the war and took the lead in the international crusade for freedom and democracy?"[47]

## Reframing History

This book shifts the frame of analysis to correct for distortions of history. The wedge of time has opened critical distance between the twentieth-century movement for civil rights and the present, reducing a grueling, daily, decades-long struggle to a list of legal, social, and political victories that disrupted American society in the 1950s and 1960s and reset the needle on racial (in)equality. Although helpful in documenting the historical record, the longer view emphasizes outcomes—a final scorecard—and skews perceptions of America's protracted racial past. The historicization of the movement diverts our attention from the painful ordeal that exacted such a high price from Black Americans since Reconstruction and before, fixing the freedom struggle in time as finished business and, most concerning for this book, obscuring the ambivalence and conscious resistance of segregationists—specifically newspaper editors and journalists—who worried that Black gains would come at the expense of white southern culture and its privileges. Although the northern white press had distinct blind spots regarding the political and material value of whiteness, southern journalism's resistance to integration had a peculiar historical dimension.

In the inevitable revisionism that followed passage of landmark civil rights legislation in the 1960s—the federal laws mandating equality in voting, employment, and housing—the freedom struggle was assigned to history and the media reframed it as a clearly defined contest between good and evil whose outcome, owing to the march of progress, was logical and predictable, even if some outlier whites resisted change. In this virtue narrative, implied in memoirs, documentaries, and press histories, the northern white journalist, the chronicler of human redemption, is often cast as a warrior for truth and social justice, standing firmly on the right side of a moral and ethical absolute.[48] In fact, in the U.S. South and much of the nation, equal rights for Black Americans were never foreordained and remained improbable through much of the 1950s, given the political and social obstacles. Looking back to the beginning of the New Deal, Jason Morgan Ward wrote, "Rather than a backlash against the unthinkable, the segregationist movement was a coordinated revolt against the foreseeable." Ward argued that resistance to *Brown* was embedded in southern culture, that segregationists were motivated not purely by the specter of school desegregation but by "longstanding anxieties over black civic equality, racial egalitarianism, and the federal government's role in promoting both."[49]

This book also shifts the frame on the history of the twentieth-century press and race. Of deep importance to this historical investigation are the ways in which the Black-white divide in journalism, specifically the segregation of news work and news audiences, worked in tandem with white southern resentment against the northern press to influence editorial decision-making and validate journalism sympathetic to Jim Crow. Central to this project, then, is the recognition that American journalism was a segregated profession attempting to report on the effort to desegregate other institutions, industries, and systems while preserving the racial exclusions that defined the American press. This analysis foregrounds this ethical contradiction to prevent white privilege from being taken for granted and disappearing from view. To that end, white editors and newspapers referenced in this discussion also are labeled by race.

Historical scholarship that discusses relations between the northern and southern presses and examines the regional divide during the modern civil rights movement must acknowledge conflicting claims about white southern identity. An extensive catalogue of scholarship recognizes, both implicitly and explicitly, that white southern-ness is a cultural identity that marks certain Americans and distinguishes them from others, with actual implications for their roles as citizens and access to the good life—though certainly not with the same consequences as a nonwhite identity.[50] In the context of this book, the regional fracture within white journalism must be viewed alongside the conclusions drawn by Matthew D. Lassiter and Joseph Crespino in their critique of the "myth of southern exceptionalism," which challenged civil rights historians' focus on southern racism to the exclusion of apartheid in the North. Their argument echoed the midcentury southern press's complaint about the hypocrisy of the northern press in acquiescing to the North's racial injustice while disparaging the South for codifying its racial inequity through law and custom.[51] Jeanne Theoharis implicated the northern press in perpetuating "the false distinction between a Southern 'de jure' segregation and a Northern 'de facto' segregation, making Northern segregation more innocent and missing the various ways such segregation was supported and maintained through law and political process."[52]

The white southern editors who complained about northern hypocrisy were not wrong; however, their motive was self-serving and neither altruistic nor democratic. Their primary goal in critiquing northern white journalism was to disparage Black people and discredit the cause of integration, not to enhance the profession, and any benefit to the common good was incidental. By invoking journalism standards to justify their what-aboutism and excuse southern racism, they affirmed the thesis of this book. Moreover, their racism foreclosed an alliance with Black newspapers, which had been making the same point about the northern white press for more than a century.[53]

## Constructing and Conferring Objectivity

By the time the American press was reporting on the *Brown* decision, objectivity—as a journalism practice, a professional value, and an assumption about how to report news—was firmly embedded in white newsroom culture and expectations. Since college-level journalism instruction began in the early years of the century, objectivity, which emphasized factual, verified, accurate, balanced, and impartial reporting, had been the norm guiding both journalists' attitudes toward their work and how routines and formulas for journalism were to be practiced in news work.[54] Columnist Walter Lippmann, in his criticisms of the press after World War I, had called for journalists to use the scientific method in gathering and reporting the news, on the theory that testing facts for accuracy, an emphasis on the process of news gathering rather than the abstract values underlying the concept of truth, would produce journalism that could be considered objective.[55] From an analysis of early journalism textbooks, Tim P. Vos found that "after 1920 the texts portrayed editorializing in the body of a news story and invention of colorful details as illegitimate practice." Vos also discovered that the framework of objectivity conferred special status on the journalist. "The texts mythologized objectivity by portraying it as a mechanical process overseen by journalists who were like scientists and professors," Vos wrote. "Objective journalists were heroic figures—homo journalisticus—who had mystical connections to the needs and desires of audiences."[56] This supports Michael Schudson's claim that in the 1920s, "the objectivity norm became a fully formulated occupational ideal, part of a professional project or mission. Far more than a set of craft rules or a set of constraints to help editors keep tabs on their underlings, objectivity was finally a moral code." To that end, the profession incorporated objectivity into its first ethical guidelines.[57]

Well before the 1950s, many news professionals also understood objectivity to be a flawed concept, one that was impractical within a profession that pursued truth and accuracy but published subjective versions of reality prepared by human beings with different life experiences. Schudson found that objectivity "as a professional value in journalism . . . seemed to disintegrate as soon as it was formulated." Objectivity's rise coincided with modernity's embrace of relativism: "It became an ideal in journalism, after all, precisely when the impossibility of overcoming subjectivity in presenting the news was widely accepted."[58] At the very least, context mattered. As the Commission on Freedom of the Press, chaired by Robert Hutchins, wrote in 1947, the press had a social responsibility to the public that included a commitment to accuracy, but "the account of an isolated fact, however accurate in itself, may be misleading and, in effect, untrue." The report noted, "It is no longer enough to report the *fact* truthfully. It is now necessary to report *the truth about the fact*."[59] Three decades later, Gaye Tuchman would theorize journalism's "Web of Facticity" and assert that "taken by itself, a fact has no meaning."[60]

Despite concerns about its limitations as a professional standard, objectivity retained its legitimacy as what Schudson described as "the chief occupational value of American journalism."[61] Stephen J. A. Ward asserted that "objectivity reached its zenith in the 1940s and 1950s," and despite the growing complexity of the news that journalists covered, "the ideal was *complete* detachment from events."[62] As such, it was easy for white southern editors, bristling at the midcentury journalism of Black Americans and northern whites, to ignore their own conflicts of interest and invoke objectivity in their defensive posture against *Brown* and civil rights activism. Although the definition of and rules for objectivity were open to interpretation, objectivity was still a firm value of the profession and a news report could be disputed and disarmed with an accusation that its reporting was biased. As David Mindich noted, designating a news subject or perspective as objective or not objective conferred either legitimacy or deviance on a news discourse.[63]

Conversely, members of the white southern press could claim objectivity in their own coverage of the race story, discrediting the counternarratives in the Black and northern presses and validating news coverage that reified the South's racial status quo. As such, southern whites who considered their own standpoint to be the only valid perspective on race were sincere in asserting that the white southern press was unbiased and reported the truth about racial conflict. David R. Davies observed that, as a methodology for reporting news about the civil rights movement and racial conflict, objectivity was wholly inadequate to the task because the divergent perspectives on civil rights foreclosed a consensus on accuracy. "Desegregation seemed, after all, to be a story that demanded interpretative reporting," Davies wrote.[64] As such, the decision by white southern editors to elevate and champion objectivity at precisely this historical juncture is significant as a marker of racial strategy.

In addition to being a vaunted professional ideal, objectivity, whose meaning was generally understood among journalists even without definition, became something of an umbrella term for the foundational professional standards in journalism, covering a range of expectations about accuracy, completeness, balance, impartiality, and fairness.[65] Journalistic discourse at midcentury conflated journalism standards, making the term "objectivity" interchangeable with the component parts of its meaning. A story by the Black or northern white press might fail a white southern test of accuracy, but the transgression was framed as a lack of objectivity, not simply an error of fact. Criticism that a story reported by a Black or northern white journalist was inaccurate or lacked balance generally assumed the reporter was advancing an integrationist political agenda and intentionally portraying the white South in a poor light. In contrast, the white southern press was deemed objective and politically neutral when it supported the racial status quo.

A debate about headline writing illustrates how this worked. All of the white editors discussed in this book were members of the American Society of Newspaper Editors (ASNE) and received its newsletter each month. In at least a dozen articles about objectivity in the *ASNE Bulletin* in the five years preceding the *Brown* decision, the concept was referred to as "deadpan" reporting, in contrast to the interpretive reporting that had evolved since the 1930s and received impetus from the Hutchins Commission's articulation of a social responsibility for the press.[66] In 1955, while the white South was still formulating a response to *Brown*, Waring, the racially conservative editor of the *News and Courier* in Charleston, joined the *ASNE Bulletin* debate about objectivity and took issue with a headline in an unidentified northern paper. His argument, which echoed his article a few months later in *Harper's*, employed objectivity as political strategy, even if it criticized the northern press for doing exactly that. "On at least one subject—race relations—the American press as a whole seems to have given up objectivity," Waring complained, taking issue with headline writers' use of the word "bias" instead of "segregation" above stories about the South. Although he conceded the utility of a four-letter word in the space allowed for a headline, Waring insisted "bias" was "a smear word." He wrote, "To defend the use of 'bias' requires belief that separation of the races is wrong in principle. If a paper wishes to take that position in editorials of course it has that right. It does not have the right to transfer editorial views to the news headlines and still claim 'objectivity.'"[67]

## Theorizing Objectivity

In this way, the concept of journalistic objectivity—when applied to reporting on race and offered as a professional standard by racially conservative white editors and journalists who claimed to be concerned primarily about news accuracy—did the ideological heavy lifting for the segregationist faction in American journalism and their enablers in the North. As with any social construct, development of professional understandings of journalistic objectivity has been historically contingent; in the case of journalistic objectivity, Michael Ryan found that the concept evolved alongside understandings of the scientific method and in response to public criticism of press standards.[68]

The concept of objectivity assumes that journalists work from a position of neutrality, a space that they can enter and depart at will.[69] As such, the journalistic understanding of objectivity used at midcentury imagined that journalists could attain a state of detachment and even ideological purity as they went about their work, specifically that journalists could step outside the strictures of their own social location, identity, and personal experience. Importantly, however, objectivity—as it was deployed in white southern journalism as a defense of racial and regional identity—assumed that objectivity was achievable only by members of the white southern press. Indeed, as a norm, and as the point of view from which truth is purportedly ascertained, journalistic objectivity implies the presence of an oppositional "other" who is not objective. White southern editors disqualified members of the Black and white northern presses from being capable of objectivity, claiming they had an inherent conflict of interest in reporting on civil rights. And yet, these critics did not recognize a similar conflict of interest in their own social location, as defenders of an embattled race-based caste system from which they benefited directly.

For the white southern editors described in this analysis, who began their journalism careers in the 1920s, 1930s, and 1940s, the professional expectations attached to objectivity were taken for granted when the postwar civil rights movement became breaking news.[70] This historical analysis does not dwell on the philosophical underpinnings of objectivity, its history beyond the period in question, or the decades-long debate over its general viability as a journalism standard. The purpose here is to examine how a group of white southern editors understood the concept during the 1940s and 1950s, and how they used its normative power as a tool within a broader ideological strategy to shape the news narrative about civil rights. The methodology used here aligns with Mindich's approach, that "'objectivity' is an active enterprise" rather than merely a theory or social construct. We can analyze its function through the uses to which journalists put it. "The criticism by 'objective' journalists of sensational and subjective journalism can tell as much about the critic as it does about the subject," he wrote.[71]

This book also is in conversation with Richard L. Kaplan's work on the history of objectivity, which affirms that "the pervasiveness of journalism's modern occupational ideal" made the standard easy to subvert for political ends. "According to [its] cultural image," Kaplan wrote, "journalism's only true duty consists in supplying factual and reliable information to the American citizenry." This position, which reflects segregationist editors' criticism of the Black and northern white presses during the civil rights movement, is a fallacy. "Indeed," Kaplan observed, "far from floating above the realm of politics, each crafted journalistic story implies a particular standpoint. The news as a construct of a detached professional is thus an unworkable illusion."[72] Southern white critics of the Black and northern white presses were correct that such journalism was ideological, but they were disingenuous in asserting that theirs was not and staking greater claim to the ethical high road.

The analysis that follows is informed by Schudson's significant contribution to the history of media sociology and professional practice but answers his concern about applying critical theory to an analysis of objectivity. He admonished scholars that "the cultural knowledge that constitutes 'news judgement' is too complex and too implicit to label simply 'ideology' or the 'common sense' of a hegemonic system. News judgement is not so unified, intentional and functional a system as those terms suggest," he wrote. "Its presuppositions are in some respects rooted much more deeply in human consciousness and can be found much more widely distributed in human societies than capitalism or socialism or industrialism or any other particular system of social organization and domination can comprehend."[73] This historical investigation does indeed posit that white southern editors' arguments about objectivity were ideological and partially explained by Gramscian "common sense," but it does so specifically to interrogate the editors' use of "objectivity" under the *guise* of news judgment, as a political strategy of resistance to historic social and political change.[74] Acknowledging the role of ideology in the subversion of objectivity as a professional standard does not minimize the complexity of the news judgment analyzed here. Rather, by tracing ideology through the consequences of white southern editors' moral and professional choices, we can assign accountability for outcomes without relying on editors' stated intentions or denials of culpability as an index of their motives.

## A Battle on Multiple Fronts

Not by coincidence did white supremacist southern editors resort to journalism standards as a political weapon in their defense of the South and its racial laws and customs in the 1940s and 1950s. Segregationists hoping to discredit those who challenged or failed to defend the southern way of life fought for their cause on multiple fronts, imposing barriers to impede integration but also to control the narrative about race and normalize white supremacy. As Black Americans accumulated piecemeal gains in court rulings and executive orders, gradually swaying moderate white opinion, segregationists pushed back to demonize the civil rights movement and align white privilege with social order.[75] The midcentury tension over journalism standards must be viewed in context, as one tactic in a broader strategy to preserve Jim Crow.

Most prominently, opponents of integration portrayed civil rights for Black Americans as a threat to democracy, not an affirmation of it, and often labeled supporters of *Brown* as un-American and influenced by communism. Jeff Woods described the ways proponents of "southern nationalism" employed anticommunism to undermine the civil rights movement: "The [red] scare thus rose and fell largely in rhythm with southern efforts to counter the struggle for black equality."[76] Segregation's defenders were so successful in attaching the communist label to the civil rights movement that the NAACP and some other organizations were neutralized by statute throughout the South after *Brown*. Segregationists argued that the white South would have continued friendly relations with its Black neighbors but for meddling by outside agitators who sowed discontentment, that the demand for civil rights was so antithetical to white assumptions that it had to be communist-inspired.[77] Even after U.S. senator Joseph McCarthy's inquisitions had been discredited, Congress and southern legislatures continued their investigations into presumed communist infiltration of the civil rights movement, spurred on by the editorial pages of segregationist newspapers, including Waring's in Charleston, South Carolina.[78]

In addition, as Aimee Edmondson has shown, segregationist police and public officials used libel suits against the northern white press to forestall unflattering scrutiny of the white southern response to civil rights, which sometimes was violent. The U.S. Supreme Court curtailed the use of litigation against the press with its 1964 ruling in *New York Times v. Sullivan*, which refined the libel standard and articulated a constitutional protection for journalists who reported on public officials. The ruling also nullified an Alabama jury's staggering $500,000 libel judgment against the *New York Times*. As southern public officials intended, the threat of extreme financial consequences produced a chilling effect on northern press coverage of southern resistance to integration and white violence against Black Americans. The *Sullivan* decision protected the watchdog function of journalism, Edmondson explained: "Without the world looking at the South through the lens of the national press, southern officials and other segregationists would have been free to continue squelching activism in their own way."[79] Within this context, the professional maneuvering of the white southern editors analyzed in this book cannot be viewed apart from organized white resistance to the freedom struggle.

The chapters in this book consider distinct chronological but overlapping episodes in white southern journalism's response to civil rights gains, roughly from 1942 to 1957. Informed by research in fifteen archives or manuscript collections, the narrative is populated by a recurring cast from the midcentury press and academia, white and Black contemporaries who knew each other or were at least aware of each other's work though segregation limited their collaboration and dictated the professional rules of the game. The critical focus of the narrative is white efforts to preserve Jim Crow through the manipulation of journalism standards, so the analysis is concerned with the ongoing marginalization of the Black press and the barriers erected by whites and their institutions to discourage Black Americans who sought to work alongside white journalists or tell their own story to an integrated national audience. This is not to minimize the important activism of the Black press during this period but to isolate the role of white racism in thwarting its work. The analysis in the chapters is anchored in the two most significant disruptions in the twentieth century, World War II and the postwar movement for Black civil rights, but it also is centered in the professional practice of journalism, where news coverage constructed and reified racial difference. In addition to the overarching segregated press, the Associated Press, a journalistic nexus, and the upstart Southern Education Reporting Service are rich sites for investigation with extensive archives.

## Chapter Summaries

The book opens with an analysis of the racial divide in journalism during the 1940s, first through white criticism of the Black press in World War II and then a failed effort to integrate the opinion pages of daily newspapers, a bastion of whiteness in the American press. In 1942, during the Black press's Double V campaign, a call for racial equality at home as the United States battled fascism abroad, southern newspaper editor Virginius Dabney, who wrote for national magazines, and syndicated columnist Westbrook Pegler, a northern ally of segregationists, branded the activism of the Black press unpatriotic and its journalism substandard. Such white disparagement of the Black press blamed Black editors, not angry whites, for the violence that followed Black demands for civil rights concessions from their "white friends." In chapter 1 we meet Claude Barnett, who founded the Associated Negro Press as a Black response to the Associated Press and other white wire services, and Charles S. Johnson, a prominent sociologist and expert on race at historically Black Fisk University. Barnett and Johnson offered the white daily press a column written by Johnson but found no white newspapers willing to run it on a regular basis. This first chapter explores the racial deference required of Johnson and Barnett as they tried to cross a racial barrier in journalism and confronted the pretense of colorblindness as white editors framed their rejection of the column in terms of professional standards and the wartime newsprint shortage. Although white editors did not value his work, Johnson won the confidence of northern philanthropies that supported his research and publishing, including the column project. Dabney and other white editors also would underestimate Johnson a decade later, during his service on the board of the Southern Education Reporting Service, the focus of chapter 5.

In the early postwar years, an ideological division emerged between white editors who believed objective and accurate journalism required that all Black news subjects be identified as "Negroes" in news stories and those who believed a racial label should be used sparingly. As chapter 2 describes, the push for racial identification in news stories was spearheaded by white southern editors who did not support integration and prioritized race in determining news values. Many white southern editors sought news that portrayed Black people as unfit for integrated society and declined to publish stories that portrayed them as normal, law-abiding Americans. Racial identification was essential to making those distinctions in news copy, where the racial identifier segregated Black news subjects on the printed page. This controversy played out within the membership of the AP news cooperative from the 1940s, when segregationists began to feel threatened by incremental racial gains for Black Americans, until the mid-1950s, when civil rights conflict made race a relevant element of many stories in the daily news budget. Chapter 2 examines the debate within the AP membership, where a continuous protest by a strident and unrelenting southern faction changed wire service policy and practice, ultimately mandating racial identification in any wire story that contained a Black news subject.

Chapter 3 explores racial gradualism as an ideological tool that allowed moderates in the white southern press to champion objectivity even as they maneuvered to control the news narrative about race and stymie desegregation in the years just before *Brown*. The analysis follows Harry S. Ashmore, editor of the *Arkansas Gazette*, through a controversy over the meaning of a speech he gave to the Southern Governors' Association in 1951. His talk, which was covered by the wire services and the Black and white presses, was widely misunderstood as an endorsement of integration. Ashmore renegotiated the meaning of the speech in correspondence with both fans and critics and during remarks to a symposium at historically Black Howard University. The gradualist position was easily misinterpreted because of its inherent ethical contradiction: the assertion that civil rights for Black Americans could coexist with segregation and that separate could in fact be equal. Ashmore, who was not a racial liberal, would edit the book *The Negro and the Schools*, a data-driven project sponsored by the Ford Foundation's Fund for the Advancement of Education (FAE). Ashmore described the project as objective journalism, a dispassionate arrangement of facts, and claimed to have no personal investment in the outcome of *Brown* despite his gradualist views on race. When the desegregation ruling was imminent, the FAE also underwrote the Southern Education Reporting Service, the objectivity project promoted by Don Shoemaker. Ashmore, a Pulitzer Prize winner who opposed integration during the 1950s, is often misremembered as a racial progressive.

Chapter 4 continues the analysis of the North-South divide, focusing on the effort by segregationist AP members, which accelerated after *Brown* in 1954 and the Till trial in 1955, to alter wire service news judgment and policy on the reporting and dissemination of news about race. For example, the segregationist faction insisted that news about unruly and antisocial behavior by Black news subjects and particularly about Black-on-white crime in the North be dispatched to a national audience, even if the stories had relevance and impact only in the community where the events occurred. White southern editors acknowledged their intention to portray Black Americans as unworthy of full citizenship but framed the argument as one of journalism standards. The civil rights story required accurate and unbiased reporting, which they insisted could be achieved only by highlighting Black shortcomings, particularly when integration produced racial tension. Ultimately, the AP capitulated to its segregationist membership; correspondence with southern members and discussion among AP staff show that the AP bent its news values to appease the white supremacists in its membership, largely because these editors framed their concerns as a defense of journalism standards. The chapter also examines the arguments that the northern white press engaged in journalistic hypocrisy by covering southern de jure racism more thoroughly than de facto segregation in their own communities, and that a "paper curtain" separated North from South and censored the segregationist viewpoint from the press.

The Southern Education Reporting Service, whose mission was the objective reporting of the race story, is the focus of chapter 5. The SERS was founded in 1954, just as the *Brown* decision was first announced, and the timing was no accident. The Fund for the Advancement of Education, the Ford Foundation entity that sponsored Ashmore's book, accepted the argument that the story of desegregation had to be managed to prevent white supremacist violence and that objective reporting, as defined by the southern white press, was the way to achieve that goal. In reality, the SERS manifested the assertion that only the southern white perspective aligned with journalism standards. Chapter 5 analyzes the journalistic mission of the SERS, which maintained an all-white, all-southern reporting staff while claiming to advance the principle of objectivity—but inverts the historical narrative to foreground Black participation. Under the direction of Don Shoemaker, the SERS board was led by segregationist editors

Virginius Dabney and Thomas Waring, and the token Black members were Charles Johnson and *Norfolk [VA] Journal and Guide* editor P. B. Young Sr. The board became enveloped in controversy when Waring insisted that Bonita Valien, a Black researcher, be fired for public comments in favor of *Brown* and for violating the SERS objectivity mission, even as white editors on the board openly defended segregation. Young quit the board in protest, and the SERS, which was condemned by the Black press, had difficulty finding other prominent Black men willing to fill his seat and that of Johnson, who died in 1956. In this counternarrative, the roles of Johnson, Young, and Valien, who are minimized in most white histories of the SERS, become the point of the story.

The book's concluding discussion explores parallels between twenty-first-century racial politics and debates over journalistic objectivity, which have been reactivated with the mainstreaming of conservative media and polarization over concepts like whiteness and critical race theory. The discussion also analyzes the AP's 2020 stylebook change, calling for the capitalization of "Black" and other racial identities, but not the "white" designation.

Each chapter challenges the white orthodoxy embedded in journalism history, which too often mirrors the bifurcation of American newspapering into a white press and a Black press. When the Black movement for civil rights threatened the southern way of life at midcentury, white southern editors weaponized journalism standards, claiming to defend the profession by maintaining the racial distinctions that constructed a white press and a Black press as separate and unequal public spheres. The white editors in this story were unable to see that their own racial stake in segregation presented a conflict of interest and undermined their claim to be concerned primarily with news values and the free press. By foregrounding the power that accrued to whiteness in American journalism, we see the incongruity of assertions by white southern editors that their racism was professionally inspired and performed a public service.

CHAPTER 1

# INDICTING (AND OTHERING) THE BLACK PRESS

RESECURING RACIAL BOUNDARIES
DURING THE WAR DECADE

When World War II exposed and exacerbated racial tensions in American society, the Black press bore witness as a chronicler of injustice and the most insistent and enduring voice for racial change. P. L. Prattis, managing editor of the *Pittsburgh Courier*, the largest circulation Black newspaper at the time, noted at the end of the war that the Black press was driven by a commitment to reporting the reality of Black experience. "The Negro press acts as it does, sometimes intemperately, because of the kind of fight it is in and all too often it must do a blasting job to get at the truth," Prattis wrote.[1] Segregation in the industrial workforce and military had constrained Black opportunity, but with America's entry into the war at the end of 1941, Black editors hoped the urgency for more soldiers and defense laborers would bring practical but meaningful racial gains. If white people could not see the moral necessity of equal opportunity at home, even as the United States fought racism and fascism abroad, perhaps the imperative for the war effort would create the paradigm shift necessary to break down racial barriers to Black Americans' full participation in the life of the nation.[2]

For more than a century the Black press had advocated an end to the racial double-standard, but such entreaties had been easy for whites to ignore in a country informed by a segregated press—with the white press writing for white audiences while Black newspapers served Black readers, largely beyond white Americans' view. With the arrival of World War II and an intensification of Black agitation for civil rights, some in the white press responded not with democratic equanimity but with suspicion and defensive attacks on the source of unwelcome reminders of America's constitutional failings. Even as the nation engaged in existential warfare on multiple international fronts, some in the white press were unsettled by the modest civil rights concessions the freedom struggle had achieved by the early 1940s. Their sudden preoccupation with the wartime content of Black weekly newspapers invites our curiosity as we anticipate the white press's response to the tectonic shift in race relations that would arrive in the 1950s.

White attacks on Black newspapers during World War II characterized Black journalism as unobjective, concerned only with the narrow interests of Black readers, and no match for the professional standards of the white press. White critics also demonized the Black press by portraying it as a threat to democracy rather than a force for the expansion of rights at a pivotal moment in U.S. race relations and world history. Most prominently, the Black press of the early 1940s received hostile scrutiny from nationally syndicated, conservative columnist Westbrook Pegler, who seemed to discover the Black press in 1942 and aggressively warned readers of white daily newspapers that, in his view, inferior Black journalism was exacerbating racial tension.[3] Pegler's vitriol, which characterized the content of the highest-circulation Black newspapers as "just trash and . . . imitative, and in a crude way, of all that is discreditable or least admirable in the white press," reached a national audience in the millions.[4] That same year, the national magazines *Atlantic Monthly* and *Saturday Review of Literature* offered a platform to editor Virginius Dabney of the *Richmond [VA] Times-Dispatch*, who by virtue of his white, southern heritage considered himself an expert on "the Negro problem" and the perceived dangers of the Black press, and was widely regarded by whites as a southern thought leader on race. In one article, Dabney warned, ominously, that Black editors' wartime demands for full citizenship were irresponsible, alienated white allies, and would trigger "explosions of serious proportions."[5]

Other chapters in this book analyze white editors' representations of their own whiteness, Black life, southern culture, and segregation in the years soon before and after the 1954 *Brown v. Board of Education* decision, when the U.S. Supreme Court declared separate-and-unequal public schools to be unlawful; however, that postwar journalistic discourse on race was rooted in a widely held white assumption, shared by some members of the white mainstream press in the 1940s, that Black Americans had not evolved socially and politically and were not worthy of civil rights.[6]

According to this logic, the content of the Black press, which did not comport with the standards of white daily journalism, was itself an affirmation of Black unfitness for full citizenship. Positioning themselves as arbiters of journalism standards and qualification for civic participation, Pegler and Dabney used critiques of the Black press to emphasize perceptions of racial difference and lay a foundation for white resistance to more dramatic Black advances a decade later, when *Brown* would mandate integration of public schools. As such, the normative dimension of these criticisms, which posited the white perspective as the American reality, formed a key rationale for the segregated American press.[7]

This targeted critique of the Black press arose on a historical continuum, of course, and its emergence at the beginning of America's involvement in the war and on the cusp of the midcentury civil rights movement is both historically logical and consequential. As Black newspapers advocated on their readers' behalf, challenging the assumptions that supported white supremacy, their white critics questioned the Black press's journalistic legitimacy. By weaponizing discourses of patriotism and definitions of journalism standards, including objectivity, white critics reasserted the historical intransigence of racial boundaries in journalism. White editors who sought to protect the racial status quo would use these tactics a decade later against the mandate for school integration and the activism for civil rights that followed *Brown*.[8] In this professional climate, in which a dominant press continued to employ and serve white readers and an alternative, oppositional press employed and served Black readers, Black journalists and editors were both invigorated by possibility and daunted by racism as they resisted and renegotiated their role as professional outsiders in an industry governed by the expectations of the white press.[9] This wartime reaffirmation of Blackness and the Black press as "other," as existing apart from the journalistic norm specifically at this historical juncture, would have bearing on the future of journalism. Without minimizing the important political labor of the Black press during this period, this chapter and those that follow expose and scrutinize the white press's contribution during and after World War II to the ideological legacy of white supremacy in journalism.

It seems prescient that Pegler, an acerbic but influential conservative voice based in New York, and Dabney, a prominent and dignified southern editor, emerged as national agenda-setters in the white rhetoric about the Black press during World War II. When the civil rights movement of the 1950s unfolded, white southern newspaper editors asserted themselves, drawing a contrast with the Black press, as the journalistic standard bearers on the segregation story, as experts on race and southern culture uniquely qualified to mediate coverage of *Brown* and its impact. Although white southern editors incessantly criticized many segments of the white northern press, their defense of segregation received a thorough hearing in northern publications because sympathetic northern allies like Pegler could be persuaded that not providing both sides of the race story—not giving segregationists equal weight in reporting—was an abdication of journalism standards. Moreover, even northern daily newspapers that scorned the southern press's defense of Jim Crow simultaneously maintained virtually all-white newsrooms.[10] This chapter also shows that when the war ended, most northern dailies preserved their editorial and op-ed pages as a white enclave, denying admission to Charles S. Johnson, a leading Black intellectual who offered them a regular column called "A Minority View." White daily journalism was decades away from integrating newsrooms, and Pegler's and Dabney's attacks on the Black press affirmed a racial status quo that left no room even for Johnson's column.

The Black press's most inflammatory affront in the 1940s was to document the irony of the United States' fighting a war of liberation abroad when Black citizenship was constrained by both de facto and de jure segregation at home. Although Black newspapers had been reporting and editorializing since 1827 on racial injustice and the democratic failings of the white press, many white people paid no attention until World War II.[11] In 1942, as the U.S. military mobilized following the attack on Pearl Harbor, the *Pittsburgh Courier* launched the Double V Campaign seeking victory over fascism abroad and victory over racism at home, and other Black papers, including the *Chicago Defender*, joined in. This tactical move underscored the democratic paradox of American racism and accelerated calls for desegregation of the defense industries and combat military, while also disconcerting those members of the white press and public who took comfort in the strictures of racial apartheid.[12] In this moment of hyper-patriotism, it was easy for Pegler and Dabney to portray Black newspapers as a threat to national security.

This chapter examines the historical context that amplified the impact of discourse about the Black press that was available to national audiences in 1942 and 1943, after the *Courier* launched its Double V campaign. To that end, the historical investigation engages the writings of Pegler, a conservative columnist for the *New York World-Telegram* whose persistent assault on the Black press appeared in daily newspapers across the country, and national magazine articles by Dabney, the reputedly more moderate Virginia editor, a defender of gradualism and the racial status quo. Pegler had just won a Pulitzer Prize in 1941 for exposing union corruption, which smoothed the rough edges of his professional reputation; Dabney would win a Pulitzer Prize in 1948 for his reasoned local editorials on race but in 1942 and 1943 wrote more strident articles about the Black press for national magazines.[13] The analysis also considers the positions of Black journalist-scholars Warren Brown and V. V. Oak, who responded to the white outcry in separate and divergent pieces for the *Saturday Review of Literature*, one of the national outlets that had published a Dabney grievance against the Black press. Finally, the chapter examines the unsuccessful effort by Johnson, the renowned sociologist at historically Black Fisk University, and Claude Barnett, owner of the Associated Negro Press news service, to provide the white daily press with a newspaper column written by Johnson. During the war Johnson affirmed his reputation as a moderate expert on race; that his superior credentials were insufficient to make his authorship of "A Minority View" palatable to most white editors in the mid-1940s provides context for the criticism of the Double V campaign. Johnson's marginalization also demonstrates how deeply Jim Crow structured American journalism, setting the stage for the white southern press's rejection of Black civil rights in the 1950s.

## A Confluence of Events

When the United States entered World War II in December 1941, most Black Americans already hoped for expanded citizenship and opportunity through employment, education, and housing, as well as an end to voting restrictions and Jim Crow segregation in public accommodations and transportation in the South. "Negroes in the United States want first-class citizenship," wrote historian Rayford W. Logan. "There is, of course, still a considerable number who are willing to settle for less. This number is, however, growing smaller: a current expression among us asserts that 'it is time for the leadership to catch up with the followship.'"[14] The Black freedom struggle had long highlighted a range of democratic inequity, even if the subject remained taboo for many white people, and the Black press of the early 1940s provided Black Americans with information and opinions about the war and the national civil rights effort. At the beginning of the war, 230 Black weeklies had a combined circulation of 1.3 million, and that number would reach 1.8 million before the war was over.[15] The call for civil rights would grow louder and more pronounced over the next two decades, but Black grievance against segregation was well established when the *Pittsburgh Courier* rolled out the Double V Campaign in 1942 and tied the Black freedom struggle to America's patriotic mission in the war, symbolized by the "V for Victory" slogan. Although prominent newspapers like the *Courier* and *Chicago Defender* modulated their tone during the course of the war, the iconic Double V defined their public position.[16] As well, several concurrent developments directly impacted the racial climate surrounding the Double V Campaign and likely amplified white fears that Black Americans were seeking to upset a social order that ensured white advantage.

Although the Fair Employment Practice Committee (FEPC) ultimately did not fulfill its mission to integrate the defense industries, its appointment by President Franklin Roosevelt in 1941, following negotiations with Black labor leader A. Philip Randolph, was a milestone in the midcentury movement for Black civil rights.[17] Randolph's activism and influence in the early 1940s signaled that even if change would not be immediate, it was coming. His leadership, which fostered the early March on Washington Movement, was noted by many Black politicians and scholars, including sociologist E. Franklin Frazier, who in 1942 described Randolph's following as "an incipient mass movement, gathering within itself the present upsurge of the Negro masses."[18] Large meetings organized by Randolph to protest America's racial "caste system" attracted twenty thousand people in New York and seventeen thousand in Chicago.[19] Frazier wrote that between the two world wars, "the isolation of the Negro has been broken down, and he has been brought into contact with a larger world of ideas. The traditional relationship of loyalty to whites has been destroyed, and race consciousness and loyalty to his race have taken its place." The Black press was an agent of change as its readers imagined a new social order, Frazier said. "While the newspapers support the country in the war, they are carrying on a vigorous fight for democracy and equality for the Negro at the present time."[20] As reported in the *Courier*, in 1942 Randolph also began lobbying Roosevelt to admit Black journalists and editors to presidential briefings, an effort that would bear fruit in 1944.[21]

Also in 1942, a meeting of southern Black academics and professionals at Durham, North Carolina, produced a position paper formally titled "A Basis for Interracial Cooperation and Development in the South: A Statement by Southern Negroes." The Durham Manifesto called for white concessions on equal education and voting rights for Black Americans and contained moderate statements of opposition to segregation and support for its *eventual* elimination.[22] Sociologist Gordon B. Hancock called the Durham Manifesto "probably the most constructive departure in race relations since the emancipation of the Negro."[23] Although he had been working on issues of race for two decades, Charles Johnson, the Fisk University scholar, came to the attention of many whites when he drafted the Durham Manifesto, which attracted attention in the white press, North and South.[24]

In addition to furthering Johnson's regional and national reputations as a thoughtful steward of racial reform, the Durham Manifesto set a historical marker for the evolution of southern Black attitudes about segregation and forced the white press to go on record. In a column in December 1942, Ralph McGill, editor of the *Atlanta Constitution*, praised the document as a call for social and economic justice that tactfully avoided a direct challenge to Jim Crow. "It will be most unfortunate," McGill cautioned fellow whites, "if the Southerner does not discuss calmly and intelligently the basis for inter-racial cooperation as advanced by this group of Southern Negroes. . . . This is the very first vocal expression by a united front of Southern Negro leadership [and] it is important and significant."[25] Clearly, "inter-racial cooperation" was euphemism for compromise that left intact the structures of American racism, but the manifesto put McGill's white readers on notice that the southern Black professional class, represented at the Durham meeting, would not indefinitely acquiesce to disparities in access to the good life and that they intended to cross racial boundaries that restricted Black achievement.

Paralleling the optimism embodied in the Double V Campaign and the Durham Manifesto was southern retrenchment on segregation, even among some of the more moderate voices in the white southern press.

In July 1942 Mark Ethridge, white editor of the Louisville daily newspapers and a Roosevelt appointee to the FEPC, stunned Black leaders and reassured segregationist whites during an employment discrimination hearing in Birmingham, Alabama, when he warned that "the Southern Negro cannot afford to drive from his side, in his march to greater fulfillment of his rights, the Southern white men of good will who have been his chief asset and chief aid." This assertion clarified the limits of federal regulation of fair employment policy during the war, but it also recalibrated the white political spectrum below the Mason-Dixon Line: Ethridge, a New Dealer who had been regarded as among the most liberal white southerners on race, now deferred to segregationists. "There is no power in the world—not even in all the mechanized armies of the earth, Allied and Axis—which could now force the Southern white people to the abandonment of the principle of social segregation," he said, warning Black leaders that it was "cruel disillusionment, bearing the germs of strife and perhaps tragedy ... to tell [Black people] that they can expect it, or that they can exact it as the price of their participation in the war." In recounting the speech, John Temple Graves, a white columnist with the Birmingham newspapers, said Ethridge was "passing no judgment, simply stating a truth." White southerners, Graves explained, considered segregation to be "a thing apart from the general issue of advancement for the Negro."[26] In the myth of separate-but-equal, Black rights and segregation were not mutually exclusive.

White reaction to the Double V Campaign was tinged with suspicion that foregrounding racism at home was not only unpatriotic at a time of national vulnerability but also subversive, anti-American, and probably inspired by communism. As Patrick S. Washburn documented, the federal government shared this concern. Agents of the Federal Bureau of Investigation visited Black newsrooms throughout 1942 and beyond, and some Black newspapers reported on this surveillance.[27] Had they known the FBI was openly monitoring Black newsrooms, many whites would have approved as this scrutiny reflected broader white concerns about Black loyalty to American democracy. In the unsettled political climate at the beginning of the war, the white press's criticism of Black journalism could be explained as a patriotic necessity. Moreover, allegations of communist influence—the white claim that Black grievance could not occur without sinister manipulation by outside agitators—would continue to dog civil rights activists and organizations, especially the National Association for the Advancement of Colored People (NAACP), throughout the postwar freedom struggle.[28] In this context, the reactionary white response to the Double V campaign said more about the uncertain status of white racial identity than Black demands for racial progress.

## Double V Blowback: Pegler Demonizes the Black Press

In his nationally syndicated column "Fair Enough," Pegler set the tone on April 29, 1942, when he argued that the Double V campaign, initiated late that winter by the *Pittsburgh Courier* and adopted by the *Chicago Defender,* two of the most "vigorous papers of the Negro press," was "exploiting the war emergency as an opportunity to push the aspirations of the Negro."[29] Pegler's assertion that Black advocacy for civil rights threatened national unity and undermined the war effort provided patriotic cover for his sneering critique of the Black press, which appeared in five columns in spring and summer of 1942 and caught Black editors off guard because Pegler had not previously focused on race.[30] Pegler, who wrote prolifically for Scripps-Howard and Hearst newspapers from the mid-1930s to the 1950s, had cemented his conservative reputation by opposing the New Deal and trade unions. By the time of his 1942 attack on the Black press, 174 daily newspapers with a total circulation of nearly 10 million had access to his daily column.[31]

A close analysis of Pegler's argument on April 29, 1942, his first direct shot at Black journalism after the start of the Double V Campaign, makes clear that his concern about the Black press had arisen "of late," not from a sustained reading; that a few issues of the *Courier* and *Defender* formed the sample for his "studying" of those publications; and that he described his own experience when he wrote that the two newspapers were "well-known among the colored population, but widely unknown to the white people." As a white man who ordinarily paid little attention to Black advocacy for civil rights, Pegler was deeply offended politically and professionally by the content of the Black newspapers he had seen. "As journalism, the Defender and the Courier compare ill with the standard white press of the country and are no compliment to the people whom they purport to represent," Pegler wrote. "They are reminiscent of Hearst at his worst in their sensationalism, and in their obvious, inflammatory bias in the treatment of news they resemble such one-sided publications as the Communist Party's Daily Worker and [Father Charles] Coughlin's Social Justice."[32] This was one of two references to the antisemitic radio priest's weekly paper, whose second-class mailing permit had been revoked by the Roosevelt administration.[33] Ironically, Scripps-Howard would terminate Pegler in 1944 because his own views on labor unions had become too strident and intractable for the *New York World-Telegram* and the chain. Despite the disparaging comparison with the Black press, Pegler would then go to work for Hearst at the *New York Journal American*.[34]

In this first column, Pegler described the writing in the *Courier* and *Defender* as mediocre and argued that the papers did not make a convincing case for Black civil rights. "In neither paper is there any writing of the slightest distinction to substantiate in the field of journalism at least, the cry that discrimination, alone, retards the colored man's progress," he wrote. Pegler made no allowance for the fact that the Black papers were weeklies and that leaders of the white daily press considered white weeklies to be substandard as well.[35] He expressed surprise that the two newspapers advertised books about sexual performance and such products as charms and skin-lightening cream, which he said appealed to superstitions and insulted readers' intelligence. Pegler pointedly described the Black newspapers that circulated to Black soldiers in the military as posing a threat to the war effort and again placed the Black publications in the same category as the antisemitic *Social Justice*: "These Negro papers agitate violently and, I think, to the same dangerous degree that was alleged against Charles E. Coughlin's weekly, particularly in their appeal to colored soldiers whose loyalty is constantly bedeviled with doubts and with the race-angling of news. If tomorrow they should win everything which they profess to advocate, they would die for lack of the segregated circulation which they exploit."[36] The pronouncement about "segregated circulation" underscored how little Pegler understood the mission of the Black press, which existed precisely because racial segregation in journalism and society at large constrained Black access to the public sphere. In 1949 the School of Journalism at Lincoln University, the historically Black institution in Missouri, would host a symposium called "Is the Negro Newspaper Here to Live or Die?" For Thomas Young of the *Journal and Guide* in Norfolk, Virginia, the answer was clear: "Self-liquidation in the final analysis is what we are really striving for."³⁷

In his second critique of the Black press, on May 11, 1942, Pegler acknowledged responses to his earlier comments on the Black press. Quoting an unnamed "colored man" who wrote to thank Pegler for "tak[ing] a crack at the yellow journalism of Negro newspapers," Pegler said he also had heard from Randolph's March on Washington Movement and claimed that the organization had misconstrued the views set forth in the April 29 column. The organization, Pegler reported, "said my analysis 'of the just grievances' of Negroes was 'vicious' when the fact is that I did not analyze such grievances at all." The partial quotation makes it difficult to judge whether the complaint squared with the text of Pegler's argument on April 29, but that first column did indeed offer a sweeping dismissal of the Black press's claim that its readers were disadvantaged by discrimination. Pegler continued his rebuttal: "This one also said I had linked Negroes in the same category as the Fascist and Communist groups although there was not a word in the whole discussion which even hinted at such a connection. This was a plain, deliberate lie." In fact, in the second and final paragraphs of the April 29 column, Pegler drew an analogy between the Black newspapers and Coughlin's *Social Justice*. In the second paragraph, Pegler also mentioned the Communist Party's *Daily Worker*.³⁸

Pegler ended his May 11 column with a diatribe against the press service at Howard University, the historically Black institution in Washington, DC, which he said had issued a statement after the April 29 piece. Pegler had been "shocked" by the press release from Howard, "which is supposed to be a center of Negro intelligence upholding the Defender and the Courier in the practices cited on the pathetic ground that they are 'heroic defenders' of the colored people." Pegler mocked the press release for arguing that any deficiencies in Black newspapers resulted from the segregated press. Black newspapers, which targeted news and advertising to Black readers, "tend to secure that segregation by exploiting a Negro world far apart from the whole community of the United States," he wrote. Pegler again argued that the Black press compared unfavorably with the white press: "It would be a pathetic admission by Howard University that these two papers do represent the best ability of colored men in journalism because if we are arguing from the basis of my professional opinion, they are very inferior to the standard white journalism."³⁹

A Pegler column datelined June 16 then reported that a Howard University official had distanced the institution from the press release, which was written and disseminated by a student without institutional review or authorization. Although Pegler had made no effort to verify the source of the press release before quoting it, he chided Howard for the mishap and congratulated himself for raising questions about content in the Black press. Pegler quoted liberally from an editorial in the *Los Angeles Tribune*, a Black newspaper that believed Pegler had performed a service:

> In brief [Pegler] decried the sensationalism of the Negro press, its "obvious inflammatory bias," its "gents' room journalism" (vulgar gossip columns), its lack of distinctive writing and the spurious contention of many of its advertisers, i.e., various claims to voodoo, hypnotic and supernatural powers.
> Although misunderstanding the reason behind all of this, Pegler wrote, in these regards, the welcome truth. Negroes have themselves complained of their newspapers; it will take, perhaps, the white light of national publicity to make the most flagrantly offensive of them mend their ways.

Pegler noted that the National Negro Publishers Association (NNPA) had placed his criticism on the agenda for its recent convention in Chicago but said he did not know how the discussion turned out.[40] Presumably, he would have been willing to contact a white organization for information to use in his column, just as he might have contacted a white university to verify the source of a questionable, mimeographed statement that arrived in the mail.

As it happened, Pegler's attack on the Black press received play in *Time* magazine's item on the NNPA meeting, which described a smoke-filled room in a Chicago YMCA basement, where the Black publishers, "full of fried chicken and Pepsi-Cola, were still wrought up about the issue of their press and race." In summarizing the NNPA's response to Pegler's complaints, *Time* reported that Pegler was condemned during the discussion as an enemy of democracy.[41] The publishers, noting national pressure to stop playing "discordant notes" during the war, resolved to use their papers for the preservation of freedom and democracy and pledged loyalty to the United States and President Roosevelt. The group did not back away from its commitment to wartime civil rights, however, and approved a resolution supporting establishment of an interracial division in the U.S. Army.[42]

Betraying no sense of irony after his assaults on the quality and integrity of the two largest Black papers and a leading Black university, Pegler next, on June 18, published a column challenging Black Americans' complaint "that the white newspapers of our daily press are unfair to the negro in their treatment of news stories, if not actually hostile to the colored man." Pegler instead described the white press's posture toward Black Americans as "scrupulously fair and sympathetic" and "friendly to the negro," and said the white press sometimes performed a service—restraint that he found unethical—by downplaying racial angles in news in order to keep the peace.[43] As chapter 2 of this book demonstrates, this complaint recurred in the white press of the 1940s and 1950s, and was directed against newspapers that did not label Black news subjects, emphasize Black-on-white crime, or portray Black Americans as antisocial.

The Black press applauded one column, datelined July 16, in which Pegler displayed uncharacteristic empathy for the plight of an unnamed Black solider who had enlisted to fight for a country that did not regard him as a full citizen. Before deployment, while he was stationed in the South and even wearing an American uniform, whites still did not regard the Black soldier as a citizen, Pegler wrote. "In Florida he still found himself . . . barred not only from the haunts of the white civilians whose very lives he had volunteered to defend with his life but forbidden even to buy a sandwich or a glass of milk in a white restaurant." Pegler wrote profoundly of the dilemma confronting this soldier: "Now, assuming that this boy comes back from the war to a victorious country, what status will he come back to? Will he be niggarized again and restricted to menial jobs, Jim-Crowed and driven back to the dreadful ghettos of our cities or will he be treated as an American?" In the column's conclusion, members of the Black press were stunned to read Pegler offer something close to an apology:

> Although my recent adventure with the Negro press has subjected me to some spiritual violence, I am glad I provoked the subject because the experience has made me realize what awful conditions our indifference has put upon these fellow Americans. If I were a Negro I would live in constant fury and probably would batter myself to death against the bars inclosing my condition. I would not be a sub-American or a sub-human being, and, in docile patience, forever yield my rightful aspiration to be a man, to work, to progress and to move out of the slums.[44]

So significant was Pegler's apparent change of heart that editor P. B. Young Sr. of the *Journal and Guide* in Norfolk quoted it at length as a milestone for the Black press, when Young gave the keynote at the 1948 Wendell L. Wilkie Negro Journalism Awards.[45]

What Young did not mention was that Pegler quickly returned to form. A year after writing his contrite and sensitive column about the injustices faced by a Black soldier in the South, Pegler attacked Black newspapers, blaming them for rioting in the North in 1943.[46] Lumping the Black press into a category of "frictioneers," along with communists and white mogul Marshall Field of the *Chicago Sun*, Pegler described Black newspapers as "propaganda" that encouraged racial discord. "The guiltiest of all agitators are those who pretend to fight against group hatreds," he wrote. "There is no element comparable to the Negro press in the promotion of race consciousness among the Negroes and racial distrust of the white population. These publications have a large circulation and they constantly remind the Negro that he is a Negro while calling on the white press to forego all such distinctions. They misrepresent the background facts of all disturbances so as to make it appear that, invariably, some white man was responsible for the trouble and the Negro Communists and fellow-travelers always receive recognition as racial leaders."[47] Ignoring the divisiveness of his own argument and the white press's continuous advocacy for white interests and readers, Pegler consigned the Black press to the margins of the journalism profession. For most white readers, who never picked up a Black newspaper or interacted with people of another race, Pegler's description of the Black press as un-American and biased stood as an official account by an opinion leader who professed concern for patriotism and racial harmony.

In sum, the single empathetic column about the Black soldier and the democratic paradox was an anomaly. In columns in the 1950s, Pegler would defend some of the most intransigent white supremacists in the southern press.[48] Privately, in 1955 he also wrote a letter of support to the attorneys defending the murderers of fourteen-year-old Emmett Till. "Your clients may be guilty," he wrote. "I am not judging." Of greater concern to Pegler was whether the white defendants could be treated fairly by the white press in the North, which he claimed actively concealed "the details of many horrible criminal assaults by negro beasts on white women in New York and Chicago."[49] This correspondence places

Pegler's attack on the Black press during World War II on a discursive continuum with the fiercest, most abject white supremacy following the *Brown* decision.

## Making the Case in the Magazines: Dabney Goes National

With Pegler's condemnations of the Black press playing in the background during the war years, Virginius Dabney prepared articles for national magazines claiming that "extremists" in the Black press were putting their demands for racial change above the nation's interests.[50] For Dabney, who ran a white newsroom in the capital of the former Confederacy, Jim Crow laws and social customs were a local framework that he and readers of the *Times-Dispatch* expected to retain. Even so, Dabney well understood, because the NAACP already had moved to integrate graduate schools and the March on Washington Movement had secured concessions from the Roosevelt administration on appointment of the FEPC, that the battle over the racial status quo would be won or lost at the national level, not on the editorial page in Richmond.[51] Although Dabney was more moderate than many southern whites and editorialized in 1943 for the integration of public transportation, he did not support an end to social segregation and certainly did not condone racial "mixing" in public schools.[52] With public anxiety about the war effort mounting and the Double V Campaign charging the political atmosphere, Dabney took to his typewriter.

Described as a "genteel segregationist" by one historian, Dabney was certainly more polished in his argument than Pegler, but Dabney's views about the Black press were not remarkably different.[53] He also shared Pegler's ambition to speak to a national audience and took advantage of the race issue, bending his career trajectory to meet the historical moment. In 1942, Dabney had published *Below the Potomac: A Book about the New South*, which he dedicated to his segregationist father. During the war, Dabney wrote more than a dozen articles for national magazines on issues related to the South; of concern here are two pieces from 1942 and 1943 that marginalized Black newspapers following the launch of the Double V Campaign and publication of most of Pegler's 1942 columns about the Black press. The first, "Press and Morale," appeared in the July 4, 1942, edition of the *Saturday Review of Literature*, which later allocated space for commentary from Black journalist-scholars Warren Brown and V. V. Oak.[54] "Press and Morale" also laid the foundation for "Nearer and Nearer the Precipice," a treatise by Dabney in the *Atlantic Monthly* on the alleged failings of Black leadership and the Black press, and his impending alienation from the Black community.

Members of the Black press who read "Press and Morale," Dabney's argument for a patriotic and constructive wartime press, might have been pleased to see themselves included under the umbrella of "the press," as part of a discussion that took swipes at such purported Axis sympathizers as the *Chicago Tribune*, *New York Daily News*, *Washington Times-Herald*, and the Hearst papers. Too often the Black press was neglected in broader discussions of journalism, with "the press" referring exclusively to white publications.[55] At the conclusion of the piece, which called for a united ideological front in the face of Axis propaganda, Dabney turned his attention to Black newspapers, which he (unlike Pegler) routinely read.

Dabney conceded, perhaps strategically, that most readers of the Black press were patriotic despite their sense of racial grievance. "The degree to which this injustice and discrimination is being emphasized by Negro editors and other leaders at this time, and the insistence with which they are demanding a complete and immediate revolution in race relations in America has aroused no little concern among their white friends," Dabney wrote, acknowledging that Black disadvantage was often caused by white racism. Even so, he continued, echoing Mark Ethridge's comments in Birmingham, their white supporters "cannot view with other than apprehension the speed with which Negro leadership, as exemplified in the Negro press, is pushing matters to a climax." Dabney argued that empathetic whites would be more inclined to help Black people raise their standard of living through "evolutionary processes" rather than immediate change, to avoid a violent and bitter reaction by less enlightened whites. It became clear that Dabney himself was one of the empathetic whites he described in the third person, whose support was in jeopardy: "The great majority of the Negroes are in the South, and it is there that normally friendly white opinion is becoming alarmed, chiefly for the future of the black man. Explosions of serious proportions, both North and South, will be well nigh inevitable, if present tendencies continue, and race relations will probably be set back for decades. This is the considered belief of men and women who are responsible for some of the major advances achieved thus far by the Negro, and who are earnestly desirous of seeing him succeed in achieving others."[56]

Although "Press and Morale" was stunning in its own right, "Nearer and Nearer the Precipice," the January 1943 article in the *Atlantic*, is the most significant of Dabney's magazine writing in this period because he imagined to a national audience that the impertinence and Double V advocacy of the Black press would not only undermine the war effort but also trigger a racial apocalypse. With "Nearer and Nearer the Precipice," Dabney, a so-called southern liberal on race, alienated Black editors who had thought him a conditional ally, documenting that his true loyalties lay with racial tradition.[57] Running through Dabney's articles about the Black press was the assumption that Black southerners, no matter how unjust their treatment, bore responsibility for white violence that resulted from Black activists' upsetting the social order by asking for too much, too fast, before southern whites were willing to accede their privilege. "Nearer and Nearer the Precipice" and Dabney's other wartime writings about race formed a strategic justification for gradualism, the white hypothesis that segregation would be eliminated organically and without political agitation or legal coercion.[58] Meanwhile, Black Americans were told, demands for change that offended white supremacist sensibilities in the South were not in their best interest and would reverse the tenuous progress they already had made. The call for Black patience to give "friendly white opinion" time to evolve is particularly disingenuous, given that Black Americans had been waiting since the 1896 U.S. Supreme Court ruling in *Plessy v. Ferguson* for their "white friends" to provide separate-but-equal educational facilities and public accommodations.

When "Nearer and Nearer the Precipice" appeared in the *Atlantic* six months after "Press and Morale," Dabney's position against the Black press had hardened. He now vilified Black newspapers without much attempt at appeasement and blamed what he regarded as radical, extremist Black leadership, specifically the March on Washington Movement and the NAACP, for the increasing strain in race relations. Dabney warned, vaguely, that the ensuing race war would have global consequences for the world war, "unless saner counsels prevail." By Dabney's reckoning, Black leaders and editors were disproportionately responsible for violence caused by racist whites. For example, he described demagoguery and deceit by southern politicians who inflamed white sentiments against Black people and spurred three lynchings in Mississippi in response to a Black candidate running for Congress. Culpability, he wrote, lay with Black leaders who should have anticipated this outcome and not incited white racists by encouraging a Black candidate.[59] Although Dabney decried the violence perpetrated by racist whites and catalogued a number of such events, he argued, essentially, that it was in Blacks' own best interest to capitulate to the mob by not causing trouble.

The Black press, Dabney argued, had an obligation to defuse the situation instead of "stirring up interracial hate" with incendiary reporting on such incidents as the 1942 police beating in Rome, Georgia, of "Negro tenor" Roland Hayes.[60] For balance, Dabney argued, Black newspapers should publish stories that described "the sincerity, the humanity, or the decency of the white race." Moderate voices in the Black press did exist, Dabney wrote. "All of the papers harp constantly on racial grievances, but that has been going on for years. Many of them are reasonably restrained in their language, and careful not to indulge in vilification or abuse. But others are so extreme that riots probably would break out if they were read widely by whites." In his analysis of the Black press, Dabney mentioned just one Black editor by name, P. B. Young Sr., whose Norfolk *Journal and Guide* he regarded as "one of the sanest and best-edited newspapers in the United States."[61]

Young was not cajoled, however, and wrote Dabney a detailed rebuttal of the argument in "Nearer and Nearer the Precipice," drawing an analogy between Dabney's position and that of prominent southern demagogues: "It is the same thing that Messrs. [John] Rankin, [Eugene] Talmadge, [Theodore] Bilbo and others say with the difference that their language is always coarse and their attitude brutal, while your language is always cultured and your attitude dignified. The result is the same." Among criticism from other members of the Black press was a retort from poet Langston Hughes, whose opinions appeared in the *Chicago Defender*. Rejecting Dabney's call for gradualism, Hughes wrote, "Mr. Dabney's article as a whole implies that Negroes, segregated, Jim-Crowed and lynched as we are, should not seek to disturb the *status quo* of racial oppression."[62]

Although Dabney was most concerned with the perceived shortcomings of the Black press, he was even-handed in calling for the white press to exercise moderation in reporting on racial matters. "Nearer and Nearer the Precipice" was followed in 1943 by "Newspapers and the Negro," a manuscript that appeared in the *Bulletin* of the American Society of Newspaper Editors and was reprinted a few months later in the *Quill*, the publication of Sigma Delta Chi, precursor to the Society of Professional Journalists. Both audiences were exclusive to the profession of journalism—including students, faculty, journalists, and editors—and were virtually all white. Even when writing for publications that ordinarily would not circulate to Black readers, Dabney's message of moderation was consistent, and he also lectured whites on their responsibility to promote racial understanding rather than stoking discord. Dabney did not mention the Black press in the *Bulletin* and *Quill* but his message is relevant here. The context of the times is apparent in his comments: "Those of us who edit newspapers can do our bit toward smoothing the points of friction, if we try to grasp the viewpoint of the thinking Negro, and seek to print the news about his race in an understanding and objective manner." Dabney encouraged white newspapers to emphasize Black accomplishment rather than misdeed. "Too many of us newspapermen think of our colored friends largely in terms of their police court performances, their crap-shooting proclivities and their virtuosity with the razor," he wrote. "We stress this side of the race and forget that there is another, a more important side." Black achievements in the arts and in service during the war should be reported, he said, making special note of the bravery of Doris Miller, "the mess boy who grabbed a machine gun at Pearl Harbor, and won the Navy Cross for heroism."[63] Of course, Dabney did not mention that Miller had been ineligible to serve in the fighting forces in 1941 because he was Black.

Dabney's attempt at balance in this trade article might have impressed his white professional peers, but his attacks on the Black press severely diminished his credibility with Black editors. Later in 1943, Dabney published editorials supporting the integration of street cars and buses, and believed, an acquaintance reported, that "these editorials had apparently restored his good status with the colored people. He thought that they had written him off as a bad risk after his severe criticism of the Negro press in the *Atlantic Monthly* article."[64] As J. Douglas Smith noted in an analysis of Dabney's editorials in this period, Dabney proposed the concession on local transportation as a strategy for increasing the comfort and convenience of white passengers, not as a stand for racial equality.[65]

## The Brown-Oak Debate

Uncertainty about the outcome of the war and its impact on race relations raised the stakes for both Black and white Americans, and national magazines were eager to provide a forum for discussion. A few months after Dabney published the article on "Press and Morale" in the *Saturday Review of Literature*, the magazine expanded the conversation in its December 19, 1942, issue with "A Negro Looks at the Negro Press" by Warren H. Brown, who had written a doctoral dissertation on the Black press but now sided with its white critics.[66] The article, which coincided with the publication of "Nearer and Nearer the Precipice," backfired when Black newspapers exposed Brown as an opportunist with an ax to grind against the Black press. Even so, the article remains in the archive and should be acknowledged with context, along with a counterpoint by Black scholar V. V. Oak, which the magazine published in March 1943.[67]

When he wrote "A Negro Looks at the Negro Press," Brown was working as director of Negro relations for the Council for Democracy (CFD), a Henry Luce–funded organization started in 1940 to increase public support for the defense buildup, and the *Saturday Review of Literature* acknowledged that Brown produced the article in his official capacity. Black newspapers quickly attacked the article because Brown had been fired from the *Chicago Defender* and lately had been unable to find work with the established Black press in New York, despite having been an assistant editor at the *Amsterdam News*.[68] Some members of the Black press reported Brown to be unreliable when the General Education Board (GEB), a Rockefeller philanthropy, vetted him in 1944 and learned that Brown had written a piece for a Black newspaper that resulted in a successful libel suit.[69] In short, Brown had been ostracized by the Black press and was a poor choice to author a serious critique of Black newspapers for a national magazine, but the white press probably did not check him out. As a result, those who read the magazine article but not the reporting and commentary in the Black press did not know that Brown was not credible. Moreover, in January 1943 *Reader's Digest* published a condensed version of "A Negro Looks at the Negro Press" under the more ominous title "A Negro Warns the Negro Press." Dabney ran the *Reader's Digest* version on the editorial page of the *Richmond Times-Dispatch*.[70]

Brown's criticisms blended Pegler's and Dabney's concerns that Black disaffection resulted from communist influence and agitation by irresponsible Black leaders and Black newspapers, which Brown described as "Negro first and American second. They foster segregation by aiming to make all Negroes race-conscious before they are America-conscious." Citing examples of what he characterized as sensational coverage of crime and exaggerations of racism against Black Americans, Brown claimed that Black newspapers did not accurately reflect Black conditions. "For giving a dishonest, discreditable picture of American Negro life, they are worse than the worst white newspaper," he wrote. "The average Negro newspaper portrays Negro life in burlesque." Ultimately, Brown said, the content of most Black newspapers was undermining the quest for equality: "The kind of justice for which the Negro strives is undoubtedly delayed by the Negro press."[71]

In the *Saturday Review*'s March 6, 1943, issue, Oak, who also had a doctorate and taught journalism and sociology at Wilberforce University, a historically Black institution in Ohio, answered Brown's attack and, therefore, the positions of Pegler and Dabney. Oak rejected the suggestion that the Black press's attacks on lynching and the poll tax meant its newspapers were pro-fascist or anti-American. Oak reviewed the mission of the Black press and argued that it provided a service to the nation. "Because the Negro press arose out of the dire need for racial leadership, it is only natural that it is strictly racial to this day," he wrote. While the white press tended to ignore news about the Black community, the Black press strengthened democracy through "its virtuous fight in behalf of its people and . . . rendering invaluable service to the cause of justice and fair play. The Pittsburgh Courier with its double 'V' campaign has made both the colored and white readers realize that we have to win victory over tyranny abroad as well as at home."[72]

Oak indirectly acknowledged Dabney's concern that the Black press had made race relations combustible, but he argued that the Black press had ameliorated anger, not incited it. The Black press, Oak wrote, functioned as a pressure valve to prevent the rage exhibited by Richard Wright's protagonist in his 1940 novel *Native Son*:

> The Negro press is rendering an invaluable service toward crystalizing Negro thought and action, and is serving as an outlet to the Negro's otherwise thwarted ambitions and repressed anger against the injustices of his white compatriots, thereby preventing the birth of more

and more "Bigger Thomases." Hounded at every turn, unable to enjoy even the ordinary decencies of what we call the "American way of living," debarred from all recreational activities and eating facilities normally open to white Americans, the Negro press is the only outlet of the intellectual Negro and the only place where even the Negro masses see themselves depicted just as they are.[73]

The recognition that some Black people were angry enough to need a pressure valve undoubtedly made some whites uncomfortable; however, Gunnar Myrdal would also make this point in *American Dilemma*, published the following year.[74] What Dabney and Pegler wanted was for the Black press to urge patience and caution, but that was not Oak's message.[75]

Pegler's attacks during 1942 had placed members of the Black press on heightened defense, prompting editors of the *Chicago Defender* and *Pittsburgh Courier* to wonder publicly whether the columnist was collaborating with the federal government and U.S. military to suppress Black journalism.[76] Then, leaders of the Black press were struck that just a few weeks elapsed between publication of Brown's piece, which was openly part of the CFD's effort to promote the war, and Dabney's astounding attack in "Nearer and Nearer the Precipice." The articles by Brown and Dabney delivered a one-two punch of sorts that seemed to confirm a coordinated assault on the Black press. In January 1943, right after the two articles appeared, Claude Barnett of the Associated Negro Press (ANP) news service found several Black editors concerned that they might be the target of a government strategy to formally limit their free expression.[77] Given FBI visits to newsrooms and the now-familiar portrayal of the Black press as a threat to democracy, Black editors can hardly be faulted for their concern.[78] Their perspective also was informed by the experience of being Black editors who advocated for democratic change during wartime, without full citizenship rights of their own.

## No Home for "A Minority View"

Anticipating postwar momentum toward civil rights, Barnett, whose news service distributed editorial content to and from Black newspapers, sought in the mid-1940s to introduce a Black perspective into the opinion pages of white-owned daily newspapers.[79] Had the project succeeded as Barnett imagined, the column would have produced a symbolic desegregation of the editorial pages of the virtually all-white, midcentury American daily press. To ensure maximum credibility with white editors, Barnett persuaded Johnson, the Fisk sociologist, to write opinion essays billed as "A Minority View" to be distributed by the ANP to a mailing list of daily newspapers. Importantly, Johnson and Barnett were able to secure funding for the project from the GEB. From 1945 to early 1948, Johnson and his staff at Fisk prepared more than sixty columns on a range of topics, most related to racial challenges in postwar America.[80] Ultimately, just a few daily newspapers ran any of the columns, and none made it a regular feature. Barnett believed, however, that even if the primary audience for "A Minority View" were white editors who rejected the column, those arbiters of majority opinion would be exposed to Johnson's perspectives, which would inform both the content of daily newspapers and the trajectory of U.S. race relations. "I am confident," Barnett wrote to Johnson's assistant in 1946, "that these articles are proving enlightening even if not printed by these various papers which are receiving them."[81]

Although historians have focused extensively on both Barnett's role in advancing the Black press and Johnson's broad influence on Black education and the sociology of race, "A Minority View" is, understandably, not mentioned in accountings of either man's accomplishments.[82] The column's failure to find an audience demonstrates just how conditional Black citizenship continued to be during and after World War II, despite Black gains toward fuller participation in military service and employment. The column proposal also coincided with the admission of the first Black journalist to the White House press corps in 1944, yet this advance did not guarantee opportunity elsewhere in journalism. Barnett's and Johnson's experiences with "A Minority View" provide sobering context for Black hopes that full civil liberties would be within reach at the end of the war. In the mid- and late 1940s, the constitutionally endowed American press still had its own Jim Crow protocol, and not even a Black intellectual of Johnson's stature could cross the racial barrier around the opinion pages of white daily newspapers.[83]

Within the context of his time, however, Barnett's ill-fated initiative was both practical and visionary, acknowledging the inability of the Black press to reach a national white audience and anticipating the eventual influence of the white press in changing white attitudes and public policy related to race.[84] In response to the segregation of American journalism,

Barnett had founded the ANP in 1919 as both a counterpoint to the Associated Press and other content services targeting the white press, and as a vehicle for sharing news and features among Black newspapers. Operating with limited resources, the ANP mailed its subscribers packets of stories gathered from Black papers as well as reporting by the ANP staff in Chicago, much of it rewritten from published reports. Despite its usefulness to the Black press, the ANP was regarded even among Black journalists as a "clipping service."[85]

Correspondence archives related to the column project make clear that Barnett and Johnson encountered significant racial obstacles, both systemic and improvised, in their attempt to bring a Black perspective to readers of the white daily press and to transcend the racial divide that structured American society generally and American journalism specifically. Most of Johnson's columns spoke to the American racial condition at midcentury, and the tone was thoughtful and moderate but frank: "Northern newspapers and individuals have made both a strategic and real mistake in labeling certain representatives from southern states like Senator [Theodore] Bilbo and Congressman [John] Rankin as peculiarly southern phenomena."[86] Challenges directly linked to the end of World War II also attracted Johnson's attention: "Despite the greatest campaign in American history to impress upon the public the meaning of freedom and democracy, there has been a most amazing public and official tolerance of racist demagoguery."[87] And sometimes the topic had a distinctly international angle: "The ex-premier of England, Mr. Winston Churchill, speaking unofficially with an official tone at Fulton, Mo., has made an appeal for Anglo-Saxon bilateralism as a guaranty against positive Soviet hegemony in Europe and Asia."[88]

The column project emerged at a historical juncture when many Black Americans began to see equal opportunity as a realistic aspiration and some whites signaled a willingness to relent, even if the gestures were tentative and token. Release of the Durham Manifesto in 1942, which stopped short of advocating desegregation, had cemented Johnson's popular reputation. As Barnett sought an author for "A Minority View," Johnson was his first choice in a narrow field of Black leaders who opposed segregation but also could communicate moderately enough to be credible with the white audience Barnett sought to reach. Through academic work on race, specifically through prolific scholarship in sociology that by 1943 had produced ten authored or edited books, and also through prominent nonprofit and governmental service, Johnson had earned the confidence of the Black community and influential white philanthropists. Johnson had pursued an activist agenda but had done so within the parameters of a segregated society; he could be conciliatory to whites who advocated gradualism or worse, and do so without being so self-effacing that he rendered himself ineffectual. In this vein, Johnson's biographers noted "his shrewd political savvy and commitment to an overarching goal."[89]

After he received his doctorate from the University of Chicago under the renowned sociologist Robert E. Park, Johnson spent much of the 1920s in New York City as director of research for the National Urban League and founder and editor of its journal, *Opportunity*.[90] In 1928 Johnson left for Nashville, Tennessee, to chair the Department of Social Sciences at Fisk. He started the Institute for Race Relations there in 1942, and in 1946 would be named Fisk's first Black president. After returning to his native South, Johnson frequently traveled north to solicit grants from funders that were interested in his work and in supporting Black education. Among them were the Rockefeller-endowed GEB, which gave Fisk more than $5 million over the years, and the Laura Spelman Rockefeller Memorial, which in 1927 made a stunning grant of $200,000, worth more than $3 million a century later, to facilitate Johnson's move to Fisk.[91] From 1942 to 1948 Johnson also was employed as codirector of the Chicago-based Julius Rosenwald Fund, which distributed the Sears fortune primarily to Black recipients. This second job required Johnson to travel to Chicago at least one week a month, where he often saw his old friend Barnett.[92] In 1942 and 1943 Johnson and Barnett began discussing "A Minority View," and Barnett assured Johnson that he was the best person to embark on this journalistic experiment: "You have had such rich experience now and your contacts are so superior to what any other Negro American has, that I believe you can render a service [of] unusual character."[93]

Although Johnson had credibility with white audiences, was an experienced editor, and was comfortable writing for nonacademic readerships, he lacked one important qualification for authoring a regular newspaper column: the time to produce articles on a fixed and inflexible schedule. A constant in Barnett's stewardship of "A Minority View" would be tension over Johnson's inability to meet deadlines, a predictable circumstance given the number and scope of his professional obligations. That begs the question of why Johnson, as an established scholar and, after 1946, a university president, would try to make time for Barnett's column project. Although Johnson, as a published academic, had conditional access to elite white audiences, the prospect of speaking to popular white audiences, which typically were placed off-limits by the white gatekeepers at the head of daily newspaper newsrooms, was something different entirely. The project also attracted the qualified support of the GEB, one of Johnson's academic patrons.

The GEB staff, in consultation with Arthur Hays Sulzberger, white publisher of the *New York Times* and a Rockefeller Foundation trustee, concluded that direct underwriting of the column was beyond the philanthropy's scope; however, the GEB's ongoing support of Johnson's scholarship might cover the research and clerical staff required for the endeavor. According to GEB records, Sulzberger was concerned that the GEB's intervention in press content might be perceived as a challenge to editorial autonomy at both the white newspapers that received the articles and at the ANP.[94] Sulzberger also expressed concern about the column on racial grounds. "Negro columns in white papers would have certain value but might tend to introduce a distinction which is not intended," reported Jackson Davis, a member of the GEB staff. "... The important point is that all this material should be in accord with the standard of the newspapers. It is also important that these articles should represent the constructive side of Negro effort and thought and not the protest side."[95] Channing Tobias, a Black GEB consultant who had attended the Sulzberger meeting, wrote Barnett that GEB officials supported the concept of a grant to Fisk, not to the ANP. "Mr. Sulzberger was decidedly of the opinion that it would not be wise to encourage special columns on racial questions edited by Negroes for the daily papers of the north," Tobias wrote. "It is his opinion that Negro news should be integrated into the news columns...." Moreover, Tobias reported, Sulzberger believed "there should be no movement toward subsidizing a Negro press association because of the handicap that this might place on the freedom of such an association."[96] Although the GEB appeared to be distancing itself from the column and challenging its racial premise, the philanthropy, which already supported Johnson's research at Fisk, made the university a $5,000 grant in 1944 and a second for $2,500 two years later with the understanding that the funds would support Johnson's scholarly publishing and probably include "A Minority

View."[97] With this arm's length agreement, Sulzberger and the foundation had plausible deniability if the column project became controversial.

As they made plans for the column, Johnson and Barnett developed different mailings for white newspapers in the South and those in the North. The ANP sent the first formal solicitation with sample columns in January 1945, but Johnson also mentioned writing a personal appeal to some more racially moderate white southern editors, and his records include an undated letter.[98] Johnson's tentative tone and language provide insight into the task faced by a Black American, even one as accomplished as Johnson, who approached white southern editors in the mid-1940s with a suggestion that he be granted space in their newspapers. This letter, which clearly enacted the social customs governing interracial social relations in the midcentury South, contrasted sharply with the formal solicitation letter the ANP mailed to editors all over the country. Johnson's personal letter, which was addressed to Alabama editor Harry Ayers in the archived copy, opened with the disclaimer that "this note is written somewhat apologetically, because it has some personal implications. These implications, however, should not be taken as a request for any personal consideration, or any consideration at all beyond the current policy and needs of the Anniston Star. They are mentioned simply as part of the explanation of a somewhat unusual circumstance and proposal."[99]

The letter then attributed not to Barnett or to himself but to Davis of the GEB, who was white, "the idea of a column that might be carried in perhaps a few of the progressive papers of the South, giving, out of a somewhat dispassionate social science background, a minority or Negro interpretive slant on certain current social issues." Johnson then directly addressed the implications of his race. "I realize that the idea itself is full of problems," Johnson wrote. "For there are many risks involved in the effort to add clarification for the public on an issue, especially if the comment comes from an unexpected or somewhat questionable quarter." He continued, "From some other points of view, however, if well done, a minority view that is not too embittered and fractious might be considered desirable, notably in facilitating the difficult process of inter-racial communication and understanding. There is, however, always the sobering thought that a venture of this sort might lack journalistic value." This was followed by an even more startling statement about his qualifications to write the columns:

Although I feel fairly secure in my access to factual material and in a reasonable amount of experience in this field, I have no illusions about the value of these personal advantages to a newspaper and its public. If you think that the idea has merit, I would greatly value your suggestions on the character, content, and slant of the articles, to make them more newsworthy. If you think the whole idea falls outside the scope of your newspaper or, for that matter, any newspaper, it will not be a major personal disaster, and I would not in the least mind your saying so.[100]

In this first-person appeal, Johnson, an undisputed expert on race and generally more accomplished than anyone on the mailing list, used a series of disclaimers to ask white southern editors for a hearing. Although he was optimistic about the project, Johnson understood that, at this moment in the history of American race and journalism, some editors would find the column proposal presumptuous, or even audacious, on racial grounds.

The approach was markedly different in drafts leading up to the third-person solicitation letter that was sent over Barnett's signature and on ANP letterhead, introducing "A Minority View" to northern daily papers that might publish it. In late 1944 Johnson revised Barnett's first draft, which perhaps went too far in avoiding deference. That version began, "The American Negro is not the only racial minority group whose activities and destinies will be of absorbing interest to newspaper readers in coming months, but he represents the most important." Before describing Johnson's qualifications and asking the editor to publish the columns, the draft also stated, "There are few subjects about which so many people think they have a great deal of knowledge but actually know as little as is generally true of the Negro, his life and his minority viewpoint."[101]

In comparison, the final, more circumspect draft mailed to newspapers framed racial tension as a postwar issue pertinent to all. "The whole of the American public," the letter began, "is concerned that the conclusion of this war should mark the beginning of an era of enduring peace at home and abroad. A significant portion of the American public is concerned lest there be a recurrence of the tragic and costly domestic incidents of racial and minority tension that ensued upon the close of the First World War." The letter then described the role of the press "as a forum of opinion on plans and proposals for post-war world organization." The letter noted the difficulty of discussing race dispassionately and proposed that it "be divested of emotionalism and presented to the general reading public on a rational basis." Moreover, "If a careful analysis of the relation of the Negro to the whole of American society were presented to the American public through the press, this would go far to clarify confused thinking on the whole involved question of minority status." Then, having buried the lede, news jargon for the main point of a story, the letter introduced Johnson as just the person to educate the public and asked the editor to consider a regular column by him.[102]

The ANP mailed the solicitation and samples to about sixty-five daily newspapers in all regions of the country in January 1945. When Barnett confirmed that the mailing had gone out and reported that the ANP had targeted "a pretty good cross section of the larger papers of the country, a paper in nearly every large city," Johnson cautioned that the newsprint shortage might be an issue. "I have heard from three or four editors, in response to my own note . . . ," he wrote. "They indicated an interest in the idea, and said that they would write further after having a chance to look over the articles. There was forewarning, however, in their reference to the paper shortage, which would make it difficult for them to include other materials at this time."[103]

Surviving responses from editors who received the solicitation are few, but a handful of letters in archives offer a sample of editors' reactions to the initial columns. Dabney of the *Richmond Times-Dispatch* politely deflected. "They reached us only a short time ago," he wrote Barnett, "and we have as yet been unable to reach a decision as to them, but we shall be happy to let you hear from us in the near future. . . . We are considerably interested in the idea, and it may be that we can work something out. We have not had an opportunity to read the columns carefully as yet."[104] Dabney did not follow up, however. R. L. McGrath of the *Seattle Times* wrote that "the samples sent are interesting, and should be effective," but asked for a list of other newspapers that had published Johnson's columns. "The problem in Seattle, with many migrants from the South, is a delicate one. We don't want our well-meaning efforts to boomerang by stirring up antagonisms that would defeat our purpose. The experience of other editors using Dr. Johnson's column may guide us."[105] Erwin Canham of the *Christian Science Monitor* declined to consider the column because his newspaper originated its own opinion articles. "We recently checked up on the way in which our bureaus within the United States have been producing Negro news and feel that, all things considered, we have had unusually full coverage," he responded, but did not elaborate on the value of including a Black voice.[106]

The two most detailed responses to the initial mailing both emphasized the wartime newsprint rationing, which had been imposed in 1943 and had restricted space in daily newspapers.[107] Indeed, many newspapers had shrunk content other than news and advertising, eliminating their op-ed pages or curtailing the number of columns they published. Ted Dealey of the *Dallas Morning News* wrote that he and others at his newspaper thought the sample articles were "clearheaded and impartial and that they might serve a constructive purpose under normal circumstances. However," emphasizing that he was not making an excuse, "we simply don't have sufficient newsprint to start running such a series, although we find nothing objectionable in them and although we think they are very well done." In addition, Dealey noted that his paper aggressively covered the race issue, presumably using white journalists, and he did not see the subject as a gap in its content.[108]

Mark Ethridge, who had returned to the editorship of the *Louisville Courier-Journal* after his tenure with the FEPC, also mentioned the newsprint shortage in his response, but his staff's analysis of the sample columns raised editorial concerns about the columns' timeliness and audience.[109] Although the columns were well written and astute, and a few presented new information and perspectives, a serious question was the essay format of "A Minority View" and the apparent fact that the columns were written "far in advance of publication and without the topical timeliness usual in newspaper columns. It would obviously be impossible for [Johnson] to be as timely as the [other columnists], for his field is limited and, important as the problem he deals with is, it would be no use to pretend that it produces a live national issue of widespread general interest once or twice a week." Readers of the Black press might have disagreed. Moreover, Ethridge said the columns were likely to appeal to the already converted, not "the audience that might be convinced. The material lends itself much better to magazine publication than to newspapers."[110]

Although racism likely was a factor in editors' lukewarm reception to "A Minority View," the column's failure was not so one-dimensional. Ethridge's assessment of the sample, a racially inflected critique about journalism standards, underscored that he and other white editors were unwilling to risk alienating white readers. The essay style of the columns would be unfamiliar to readers of daily newspapers, and the undated nature of the sample columns, which addressed general topics without, in some cases, a clear peg to recent news, did not meet daily journalism's expectations for timeliness. The distribution framework that Barnett and Johnson proposed followed the ANP model, which set up a conflict with the professional norms of deadline-oriented daily journalism. Johnson mailed a column to meet a weekly deadline at the ANP headquarters in Chicago, then Barnett sent it to newspapers on the mailing list. By the time a column reached a daily newsroom, at least a week had passed since Johnson mailed it from Nashville and facts surrounding a topic might have changed. In fact, correspondence between Johnson and Barnett indicated that during the life of the project, Johnson or his staff often sent multiple columns at a time, possibly compounding the timeliness perception for white editors. Even so, daily newspapers in the 1940s received other weekly feature content by mail, raising questions about whether the ANP's inability to transmit content by wire was truly disqualifying or was a contrived racial barrier.

As he attempted to manage the project, Barnett was routinely frustrated by Johnson's inability to meet the agreed-upon schedule, most notably by Johnson's long lapses in sending submissions at all once it became clear to Johnson that demand for the columns was light. This should not have come as a surprise to Barnett; Johnson had been a frequent ANP contributor and Barnett had long familiarity with Johnson's routine overcommitment of time and energy. For example, Barnett had been unable, despite reminders over several months in 1944, to get Johnson to supply a review of Gunnar Myrdal's *An American Dilemma*.[111] During 1945, when Johnson submitted columns intermittently, he reflected on the challenge of writing a column for the white daily press.

> As you can tell by my last editorials, I have had some difficulty getting into the channel for the rigid deadline of a real news service, but I hope I am improving (even if, unfortunately, at your expense).
>
> Last night I sent off four fairly timely articles. That catches me up, I hope, and sets me forward a trifle.
>
> You will note from the general character of the last seven or eight that the style and subject matter have been slightly altered, still feeling for the standard of acceptance by the general press.[112]

Although Johnson was more comfortable writing for magazines, his comments are remarkable given Ethridge's feedback In noting the deadline standards of the daily press, Johnson suggested that four articles, to be sent out one at a time over a month, could be considered "timely."

The frequency of "A Minority View" improved in spring 1946 while Johnson was on a U.S. State Department mission to study the educational system in Japan. The GEB grant had assumed that Johnson would hire a research assistant, and Bonita Valien, who had done graduate work in sociology, began ghostwriting the columns during this period.[113] Correspondence between Barnett and Valien, and occasionally from Johnson, documents that Barnett received at least a dozen columns during the rest of 1946 and again in 1947 but also sometimes was without material to distribute.[114] Notably, Johnson's professional obligations increased dramatically in October 1946, when he was appointed president of Fisk University. During this period, moreover, he published a book and continued service to the Rosenwald Fund and other organizations.

The number of daily papers that ran Johnson's column even occasionally could likely be counted on one hand, though this uncertainty complicates a precise analysis of "A Minority View." Sending tearsheets of published columns, particularly when requested by another editor, was protocol in the 1940s—assuming that white daily newspapers extended the same courtesy to the ANP. Few clippings of Johnson's bylined column made their way to the archives at Fisk or the ANP, and just a few more can be recovered from databases of digitized newspapers, where stories about Johnson's appointment as Fisk president, speaking engagements, and travels are numerous and easy to locate.

Soon after the initial solicitation letter by Barnett, the *Kansas City Star* published a column in the sample packet and the *Des Moines Register* featured a piece "condensed from an article" by Johnson.[115] In February 1946 the *Milwaukee Journal* ran a column on the impact of automation on southern agriculture.[116] The heaviest documented use of the column occurred that spring, when editor Carroll Binder of the *Minneapolis Star-Journal and Tribune*, who wanted Barnett to know that he recently "had the supreme pleasure of hearing Paul Robeson sing," ran the column at least four times, two of them when syndicated columnist Walter Lippmann was on vacation.[117] Barnett was heartened by Binder's interest in the column and even discussed expanding the mailing.[118] Ironically, the largest reader response to "A Minority View," documented in the ANP Chicago office, followed a reference by the newspaper *PM* to a February 1947 column. Of interest was a Johnson essay titled "Billions for Science, Pennies for People," a think piece about the willingness of government and industry to support the natural sciences but not the social sciences. The column did not mention race. This reference to Johnson's views generated at least eight written requests to the ANP for reprints of his columns.[119]

In 1959 the Fisk librarian, while cataloguing Johnson's papers three years after his unexpected death from a heart attack, discovered the columns and wrote Barnett seeking context for "A Minority View."[120] In his response to the librarian's query, eleven years after the final installments had been written, Barnett had clearly put the experience behind him. He recalled the column project targeted to white daily papers as lasting six months, not three years. "We were able to sell so few that we gave the project up . . . although we had hoped to revive it," Barnett wrote. "I cannot tell you what papers used the material although there was one paper in Minneapolis or St. Paul which did."[121]

The failure of "A Minority View" to find a mass audience of white newspaper readers is a pointed demonstration that American journalism remained intractably segregated at midcentury. With historical perspective unavailable to Barnett and Johnson, "A Minority View" clearly was doomed from the outset. Barnett and Johnson had deep familiarity with racism, in both its overt and subtle forms, and Johnson knew he had to treat white editors, particularly southerners, with special consideration, but they did not fathom that daily newspapers were decades away from easily welcoming nonwhite journalists into newsrooms. And even when, in the 1970s, the daily newspaper industry began its push for newsroom integration, nonwhite hires, who brought different perspectives to the process of doing journalism, would confront deep suspicion about their ability to practice a craft that had been a white domain.[122] For some newspapers, the editorial pages, where the newspaper's voice and authority were thought to reside, would be slower to integrate than the staffing of the news section. Even the op-ed page was a carefully controlled space. In his memoir, Carl T. Rowan, one of the first Black Americans to receive a syndicate contract for opinion, described holding a press conference in 1965 to announce that he had been hired by the *Chicago Daily News* and Publishers Newspaper Syndicate to write three columns a week. "It seems like nothing today, but on August 5, 1965, the Washington press corps was caught up in the story of a black guy breaking the barrier against newspaper syndication," Rowan wrote.[123] Not until 1993 did the *New York Times*, Sulzberger's newspaper, make Bob Herbert its first Black columnist.[124]

Racism was a factor in editors' rejection of "A Minority View," but it was not the only factor, which complicates an analysis of circumstances that influenced newsroom decision-making regarding the column. The newsprint shortage was real, but it also presented a convenient excuse for not publishing the column. In addition, the timeliness and format issues would have given many white editors pause, even if ample space had been available in their daily papers, but there is no way to isolate race from these considerations. Would editors have rejected Johnson's column if newsprint had not been a factor? Or if the column had been delivered more quickly? If editors had felt an ethical imperative to integrate their opinion pages, would they have been less critical of the essay style of the column? All things being equal, would editors have rejected a column written by a white sociologist of comparable reputation? Without question, race and racism were at the core of the column project: racism was the reason the column needed to be written, and Johnson's race was the reason he needed to write it. Race and racism also were the reasons white editors could not evaluate "A Minority View" on its merits.

## Conclusion

The call for "national unity" during the war, one of the key rationalizations for the Pegler and Dabney critiques of the Black press in 1942 and 1943, exposed the democratic irony of simultaneously denying full rights to and demanding loyalty from an oppressed segment of the citizenry. Following Black activism for civil rights and especially the Double V campaign, Pegler and Dabney framed the Black press as unpatriotic and engaged in self-serving activism to the detriment of the nation. Their concern about the patriotism of Black editors was a pretext, a rationalization for questioning the legitimacy of the Black community's primary source of information about America's democratic failings. Although their criticisms were anchored in wartime, their fundamental objection to the Black press transcended the moment. Pegler and Dabney spoke for many white Americans when they used their national platforms to remind the Black press and Black citizens of their place.

In developing "A Minority View," Barnett and Johnson knew they were challenging a racial barrier, but they did not fully understand that, for many white editors during the 1940s, the column proposal set a depth charge beneath daily journalism's status quo. Barnett and Johnson also underestimated the extent of many white editors' disregard for the Black press with which Barnett was directly associated. As white editors weighed whether to give Johnson access to their white readers, it is reasonable to see Johnson's race and the column's affiliation with a Black news service as factors in the chilly reception. American journalism had emerged from World War II with the racial segmentation of its press undisturbed, with a white press and a Black press speaking to different audiences and the standards of the white press functioning as an immutable and exclusionary norm. Although no longer a threat to the war effort and with some victories of professional access under its belt, the Black press remained a voice from the margins as the modern civil rights movement began to unfold. The assertion that the Black press and other challengers of the racial status quo were un-American would continue to be a central trope of white resistance to the freedom struggle.

For Johnson, a person of vast accomplishment, "A Minority View" was a minor project of little professional consequence. He seemed fascinated by the prospect of writing for the white daily press and believed the editorial pages of daily newspapers held sway over white thought. He also was loyal to Barnett. Nonetheless, his letter to Jackson Davis in February 1946 seeking a second GEB grant suggests that he was looking past the column to other opportunities for his research program. Johnson described the column as being "editorially acceptable to a fairly large number of papers" but wrote that editors declined to run it because of newsprint supply. Instead, Johnson noted, the editorial operation supporting the column had been put to other good uses.[125] Indeed, in awarding a second grant, the GEB concluded that "the incidental features of this editorial service have assumed considerable importance in ways not originally taken into account."[126] The data compiled for the columns had been published as pamphlets or used in speeches and other articles, and Henry Holt and Company had requested a textbook on *The Negro and Race Relations*. Moreover, the material had found its way into editorials that appeared in *A Monthly Summary of Events and Trends in Race Relations*, a publication that Johnson's Institute for Race Relations at Fisk had prepared for the Roosevelt administration.[127] As such, Johnson and Barnett could take solace: some content of "A Minority View" was reaching broader audiences, with or without the help of white newspaper editors.

In addition, Johnson's *Monthly Summary* was the model for *Southern School News*, the "objective" monthly roundup of school desegregation reports launched by the Southern Education Reporting Service (SERS) in 1954. That journalistic project, whose mission was objective reporting on the South's response to *Brown v. Board*, is discussed in chapter 5. There, Virginius Dabney, P. B. Young Sr., and Charles Johnson crossed paths again as members of the SERS Board of Directors. And Bonita Valien, Johnson's ghostwriting research assistant, became a racial target for violating the SERS's standard of objectivity. For the American press, Black and white, the racial tensions of the war decade were prologue for the civil rights conflict of the 1950s.

CHAPTER 2

# THE AP AND THE NEGRO IDENTIFIER

AN IDEOLOGICAL BATTLE FOR
JOURNALISM STANDARDS

The arrival of the Ypsilanti triplets produced a light, human-interest item for the Associated Press's national wire. On December 7, 1948, thirty-four-year-old Charles Logan of Wayne, Michigan, whose wife had suddenly given birth at home to two boys and a girl, drove mother and newborns to the hospital. "I've got a basketful of babies," Logan told the first nurse he encountered. The AP's Detroit bureau picked up the story, the news service dispatched it nationally, and variations of the report, datelined Ypsilanti and highlighting the nurse's surprise at the contents of Logan's basket, appeared in newspapers across the United States.[1] The Ypsilanti triplets feature would have been an inconsequential feel-good story except the AP neglected to note, when the item first moved on the national news wire, that the Logan family was Black. Many newspapers, including some in the South, published the dispatch before an AP Wirephoto, transmitted by the glacial technology available at the time, caught up to the story later in the day and provided visual evidence that the beaming father, shown gazing through the window of the hospital nursery, was—in the parlance of the day—a Negro.

Thus, the Ypsilanti triplets became a momentary flashpoint in an enduring controversy over journalistic standards of objectivity, accuracy, and news judgment, specifically when the news was about Black Americans. As the civil rights movement celebrated early victories, including President Harry Truman's desegregation of the U.S. military in 1948 and court rulings that laid the groundwork for desegregated education, white editors and journalists increasingly clashed with wire service executives over questions of when exactly Black Americans were newsworthy to the white readership AP news reports targeted, whether a story could be considered accurate and complete if it did not label all Black news subjects as "Negroes," and whose judgment determined the answers to these questions.[2] Although journalistic objectivity had been critiqued as an elusive and unattainable ideal, it remained at midcentury a cherished professional standard for many in white journalism; racial identification, some editors argued, provided the full information necessary for accurate reporting and objective newsroom decision-making by white news professionals.[3] To withhold it, they maintained, particularly but not solely from pro-segregation newsrooms in the South, was to omit relevant information and bias the news in favor of Black Americans by implying their equality with whites—whose race was not designated in news stories but was assumed. For example, at the *St. Louis Post-Dispatch* executive editor Ben Reese was adamant that Black Americans be identified by race in all news copy, and his staff was outspoken on this subject in frequent correspondence to the AP in the late 1940s and early 1950s.[4] In a letter two months before the triplet story appeared, one of at least five such complaints from the newspaper in 1947 and 1948, *Post-Dispatch* news editor H. T. Meek admonished AP news executives that "failure to identify Negroes as Negroes (thereby creating a false presumption that they are white) is, in some large sections of the country at least, the equivalent of mislabeling a drug or misbranding a can of beans—a practice which often covers adulteration and fraud."[5]

In the case of the Ypsilanti triplets story, a strong objection to the AP's delayed racial identification came from editor W. S. Kirkpatrick of the *Atlanta Journal*, whose staff, assuming the babies were white because the initial wire copy did not indicate otherwise, selected the story for the newspaper's December 7 front page. "Later that day," Kirkpatrick complained to the AP's New York office, "the attached wire photo came along which for our readers completely ruined the story. Maybe it should not have done so, but it did."[6] By 1948 the AP staff was accustomed to the demand for Negro identification from newspapers in states where Jim Crow was enforced by law and custom, and race was a criterion in local news judgment. For example, at the meeting of the Associated Press Managing Editors (APME) the previous month, Reese of the *St. Louis Post-Dispatch* had asserted that his newspaper, as a matter of policy, "subordinates Negroes, but sometimes we are out on page one with a story about black people, assuming they are white."[7] Accordingly, AP staff had scrambled when the Ypsilanti Wirephoto materialized to alert newspapers across the country that the father of the triplets was not white. In explaining the steps taken to correct the initial oversight, Alan Gould, the AP's executive editor, wrote Kirkpatrick in Atlanta to assure him that staff in the Detroit bureau realized that the babies' father was Black about two hours after the story first moved on the national wire. "As soon as the bureau did find out," Gould wrote, "we corrected the first paragraph of the story to read: 'Nurse Dorothy Heath was startled early today when <u>a young negro</u> approached her etc.'"[8]

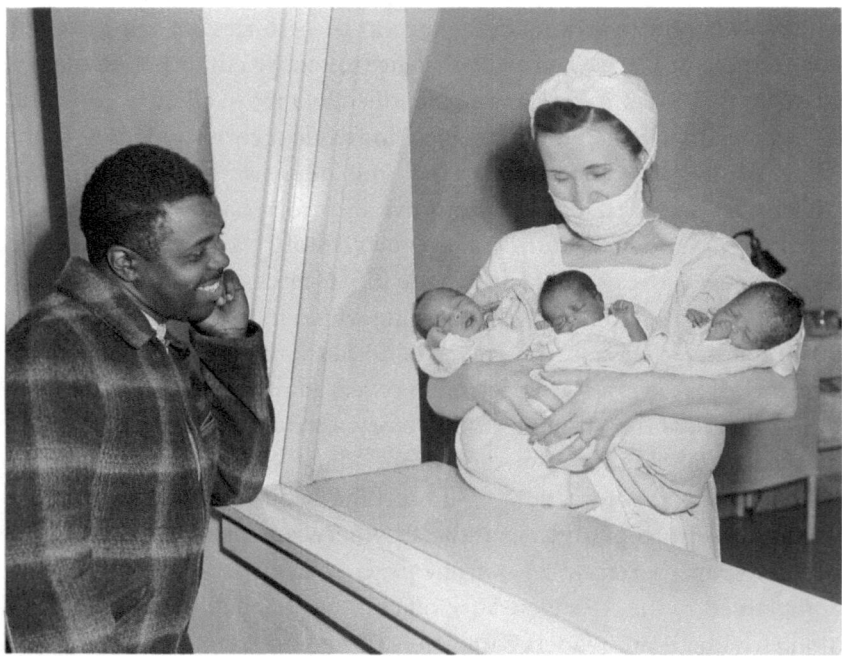

This 1948 Associated Press Wirephoto created controversy in segregationist newsrooms that published a light-hearted story about newborn triplets without realizing that the babies were "Negroes." The AP wire story did not designate the race of the babies, which became apparent when the photo arrived in newsrooms later in the day, after afternoon papers had gone to press. The original cutline read, "Nurse Elizabeth Hanawalt shows proud papa, Charles Logan, 34, the triplets he brought to the Beyer Hospital in Ypsilanti, Mich., early Tuesday, Dec. 7, 1948. Logan approached a nurse in the hospital corridor and told her 'I've got a basketfull of babies' (AP Photo/Preston Stroup)." Reprinted by permission of the Associated Press

Kirkpatrick's complaint that the Wirephoto "ruined" the story for white readers in Atlanta warrants further reflection. In 1948 the birth of triplets was still unusual enough to trigger local coverage in newspapers where the births occurred. The Ypsilanti feature was elevated to the national wire because it fed the AP's need for a mix of light content with the serious and, because the mythical stork delivered babies in a basket, the story had a magical and innocent quality. At least one newspaper, the *Baltimore Sun*, used that angle in the headline: "Triplets Born, Dad Is 'Stork.'"⁹ Until photographic evidence suggested the triplets and their father were Black, visually marking a racial difference, the *Atlanta Journal*'s editors deemed the story worthy of page one. News values, the standards and criteria white news professionals used to determine whether a story should be published and how it should be played, shifted abruptly when the AP redefined the babies as "Negro." Importantly, the triplets feature was a story about happy domesticity, which is one reason Kirkpatrick responded as he did. White southern readers generally did not want to see Black people featured in their newspapers. If Black news was important enough to appear in print, whites expected the coverage to affirm racial stereotypes about Black irresponsibility and criminality.¹⁰ The Ypsilanti story, starring a nuclear Black family with an employed and present father, was off script.¹¹

Although the Associated Press routinely placated its critics in the South and at border-state newspapers like the *St. Louis Post-Dispatch*, there was no national consensus on racial identification among the AP membership.¹² White editors, journalists, and wire service personnel in the North often did not include the "Negro" designation in their own stories even when they knew a news subject was Black, and some resented having to edit it out of AP stories when they deemed it irrelevant. For example, John Whalen, wire editor at the *Daily Republic* in Mitchell, South Dakota, complained to the AP following the Ypsilanti triplets story of "being irked every other day by the unnecessary mention of the fact that four victims of the southern flood were Negroes, a Negro father was being investigated as a possible arsonist following the burning of his home in Detroit, bringing death to several of his children, etc., although in none of the cases was the race of the persons involved pertinent to the story." As for the corrected lede regarding the triplets' father, Whalen wrote, "We here cannot in the slightest understand why such a follow-up note should be filed."¹³ Although Whalen and other more racially liberal editors made their case during the 1940s and 1950s for more equitable treatment of Black news subjects, their voices were drowned out by the strident insistence of racial conservatives, particularly at newspapers in Jim Crow communities, that nonwhite racial identification preserved the integrity of the news report.

The midcentury debate within journalism regarding the use of racial identification in news copy exposed racism in American daily journalism but it also signaled a progressive step toward recognition of Black Americans as news subjects worthy of ethical consideration. The question of whether to include racial identifiers became controversial because some white editors raised objections to the practice and their openly white supremacist peers pushed back. The conversation could not have occurred a decade earlier, before the early civil rights milestones shifted the racial ground beneath Americans' feet. Many white news workers were willing to bend to political change but others, particularly in southern newsrooms, perceived an existential threat to the racial status quo and resisted any concession to desegregation. The fight over racial identification in AP dispatches was a manifestation of white backlash.[14]

The racial identifier discussion also was the fruit of advocacy by the National Association for the Advancement of Colored People (NAACP), begun in the 1920s to persuade daily newspapers to capitalize the "N" in Negro, a first step toward treating Black news subjects with respect, and later to minimize racial identification in news content.[15] Although the NAACP's primary target was the northern daily press, the effort also had success with white southern editors at less racially strident papers who were willing to extend this courtesy in the 1920s and 1930s.[16] Despite his criticism of the Black press during World War II, Virginius Dabney of the *Richmond Times-Dispatch* also proposed in 1943 that white newspapers show Blacks consideration by capitalizing the "N." The white press should be "fair, just and objective in their handling of Negro news . . . ," Dabney wrote. "It has been demonstrated that this approach allays friction, quiets apprehension and helps to create cordial relations and a spirit of national unity." Dabney also advocated abandoning extraneous use of racial identification, though he certainly did not suggest eliminating it from news copy as some racially progressive editors suggested after the war. He also overplayed the impact of the token "N" accommodation in newspapers like his that defended Jim Crow and white privilege, assuming that polite segregation, a mark of southern gentility, pardoned the sin.[17]

During the 1930s and 1940s, the NAACP shifted its emphasis from the capital "N" to overuse of racial identification in crime stories. Archived NAACP correspondence makes clear that the organization, often through the advocacy of local chapters, again targeted newspapers in northern cities, urging a change in policy and raising awareness among northern editors that Black Americans perceived the Negro identifier as an equity issue. For example, in 1936 the NAACP wrote to major newspapers, asking them to stop labeling Black Americans in police stories.[18] The NAACP's activism may have rankled columnist Westbrook Pegler, discussed in chapter 1. In developing his attacks on Black newspapers and the Double V Campaign, Pegler discovered Black complaints about the white press using racial identifications for Black people accused of crimes and other failings, when the racial identity of unlabeled news subjects was assumed to be white. In 1942 Pegler accused Black Americans of holding an inconsistent position on racial tagging. "There is never any objection to pointed mention that Marian Anderson or Joe Louis is a negro," he wrote.[19]

In 1946 the NAACP campaign marked an important victory with the white daily press, when the *New York Times* editorialized that singling out Black Americans for racial identification in crime stories was unfair and professionally irresponsible:

> The press, we believe, has a special and heavy responsibility.... Some newspapers treat news about Negro citizens in separate sections or columns, extending Jim Crowism to the printed page. In others discrimination is less flagrant, but Negroes are often identified, whereas members of other races are not.
>
> This may seem a small thing. The Negroes do not think so. This newspaper has considered its obligations to its readers in light of these facts and principles. This consideration has led us to adhere to the rule that the race of a person suspected or accused of crime shall not be published unless there is a legitimate purpose to be served thereby....
>
> News that encourages racial discrimination may sometimes be of interest, but responsible journalism has a higher law than a passing interest.[20]

In 1952 the New York branch of the NAACP persuaded the New York City Council to pass a resolution asking all New York daily newspapers to discontinue racial identification in crime stories.[21]

A similar public discussion was taking place in Chicago, a city that had seen its Black population swell as Black southerners migrated north for employment and safety. In 1950 the civic organization City Club of Chicago released a report titled "John Smith, Negro, in the Tribune," which noted that all but one citywide newspaper in Chicago had minimized offensive overuse of the racial identifier. Colonel Robert McCormick, *Chicago Tribune* publisher, declined to meet with the City Club's Race Relations Committee, which then published its criticism of the newspaper. Sampling racial identification in the *Tribune*, the City Club offered pointed and detailed analysis of the issue. "Instances in which the word has been used with repeated and hammer-like effect demonstrate the point that it is difficult to use such a poison in moderation," the report said. The City Club summarized its objections to the newspaper's use of racial tagging because "in a paper that emphasizes crime and violence as the Tribune does there are inevitably many news stories connecting Negroes with such crimes. The inference is drawn by readers that Negroes have an inherent biological tendency toward such crime." The report concluded that the paper was undemocratic. "The concept of a free press necessarily involves the correlative concept of a responsible press," it stated. "A paper like the Tribune which prides itself on fighting for freedom of the press owes a special obligation to avoid practices which hamper the freedoms of some citizens."[22] The report also drew an analogy with the Nazis' use of the Star of David to identify Jews during World War II and argued that the racial label was "feeding the vulgar appetite for a scapegoat."[23]

Although the *New York Times* and some other metropolitan dailies staked out a position that informed practice at many other newspapers in the North, most newspapers in the South considered such thinking an affront. Given this divide, the AP attempted to hold firm in the slippery middle, prevented from adopting a definitive national policy by its cooperative ownership structure and pretense toward neutrality.

## Constructing Racial Difference on the AP Wire

The racial identifier debate has been mentioned by other journalism historians and this chapter is in conversation with previous scholarship; however, the argument here ascribes greater significance to the issue, defining it not simply as an anachronistic and now abandoned professional routine but as a primary site of contested representation, a central ideological battle in the civil rights–era struggle over meaning and racial identity in the news narrative.[24] Although the issue of racial identification in news copy was pervasive in postwar daily journalism, this analysis situates the discussion within the Associated Press, a normative institution that imposed journalism standards on the twentieth-century press.[25] This research demonstrates how the debate over the Negro identifier changed policy within the AP and, consequently, impacted newsrooms across the country, even those led by racially liberal editors. The discussion is grounded in an extensive review of documents in the Associated Press Corporate Archives, primarily member correspondence with AP personnel during the 1940s and 1950s. By design, the letters singled out for analysis here are representative of topical threads that run throughout the archive and focus not on major news stories but regular, everyday reporting. Using this approach, the analysis shows that the ideology motivating segregationist editors to demand the Negro identifier in news copy became ingrained into the news philosophy and daily operations of the AP, affecting work routines and decision-making in newsrooms and bureaus throughout the United States and in the corporate offices in New York.

The AP found itself at the center of the racial identification dispute because, as a leading wire service for U.S. and world news, the AP was an arbiter of journalistic norms and in theory distributed to U.S. clients both national and regional news reports that could be deemed credible by white readers of various political leanings in every area of the country, including the Deep South. The analysis shows, however, that AP leadership capitulated to the news service's strident segregationist faction, and through policy and practice, specifically daily content choices, forced members like John Whalen, the wire editor in Mitchell, South Dakota, to acquiesce to southern racial ideology, as odious as he may have been found it. The AP's posture of appeasement, which hardened over time in response to continual berating by white supremacists in the membership, treated support for Jim Crow as a legitimate and rational position in the civil rights debate. Under the rubric of objectivity, which called for both sides of a story to be told, the AP created a false equivalency between the pro- and anti-segregationist positions, assuming that neutrality on racial justice was a sustainable position. Journalism ethics codes would not take a definitive position on race for decades, but the *Brown* decision would declare segregation illegal in 1954, which complicated the AP's refusal to take sides.[26]

Throughout southern journalism and in some racially conservative northern and border-state newsrooms, the social customs of Jim Crow permeated even the professional standards of journalism. The AP, with its adherence to the inverted pyramid story structure, a formula for prioritizing information in the news report, and its protocols for verification and balance, offered the unquestioned model for the application of journalistic objectivity and verification of accuracy within a daily newspaper industry that in 1948 employed almost no Black editors and journalists and served a predominantly white readership.[27] During the 1940s and 1950s many southern newspapers still segregated text and images by placing Black news on separate pages or even by publishing special "black star" editions that circulated only to Black readers and preserved the daily newspaper as a space for the white audience.[28]

Accordingly, when the AP presented racial news in a way that appeared to treat Black Americans equitably or to legitimate their demand for civil rights, white supremacist members protested the discrepancy between their perception and the news report, charging bias and insisting that their view, not the AP's, represented objectivity and accuracy. And, because news outlets that received AP news copy were member-owners of the nonprofit cooperative that operated the wire service, the editors' views held sway. Officials in the AP headquarters in New York and in bureaus across the United States, who were in effect employed by the AP membership, met criticism about racial coverage with changes in practice, as they did in 1948 when they transmitted a clarification about the Ypsilanti triplets' race. During the 1950s, when civil rights activists elevated demands for racial equality, school desegregation and other civil rights issues often dominated the AP's daily report. The ideological framework for news judgment was redefined by southern editors' continual agitation against positive news representations of Black Americans and negative portrayals of the white South's response to their legal gains. By vigorously protesting the wire service's perceived acquiescence to evolving racial norms in the North, and forcing the AP to cede to their demands, racially conservative editors anchored the segregationist status quo within the definition of journalistic objectivity and standards of news judgment and accuracy.

As such, the AP membership's midcentury debate over racial identification in daily newspapers is but one manifestation of a broader pattern of strident reaction by segregationists in the white daily press, particularly in the South, who recognized that rigid social and political demarcations along lines of racial identity were under challenge and invoked journalism standards to maintain racial distinctions and manage the news narrative about race. Our chapter opens in 1948, early in a wave of radical change in the legal status of Black Americans, but by 1954, when the *Brown v. Board of Education* decision declared racially segregated schools to be unconstitutional, the racial stakes for white southerners and their northern allies also intensified. As a result, some racially conservative white editors, believing that the daily record of the AP news report defined social and political reality, made it a priority during the 1950s to monitor and debate the standard of objectivity employed by the news service on racial news. These activist editors became fixated on the inclusion and omission of the Negro identifier in news stories and critically and relentlessly monitored the wire. Surveillance of the AP by white supremacist members expressed a fear that daily newspapers would become unwitting accomplices in the effort to normalize Black participation in social and civic life, and would erase the racial distinction and power differential that subjugated Blackness to whiteness.

Obsession with the Negro identifier in news copy, which laid siege to the AP for more than a decade, was part of a broader ideological campaign in white southern journalism to defend the racial status quo. Following *Brown v. Board of Education*, southern editors and journalists intensely critiqued the objectivity of the northern press in reporting on racial tensions in the South, and some also became prominent advocates for southern racial tradition—working behind the scenes politically, writing books and magazine articles pleading the case of the white South, and using the news columns as well as the editorial pages of their newspapers to advance the cause of segregation.[29] As well, southern advocates for continued segregation and their northern allies battled the Associated Press management for the better part of the 1950s over perceived disparities in the news service's coverage of racism in the North versus the South. AP officials in New York spent a good deal of their time during the decade fielding southern complaints about failures to include racial identification, reassuring southern members of the AP's neutrality on the issue of desegregation, and defending the objectivity of the wire service against claims that its reporting on local and regional racial tensions was biased against the South and in favor of the North.[30]

Significantly, by the mid-1950s pro-segregation journalists and editors in the white daily press, who were reporting on the seismic social change that *Brown* and other legal gains had initiated for Black Americans, were also contending with the civil rights movement's consequences for their own racial status, which had historically depended on perceptions of Black inferiority. The scope and depth of the impending upheaval in the southern social order was disconcerting to many white journalists and editors, whose allegiance to segregation had been sanctioned not only by law prior to *Brown* but also by the revered regional history and way of life that now were under direct attack. When Thomas Waring of the white supremacist *News and Courier* in Charleston, South Carolina, editorialized that integration and racial amalgamation would mean the end of white civilization, he was not engaging in hyperbole; he believed this to be true.[31]

The preoccupation with the racial identifier in AP wire copy flowed from this cultural logic. In the late 1940s, when the early signs of a vibrant civil rights movement manifested, many white editors who believed separation of the races to be the appropriate social order felt insecure in the privileges that accrued to their own white identity and insisted that the Associated Press police a discursive racial boundary keeping Black Americans in their place and marking them as "other." Every time the Negro identifier appeared in an AP news report, race was inscribed onto the body of a Black news subject, interpellating that person into subjugated Blackness, and preserving whiteness as the assumed and, often, unmarked norm.[32] Every time this occurred, the AP affirmed a racial binary in which separate was not equal and legitimized the white supremacist intent of many in the southern white press. By challenging the objectivity and accuracy of journalists, editors, and wire service executives who did not share their assumption of a segregated society and did not see the relevance of racial identity in every news story, segregationists developed a professionally expedient tool for embedding their views into the AP's daily news report. Moreover, when Black Americans were labeled as Negroes, white editors had the means, when selecting wire content for their own newspapers, to prioritize stories about Black crime and poverty and ignore stories about Black normalcy and accomplishment, ensuring that stereotypical deviance was associated with the Black community. Specifically, the Negro identifier would prevent Black Americans like Charles Logan, father of triplets, from passing for white on the pages of daily newspapers.[33]

## The AP Framework

With bureaus across the United States, the AP served its members at daily newspapers by transmitting news along national, regional, and state wires. At midcentury, the AP's professional culture was shaped through national and regional communication loops that included internal publications and news logs, memos and directives, programming and discussion at national and state meetings of the Associated Press Managing Editors organization, and routine correspondence and conversation among AP members and the staff in wire service bureaus and offices. Because the cooperative was owned by the news outlets that contracted for its services, AP membership carried the expectation of ready access to staff in bureaus and even to executives in the New York headquarters. Questions and complaints from members were prioritized such that letters were answered quickly, copied to peers and superiors, and archived. Members had direct telephone access to bureau personnel and could query for details about news stories and seek coverage of events and issues by sending messages up the wire. Many members felt intense loyalty to the AP, which provided professional development and fellowship, but they also perceived that membership came with professional privileges.[34]

At midcentury, daily newspapers also could subscribe to the United Press (UP) wire service, which was owned by the Scripps-Howard chain and would become United Press International (UPI) in 1958, following a merger with Hearst's International News Service. In their internal communication during the 1950s, members of the AP workforce referred to UP as "the opposition" and kept score on its errors and scoops. The UP tilted its news cycle toward afternoon papers, which ultimately was its undoing, and operated on a lower overhead than the AP, a resource challenge that sometimes compromised its coverage and accuracy. Even without the cooperative ownership structure of the AP, which gave southern members direct influence over editorial decisions, the racial identity of news subjects was an occupational concern for UP. In his memoir, John Herbers, who headed UP's Jackson, Mississippi, bureau during the 1950s, recalled that some southern UP clients refused to use stories about Black news subjects and civil rights, which discouraged his bureau from covering such news.[35] UP also aggressively pursued racial detail in stories that stereotyped Black news subjects, and AP members who subscribed to both wire services sometimes realized that the AP had lapsed when racial identification appeared in UP coverage but was missing in the AP's version.

A typical complaint came from Tanner Hunt of the Beaumont, Texas, newspapers, who noted in 1956 that the AP had moved a Wirephoto of a dark-skinned man arrested in San Francisco without a racial identification in either the story or cutline: "Our observation is that the Associated Press is guilty of more omissions, such as in the attached, than are some of the other services, particularly the UP."[36] In another such incident in 1955, the Kansas City bureau chief received an "emphatic protest" about the AP's handling of a story about six fatalities in a Detroit fire. He wrote Alan Gould, the AP's executive editor, that "the Star originally had planned to play up the story, but when the United Press came in with the negro designation the Star, after confirming through a message the UP information, changed its plans. They feel that this information should be carried as a matter of information in all such stories, saying the decision on whether to publish should lay [sic] with the individual papers."[37] Competition with "the opposition" increased the pressure on AP staff and executives and provided segregationist AP members with additional leverage.

AP membership also carried a reciprocal component, a requirement that individual newspapers shared their content with the wire service. Although staff in AP bureaus and offices did their own reporting on many major news events and those for which a member could not provide coverage, much of the content distributed by the Associated Press originated in local newsrooms, where local news judgment and attitudes about race influenced framing and content. In particular, local standards regarding the Negro identifier determined whether a local story shared with the AP initially contained this information and whether, in stories received on the wire, it would be edited out of a story. In racially conservative newsrooms, editors who suspected the racial identification was missing often demanded, in an inquiry to a bureau or executives in New

York, that it be supplied. Ultimately, segregationist local editors used the racial identifier to calibrate the Black presence on their news pages, erasing Black achievement from the day's news reports, highlighting Black failings, and reinforcing damaging Black stereotypes. These editors' insistence on racial identification continually reminded AP executives and staff of their fundamental objection to integration and embedded white supremacy within the concept of objectivity.

Although the twentieth-century AP engendered an orthodoxy on journalism standards and inflexible rules for punctuation, grammar, abbreviations, and usage, all of it institutionalized in successive editions of the AP stylebook, member newsrooms exercised autonomy over local content, which was reflected in their contributions to and editing of the AP's daily news report. The first edition of the AP stylebook, published in 1953, offered a short entry that defined capitalization rules for races: "Caucasian, Negro, Indian, Chinese, but white, black, yellow, red," and proscribed use of "colored." The instruction on capitalization aligned the AP with the NAACP position, that the "N" in Negro should be capitalized. In addition, the 1953 entry stated that "identification by race should be made ONLY when it adds something to the story or is required."[38] The guidelines were little changed in the stylebook's second edition in 1960, which said the word "Colored" was allowed in organization names: "Identification by race should be made when it is pertinent."[39]

The question of pertinence, a subjective determination based on local interpretation, had been AP policy since at least 1940, when Executive News Editor Byron Price became concerned about the AP's legal exposure for incorrectly identifying white people as Negroes, which was grounds for libel in many southern jurisdictions, and issued a directive regarding this "constant problem" for the AP.[40] "Hereafter make no mention of racial identification in any story unless essential to the news," he wrote.[41] Price did not define "essential" but framed the issue as one only of legal liability, not social justice, and underscored the need to verify racial labels in crime stories.

In its concern for pertinence, the wire service appeared during the 1950s, when civil rights activism kept race at the forefront of the daily news budget, to acknowledge the implications of identifying Black Americans in news copy at the same time that it carved out a position of deference to southern racial attitudes. The AP Reference Book, a manual for personnel, contained this 1954 guideline, establishing the relativity of the pertinence definition and granting latitude and legitimacy to regional, or "sectional," interpretation:

> The AP does not have a hard and fast rule on racial identification of persons in news stories. The practice is to name a person's race whenever such identification is pertinent to the story.
>
> It is important to remember that in some sections racial identifications affect story values. That is a factor in determining the pertinence of the identification. Good taste is another factor; we must avoid the use of racial identifications that have the effect of holding the race up to ridicule.[42]

The racial identification issue, which Gould described as a source of contention at Associated Press Managing Editors gatherings for more than a decade, boiled to the surface in 1954 and 1955, as the South anticipated the impact of the U.S. Supreme Court's school desegregation ruling in *Brown v. Board of Education*. In a memo, Gould described a "fairly heated discussion" at a midyear APME meeting in April 1954, "with southerners generally demanding that stories say when persons are Negroes, mainly so they can judge the play (or non-use) accordingly." In Gould's account, the AP did not challenge the southern position on grounds that including the racial identification in every story was necessarily unfair to Black Americans but countered that the wire service's reliance on stories from member newspapers from across the United States made it impractical: "It was pointed out, both by some managing editors and by AP men, that in many sections of the country, papers do not carry such identification so the AP does NOT know." Gould also noted that "southern state wires could adopt their own style in such matters, but that the trunk wires," which distributed news beyond a region, "had to conform to a national style most suited to the largest number of members." In sum, he wrote, "No conclusions were reached and nobody was convinced."[43]

Proceedings of the April 1954 APME meeting that Gould described were outside the purview of *The APME Red Book*, which offers a record of the organization's national annual meetings held each November. The 1954 *Red Book* contains no mention of a racial identification debate that year, but the 1955 volume offers the following summation in the Domestic News Committee Report: "During the year's work, considerable controversy developed over whether racial identification was essential in AP stories. The question revolved around the matter of pertinence and it developed there was a wide difference among editors as to when such identification was pertinent." The committee concluded, in circular fashion, that "in the interest of complete reporting, the AP should continue its present policy of making such identification whenever it is pertinent."[44] The report pointedly offered no clarification of the definition of pertinence, which now functioned as an obscure news value. This remarkably brief notation about a significant and ongoing disagreement among the APME membership is important for its failure to judge the issue on its merits. Moreover, by invoking "the interest of complete reporting," the APME deferred to southern insistence that racial identification, which distinguished Black news subjects from white and marked them as "other," was always necessary for accurate news reporting.

## Developing the Party Line

Despite their executive status, Gould and other top staff in New York personally reviewed much of the member mail, including letters from many editors during the 1940s and 1950s regarding the Negro identification issue. Although some members objected that racial identification was extraneous to the news or insulting to Black Americans, a review of the archive suggests that far more correspondence came from southern editors angry to discover that racial identification was missing in a story that included Black news subjects.[45] Many members wrote the AP brass directly but member correspondence to bureau chiefs on the matter also was routed to Gould and the executive staff, who generally acknowledged those concerns with a personal letter. As Gould managed this issue over the years, his position required him to be politic in dealing with members from all regions of the United States, and he generally struck a pose of neutrality. "I readily admit," he wrote an editor at the *Boston Herald* in 1954, "that what is 'pertinent' is subject to various interpretations, by the staff as well as by the members."[46] At the same time, responses from Gould that defended omission of the racial identifier and asserted that it was not pertinent are hard to find in his correspondence with southerners. Although this faction generated the most heated comment on this issue, it comprised a minority of the AP membership. Even so, Gould's stance, and that of the wire service, was to accommodate the southern demand for Negro identification, to the extent that the information could be obtained from members who supplied stories to the AP.

The AP's executive correspondence with complaining members offers a steady iteration of the pertinence policy and documents the AP's continuing acquiescence, throughout the 1950s, to demands for racial identification in stories of any consequence, large or small, and its instructions to bureaus to comport with southern preferences. In a typical example from 1956, David Tenant Bryan, publisher of the *Richmond Times-Dispatch*, took issue with missing Negro identification in coverage of a lecture by a sociologist. "Unless the AP identifies such speakers by race, the story is really meaningless," Bryan wrote, though he presumably would not have complained if the expert had turned out to be white.[47] In his response, Paul Mickelson, the AP's general news editor, agreed that the race of the speaker should have been included by the member newspaper that provided the story: "It was highly pertinent under the circumstances, and we have told our Cincinnati bureau so."[48] Harmon Phillips, an editor at the *Tulsa Tribune*, also complained that a wire story about an Oklahoman murdered in Washington, DC, should have said the victim and killer were Black:

> I naturally became interested and telephoned our Washington bureau to get to work and have a good story for us in the morning, plus pictures if possible.
> I was a little disappointed to learn through our bureau that the persons involved were both Negroes.
> Now we have nothing against de-segregation. (I have no children in school who will be square dancing and swimming with the little darkies.)
> But I assure you I would not have spent money to rout our Washington folks out at night to get me a story of a Negro shooting. And I'm sure a lot of other managing editors feel the same way.[49]

If Gould winced, he did not convey discomfort in his reply. Gould responded that Phillips was "correct about the need of Negro identification in the Washington story" and explained that an editor in the Washington bureau had deleted a line in the story that said, "Both men were Negroes." Following that omission, Gould noted that the AP "circulated a new reminder to Washington desks that the negro identification should be carried in all stories in which (a) it is a pertinent part of the story and (b) identification is certain."[50]

As AP executives deferred to the concerns of editors who wanted the Negro label applied in all stories, the record shows that the AP management was unpersuaded by requests for less emphasis on racial identification from more racially liberal editors. In one case, Tippen Davidson of the *Daytona Beach Morning Journal*, complained about "the Southern AP's habitual disregard of the rights of the Negro citizen to the dignities of proper address." Davidson, whose Florida newspaper was on the South's regional wire and received news crafted to please a majority of southern editors, objected to the repeated use of the word "Negro" in a crime story. "There are, after all, other synonyms," Davidson wrote. "'Man' would have been a useful one, if you could persuade your writer to think of a male Negro as a human being." Davidson also complained of the indiscriminate application of the racial identifier, including "that genetic marvel, the Negro apartment house. And in the past week we had a Negro bathing beach (black sand?), a Negro amusement park, a Negro bus and a Negro grocery store."[51] The Miami bureau chief who received Davidson's complaint conceded that the Negro identification, which appeared four times in five paragraphs, "was badly over-done" in the story Davidson initially mentioned but disagreed that it signaled disrespect by the reporter. "Of all the people I know in the South, Malcolm [Johnson] is one of the last I would regard as holding Negroes in low esteem," the bureau chief wrote. "It happens that he has an extraordinarily wide acquaintance and friendship among Negroes of the Tallahassee area, notably at Florida A. & M," the historically Black university.[52] When the reporter also responded to Davidson, he attributed the redundancy in use of the Negro identifier to "sloppy writing . . . rather than any racial prejudice," and noted that he was from Idaho.[52]

In another complaint about the inclusion of racial identification, Ben Leuchter, an editor in Vineland, New Jersey, wrote, "Some years ago we at the TIMES JOURNAL decided that the identification of people by color was a form of discrimination in that it added nothing to the story, and since that time we have been tailoring Associated Press copy to conform to that policy." Leuchter explained to Samuel Blackman, the New York bureau chief, that his newspaper routinely deleted gratuitous references to race in stories irrelevant to race. "We do not identify a man when he is white, and therefore there is no reason to identify him when he is a negro," Leuchter wrote. What prompted his complaint was a story about a fatal fire in which the racial identification was extraneous to the news.

> The fact that twin babies burned to death in a fire in a South Philadelphia apartment was important enough to get the Associated Press to file a story about it. It was important because there were two human beings and because the story touched the heart. The last line in which the reader was told that the family was negro added absolutely nothing, and yet, because some people are still bigoted, the line actually may have detracted somewhat from the story. I am sure that some people after reading the entire story got to the last line and thought to themselves: "Oh, what the hell, they were only niggers, so it wasn't so bad after all."[54]

Blackman's response restated the AP's policy of providing racial identification and letting editors decide whether to use it. "Is it essential to the story?" Blackman asked. "One editor will say yes; another no."[55]

AP executives also turned aside attempts by staff to present alternate views on the issue of racial labeling. In 1954 Gould foreclosed an effort by Lew Hawkins, the Atlanta bureau chief, to minimize use of the Negro identifier under the pertinence policy. After the bureau transmitted a story shared by a member newspaper that erroneously identified a white automobile accident victim as Black, Hawkins issued a memo instructing Atlanta staff to "omit the racial identification in run-of-the-mill accident stories." Citing the risk of getting an identification wrong in a story that lists multiple news subjects, Hawkins said, "I know that one reason we have done this is member pressure for it—because having racial identification often influences the way a story is played."[56] Apparently believing he had autonomy to make such decisions for his bureau, Hawkins wrote Gould to share his staff memo and explain that the erroneous information had been supplied by the *Atlanta Constitution*. "With this [error] as an example," he wrote, "we're going to omit this sort of identification—and see if we can make it stick with the membership. . . . It is a sound peg on which to hang a change in policy."[57] Gould's response to the memo was swift, even dispatched by airmail. "If followed to the letter, it is pretty certain we'd get in deeper trouble than we may now be risking," Gould wrote. "We never expect to hit on a formula to please all sides of the negro identification controversy, but we have done just about as well as reasonably can be expected." He then repeated the guideline to use the identifier only when it was pertinent and to rarely place it in the first paragraph: "Your staff, of course, will have to decide if such identification is pertinent, but if any newspaper asks for it, then supply the information."[58]

As Hawkins had noted, the push for racial identification in all stories created opportunities for errors in reporting. AP executives also received the detailed reports mandated of reporters and bureau chiefs who were responsible for errors that made it onto the wire, and this included stories that incorrectly identified a white person as Negro. AP's procedures for documenting errors and corrections, especially those that resulted in "killed" stories pulled from use after members had already received them on the wire, entailed a detailed memo to the executive leadership from every employee who handled that news copy. The correspondence up the chain reveals how easily errors of racial identification occurred and the legal jeopardy the news service was willing to endure in the mid-1950s, a sharp departure from Byron Price's 1940 policy, to now supply this information to newspapers that demanded it. Often errors in racial identification occurred when a police dispatcher gave biographical information about news subjects over the phone, along with details of an arrest or automobile accident. In one case, involving the Mobile, Alabama, bureau in 1956, a story about an indictment incorrectly listed a victim of mortgage fraud as Negro. Stan Atkins, the bureau chief, wrote Gould a detailed chronology of the error and steps taken to correct it on the wire and stave off a lawsuit. Atkins reported that the information about the victim came from an assistant district attorney, who "supplied me with various background on the case. He repeatedly referred to her as a Negro woman." After the error had been published, the assistant district attorney "said he was completely convinced the woman was a Negro and added that one of the investigative officers had referred to her as a colored woman. He said, with some understatement, 'I hope I haven't fouled you up.'"[59]

By the mid-1950s Negro identification was in most of the news copy that moved over the AP wire, and it was widely understood that newsrooms that did not want to use the racial designation would have to remove it from those stories. In correspondence with a member, Paul Mickelson, the AP's general news editor, wrote, "We have found little to no objection from any newspapers if we handle negro identification with some finesse. If we use the word 'negro' in the first sentence of a story, we can be sure of beefs from the antis. If we slip the identification between commas in the second or third graf, where it almost always belongs, we seem to satisfy all sides. In other words: don't slap the reader in the face with it." Mickelson indicated that this guideline had evolved after AP experimented with different ways of signaling the racial identification: "Once we tried handling such identification in notes to editors following transmission of a story, but were appalled to see the note published as a shirt tail in a couple of papers!"[60]

Ironically, the civil rights movement, which foregrounded race in order to challenge inequality, increased the likelihood that an editor at an AP-member newspaper would think racial identification was pertinent to a news story. It also produced news copy in which whiteness, which usually had gone unreported, became evident in a narrative, though the visibility of whiteness alongside Blackness did not imply racial equality. In 1959 Samuel Blackman, then the AP's general news editor, explained that racial identification was appearing more frequently in AP news reports about daily events. Although the pertinence standard still applied, race had become more relevant. "We now use it more than we used to," he wrote. "That is because, with the tensions built up mostly by the school integration controversy, more and more newspapers want to know whether the persons involved in news stories are Negro or white." Acknowledging that some newspapers routinely edited the racial identification out of stories, he explained that the AP was still structuring news stories to allow the local editor to exercise local preference. "Except in stories where conflict between the races is the major element, we try to make all identification unobtrusive," Blackman wrote. "Very often it is a separate sentence, or even a separate paragraph, which can easily be deleted by newspapers which do not want to use it."[61]

In practice, this policy meant that AP personnel in the North who did not believe racial identification was always pertinent were subject to southern sensibilities. After a complaint about the omission of the Negro identifier in a 1956 story about an unsupervised child who froze to death after wandering outside during winter, Mickelson admonished Cy Douglass, the Des Moines bureau chief, that the race of the child had been pertinent simply because a southern newspaper had wanted the identification. "We will be guided accordingly in future developments," Douglass replied. "Currently in this area there is a distinctly different view about the pertinency of this descriptive, generally. For instance, the largest newspaper in the state has not yet used the word in connection with the story."⁶²

That same year, the New York office engaged in detailed correspondence for a week with staff in the Cleveland and Columbus, Ohio, bureaus over a breaking story about a crime and three arrests, initially supplied by the *Toledo Blade* without racial identification. After the AP dispatched the story over its wire, United Press identified Black subjects in its version, prompting complaints from southern AP members. In the detailed postmortem of the lapse, several bureau personnel explained the chain of events that led to the missing racial identification and engaged in discussion of the policy and the challenge of implementing it. "We had no intent to deceive," wrote correspondent Miles Smith of the Cleveland bureau. "The story was handled in extreme haste. We knew from the state message that the opposition had some kind of story out. The Blade wasn't speedy, but when it finally came through it had a coherent account of a very complex series of events." Although the bureau added racial tags in updates to the story, Smith conceded that this had not been his journalistic priority. "We filed the racial identification after making the check with the Blade," he wrote. "A member request was sufficient justification for taking this action. But what would have happened if we had learned the race identification, and there was no member request? Would we have inserted it? I don't know. . . . We have 'cops and robbers' around here pretty often, and neither the whites nor the blacks have a monopoly."⁶³

Hawkins, the Atlanta bureau chief, was looped into the correspondence because he had queried the Cleveland bureau on behalf of southern members who had suspected that the racial identification was missing and now responded to Smith as a veteran of the racial identification controversy. In the two years since Gould had rebuffed Hawkins's attempt to limit racial identification in stories handled by his bureau, Hawkins had shifted his orientation and now, in analyzing the situation with the Toledo story, articulated and rationalized the AP pertinence policy to his Ohio colleague. Hawkins affirmed a false equivalency between the two primary sides of the race story and drew an interesting distinction between professional responsibility and the practical demands of moving news copy through a wire service that served multiple regions of the United States:

I wonder if you aren't approaching the problem more from the standpoint of a conscientious newspaper editor than as an AP man.

As you note, there is an honest difference of opinion among newspapers as to whether racial identification belongs in a story such as the one in question. Some say yes, some say no and I'm sure you agree it's not our proper role to say which is correct.

But when we omit racial identification in a major crime like this, aren't we very effectively resolving the question in favor of the negative? If we use the identification those who feel it should not be used can strike it out. When we omit it, those who feel otherwise can't put it in. . . .

It is a fact that we have a <u>standing</u> request, both explicit and implicit, from literally scores of Southern members. Whenever we don't meet that request without waiting for a reminder, we are inviting criticism.[64]

By 1956, a year after the second *Brown* ruling instructing public schools to desegregate "with all deliberate speed," the AP had internalized the segregationists' demand for racial identification.

Although the Wirephoto technology had improved since the Ypsilanti triplets story in 1948, in the years after *Brown* photos of dark-complexioned news subjects that were shared by members without racial identification in the cutline forced AP personnel to resolve the missing racial detail and avoid creating an error. Smith in the Cleveland bureau also explained that dimension of the crime report. "The two of us who handled the Toledo story—desk man Bill Newkirk and myself—didn't know until we received your message that the three men were Negroes," he told Hawkins. "I knew Toledo had moved two pictures on the net, so I went to Wirephoto and got the prints. Obviously all three had very dark skins. I said to Bill that there was one who might just possibly be from San Juan. I suggested that rather than make assumptions he'd better phone the Blade. He did, and their desk checked someone and confirmed all three were Negroes."[65] This requirement that AP employees and members assign race to news subjects directly implicated news workers in the maintenance of racial categories in the daily news report.

Although a member newsroom had the option of editing the racial identification out of a story received on the wire, the AP had standardized news copy according to the specifications of southern members. By prioritizing racial identity and requiring bureau personnel to chase and verify this biographical detail, the AP had allowed white supremacist ideology to skew not only reporting standards but also journalistic resource decisions. The policy forced local newspapers that did not want to label racial distinctions to do the extra work of removing them from news copy, when time on deadline allowed, and it forced AP personnel to do the extra work of including racial detail, even if most editors in the North and West thought it irrelevant. In large measure, the AP's executive leadership had ceded news judgment about race to the strident segregationist press.

Ironically, the segregationist victory in standardizing the Negro identifier presented southern AP members with a dilemma. In 1953 many southern newsrooms had ignored the recommendation in the first AP stylebook to capitalize the N in Negro, but once the AP attached a racial label to every mention of a Black person, the wire filled with references to "Negro" news subjects. White supremacist editor Thomas Waring, who insisted on racial identification, said his Charleston, South Carolina, newspaper adopted the capital N on Negro for practical reasons, not because it softened its racial philosophy. "There is little (if any) justification for it," Waring wrote in 1955. "We do it as a sop to the Negro readers, who seem to set great store by that." He continued, "The AP capitalizes Negro, and for uniformity in style we would have to reset a lot of lines to use the small N. Even a newspaper publisher will succumb to the pressure of a buck."[66] Yet resetting type was exactly what Waring and other segregationists—as well as AP leadership—disingenuously expected of northern editors who wanted to erase the racial label that pervaded the AP news report by the mid-1950s.

## Allegations of Regional Bias

As the AP acquiesced to the ongoing demand for Negro identification, the wire service also bent its coverage in response to southern complaints that racial incidents in the South were covered disproportionately to those in the North, where, southerners insisted, race relations were no better. Southern editors bristled at the northern press's fascination with southern resistance to desegregation and argued that racial discrimination and even de facto segregation were the norm in the North.[67] Southerners insisted that the AP's transmission of negative racial news about the South, while racial problems and Black crimes in the North went unreported, was hypocritical and produced a biased news report. Southern editors further complained that the northern press played up white-on-Black racial violence in the South and demanded that the AP supply news of Black crimes against whites in the North. Under this strategy, Negro identification was essential in stories originating in the North, to allow southern critics to monitor both the AP and northern newsrooms that generated many of these stories for a lack of objectivity. Imposing the Negro identifier on news about Black crime and poverty in the North also ensured that southern papers would be able to highlight Black deviancy in making their case against integration. "The designation of Negroes as such," wrote J. Q. Mahaffey, segregationist editor of the *Texarkana [TX] Gazette*, "is always a pertinent part of stories in the south and southwest, inasmuch as it generally determines the type of play the story will receive in papers in this part of the country."[68]

As the 1950s wore on and southern resistance to desegregation intensified, the unrelenting agitation of southern editors eroded the disposition toward balance that AP executives had exhibited prior to *Brown*. As seen through changes in AP policy and practice, the racially conservative southern viewpoint, though it spoke for a minority of the overall AP membership, strongly influenced news values at AP headquarters in New York. In 1956, just months after the lynching of Chicago teenager Emmett Till in Mississippi and saturation coverage of the crime and trial focused negative national and international attention on the South, the *Chattanooga [TN] News-Free Press* editorialized against both the Associated Press and its rival, United Press, for omitting racial identifications from a story about two Black teenagers who assaulted a white teacher in Chicago—until pressed to do so by the newspaper.[69] In a memo to AP staff, Gould repeated the pertinence policy and quoted from the Chattanooga editorial: "'The fact these thugs were Negroes was an essential part of this story, especially since it was a school story and since the Supreme Court and others up North, including editors who are poorly informed on the subject, are trying to force the South to mix white and Negro students in the public schools.'" In the policy statement that followed, which AP staff and executives would cite in coming years as the wire service's position on labeling Black Americans in news stories, Gould validated the Chattanooga newspaper's complaint, even though racial identification had not been available when the story initially moved on the wire:

We naturally take no sides in the controversy over segregation. We must recognize, however, that it does make even more important than ever our roll [sic] as <u>reporters</u>. We must provide the facts from all sections and regardless of local practices or ideologies.

The Chattanooga editorial makes a good point. It <u>was</u> pertinent that the two teen-agers who beat up a white teacher were Negroes. If it is pertinent in Mississippi it is pertinent in Illinois. Such identification in stories involving members to two races does not have to be in the first paragraph and it does not have to be emphasized. But the facts should be in the story somewhere.[70]

Interestingly, Gould echoed the Chattanooga paper in equating, in the reference to Mississippi, the news values of the Till lynching and the nonfatal assault in Chicago, even though the Till story involved racial terrorism and murder; the story gained added significance when the teenager's mother displayed her son's corpse for the Black press, and Till's white assailants flaunted their guilt after their acquittal.[71]

Often, editors asked the AP to verify racial identification because something in the circumstances of a story made them wonder whether the subjects were Black but not identified as such. Sometimes, as in the case of the story about the Ypsilanti triplets, a Wirephoto depicted a subject who appeared to be dark-complexioned but the cutline and the story did not mention race. A Texas editor complained that a Wirephoto of a Black man sitting in a police car, having been arrested after a shooting spree in San Francisco, accompanied a story that was missing racial identification. In his response, Gould agreed that racial identification should have been included but explained that the San Francisco newspaper that supplied the story typically did not include the information. "Our practice is to use Negro identification whenever it is pertinent to a story, which it is in all cases of riots and unusual disturbances," Gould wrote, validating the stereotype that Black people were unruly and deviant.[72] And sometimes white editors were chagrined when the AP could not provide photos of racial conflict or unrest. Such was the case when Robert Brown of the *Columbus [GA] Ledger* wrote Lew Hawkins in April 1956 to ask why "Wirephoto provided no pictures of the interracial fisticuffs between white and Negro high school students after the Detroit–Kansas City baseball game."[73] It is not clear why Brown expected to have photo coverage of a brawl that occurred half a continent away and presumably was unscheduled. What made it newsworthy to a Deep South newspaper was the prospect of documenting racial friction in the North.

## Conclusion

For Associated Press newspaper members in the 1940s and 1950s, the wire service was a crucial link to the outside world. Member newsrooms sent and received news stories that defined and validated the reality shared by literate whites during postwar years of historic social and political change. Even if white-owned daily newspapers had Black readers, their editors culled news from the wire to meet the expectations of a white audience.[74] This was true in daily newsrooms throughout the United States but particularly so for southern editors and those in racially segregated communities like St. Louis, where the normative function of the press took on added significance during the postwar civil rights years. Those editors understood that the first draft of an unwelcome history was being written in the wire copy that flowed into their newsrooms, primarily from the North. The racial markers in news stories about Black Americans were a primary site of contention in this ideological dispute. In addition, for many white southern editors, the new social order augured by *Brown v. Board of Education* was so counterintuitive that it seemed logical to argue journalistic bias whenever a news story presented integration as a reasonable alternative to separation of the races and segregation as a violation of the law, as decreed by the U.S. Supreme Court. Unable to resolve conflicting regional assumptions within its membership, the AP leadership sought, impractically and awkwardly, to strike a balance on the matter of racial identification.

Two kinds of stories, both of which triggered disputes over racial representation, caused racially conservative southerners the greatest consternation. The first category of reporting is the primary concern of this chapter, namely daily news coverage that seemed to represent Black Americans as normal, as equal participants in social and civic life, or flagged them as criminal, unruly, and unsuited for integrated society. No representation of a Black American in a news story was too insignificant to be dismissed without scrutiny. Racial identification provided information necessary to determine news values in a segregationist newsroom, where positive information about Black Americans was less newsworthy than stories that played to negative stereotypes and fear of racial change. In the second category of news, coverage related to civil rights and public racial conflict, editors who supported Jim Crow were angered to see, day after day, their fellow southerners and their regional laws and traditions, specifically their discriminatory treatment of Black Americans, portrayed as deviant in wire service stories that were disseminated across the United States and even around the world. They sought racial identification in news stories to ensure that the northern press, including the AP, was not glossing racial discrimination and conflict in the North. This second category of reporting is analyzed in chapter 4. These ideological struggles over representation, and hence identity and meaning, were stakes in the AP membership's dispute over the Negro identifier.

Significantly, member debate over racial identification began well before the modern civil rights movement hit its stride in the 1950s and segregationists perceived a direct threat to their way of life. The racial identification dispute was always about marking Black Americans as "other" and preventing them from slipping into the daily news report as if they were white, a concern that certainly intensified after *Brown*. According to this logic, in news about accomplishments or crimes, or feature stories about daily life, all of it the routine content of the daily news report, the Negro identifier took the place of pigment, replicating on the newspaper page the visual racial distinction that governed daily life. The policy statement released by AP Executive Editor Byron Price in 1940, instructing AP staff to provide racial identification only when it was "essential to the news," makes clear that wire service leadership did not believe before World War II that any justification for labeling Black Americans was worth the risk of libel suits when there were errors. In the years following Price's memo, however, as Black Americans pressed their case for equality, the tone and content of the discussion was sharply different. AP management would abandon a pragmatic concern for avoiding litigation and acquiesce to the strident and persistent faction of AP members who argued that racial identification was an essential component of an accurate and objective news report.

But for the agitation of southern membership, Gould and other AP executives might have moved in a different direction on the issue of racial identification. The AP management's posture of neutrality and deference to demands for routine use of the racial identifier was clearly an organizational decision, codified by policy and practice, and it made the wire service complicit in the segregationists' strategy. AP executives allowed the southern and border-state membership to define the debate as one over journalism standards, news values, and objectivity. Stunningly, the news organization that created and enforced a uniform system of newspaper style would, on the more significant matter of racial identification, defer to a minority of members by declaring that news values were relative. By serving a vocal and unrelenting faction and ignoring the preferences of a majority of wire service members, the AP management imposed the segregationists' news standards on all members. Newspapers that did not want to use racial identification in their stories were supposed to supply it anyway when they shared stories with the AP and had to edit it out of the daily news report when they received wire content.

Although the Associated Press may have viewed this as a compromise, the policy made racial identification a standard element of the AP news report and legitimized segregationists' views as compatible with journalism standards. In a parallel development during the early 1950s, Little Rock editor Harry Ashmore, a noted racial gradualist, championed objectivity in his defense of the racial status quo. Sometimes referred to as "moderates" or mischaracterized as "liberals," gradualists supported separate-but-equal with the prospect of *eventual* desegregation, a nuance that distinguished them from intransigent defenders of Jim Crow like Thomas Waring. What Ashmore and diehard white supremacists had in common, however, were a fundamental belief in social segregation and long practice at manipulating objectivity to obscure racial activism. The gradualist news narrative and its neutral pose are our next points of curiosity.

CHAPTER 3

# THE POLITICS OF MEANING

HARRY ASHMORE AND THE
GRADUALIST NEWS NARRATIVE

Harry S. Ashmore was an unlikely standard bearer for both journalistic objectivity and racial moderation as southern society transitioned from World War II into the upheaval wrought by the modern civil rights movement. Ashmore, the white executive editor of the *Arkansas Gazette* in Little Rock from 1947 until he left journalism and the South twelve years later, invoked objectivity in defense of Jim Crow—yet his legacy, owing to happenstance and historical license, often miscasts him as a defender of civil rights for Black Americans. "It has always seemed to me a remarkable and melancholy fact that I became an author in the field of race and education not by design, desire, or special interest, but by default," he reflected in *An Epitaph for Dixie*, a book published in early 1957.[1] Like many white southern moderates of his generation, Ashmore was ambivalent about racial justice, and as a prominent figure in 1950s journalism, he performed his internal contradictions in public—on the printed page but also in speeches and press interviews about race. Although he conceded Black Americans certain constitutional rights, his was a worldview framed by white supremacy and "the southern way of life," and he did not, during his time in the South, betray those allegiances. Even as he championed impartiality as a journalism standard, Ashmore was overtly partisan—ideologically and politically. In addition to defending social segregation and separate-but-equal public education, Ashmore openly collaborated with Democrats on policy and election strategy. He obscured such conflicts of interest, including his own stake in southern whiteness, by shrouding them in a claim of objectivity.

As a midcentury newspaper editor, Ashmore gauged objectivity as a balance of praise and criticism, following the journalism adage that attacks from both sides of a conflict proved an editor's impartiality. As such, when the controversy was about race and civil rights, Ashmore used objectivity to elevate himself above the fray. In 1948 he wrote Walter White, executive secretary of the NAACP, describing himself as "the man in the middle who is quite likely to be denounced by people on both sides in this complex issue."[2] When both integrationists and Dixiecrats criticized Ashmore's journalism, when neither side was satisfied that he had framed its narrative correctly, Ashmore believed he had done his job as an editor. But instead of documenting his racial neutrality, the maneuver in his letter to White was an argument for journalistic and moral equivalence, one that excused him from taking a clear stand on America's defining ethical issue. Objectivity provided cover when Ashmore planted his feet on the wrong side of racial history, then punctuated his career with nonjudgmental reminiscences about the white South and his own role in 1950s journalism.[3]

In 1947 *Arkansas Gazette* editor J. N. Heiskell hired Ashmore as his editorial writer and soon promoted him to executive editor. Ashmore shared his employer's gradualist position—the belief that pushing the white South too far and too fast toward racial reform would antagonize segregationists and undermine Black aspirations for full citizenship. This was a cynical position, a less inflammatory expression of white supremacy that still assumed Black Americans were inherently unequal to whites. "For the Negro leaders," Ashmore wrote in *An Epitaph for Dixie*, "rejection of gradualism as a philosophical concept does not alter its validity as a fact of life.... While a right may be defined by a court of law, it will not be secured until each individual has earned it."[4] Gradualism, in his view, was meritocratic preservation of a racial order that depended on Black subordination.

Within the rubric of midcentury journalism standards, gradualism could be explained as a balance between two extremes, seemingly compatible with professional objectivity, neutrality, and impartiality. This approach did not mollify intransigent segregationists who eventually condemned Ashmore, but it was plausible to many northern whites who were essential to Ashmore's professional ambitions. During his Arkansas years, Ashmore laid the groundwork for a future above the Mason-Dixon Line and actively pursued the national spotlight by writing magazine articles and making radio and television appearances, venues where a certain racial tolerance was required. In addition to his commentary on southern politics, Ashmore gravitated toward direct political engagement that was incongruous with objectivity. For example, in 1956, while his readers were making sense of the *Brown* ruling, Ashmore took a ten-month leave from the *Gazette* to work on Adlai Stevenson's presidential campaign. Although the newspaper profession was more accommodating of an editor's direct political involvement in the 1950s, that diversion complicated Ashmore's effort to provide steady and clear-eyed editorial leadership for his newspaper at a time when southern society was being turned inside out.[5] Historians also have noted Ashmore's ministrations on behalf of gubernatorial candidate Orval Faubus, including authorship of a speech that salvaged Faubus's political career in 1954.[6]

Moderate editorials during the 1957 Central High School desegregation crisis brought a Pulitzer Prize, but Ashmore secured his reputation as a national expert on race through editorship of *The Negro and the Schools*, an ostensibly nonpartisan and objective interpretation of data on southern public education that was sponsored by the Fund for the Advancement of Education (FAE), a new arm of the Ford Foundation. The book, often referred to as the "Ashmore Report," was published in May 1954, coinciding with the U.S. Supreme Court's ruling in *Brown v. Board of Education* and cementing Ashmore's place in the civil rights canon.[7] When *The Negro and the Schools* offer fell into his lap in 1953, Ashmore was just thirty-seven years old but was already a journalist of some reputation in the South. In a pantheon of southern editors who spent their lives in the newsroom, Ashmore's career lasted just a decade but was still significant for its accomplishment and impact.

Prior to his work on *The Negro and the Schools*, Ashmore had been swept up in disputes about the threat of desegregation that forced him to placate racial conservatives he offended and distance himself from Black activists and white liberals who mistook him for an ally. His gradualism became controversial in a speech he gave to the Southern Governors' Conference in late 1951 and another delivered six months later to national civil rights leaders—among them Thurgood Marshall of the NAACP Legal Defense Fund—who gathered at Howard University to strategize the end of separate-but-(un)equal public education. Engagement with these diametrically opposed audiences—virtually all-white and predominantly Black, pro-segregation and pro-integration—pushed Ashmore to the right, at least on paper, and documented that his gradualism was indeed a defense of Jim Crow. These speeches also demonstrated the utility of objectivity as a framework for *The Negro and the Schools* and Ashmore's work in journalism. Objectivity's both-sides approach mandated deference to white supremacy as one position on a public controversy, legitimizing social segregation as an option for the post-*Brown* South.

Ashmore was anything but neutral on the school integration question and thus a peculiar choice to lead and edit the FAE's first southern objectivity project. More perplexing is the legacy that defines him as a racial liberal, a perception fostered by historical literature about the 1950s and journalistic remembrances, including Ashmore's own. As editor, Ashmore did take certain actions that would have been consistent with a belief in social justice, such as modifying the *Gazette*'s policy on courtesy titles (Mr., Mrs., Miss) to prevent offense to Black news subjects. This he explained as a decision for consistency in newspaper style, not a stand for civil rights, but the change aligned with campaigns by the NAACP to ameliorate racial indignities in newspaper representation and could be construed as racial sensitivity.[8] During the Central High School confrontation, the *Gazette* also endured a subscriber revolt because its endorsement of gradualism suggested that Jim Crow might be eliminated eventually and inflamed strident segregationists.[9] In context, such actions distinguished Ashmore from the most intractable white supremacist editors, but he remained a gradualist, urging compliance with *Brown* because it was the law of the land, not as a moral imperative.[10] His Pulitzer Prize–winning editorials regarding the confrontation at Little Rock's Central High School were hardly an integrationist manifesto. In them, he simply urged his readers to accept, rather than resist, the desegregation rulings. "Somehow, some time, every Arkansan is going to have to be counted," Ashmore wrote in a front-page editorial on September 9, 1957. "We are going to have to decide what kind of people we are—whether we obey the law only when we approve of it, or whether we obey the law no matter how distasteful we may find it."[11]

Despite casting himself as a racial expert "by default," Ashmore encouraged northern white journalists to perceive him as an authority on civil rights and the white southern dilemma. He was by all accounts a gracious and engaging host to reporters passing through Little Rock during the 1950s, a raconteur who enthralled his audiences, usually over bourbon, and a ready source of background about the racial news of the day.[12] Ashmore also was available until his death in 1998 to help historians shape public memory about his short career in journalism. The authors of at least three significant civil rights–era histories incorporated interviews with Ashmore; significantly, the comprehensive history *The Race Beat: The Press, the Civil Rights Struggle, and the Awakening of a Nation* draws on at least five conversations.[13] Although Ashmore's influence over their narrative is clear, authors Gene Roberts and Hank Klibanoff assessed his racial politics accurately, placing him "at the forefront of that small group of white southern editors who would fight to open the southern mainstream to Negroes and to bring the South into the national mainstream," but noted that "nothing Ashmore was advocating constituted a breach in the social separation of the races."[14]

Because Ashmore was not outspoken in his racism and offered a counterpoint to the enraged white people who accosted the Little Rock Nine as they tried to enter Central High School, his gradualism could be mistaken for something more innocent than support of social segregation. In condoning separate-but-equal, the gradualist position asserted that segregation and civil rights were not mutually exclusive. "Most of us believe in the separation of the races," Ashmore said in 1948, "and we also believe that this can be done, and in most cases is being done, without any injustice to the Negro."[15] While this argument made sense to southern whites who clung to the racial status quo, it seemed logically and morally inconsistent to supporters of civil rights, who did not know how to categorize it.

The false impression that Ashmore was a racial progressive also has an uncanny half-life, which may explain a 1999 *New York Times* headline a year after his death describing him as "a laughing liberal" and an NPR retrospective, "Little Rock Editor Faced Down Segregationists." The latter coincided with publication of *The Race Beat* and referred to Ashmore vaguely as a "moderate," a term whose white-supremacist euphemism is lost on modern audiences.[16] Indeed, a *New York Times* review of *The Race Beat*, written by a prominent historian, foregrounded Ashmore among other journalists discussed in the book and resituated his politics, suggesting that "readers should pay particular attention to . . . the liberal Arkansas editor who gained national attention during the 1957 Little Rock crisis."[17]

Such confusion over the meaning and implications of gradualism muddied contemporary understandings of Ashmore's positions on race. This is apparent in the public reception of two speeches he gave prior to *Brown v. Board of Education* in which he opposed integration of the public schools but positioned himself as an objective commentator, "the man in the middle" striving for objectivity and balance on a difficult moral issue. By taking the same gradualist position before an assembly that included uncompromising white supremacists and in an address to Black leaders of the postwar freedom struggle, Ashmore invited criticism from both sides, a *prima facie* index of impartiality in 1950s journalism. The "man in the middle" pose also anchored his work on *The Negro and the Schools*, and it is there that our historical analysis begins. Ultimately, Ashmore's racial partisanship—which inflected his journalism, his research for the FAE, and his speechmaking during the 1950s—could not be erased by his performance of objectivity.

## The Negro and the Schools

Ashmore's political engagement was hardly confined to his editorial page in Little Rock, yet he embraced objectivity as a journalism standard, defining it as "factual and unbiased" reporting. "It may be that it is humanly impossible to achieve the ideal," he told a reader in 1950, "but I, at least, am determined to go down trying."[18] When he described *The Negro and the Schools* as an objective presentation of research on race and education, he understood that the appearance of neutrality, which implied acquiescence to the segregationist status quo, was important when the subject was race and the audience was southern. As an affirmation of the project's mission to be objective and impartial, Ashmore emphasized that its data, which researchers collected prior to the *Brown* decision, were intended to help both the public and local school officials move forward, whether the Supreme Court affirmed or overturned *Plessy v. Ferguson*, the 1896 ruling that sanctioned separate-but-equal public education.[19] Citing a "great need for objective information," Ashmore wrote that "there were not available even the basic data for measuring the physical disparity between white and Negro schools and thereby computing the cost of equalization—whether this be done by merging the two systems or continuing them separately." Ignoring the conflict of interest in his own standpoint, Ashmore continued, "Much had been written on the subject, it is true, but most of it was the product of advocates on one side or the other of the central moral issue and was colored by their views."[20] Merely broaching the subject of race except to support Jim Crow was so controversial in the former Confederacy that the Fund for the Advancement of Education could not find a southern university to undertake even a project committed to objectivity and instead hired Ashmore to craft the summary from information gathered by a team of forty FAE-sponsored scholars and analysts.[21]

Framing *The Negro and the Schools* as an exercise in objectivity allowed Ashmore and his newspaper to maintain their opposition to forced and immediate school integration, even if the research documented flaws in separate-but-equal public education. The claim to objectivity relieved Ashmore from an obligation to engage the data beyond a presentation of fact. In the book's introduction, he described his work in professional terms: "I began with the assumption that I would serve simply as an editor; in the end I found myself operating as a reporter—performing the essentially journalistic function of briefing the mass of research data and fitting it, as best as I could, into the larger context of the developing pattern of American race relations."[22] Although acknowledging that arranging facts into a narrative was an inherently subjective process, Ashmore assumed, naively, that the claim of objectivity would shield him from both white-supremacist and integrationist critiques. Reflecting in 1957 on the political implications of his decision to write and edit *The Negro and the Schools*, even within the pretense of objectivity and under the banner of gradualism, Ashmore described being ostracized and no longer invited to give speeches to white southern audiences. A retired southern politician, when told that Ashmore was writing a summary report on segregated public schools, characterized Ashmore as "a man running for son of a bitch without opposition."[23]

Ashmore and the FAE board, which included columnist and objectivity advocate Walter Lippmann, strategized to ensure the American press would regard *The Negro and the Schools* as factual and impartial.[24] Before the book's publication date of May 17, 1954, the Monday on which the *Brown* ruling appeared, editors of daily newspapers and prominent magazines had an embargoed copy of the book in hand, giving them time to read and reflect on its findings.[25] The FAE gathered reviews printed during the following week, and none of the editors North or South, conservative or liberal, disapproved.[26] That said, the simultaneous release of the *Brown* decision left editors with much more to process than the appearance of the "Ashmore Report." In an assessment on May 19, "Dred

Scott Ashmore" assured the FAE that the white southern press had "acted with complete responsibility" in communicating news of the *Brown* decision and did not immediately incite opposition.[27] Ashmore took a bit of license with cause and effect and credited the purported objectivity of *The Negro and the Schools* for the reasoned editorial response to both the book and the ruling. "Put this down to undue immodesty if you will, but I am convinced that the project had a lot to do with it," Ashmore wrote. ". . . While I have by no means seen all the Southern reviews of the book I have looked over a couple of dozen. All are favorable, and most important of all, everywhere we are being credited with objectivity."[28]

Ignoring the irony, Ashmore then segued from discussion of his own objectivity to praise for the Supreme Court's framing of the desegregation order. "The manner in which the Court handed down the decision was magnificent—so much so that I am thinking about writing a fan letter to the Chief Justice, if I can only figure out the protocol in the matter," he wrote. Ashmore believed the unanimous opinion "spiked many a gun" in the white South and described the division of the 1954 precedent from the 1955 implementation decree as "a master-stroke," a move that could benefit the cause of gradualism and open the door to something less than full integration, which he likened to the end of the world. "It gives everybody time to get used to the idea," he wrote, "and opens up the possibility of intelligent and specific argument on ways and means before the Court which was impossible while the advocates [for desegregation] felt they would have to concede their major point if they discussed anything less than Armageddon."[29] As it happened, Ashmore did send a fan letter to Earl Warren a year later, after the second *Brown* ruling vaguely suggested schools be integrated "with all deliberate speed" and the Court did indeed accommodate the gradualist position.[30] In the letter, Ashmore called Warren's handling of the *Brown* cases "the greatest act of judicial statesmanship in the nation's history."[31]

Although association with *The Negro and the Schools* cost Ashmore political standing in the white South, it opened other opportunities as the Ford Foundation shifted its agenda and became interested in social issues. Ashmore had been in the right place at the right time when the new Fund for the Advancement of Education developed a series of initiatives on southern education in the late 1940s and early 1950s and sought Ashmore's collaboration on an Arkansas Teacher Education Program.[32]

His subsequent work on *The Negro and the Schools* cemented a working relationship with the FAE, which also would underwrite the Southern Education Reporting Service (SERS) to report objectively on the South's response to Brown. That project, which was authorized before the *Brown* decision was handed down, is the subject of chapter 5. Although Ashmore did not directly participate in the SERS, he helped organize it. For that initiative, Ashmore also endorsed objectivity as a central tenet of journalism and plausible goal of a foundation looking to support social change without appearing to intervene in racial politics.[33] As such, the objectivity label also insulated the FAE, whose officers worried about public relations fallout for the Ford Foundation and the Ford Motor Company, should *The Negro and the Schools* generate controversy. This was not an irrational fear. In 1953 South Carolina governor James Byrnes, a white supremacist, privately raised a concern with Henry Ford II about the as-yet-unpublished "Ashmore Report," validating the paranoia of southern academics who declined to associate publicly with the project.[34]

The contribution of *The Negro and the Schools* to the debate over segregation is beyond the scope of this book; however, its claim of objectivity drew Richard Kluger's attention—and critique—in *Simple Justice*, the definitive history of *Brown v. Board*. The Ashmore Report privileged white "community attitudes" toward race and stated, "It is axiomatic that separate schools can be merged only with great difficulty, if at all, when a great majority of the citizens who support them are actively opposed to the move. No other public activity is so closely identified with local mores."[35] For many segregationists in Ashmore's southern audience, local sentiment about racial "mixing" did not allow a neutral position, and Ashmore provided fodder for defense of the status quo. When the Supreme Court invited briefs in anticipation of the second ruling in 1955, which would implement the 1954 decision declaring separate-but-equal unconstitutional, the southern states cited Ashmore as an authority "on local mores." Kluger explained that "the attorneys general of the South read those words, underlined them, and called them to the attention of the Supreme Court," even though Ashmore had drawn data from a narrow set of communities and extrapolated them into a caution against broader integration. Kluger summarized this response: "The process must not be shoved down our throats, said Southern officials, invoking Ashmorean moderation."[36] Although Ashmore and the FAE believed their book was objective, Kluger, whose history is sympathetic to the NAACP Legal Defense Fund and plaintiffs in the five *Brown* cases, recognized *The Negro and the Schools* as a defense of gradualism that rationalized segregation as a means of preserving social order and blamed civil rights activism, not white supremacy, for any interracial strife or violence that followed the rulings.[37]

The NAACP lawyers did not have to conjecture about Ashmore's views on race. Many of them had been in the audience at Howard University in 1952 when he defended gradualism to a conference of civil rights leaders and strategists. His defense of gradualism also was controversial in 1951 when he took a similar position before the pro-segregation Southern Governors' Conference and appeared to waffle on Jim Crow. In both addresses he feigned a certain neutrality on the question of desegregation, pleasing neither the strict segregationists nor the racial reformers. His gestures toward objectivity in these speeches, staking out gradualism as a middle path, are worth exploring in detail.

### Lecturing the Southern Governors about Race

On November 12, 1951, Ashmore addressed the Southern Governors' Conference, which had convened at Hot Springs, Arkansas, and pointedly called for the South to comply with the separate-but-equal doctrine in *Plessy v. Ferguson*—or accept the inevitability of court-ordered integration of the public schools.[38] Although Ashmore believed Black Americans should have basic civil rights, including the franchise, and should be admitted to graduate programs, his speech to the governors was no radical call for an end to segregation. In fact, Ashmore later insisted that the main objective of the speech, with a presidential election a year away, had been to avoid another third-party rebellion like the Dixiecrat movement, which splintered the white southern voting bloc in 1948, or mass defection to the Republican Party for the 1952 elections, threatened by Governor Byrnes of South Carolina and others.[39] Ashmore used the speech to outline a gradualist compromise that called for both the equitable treatment of Black Americans and accommodation of Jim Crow, two outcomes he did not see as incompatible.

Ashmore's conditional and limited support for civil rights was widely perceived as backpedaling on strict segregation, and he simultaneously rankled conservative white southerners and caused advocates for integration to mistake him for one of their own. Ashmore would attribute confusion over his position on civil rights to press coverage of the speech, much of which misconstrued his intent; however, his gradualism, a contradictory position on race, mixed the message. Moreover, by stepping up to the microphone at the Southern Governors' Conference, becoming part of a newsworthy event and doing so with a clear political agenda, Ashmore complicated his advocacy for journalistic objectivity. The white southern press would have condemned similar activism by a Black or northern white editor as a breach of journalistic protocol. It is, therefore, useful to view Ashmore's speech within its historical and political contexts and against news and editorial coverage of the governors' conference. Much of this journalism condensed and oversimplified a nuanced argument, one that lacked the racial absolutism that integrationists and segregationists each sought from public commentators. Confused by his moderate approach, readers interpreted Ashmore's address to suit their own anxieties about the future of a South whose racial traditions were under challenge, even with the U.S. Supreme Court's rulings in *Brown v. Board of Education* still a few years away.[40]

In the weeks after regional and national news reports summarized the address, Ashmore generated a series of letters that reframed the speech for newspaper readers of various leanings on the issue of segregation and even for some of the southern governors who had been in the audience at Hot Springs and chafed at his message. The speech clearly challenged the southern governors' recalcitrance on fulfilling the mandate of separate-but-equal, but it also argued that separate-but-equal could be a just alternative to forced integration. Years later, when writing books about the civil rights era afforded opportunities for revisionism, Ashmore did not recast himself as an advocate for integration or claim a subsequent conversion to social justice. The speech was, he wrote in 1982, "a dispassionate appeal for moderation. It fairly represented my personal convictions."[41] There and in his other recollections about the early 1950s Ashmore described his southern heritage and the evolution of southern politics and culture without disowning his defense of social segregation.

Ashmore collaborated with Arkansas's elected leaders, including both Congressman Brooks Hays and Senator J. William Fulbright. He also was on good terms with Arkansas governor Sid McMath, who invited him to address the governors' conference when it met in Arkansas. Ashmore had assisted these politicians on various matters, including a proposed compromise to President Harry Truman's civil rights initiatives, so Ashmore was privy to their political strategy.[42] White southern distrust of the Truman administration had come to a head in 1947, when the President's Committee on Civil Rights issued the report titled *To Secure These Rights*, whose recommendations included federal antilynching legislation, voting rights, a permanent Fair Employment Practices Commission (FEPC), and desegregation of the military and federal workforce.[43] When southern members of Congress stalled the legislation, Truman desegregated the military and federal workforce by executive order, alienating the southern Democratic Party and provoking the Dixiecrat rebellion of 1948.[44] Hoping to forestall another insurrection or an exodus to the Republicans in 1952, McMath invited House Speaker Sam Rayburn and other national party leaders to the governors' conference to shore up support for Democrats in the South.

McMath also asked Ashmore to focus his remarks specifically on civil rights. Ashmore later described his inclusion on the program as an attempt to "smoke out the opposition" who saw the party as wavering on support for segregation. Presumably, the malcontents would have a choice to directly challenge Ashmore's gradualism with the national press in the room, or keep quiet.[45] The speech was therefore intended to be provocative, following a morning session on southern higher education with a biracial panel and setting the stage for Rayburn's speech that evening. About fifty white journalists, representing the southern and national press, arrived in Hot Springs to cover the anticipated eruption by southern Democrats.[46] Registered for the conference were representatives of southern newspapers and broadcast outlets as well as a national press corps that included Don Whitehead of the Associated Press, Doris Fleeson of the *Washington Star*, Johnny Popham of the *New York Times*, George Harris of *Time* magazine, and syndicated columnist Thomas L. Stokes of Scripps-Howard.[47]

Ashmore opened the address with his southern *bona fides*—he claimed two Confederate grandfathers and residence over his lifetime in seven southern states—then broached "the profoundly complex problem of race relations," a distinctly southern concern because of the legacy of slavery and the large Black population in the region. "We here in the South will have to live with it, and wrestle with it, for generations to come—and we should understand by now that we will not have the privilege of doing so without outside interference." Moreover, he noted, many northerners who criticized the South had little contact with Black Americans. "We have good cause to resent many of the strange manifestations of national concern over the racial problems of the South." Empathy with his audience thus secured, Ashmore shifted to the meat of his speech.[48]

He deflected blame for the plight of Black Americans to historical circumstance and portrayed it as a national rather than strictly regional problem, invoking Gunnar Myrdal's postulation of an "American dilemma."[49] In the South, "the high cost of segregation," of operating segregated school systems in a region whose economy relied on unskilled labor, presented a particular set of challenges, he said. In framing his argument, however, Ashmore set up a mixed message. Although he denied "sentimental concern over the black man's burden," he also made the potentially inflammatory argument that "we cannot refuse to recognize that the Negro, more often than not, has been the exception to this nation's moral and ethical code, and even to our religious precepts."

With many of the Dixiecrat instigators seated in his audience, Ashmore acknowledged that "the makings of another great political rebellion are here in this room and again it is the peculiar institution of the one-party South—with its roots in the basic problem of race relations that is its cause." He then offered a complicated defense of Jim Crow. Racial segregation, which was not unique to the South, "is considered essential by the vast majority of the white population" and should endure, he said. "The practical problem before the South, then, is to preserve social segregation while at the same time meeting the conditions of a Constitution and a national tradition which demand that full civil liberties and full equality of opportunity be extended to all citizens without discrimination." He warned against reactionary responses to the Truman civil rights initiatives, particularly by the demagogue, whom he characterized as a "radical or cynical opportunist who exploits the race question for his own ends," and fueled perceptions in the North "that we are all misbegotten racists who will respond to nothing less than federal coercion." Without naming any of the governors in his audience, Ashmore said, "It is the melancholy truth that some of those who—I suppose, sincerely—have cast themselves in the role of protectors of Southern institutions are in fact the region's most dangerous enemies."

The second half of the speech entailed a prescription for granting Black Americans civil rights within a segregated society, in accordance with *Plessy v. Ferguson*. This included "the right to vote, the right to serve on juries, freedom of worship, protection of the person." Then taking aim at the Fair Employment Practices Commission, which he categorized among "impractical and dangerous experiments," he emphasized that civil liberties for Black Americans did not include "the right to a job," which he conceptualized as state interference with a private relationship. An employer's right to choose his own employees "according to his own lights must be inviolate if our other individual freedoms are to endure." Ashmore's exemption of the private workplace was an important distinction that validated the racial exclusions in every white-owned private business, including the white press. Although he supported integration of the graduate school at the University of Arkansas, Ashmore defended segregation "at lower levels of public education" but warned that "a guarantee against forced intermingling of the races" would be achieved only if "in fundamentally public activities—and the test here would be their support by tax funds—the Negro must either be treated without official prejudice or in absolute, incontrovertible fact be provided with separate but equal facilities." Doing so, Ashmore argued, would place segregation "beyond the reach of the law."

Notably, audience reaction was measured as some in the room held their applause. In correspondence following the speech, Ashmore quibbled with a characterization of the audience response as "frigid," and said he preferred to describe it as "mixed," noting that "several of the governors told me privately they agreed."[50] Recalling the experience decades later, Ashmore wrote, "The real significance lay in the fact that the reaction was so restrained," and called McMath's strategy, which marginalized critics of Truman and the Democratic Party, a success. When the 1952 presidential election arrived, Ashmore wrote, "the GOP landslide stopped short of the Southern heartland, reaching only to Virginia, Tennessee, Florida, and Texas."[51]

No one who saw Ashmore listed as a luncheon speaker should have been surprised by anything he said to the governors. Not only were Ashmore's views on race well understood in Arkansas but he also had shared them with southern and national audiences. In 1948, in an article in *Nieman Reports* that even mirrored some of the language of the speech,

Ashmore asked his fellow southerners to "accept, without reservation, the special responsibility that falls upon the dominant race and discharge it in good faith—giving the Negro educational, economic and political opportunities not because we are forced to but because we recognize his right to them."[52] Then, in October 1948 Ashmore delivered an address to the Southern Political Science Association, later discussed by nationally syndicated columnist Peter Edson. "Segregation can be defended, but the denial of civil rights that has always gone with it has become indefensible," Edson quoted Ashmore as saying.[53] That argument was adapted for reprint in the literary magazine the *Southern Packet*, and there Ashmore declared "enfranchisement of the Negro inevitable . . . although there is no reason to believe that segregation itself will disappear in accordance with the impetuous schedule laid down by the National Association for the Advancement of Colored People."[54]

Even so, many in Ashmore's defensive audience at the 1951 conference luncheon, which included governors who stridently opposed Truman's civil rights reforms, believed the speech challenged racial commonsense and contradicted the *Gazette*'s support for continued segregation. At the same time, some in the press corps and national news audience, looking for a white southerner to champion integration, heard Ashmore's declaration that Black Americans were entitled to certain basic rights and extrapolated it to mean he was that champion. The Black press interpreted the speech using its own frames about the race story; Black scholars and civil rights activists working on the school integration issue paid attention as well. Despite his pretext of objectivity, Ashmore would learn that the racial middle ground could be difficult to explain and defend.[55]

## How the Speech Was Covered

Although many southern newspapers sent their own journalists to the governors' conference, information about Ashmore's speech reached both national and regional audiences primarily through four sources: the Associated Press and United Press wire services; the Black press, which published stories and editorials about two weeks later; and the nationally syndicated column of Thomas Stokes, who was based in Washington for the Scripps-Howard chain. Most coverage emphasized Rayburn's appearance and the governors' reactions to it, and accorded just a few paragraphs to Ashmore's speech. As such, most readers derived an impression of Ashmore's remarks from a few direct and isolated quotations extracted from a much longer and complex argument. Those who read Stokes's column, which focused squarely on Ashmore's address, had a different experience. Stokes heavily excerpted the speech to support a fawning argument that Ashmore was a rare voice of reason in the South. Members of the press registered for the conference received individual copies of the full text of Ashmore's speech on which to base their reporting.[56]

In coverage that moved on November 12, the day of the speech, and was available for afternoon newspapers, Don Whitehead of the AP, a white southerner recently returned from assignment in Korea, emphasized the civil rights discussion on the conference's opening day, folded in Ashmore's remarks, and quoted him as saying that "the problem before the South, then, is how to preserve social segregation while at the same time meeting the conditions . . . which demand that full civil liberties and full equality of opportunity be extended to all citizens without discrimination."[57] Whitehead incorporated Ashmore's remarks into those of Mississippi governor Fielding Wright, who spoke later and defended his state's segregated schools. Although Whitehead referred to the "politically red-hot subject of civil rights" and quoted Ashmore as saying that "the high cost of segregation has held back the overall development of our educational institutions," the story as it appeared in various newspapers, even when edited and shortened for local use, was generally balanced and did not exploit the conflict between the two speakers. By the next news cycle, for the newspapers of November 13, Whitehead's reporting focused on the conservative response to House Speaker Rayburn's dinner address, and Ashmore's speech had disappeared from national AP coverage.[58] The AP's Little Rock bureau gave detailed coverage of Ashmore's speech in a separate story, which got little traction outside Arkansas.[59]

The reporting by United Press, which registered Washington-based reporter John Cutter for the conference, sensationalized the civil rights discussions. For the evening papers of November 12, UP moved a story that described a speech by the "fiery young editor" and contrasted Ashmore's comment that "the high cost of segregation has held back the overall development of our educational institutions" with Governor Wright's insistence that "the segregated education system shall be maintained," a position not actually at odds with Ashmore's. The UP story placed Ashmore and Wright in "a dispute on segregation in the schools," casting Ashmore as a racial liberal. Although the UP story later said that Ashmore had "cautioned . . . that it is up to the South to find its own way to preserve 'social segregation' while extending the full benefits of civil liberties and equal opportunities to all citizens without discrimination," it misrepresented Ashmore's stated position on school desegregation.[60]

There is no evidence that Black reporters were invited or allowed to cover the proceedings, but some Black weeklies gave the speech news and editorial treatment later that month. In its summary, the *Pittsburgh Courier* portrayed Ashmore as a proponent of integration. In contrast with the Mississippi governor, who said segregated schools would be maintained, Ashmore reportedly "spoke his mind" and "called for a realistic step forward dealing with the race problem in the South." The story continued,

> Ashmore pointed out that the South should meet the demands of the Constitution which called for and "demanded full civil liberties, and full equality of opportunity be extended to all citizens without discrimination."
>
> Mr. Ashmore further stated that his understanding of civil rights was that which involved "the right to vote, the right to serve on juries, freedom of worship, protection of person and the like."

The *Courier*'s story did not mention Ashmore's endorsement of separate-but-equal.[61] The *Chicago Defender*'s reporting was more complete, noting in a front-page story that Ashmore had "advocated a positive and realistic program of race relationships in the South," and then "went on to blast FEPC and other federal safeguards as 'impractical and dangerous experiments.'"[62] In an editorial, the *Defender* said Ashmore "had the right slant when he warned the Southern Governors conference meeting . . . that if the South didn't produce a realistic race relations program that would insure equal rights, then they may as well expect continued Federal interference."[63]

Many Black newspapers used an Associated Negro Press story that characterized the *Arkansas Gazette* as the "most liberal of Dixie's publications" and said its editor's speech "created a furore among the governors . . . when he took a most implacable stand against the general policy of segregating Negroes throughout the South." The ANP selected as its most prominent direct quotation this statement from Ashmore: "We cannot turn our backs upon injustices simply because a black man is its victim, nor can we find a safe retreat in the sort of legal buck-passing that recognizes the existence of evil, but insists it is somebody else's responsibility." The ANP story reported that "Ashmore's liberal tendencies have done much to promote better racial relations in Arkansas," and attributed that assessment to the president of historically Black Philander Smith College.[64]

Readers of Black newspapers also may have seen a column that NAACP leader Walter White wrote based solely on news coverage. White enclosed a copy of his column, dated almost two weeks earlier and already distributed, when he wrote to Ashmore in December seeking the full text of the November 12 speech and expressing concern that most newspapers had not "quoted copiously" from it.[65] Although White used a direct quotation that included "the practical problem before the South is to preserve social segregation while at the same time meeting the conditions of a Constitution and national tradition," thus capturing the equivocation in the speech, he made assumptions about the rest of the argument as he paraphrased liberally. He read into news reports "an obvious reference to the psychotic anti-Trumanism" of southern governors, who White imagined "squirming" as Ashmore "ridiculed" them.[66] The Black press was disadvantaged by not having access to the meeting or Ashmore's script.

With the exception of reporting by the AP and UP wire services, the single source of speech coverage with the widest distribution appears to have been the syndicated column of Tom Stokes, a white native Georgian whose commentary was distributed by the International News Service. Ashmore's correspondence indicates that much of the misperception that he had championed integration came from the Stokes column, which appeared in white newspapers across the country the week of the speech. The column opened under a Hot Springs dateline: "It was good to come back home to the South again for the privilege of hearing a native born Southern newspaper editor boldly project a ringing note of sanity and sound sense into the Southern Governors Conference here, which seethed with another incipient political revolt." Calling Ashmore "courageous," Stokes summarized the speech, omitting Ashmore's defense of segregation and calls for making good on separate-but-equal, and portrayed the argument as an affront to the governors:

> Then, later, this bombshell right into the midst of the meeting of governors at which he talked:

"It is the melancholy truth that some of those who—I suppose sincerely—have cast themselves in the role of protectors of Southern institutions are in fact the region's most dangerous enemies."

Some who might be included in that category were recognized in his audience. That probably accounted for the tense quiet as he spoke. When he finished he got only what might be called courteous applause....

Four governors did not join in at all, sitting frigidly with hands still.

Stokes extracted direct quotations from the speech that, taken together and without the context of the rest of the argument, portrayed Ashmore as an enthusiastic and caustic advocate of civil rights reform. Heaping praise for Ashmore's willingness to confront elected leaders, Stokes argued that the speech's audience made the address remarkable: "What he said would not be considered in any way daring anywhere outside the South, and, as a matter of fact, would be accepted rather widely in the South, itself, beyond the strictly political sphere."[67]

From this coverage, readers of either the white or Black press likely received an incomplete or skewed impression of Ashmore's position and how he constructed and supported his argument. Lamenting this circumstance to another white southern editor, Ashmore wrote, "I have learned the first lesson: that no man should bring up the subject of race unless he has a clear field and at least an hour in which to define his position."[68] But the problem was not the length of time available for the speech. After all, members of the white press corps at Hot Springs had access to the text. Rather, if newspapers were to summarize it, the message would be conflated and incomplete.

Importantly, more was missing from national reporting than the segregationist nuance in Ashmore's argument. One of the most significant aspects of the first day of the conference was McMath's scheduling of the morning session, a joint meeting of the governors' conference and the Board of Control for Southern Regional Education, which gathered representatives of historically Black colleges and Black trade and professional schools for a discussion about the future of regional higher education in the South. The Black press acknowledged the importance of holding this biracial meeting during the Southern Governors' Conference; indeed, "Dixie governors" attending an "unsegregated confab" warranted a banner headline in the *Pittsburgh Courier*. The *Courier* included a photo of white and Black attendees meeting around a table and drew attention to Georgia's "Gov. Herman Talmadge, who sat throughout the meeting, without difficulty, at a non-segregated table of leaders of both races."[69] In Jim Crow Arkansas in 1951, the eleven Black college presidents were also photographed eating a segregated lunch, not at the Majestic Hotel where the governors convened and Ashmore spoke but at the National Baptist Hotel, which accepted Black clientele.

The *Arkansas Gazette*'s coverage of the governors' conference included a front-page sidebar that used the biracial meeting to highlight its reporting on Ashmore's speech.[70] And at least one southern newspaper alluded to the biracial session without mentioning that it was biracial. The *Greenville [SC] News*, which emphasized South Carolina governor James Byrnes's role in the conference, noted that he participated in a discussion about professional education. "Mr. Byrnes added that he would like to see more colored medical students in the South" because the "provision of more doctors would go far to answer the complaints of those who advocate socialized medicine."[71] But most white press coverage was silent on the racial composition of the morning session. Not even Whitehead, whose balanced and comprehensive AP reporting focused on the "politically red-hot subject of civil rights," mentioned the biracial panel on education that preceded Ashmore's luncheon address on the conference's opening day.

The tentative and conditional regard for Black news subjects in white reporting on civil rights and policy is both important and unsurprising. Including Black experts in the news narrative about public education would have presented them as qualified to plan for the South's future and contribute to an integrated American society. By minimizing their role in the conference, or erasing them from the program, much white press coverage presented an inaccurate picture of the event and framed the future of separate-but-equal as a white conversation.

## Reframing the Message

In the days and weeks following the address at Hot Springs, Ashmore received a number of letters from readers of newspaper coverage of the speech, and through his replies and depending on the political leanings of the correspondents, affirmed or redefined their impressions of his views. In addition, more than a dozen letters came from readers who wanted copies of the speech to help them place Ashmore's remarks in context. Moreover, the correspondence archive makes clear that within the moderate wing of white southern journalism, Ashmore had cemented himself as a member of the club. Jonathan Daniels of the *Raleigh [NC] News and Observer* offered "enthusiastic applause," Ralph McGill of the *Atlanta Constitution* telegraphed his commendation for "a really courageous intelligent speech," and Nelson Poynter of the *St. Petersburg [FL] Times* wrote to say, "I hear it was a wow."[72] Although his coverage of the governors' conference emphasized national politics rather than Ashmore's speech, native Virginian John Popham of the *New York Times* congratulated Ashmore on winning the admiration of the press corps. "I can't begin to tell you, also, just how enthusiastic all the newspaper boys were in expressing in their little groups for several days the high regard they had for you . . . ," Popham wrote. "You were one hell of a hit with the gang, Harry."[73] Even William Workman of the Charleston, South Carolina, *News and Courier*, a states' rights supporter, expressed pride in seeing a fellow native of Greenville, South Carolina, "beard the lions in their very den."[74]

On the contrary, Ashmore's speech alarmed racial conservatives in the South, and he sent identical letters to at least two of the governors who attended the conference, distancing himself from most news accounts of the speech, reclaiming the middle ground, and invoking the classic both-sides framework of objectivity. "The speech was—as such speeches always are—widely misinterpreted," Ashmore wrote. "I've been simultaneously condemned for being too radical and too reactionary, a circumstance from which I draw some comfort."[75] Governor Wright of Mississippi seemed placated by Ashmore's explanation: "I can understand that any speech of this kind is often misinterpreted by those who desire to misconstrue the truth."[76] In correspondence with *Birmingham [AL] Post-Herald* columnist John Temple Graves II, who had not seen the full text of the speech, Ashmore reassured him that "the digested news service reports" had misrepresented his views. "As usual, I am being condemned simultaneously as a radical and a reactionary, a circumstance from which I draw some comfort," Ashmore wrote to Graves, a segregationist who had supported the Dixiecrats. ". . . I have always had an idea we probably weren't too far apart on the basic elements of the race matter."[77] After seeing the full text of the speech, Graves acquiesced. "When I read the account of your speech I thought you had moved over somewhat, but now that I have seen the whole thing, I realize you have not. I think it was a perfectly magnificent speech and it confirms my estimate of you as one of our most clear-headed, brave, honest and eloquent."[78]

Ashmore also clarified his position in responses to racial liberals who perceived from news coverage that he supported integration. Among them was James Dombrowski, director of the Southern Conference Educational Fund (SCEF), whose pro-integration agenda segregationists had accused of being communist-inspired. "Judging by the one press report that I have read," Dombrowski wrote, "you made a very fine statement before the Southern Governors Conference."[79] Ashmore declined Dombrowski's invitation to judge a student editorial contest, saying that his "own views on segregation and those of the SCEF are pretty wide apart."[80] Ashmore also turned aside praise from Fleur Cowles, an editor of *Look*, *Quick*, and *Flair* magazines, who had seen the speech reprinted in full in the Cowles's *Des Moines [IA] Register* and interpreted it as challenging Jim Crow. "I don't believe I have ever read a statement run by our paper of which I was more proud; you have put into words, and acceptable words to both southerners and northerners, a remarkable statement about segregation," she wrote. "This is one of the few fan letters I have ever written."[81] Ashmore rebuffed her praise in a reassertion of his claim to objectivity. "It might interest you to know," he wrote Cowles, reinterpreting the correspondence in question, "that in the same mail I received a letter from Gov. Fielding Wright of Mississippi in which he endorsed virtually all of the sentiments expressed in the speech."[82]

Ashmore's responses to Black Americans who wrote to applaud the message in news reports were brief and perhaps strained. For example, Lawrence A. Davis, president of the Agricultural, Mechanical and Normal College at Pine Bluff, Arkansas, a historically Black institution, commended Ashmore for a "very excellent and courageous speech." Davis acknowledged the difficulty of giving a speech that was acceptable to people holding a range of opinion on race: "We must, in positions such as you and I hold, realize that we are always between extreme forces, sometimes of tremendous power, and we will always find it difficult to maintain acceptable positions."[83] As with the note to Cowles, Ashmore's noncommittal response to Davis's letter put distance between himself and Davis's impression of the speech, asserting his professional impartiality. "As you recognized," Ashmore wrote, "I was not trying to express personal opinions, but trying to establish some tenable ground for all men of good will."[84]

## The Howard Conference

Harry Ashmore's speech drew the attention of Black academics and civil rights strategists outside Arkansas. Within a few weeks, Charles Thompson, dean of the graduate school at Howard University and a collaborator in the NAACP Legal Defense Fund's court challenges to segregated schools, invited Ashmore to speak during a national conference on "The Courts and Racial Integration in Education" in April 1952. Thompson, as editor of the *Journal of Negro Education*, planned to compile proceedings of the conference, to be held at Howard, in an upcoming issue.[85] Ashmore agreed to prepare an address on the topic of "Some Major Problems Involved in Racial Integration with Especial Reference to Education in the South."[86] Upon hearing that Ashmore would address the conference, an official with the Rockefeller-endowed General Education Board, which funded Black educational initiatives in the South, wrote Ashmore to underscore the event's importance: "Since this conference may have significant implications for further developments in the education of Negroes, I am sure there will be interest in what you have to say."[87] Ashmore instead used this speech before a predominantly Black audience of more than three hundred to cement his public support of continued school segregation.

Thompson's biographer, who devotes a chapter to the 1952 conference, describes the three-day event as part of Thompson's strategy to build momentum for reversing *Plessy v. Ferguson,* which he believed the U.S. Supreme Court would be willing to do when presented with the appropriate court challenge. Thompson hoped that thoughtful debate among those holding a range of opinion on segregated schools would bridge differences and sought, perhaps naively, to create a national forum on the issue. Given the political hazards attached to public discussions of integration by white southerners, that aspect of the conference program failed definitively. Although representatives of every southern school district were invited, few whites attended. As a gradualist, Ashmore provided a candid assessment of white southern attitudes toward the prospect of integration.[88]

The gregarious Ashmore was, at the very least, aloof in his dealings with his Black hosts at Howard, declining to participate in the conference beyond his delivery of the address. Ashmore planned to attend the annual meeting of the all-white American Society of Newspaper Editors (ASNE) in Washington, DC, that week and did not appear interested in communion with others who attended the Howard meeting across town. After accepting the invitation to speak, he appeared to distance himself from the obligation as he was slow to respond to the hospitality Thompson extended. In Ashmore's defense, he may not have known that a keynote at an academic conference entailed, at least from his hosts' perspective, more formality and preparation than the speeches Ashmore gave to clubs and organizations. Over the interceding months, he probably exasperated Thompson, who expected to pay Ashmore's expenses, with tardy responses to requests for information necessary for conference planning. For example, Ashmore wrote Thompson on April 12, after long silence and just four days before his scheduled address, to say that he did not have his paper done for distribution to others on the program, including the assigned discussants; would not stay in conference accommodations; would not participate in other parts of the conference; and otherwise would attend the ASNE meeting during his trip to Washington.[89] Ashmore's failure to send Thompson a copy of his remarks before the Howard conference contrasts with his address at Hot Springs, where he cooperated with the planners and provided an advance script of his speech to the white press and southern governors.

Because the meeting was attended by postwar academic and legal experts on civil rights, Ashmore presented a strong counterpoint to the views of most members of his audience. Among them were Thurgood Marshall, legal counsel to the NAACP; Walter White, executive secretary of the NAACP; Lester Granger, executive director of the National Urban League; and presidents of historically Black colleges and universities. Moreover, the event was titled "A Conference on the Courts and Racial Integration in Education," with emphasis on integration, whereas Ashmore framed the debate in terms of segregation.[90]

Following his defense of separate-but-equal public schools alongside an affirmation of the white South's theoretical commitment to equitable education for Black Americans, Ashmore denied that segregated schools necessarily impinged on civil rights and equated the effort to repeal *Plessy v. Ferguson* with radicalism. Taking clear aim at the NAACP strategy to integrate public classrooms through litigation, Ashmore argued, "For a new generation of Negro leaders, far more militant than their predecessors, the school issue has been seized upon as an opportunity to exploit the whole of their racial grievances." He then critiqued the assumptions underlying the conference:

> The conference prospectus contains this statement: "Negroes are determined, and all but the most reactionary whites are resigned to the fact, that enforced segregated schools must go in the very near future." I would take sharp issue with this statement insofar as it applies to the white South. The reactionary whites, who are in a considerable minority, frequently oppose even the equalization of school facilities. The conservative whites—who insofar as this issue is concerned make up the great majority of Southern whites—are a long way from being resigned to the abandonment of segregation in the public schools.[91]

Ashmore cautioned against inferring that muted white reaction to the court-ordered integration of some graduate programs, which affected a limited number of southerners, meant that whites generally would not resist desegregation of the public schools, which he defined as "the most sensitive area."[92] To suddenly integrate primary and secondary schools by decree, he warned, "would involve a social revolution, touching not a few persons of advanced educational attainment, but the mass of the Southern people."[93]

Ashmore did not foreclose the possibility that southern schools could be desegregated eventually and noted that race relations in the South had evolved in recent decades. "Mine is still the classic doctrine of the gradualist," he concluded, cautioning against a strategy that would force white southerners to integrate their elementary and high schools. "What we are dealing with finally is a state of mind which is, and is likely to continue to be, beyond the reach of any court order."[94]

Although the audience and objective for the speech were different, Ashmore's remarks at Howard University clearly aligned with the position he had expressed to the virtually all-white Southern Governors' Conference. At Howard, however, the political drama and national interest that had animated the audience at Hot Springs were missing and press coverage was limited. Local white newspapers covered the first day of the conference. The *Washington Post* sent Simeon Booker, its first Black reporter, and published a ten-paragraph story at the top of page 2B, in the local news section. Booker's account, which recognized the gathering's significance for civil rights strategy, did not lead with Ashmore's speech but with a pointed call for desegregation by Horace Mann Bond, president of historically Black Lincoln University in Pennsylvania: "We need to struggle to open all doors now closed; to integrate Negro students into all schools, and Negro teachers into all faculties, and Negro board members into all private and public, local, state, and national boards."[95] Although Booker quoted Ashmore, who was one of four speakers in the opening session, he did not treat him as the primary keynote. The *Washington Evening Star*, however, ran a six-paragraph story buried deep inside the paper that listed some of the other speakers but summarized only Ashmore's defense of segregation.[96]

The Black press covered the Howard gathering as well. A *Pittsburgh Courier* synopsis of Ashmore's speech a week after the conference led by quoting him as saying, "Public opinion in the South today favors equal education, but any attempt on the part of the courts to change the prevailing system of separate schools would arouse a deep-seated opposition that would do the Negro more harm than good."[97] A similar story, which noted that prominent Black speakers "offered somewhat different views than those offered by Ashmore," appeared in the *Alabama Tribune*, a Black weekly in Montgomery.[98] These papers offered a fair summation of Ashmore's position, even if those remarks contradicted the conference's goal of strategizing an end to segregated schools.

In submitting expenses for his trip to Washington, Ashmore thanked Thompson and acknowledged that he had been "in the position of representing a minority view at a session dealing with minority problems."[99] Thompson returns to our story in chapter 5, when the Southern Education Reporting Service frantically cast about in 1956 to recruit prominent Black men to fill the token Black seats on the SERS board following a director's death and another's resignation in protest of SERS racism. The SERS, founded to report on the South's response to *Brown*, would be the second Ashmore-affiliated objectivity project underwritten by the Fund for the Advancement of Education. As a leading Black intellectual, Thompson was an obvious target for SERS board membership. Although Thompson would have several reasons for declining the invitation, including the Black press's eventual condemnation of the SERS, his orientation toward the invitation might have been different if Ashmore, a reporting service founder, had exhibited greater professional deference in 1952. The Howard conference had provided Ashmore an opportunity to collaborate across racial lines, but he rejected the chance to learn more about civil rights goals and strategy—even as Thompson was willing to put him on the program to provide ideological balance and to learn from him. Ashmore might have rationalized his exposure to differing viewpoints as necessary for the objective discussion of race.

For a white southern editor who opposed social integration, Ashmore's Howard address was a safe speech, validating the racial status quo before a sizeable audience of Black Americans, many of whom were the activists propelling the civil rights struggle. In a brief reflection in 1982, Ashmore contrasted them with the Black traditionalists who had acquiesced to gradualism instead of pressing for reform. He wrote that "the split between the black militants and accommodationists came into the open" at the Howard conference, using defensive white language to frame the NAACP litigation effort as extremist and the audience as radical.[100] In fact, the Howard gathering in 1952 was attended by Black educators, academics, and attorneys—a cross-section of the postwar Black professional class and intelligentsia. Ashmore's position in this speech was essentially the same one he had offered in public for at least four years, including the address to the governors, but at Howard University before a predominantly Black audience, Ashmore's ideological distance was apparent in the juxtaposition of his remarks with those of school integration advocates on the program. He had encountered a similar circumstance at Hot Springs, when his argument did not conform to his audience's assumptions. Where Ashmore's call to the governors to comply with the separate-but-equal doctrine seemed to challenge white supremacist orthodoxy, his endorsement of separate-but-equal schools in the Howard speech now positioned him as a defender of that status quo.

His entreaty for civil rights leaders to exercise restraint was pointedly ineffective. In his history of the *Brown* litigation, Richard Kluger noted that Thurgood Marshall and other plaintiffs' attorneys in the NAACP desegregation lawsuits heard Ashmore indulge the recalcitrance and defiance of southern racists and warn Black activists against demanding more rights than the white South was prepared to concede. This was a familiar scare tactic—deployed against the Black press in World War II, for example—that rationalized gradualism as a palliative to keep southern whites from turning violent. "What Marshall heard there might have given pause to a less determined man," Kluger wrote. Instead, Marshall embarked on "a far stronger and more determined effort . . . to convince the Supreme Court to strike down segregation."[101] Two years later the U.S. Supreme Court would issue its first ruling in *Brown*.

Oddly, Ashmore gave the Howard speech only brief mention in his autobiographical histories of race in America, even though the meeting was concretely more important than the governors' conference in terms of its impact on the civil rights movement and its place in history.[102] The value of the Howard conference might not have been clear to the gradualists in the 1950s, but when Ashmore published reflections on the South and civil rights in the 1980s and 1990s, the appraisal of racism had shifted. By then, Marshall had been on the Supreme Court since 1967 and the *Brown* decision was established as the law of the land, making the link between the litigation and "militancy" appear strained. Ashmore seemed unaware that his defense of gradualism at Howard had backfired and had in fact strengthened Marshall's resolve to integrate the schools.

## Waiting for the Racial Future to Unfold

When he returned to Little Rock after his Howard speech, there were no letters asking Ashmore to clarify his message as there had been five months earlier when his address to the southern governors was covered by the national press. That summer, editor Virginius Dabney of the *Richmond Times Dispatch*, a fellow gradualist, sought Ashmore's input on likely southern reaction to a possible Supreme Court ruling desegregating the public schools, and Ashmore sent him a copy of the *Journal of Negro Education* issue containing his remarks to the Howard conference.[103] Dabney's response contrasts Ashmore's position and that of Horace Mann Bond, who preceded Ashmore on the program and was quoted in Booker's *Washington Post* story. Bond, whose twelve-year-old son Julian would become a prominent civil rights activist, offered an impassioned endorsement of the NAACP strategy "to sue, and sue, and sue, for access to every opportunity available to every other American."[104] In his reply to Ashmore, Dabney, who also was misperceived as a racial liberal at this point in his career, illustrated the gulf between gradualism and the racial equality sought by Black Americans at the conference.

Ashmore's "address to the Howard University conclave is just right, it seems to me," Dabney wrote. "At first, I got confused and read Page 249 as part of your remarks, and concluded that old Ashmore sure had gone overboard, but after scratching the Dabney dome for awhile, I waked up to the fact that some other brother, doubtless with Senegambian ancestry, had cut loose with that blast."[105]

Like John Temple Graves and other racial conservatives who expressed concern about what, exactly, Ashmore had meant in his remarks to the governors, Dabney's ribbing about the Howard conference reminded Ashmore of the ideological line that a gradualist dared not cross if he hoped to retain credibility with his white southern audience—and with many of his fellow white editors. Even before *Brown v. Board of Education* intensified the ideological surveillance of the white press by white southerners, discussed in chapter 4, white editors experienced unrelenting scrutiny of their positions on race for deviations from the racial status quo. The normative effect of this boundary policing is unmistakable: Many white southerners chose their words carefully, or remained silent, to avoid being branded as disloyal.

Although Ashmore might have understood that desegregation was inevitable eventually, any assumption that he ever supported the social or legal outcomes sought in *Brown* is revisionist conjecture. In his remarks to the Howard University conference in April 1952, he was sharply critical of the NAACP litigation strategy and tried to dissuade his audience that desegregation of graduate schools meant southern education at any other level could be integrated without white defiance. Two years later he also insisted that his editorship of *The Negro and the Schools*, whose data reported on educational resources and outcomes under the separate-but-equal doctrine, was objective journalism, not political engagement, that he merely arranged and contextualized information supplied by others.[106] After the book's publication, he screened invitations to participate in discussions and media events about *Brown*, accepting those that might not compromise his newly acquired neutral pose and rejecting those that were politically treacherous.

In October 1954 he appeared with Kenneth Clark, the Black psychologist whose research informed the *Brown* litigation, on a University of Chicago *Roundtable* broadcast on NBC Radio. Although Clark was the expert and Ashmore was a journalist, Ashmore dominated the conversation.

Even after the *Brown* ruling, this was a politically safe discussion because Ashmore was the counterpoint to Clark's racial liberalism.[107] The previous June he had turned down an invitation to appear on the radio program hosted by Walter White, the NAACP's executive secretary. Ashmore invoked the principle of objectivity in his reply:

> As to appearing on your broadcast I think frankly that it would be unwise for me to do so at this time. The Supreme Court decrees, of course, are still pending, and your organization is still identified . . . as an advocate. I have tried in [*The Negro and the Schools*] and in other statements I have made publicly to maintain objectivity. I rather doubt, of course, if this is humanly possible, but at least I am working on it. I feel that identification with the NAACP, or for that matter with something like the emergency governors conference at Richmond on the other side, would be a mistake. I hope you will appreciate my feeling in the matter.[108]

Claiming a full schedule, Ashmore also declined an invitation from Myles Horton, leader of the biracial Highlander Folk School in Tennessee, to be a discussion leader at a workshop on school desegregation a month after the *Brown* ruling and publication of *The Negro and the Schools*.[109] A year later Rosa Parks and other civil rights activists would be trained at Highlander; in 1957 the Reverend Martin Luther King Jr. also attended a meeting there.[110]

Ashmore's stated interest in the public appearance of neutrality and objectivity had emerged since his speeches to the 1951 Southern Governors' Conference and the Howard symposium the following spring. The audience at the Richmond event in the example Ashmore mentioned to White was the same cohort he had addressed at Hot Springs. Now Ashmore's association with *The Negro and the Schools* allowed him to claim neutrality when mandated integration became reality, but its affiliation with the Ford Foundation raised suspicion among white supremacists who worried that the northern philanthropy, newly interested in Black education, had made a leftward turn and taken Ashmore with it. Ashmore never wavered in his gradualism, but the strict segregationists eventually regarded him as a breed apart.

What irrevocably alienated Ashmore from the conservative white South was *An Epitaph for Dixie*, which W. W. Norton published in 1957 before the Little Rock crisis. Although a far less ponderous work, *Epitaph* belongs to the genre redefined in 1941 by journalist W. J. Cash in

*The Mind of the South*, a self-reflexive and soul-searching analysis of southern white identity that Ashmore described as "profound." Although he still hedged on integration, Ashmore conceded the inevitability of racial change and, like Cash, lamented the price of southern obstinance throughout history. "It would seem that those who resolutely turn away from the future would at least be able to read the first lesson of the South's past: When responsible men default, irresponsible men take power," he wrote. "This is the ultimate price Southern leaders, and the Southern people, may yet have to pay before the stiff necks bend and defiance gives way to the inevitable compromise." Ashmore noted that he had lost favor in the white South, "not by fervently crusading for the downtrodden blacks, but simply by insisting that no Southern newspaper could possibly ignore the most pressing social issue its readers face, and that these matters must be fully reported and dispassionately discussed." Attempting to balance the demands of objectivity, he continued, "It seems to me, indeed, that I have done no editorial battle at all; my role, rather, has been that of a man trying to preserve order at an incipient riot . . . and to see to it that calm and reasonable voices are heard above the clamor of willful and ignorant men."[111]

*Epitaph* and its author were condemned by white supremacists whose racism lacked the nuance of Ashmore's. For example, in a syndicated column distributed in January 1958, Westbrook Pegler, by then working for King Features Syndicate, took aim at the perceived liberalism of Ashmore and Hodding Carter Jr., another gradualist. Carter, editor of the *Delta Democrat-Times* in Greenville, Mississippi, reviewed *Epitaph* for the *New York Times Review of Books* and described massive resistance advocates Thomas Waring of the *Charleston [SC] News and Observer* and James J. Kilpatrick of the *Richmond News Leader* as "apostles of neo-secessionism." Ashmore had singled them out for unscrupulous editorial leadership.[112] Defending Waring and Kilpatrick, Pegler wrote, "These are two of the best journalists in the country. Both are gentlemen and neither Ashmore nor Carter is fit to run their copy."[113] A few months later, columnist George Sokolsky, a right-wing anticommunist with a national platform in both print and radio, also excoriated Ashmore, assumed to be an "integrationist," for being a hypocrite who did not hire Black reporters and still segregated "Negro news" within his newspaper.[114]

In these and other cases, Ashmore's critics assumed him to be far more liberal on the question of desegregation than the record would indicate. Even so, circumstances in Little Rock made it uncomfortable for him to remain at the *Arkansas Gazette* after the Central High School confrontation. When he left the South in 1959, he was able to trade on contacts he had made in the North. He first went to work on Ford Foundation projects and in 1960 was named editor of the *Encyclopedia Britannica*. He later joined a California think tank underwritten by Ford's Fund for the Republic and run by Robert M. Hutchins, the former University of Chicago president who headed the Committee on Freedom of the Press and authored its findings in 1947, commonly known as the Hutchins Report.[115] By the time of Ashmore's death in 1998, he had written eight more books.

Ashmore's public position on race remained murky, even as he wrote frequently about civil rights. Although he generously inserted autobiography into his books, describing his poor white upbringing in segregated Greenville, South Carolina, he presented himself as a frontline observer of the white South's evolving relationship with its Black citizens, not as a partisan—an objective pose he had developed for *The Negro and the Schools*. He also made few public statements that would betray his personal philosophy. Even in later decades, when disavowing one's previous support of segregation was fashionable, if not required, Ashmore remained a circumspect eyewitness to history. He drew a sharp contrast to the opportunistic Kilpatrick, who renounced his racism after leading the Massive Resistance movement following *Brown* so that his column could be nationally syndicated and he might provide commentary on network television.[116] Ashmore was certainly more racially tolerant than many of his peers in the white southern press, but he was not the integrationist his detractors condemned. In his statements in the late 1940s and early 1950s, Ashmore repeatedly acknowledged that the South's treatment of Black Americans had been un-Christian and insisted that they were entitled to certain civil rights; however, there is no evidence that Ashmore believed Black Americans were his equals. When he quoted from the 1951 governors' conference speech in his books, even decades later, his excerpts foregrounded his support of separate-but-equal schools as an alternative to integration.

In short, Ashmore did not renounce positions he held before *Brown*, even decades later when cultural norms changed and those views became odious in most circles. This raises important challenges for the historian evaluating a record that spans decades in both the life of Harry Ashmore and a racialized society upended by the civil rights movement. Ashmore's views on race undoubtedly had adapted to the norms of the broader culture, but how much and in what ways is not clear. As late as 1980, when Ashmore was working on *Hearts and Minds: The Anatomy of Racism from Roosevelt to Reagan*, Ashmore had not eliminated racial slurs from his vocabulary. In a most stunning note to longtime friend C. A. McKnight of the *Charlotte [NC] Observer*, who was the SERS's first executive director, Ashmore referred to "the book I am finishing for McGraw-Hill—which should, but won't be, entitled Niggers I Have Known."[117] The language is not open to interpretation and suggests that Ashmore had not moved past the racism that manifested in his defense of segregation in the 1950s. That letter was not a fluke. Earlier that year, Ashmore had written McKnight that he was "at work on another book, this one being a more or less personal reflection on the course of race relations in the twenty-five years since you last played 'Nigger-Loving Boogie' for Thurgood Marshall and Mrs. [Ogden] Reid. It often brings you to mind."[118] The correspondence refers to a party hosted by the editor of the *New York Herald Tribune*, following a forum on *Brown* that had been sponsored by the newspaper. Marshall and Ashmore had attended the party because they participated in the forum; McKnight was there in his SERS capacity. In a published reflection, Ashmore described the song as an original composition by McKnight, an amateur jazz pianist, though it is unclear whether party guests were told what song he played or it remained an inside joke.[119]

Ashmore found the reference poignant in recounting the episode. Nearly three decades after he stood before the southern governors and the civil rights leadership at the Howard conference, his disdain for the history he was writing and the people at the center of the story undermined his performance of objectivity on race and civil rights. But Ashmore was not the only white southern editor who lost his ethical bearings in the mid-1950s. When the *Brown* decision declared the racial status quo unconstitutional, many of Ashmore's peers invigorated their efforts to control the news narrative about race. Fortifying their ideological battlelines and calling out a familiar enemy, southern white editors took aim at the journalistic scallywags north of the Mason-Dixon Line. The Associated Press news service would again be drawn into the fray.

CHAPTER 4

# SOUTH VERSUS NORTH

THE MASON-DIXON LINE
IN JOURNALISM STANDARDS

For whites across the American South, the end of legal school segregation in 1954 signaled a historic disruption of the region's culture and politics and provoked a response that was often fearful and sometimes even violent. At the vanguard of white southern reaction to the U.S. Supreme Court's ruling in *Brown v. Board of Education* were white editors of daily newspapers, many of whom saw the mandate as an attack on southern values and the political autonomy entailed in states' rights. As their readers grappled with desegregation's impact on the "southern way of life," a social framework that depended on Black subordination, many editors vigorously defended the honor of the South, a region long maligned as benighted and backward, against intensified scrutiny by the northern press.[1] National news coverage of the Emmett Till lynching in 1955 and the exoneration of his white killers amplified northern derision of white supremacy and in turn animated defensive southern resistance to such scrutiny. In many communities in the South, the end of legalized Jim Crow came uneasily; white supremacist venom and interracial clashes made for titillating news copy in the North, where southern racial traditions registered as deviant.[2] Such reporting, according to many white editors in the South, was journalistic hypocrisy. This central trope of the white southern response to *Brown* held that northern racial bias and the inequity it perpetuated in housing and jobs were as effective at separating the races as the South's Jim Crow laws, but the northern press was fixated instead on racism in the former Confederacy.

An inviting target for white southern outrage was the Associated Press, the New York–based wire service that distributed national news to the South, much of it generated by northern newspapers that did not, as a matter of routine, assign significant news value to racial inequity in their own communities or intentionally emphasize stories that portrayed Black Americans in a negative light. Importantly, the AP also transmitted news from the South to member newspapers in the North, where reports of white animosity toward integration affirmed the South's low esteem above the Mason-Dixon Line. As the most pervasive U.S. news infrastructure at this juncture in American history, the AP was an indisputable nexus in the ideological battle over representation that shaped civil rights discourse in the mid-twentieth century.

Suspicious of the AP's agenda-setting protocols for selecting news for the regional and national wires and convinced that the AP's news judgment was biased against the South, white editors at many newspapers in the region—or "section," in 1950s idiom—judiciously monitored the wire service for offending news copy. Many also participated in a campaign— through correspondence and phone calls to AP executives and bureau personnel, messages on the wire, editorials in their own newspapers, and grievance sessions at professional meetings—to intervene in news judgment about racial discord and discrimination in the North and to ameliorate negative news coverage of the South's response to *Brown*. Particularly effective over time were white southern accusations that the AP, in prioritizing and framing racial news from North and South, engaged in a journalistic double standard and violated its own standards of balance and objectivity. In this vein, Joe Parham, white editor of the *Macon News* in Georgia, complained to the AP's Atlanta bureau in 1956 that the wire service, whose board of directors was dominated by representatives of large northern newspapers, had to be "needled into" reporting on racism in the North. Parham wrote, "The NAACP, as you well know, will raise unshirted hell at the drop of a comma, and raise it where it will do some good, while us poor old Crackers continue to entertain five or six visiting reporters doing an expose tour of the South every week and continue to wonder what's going on up North in racial relations."[3]

This chapter examines tensions evident during the 1950s in correspondence and other artifacts in the Associated Press Corporate Archive, which illustrate the oppositional dynamic between segregationist white editors in the South and AP journalists and decision-makers. Drawing on southern complaints about the handling of AP stories and the AP's policy responses, this discussion builds on chapter 2's analysis of the controversy that had erupted in the 1940s over racial identification in AP news copy and documents the clear impact of segregationist advocacy on story selection for the daily wire report. Although this ongoing agitation did not erase the national news value of white southern resistance to desegregation, it most certainly recalibrated the AP's news judgment pertaining to racial conflict and discrimination in the North. This reactive change in journalism standards is apparent in AP policy statements, staff responses to aggrieved southern members, and internal memos to and from AP bureaus. For example, writing from the wire service's executive offices in New York in 1957, Paul Mickelson, the AP's general news editor, confirmed for an AP reporter in Montgomery, Alabama, who was on the frontline of southern editors' anger and suspicion about the wire service, that stories about racial disharmony in the North were receiving higher priority because of complaints from southern members. "All of us here are aware of the necessity of expediting such coverage southward though we miss occasionally through lapses on the part of northern bureaus," Mickelson wrote.[4] In this exchange Mickelson confirmed that the AP was imposing segregationist news values on AP members and wire service personnel in the North. In short, white southern editors had succeeded in deploying journalistic standards of accuracy, objectivity, and balance as weapons in an ideological battle exacerbated by the end of legal Jim Crow.

From the mid-1950s onward, AP executives in New York and the staff in bureaus and offices across the United States were on notice that many white southern editors were surveilling the flow of news to and from the North, prepared to challenge the transmission of racial news that reflected poorly on the South. Of greatest concern to the segregationists were stories that glossed racial inequity in the North and failed to play up criminal and antisocial behavior by Black Americans, which in their minds justified Jim Crow and rendered Black people unqualified for full citizenship. These editors also objected to the South being singled out for its culture of white supremacy, which had been sanctioned by de jure segregation even as de facto segregation persisted in the North. In the years after the *Brown* decision, some white editors continuously inventoried the wire for evidence of this hypocrisy and assumed in their frequent correspondence with AP staff that the wire service intentionally emphasized stories about white southern resistance to integration and suppressed news of racial tension from the North. If stories with a racial angle in the North were delayed or moved only on a regional wire, rather than given national distribution, or lacked racial detail that affirmed the stereotypes about Black criminality, deviance, or irresponsibility that appealed to white southern newspaper readers, these editors charged the AP with journalistic bias.

This was the case in 1957, when Kentucky editor Edgar Arnold Jr. of the *Madisonville Messenger* corresponded with AP bureau chiefs in Chicago and Louisville, as well as AP executives in New York, about the suspected omission of a racial angle in a story about teenage gangs in Chicago. Presenting his case as a defense of journalism standards, Arnold wrote,

> I am aware that there are many misguided agencies and newspapers who apparently hold the view that racial troubles will disappear if they ignore them. This is another form of censorship which we must resist.
>
> The people of the South are sick and tired—and justly so—of having the accusing finger pointed at them daily from the front pages of big, Northern newspapers while these same papers willfully suppress any news with a racial tinge in their own back yards. This is the thing which I want our Associated Press to be on guard against.... After all, we are working for the same aim—a fair and impartial report of the news.[5]

Arnold assumed that the story, which mentioned only the murder of a Black teenager by a white gang, had intentionally omitted the criminal activities of Black gang members and details about white victims of Black violence.[6] Alan Gould, the AP's executive editor, was among AP personnel who responded to Arnold's complaints. "I agree thoroughly with the general premise of your letter . . . ," Gould wrote. "We should not have double standards of news coverage" on stories about race.[7] In a letter that might still have been making its way through the U.S. mail, Alvin Orton, the Chicago bureau chief, had written Arnold a day earlier to refute his claim and clarify that "with the exception of the killing of . . . a Negro, all crimes mentioned in our March 21 story involved only whites," and reported that the white gang's confessed motive for killing its Black victim was "race hatred."[8]

Gould, unaware of Orton's explanation in the other thread of correspondence and, by 1957, well-practiced in deference to southern complaints, took a position that aligned with Arnold's. "I think you make a very good point," Gould wrote. "I would be very much surprised, as you would, if all the other incidents mentioned in that story involved only white youths, and if the only Negro in all the cases mentioned was the one beaten by a gang of whites. . . . I think we must admit that the story, as written, gave a false impression." He then suggested that "the racial angle in the Chicago story needed treatment in a separate paragraph or two. I doubt that all the young hoodlums were black, or all white, or that all the fights were between racial groups, but we should have brought out to what extent the two races were involved."[9] After receiving the Chicago bureau chief's clarification, and apparently before Gould's letter arrived, Arnold acknowledged that his assumption had been in error. However, Gould's equivocation remained on record as his last word on this complaint.[10]

In this exchange of letters, which lasted more than a week and was complicated by responses from multiple AP staff crossing in the mail, Arnold received from Gould, the AP's top editor, an affirmation of news values that were different from those applied by the pivotal bureau in Chicago. Moreover, Gould suggested that reporting on criminal behavior by whites in the North should be balanced by reporting on criminal activity by Blacks. That the correspondence centered on a faulty assumption, by both the southern editor and Gould, makes it all the more significant. In 1957, having endured many similar rounds of criticism from segregationist AP members, Gould reflexively acquiesced to their complaints and conceded Arnold's argument before knowing the particulars of the story and how it had been reported. Moreover, because the AP was highly transparent in discussion of news values and practices, most of the AP correspondence with white southern editors was copied to other wire service employees in New York and in relevant bureaus. In addition, editors and bureau chiefs were often asked to reply directly to members, clarifying their handling of stories that generated complaints, and were present when members voiced suspicion about a North-South double standard at national and regional meetings of the Associated Press Managing Editors (APME).[11] As a result, positions taken by AP executives in response to criticism by southern members were understood throughout the staff and membership network and set policy for the organization.

## The AP as Arbiter of a Regional Dispute

Many white southern newspapers also subscribed to the United Press (UP) wire service, renamed United Press International (UPI) after its merger in 1958 with the International News Service, but many white editors had greater allegiance to the AP, which became the standard bearer for the American daily press as UPI succumbed to financial challenges and as journalism education emphasized AP style rules.[12] The AP was a member-owned cooperative, meaning the AP workforce, including the editorial staff in bureaus and the executive officers in New York, were accountable to all the newspapers—North, South, East, and West—that received the AP's news service. It was, in membership and personnel, a virtually all-white organization. As part of a reciprocal agreement, AP members were obliged to share their locally generated news content with the wire service for dissemination to all other members; when local newsrooms could not provide coverage or a monumental story warranted extra attention, AP personnel in state and metropolitan bureaus stepped in to report. Throughout the day and night, the AP gathered and generated news from throughout the United States and around the world, making judgments about news value and listing stories on news budgets, determining whether these stories had national, regional, or state importance, and issuing bulletins and updates as developments warranted. A breaking and developing story might receive a succession of new "ledes," newspaper jargon for the lead paragraph of the story, creating a shared experience for members working on deadline across the country, even as they edited the wire copy for their own readers. In addition to the clear agenda-setting function of the AP process, the normative impact of this mechanical reproduction of the news was significant. Copies of the same story appeared simultaneously in many newsrooms, formatted according to AP's style rules and the inverted pyramid story structure, which foregrounded certain facts over others. The global power and pervasiveness of the AP news report were not lost on white southern editors, whose work routines were modulated by the clatter of the teletype machines in their newsrooms.[13]

News judgment, the determination that an event or issue was worthy of coverage, was imposed when an editor first assigned a story to a reporter, but the AP also exercised news judgment when it transmitted stories into member newsrooms along a hierarchy of wires that prioritized the most pressing news of general interest to the national wire and directed stories assumed to have more limited news value to state and regional wires. Without an editorial decision by the AP, newspapers in California or Georgia would not receive the same news report as members in New York. The story selection and news-routing functions of the wire service became a point of sharp ideological conflict as white southern members worried about discrepancies in the reach and play of stories about racial issues and incidents reported from and about the North versus the South. Archived AP correspondence documents that during the years immediately following the *Brown* decision, AP staff in the corporate headquarters in New York and in bureaus across the United States prioritized these complaints and responded diligently and thoroughly to segregationists' concerns. Although the southern critics were a minority of the membership and were politically out of step with most of their editor peers in newsrooms outside their region, they were vocal, energized, and unrelenting. By positing their arguments as a defense of journalism standards instead of the racial status quo, they forced the wire service and its members across the country to confront the segregationist perspective while reporting and editing the daily news.

For white southern editors, the motivation was simple: as they managed the story of race from their newsrooms, from the vantage of a region under siege and with an inflamed sense of grievance, journalism standards offered a convenient tool to control the news narrative about race and southern culture. By 1954, when the *Brown v. Board of Education* decision declared racially segregated public schools to be unconstitutional, the racial stakes for white southerners had intensified and their dominant status in the racial binary governing the South was uncertain. As a result, pro-segregation journalists and editors in the white press, who were reporting on the social change that *Brown* and other legal gains had initiated for Black Americans, were also contending with the freedom struggle's consequences for their own racial status, which had always been defined by the exclusions of Jim Crow. White southern editors, whose grandfathers might have been Confederate veterans, also had experienced, either during their careers or as cultural memory, the scorn incited by national press coverage of the Scopes trial in 1925 and understood that the national news portrayal of the white southern response to

*Brown* would shape their political reality. Perceiving an existential threat to white culture, segregationist editors very intentionally monitored the wire service's coverage of race and debated with AP staff the standards of objectivity, accuracy, and balance, based on how the news coverage reflected on the white South. Ultimately, this organized surveillance of the AP news wire was a political effort to maintain the racial distinction and power differential that historically had subjugated Blackness to whiteness. Journalism standards were never the actual point.

## Journalistic Equivalence

Fueling southern scrutiny of northern news values during the 1950s was northern derision of illiberal and cruel southern racial practices. In addition to their alarm about reporting on the *Brown* decision, many white southern editors resented saturation coverage of the 1955 Emmett Till lynching and the trial of the two white men accused of murdering him, which became a national and international story. The Till murder in Mississippi initiated a wave of northern journalists who converged on the South to cover segregationists' reactionary and sometimes violent response to *Brown*. Objecting to their region being portrayed as backward and racist in the northern press, white southern editors lobbied the AP for national dissemination of stories that highlighted racial tension in the North. In particular, they insisted on news coverage that portrayed the Black Americans living there without the constraints of southern Jim Crow as criminal, unruly, and prone to riot.[14] This aligned with a theme emerging in conservative publications that integration unleashed social problems that segregation had kept in check. As *U.S. News and World Report* asserted in the title of an article, "When Negroes Move North: Many Problems of the South—and Others, Too—Come with Them." Moreover, the magazine insisted, liberal northern newspapers were keeping this a secret.[15]

Such coverage coincided with the 1956 campaign by Grover Hall Jr., editor of the *Montgomery Advertiser* in Alabama, to assert in editorials and news stories the existence of racial problems in the North, the northern press's complicity in concealing them, and the hypocrisy of northern critics of race relations in the South.[16] In addition, by 1956 James J. Kilpatrick, editor of the *Richmond News-Leader*, had begun to complain about a "paper curtain" that separated North from South and allegedly prevented a fair hearing in northern newspapers and magazines of southern views in support of segregation.[17] Their representation of a censoring northern press quickly gained traction with their peers in southern newsrooms. In an editorial, Joe Parham, editor of the *Macon News*, heralded Hall and Kilpatrick as southern heroes and called on members of the white southern press to follow their example. "Southern newspapers edited for Southern people by Southern editors ought to be inspired and enrolled in this fight against the hypocrisy of the northern press," Parham wrote.[18] That same year, Thomas Waring Jr., segregationist editor of the *News and Courier* in Charleston, South Carolina, also joined the "paper curtain" crusade, editorializing that the "anti-southern slant" in the northern press constituted "a powerful blast of propaganda" and compared it to the impact on attitudes toward slavery of *Uncle Tom's Cabin*, the 1852 novel credited with shifting northern opinion toward entering the Civil War.[19]

Even as the "paper curtain" argument appealed primarily to white southern audiences, Hall, who has been described as "a master at teasing the national press," garnered a good deal of attention from AP executives and staff members, whom he exasperated.[20] In a 1956 memo to executive editor Gould, Lew Hawkins, the Atlanta bureau chief, wrote that Hall "is working hard selling the proposition that northern papers suppress or play down their racial troubles while playing up those in the South and that AP is going along in the same pattern."[21] Parham and other southern editors believed that thirty-two installments in "Tell It Not in Gath, Publish It Not in the Streets of Askelon," the *Montgomery Advertiser*'s series of case studies on northern racism and the perceived hypocrisy of the northern press, should have been picked up by the AP and moved on the national wire. Historian Douglas O. Cumming, who analyzed Hall's work during this period, concluded, "The installments were typically based on a single long-distance phone call, tendentious questions, and unsurprising answers."[22] Although many newspapers in the South reprinted the series, which emerged after the Till murder trial and continued during the Montgomery bus boycott in 1956, the AP declined to do so. In explaining the AP's decision to Parham, Hawkins noted that the AP had assigned its own enterprise reporting on race relations in the North.[23] In framing his argument for Parham as a counterargument for journalism standards, Hawkins also attempted to draw a distinction between reporting and opinion: "A good many of [Hall's] pieces have been almost purely editorial and consisted largely of his opinions about the ethics and professional morals of various northern papers. I assume some northern papers have been critical, from time to time, of the way some southern papers report the news. But I'm sure their editorial views haven't been carried as news by the AP. We just don't get messed up in such intramural name-calling except in very unusual situations."[24] In the lengthy exchange with Hawkins, Parham wrote, "I am quite candid in stating that the Montgomery Advertiser has been printing information we want and we believe our readers want and with teletypes clicking away in our wire room, we don't believe we should have to wait until yesterday's edition of the Advertiser arrives [by mail] to get that information."[25] Although the AP's top management avoided direct and public engagement with Hall, the executive and bureau staffs were not immune to the unrelenting criticism by Hall and his southern peers.

In February 1956, less than two years after the *Brown* decision rocked the South and just months after the end of the Till murder trial, Alan Gould issued a policy statement that rejected the colorblindness practiced by many northern newsrooms in reporting stories about Black Americans who were charged with crimes or engaged in antisocial behavior. Gould's memo to the entire AP staff, which also addressed the racial identification controversy discussed in chapter 2, responded to an editorial in the *Chattanooga News-Free Press* that complained of "a conspiracy of silence on the part of important parts of the nation's press to protect the Negro race from unfavorable publicity resulting from vicious crimes committed by Negroes." The Tennessee newspaper, edited by segregationist Roy McDonald, had singled out an AP story that did not label as Negroes two teens who assaulted a white teacher in Chicago. The editorial asserted that "it is a simple and inescapable fact that, supported by police records all over the country, that [sic] the lawless element of the Negro race is responsible for a highly disproportionate number of crimes of violence every year. It is true in Chicago. It is true wherever there are large Negro communities." Moreover, the editorial warned, "If [people] do not know about it, they cannot be adequately informed on one of the serious problems confronting our society."[26] The editorial further complained that the northern press and wire services had not hesitated to report crimes by southern whites against Black Americans, including the Till murder, and demanded comparable reporting of Black-on-white crime in the North. In a memo to AP staff, Gould acquiesced and called for a journalistic equivalence between stories about race that were generated in the North and those that were reported from the South, even conflating more routine crimes by Black northerners with racial terrorism by southern whites. "We must provide the facts from all sections and regardless of local practices and ideologies," he wrote.[27]

By capitulating to white southern criticism, Gould imposed segregationist news values on the Associated Press. In addition to his February 1956 policy in response to the Chattanooga editorial, Gould began requiring AP bureaus to do additional reporting to supply racial angles that were missing in news stories shared by newspapers in the North. Unwilling to accept that some white northern editors and journalists simply did not believe Black identity was the primary index of news value in routine stories, segregationist members concluded without clear evidence that northern newspapers were in league with civil rights organizations and intentionally obscured news about racial friction to advance the cause of integration and to avoid provoking tension and violence in their own communities. This, segregationists believed, violated journalistic principles, and Gould took their side.

In the mid-1950s newspaper markets in which member newsrooms routinely gave less emphasis to race included Detroit, Chicago, St. Louis, and New York.[28] In April 1956 Gould instructed chiefs of bureaus in those cities to compensate when local members submitted stories for transmission on the wire and omitted racial details. Gould acknowledged that his directive was prompted by heat from southern members. "Conversations with editors and publishers at recent meetings in Washington and New York convince me that this is an extremely important point in the eyes of many of our members," Gould wrote. "It has been the subject of editorials, speeches and news stories." Gould directed northern bureaus to cover racial angles fully, with the expectation that local stories about racial conflict in the North would move on the national wire for use by southern members, and that bureaus would be asked to supply the information anyway if a southern member found it missing and requested it. Northern newspapers that did not want to use wire stories about racial issues or preferred to deemphasize racial angles could exercise editorial judgment, he continued. But he clearly expected stories dispatched by the

AP to align with segregationist sensibilities, requiring more racially tolerant newsrooms to opt out of the policy whenever they edited wire stories. "I am not suggesting that every fist fight between members of different races is worth the A [national] wire," Gould wrote. "We need perspective and balance in coverage both North and South. But we need equality, too. A good test might be to ask yourselves: Would this be an AP story if it happened in Birmingham?"[29]

## "Intersectional Hullaballoo"

Managing the southern membership during the 1950s was particularly challenging for AP decision-makers because many of the editors who complained held intractable views on separation of the races and, after *Brown*, advocated a position that the U.S. Supreme Court had declared illegal. Moreover, their assessment of the AP's performance on racial coverage was often at odds with northern expectations for sound reporting. In 1955, when the second *Brown* ruling was still pending and the white press was feeling its way into the race story, editors North and South found fault with AP coverage, and Hawkins, the Atlanta bureau chief, moderated many of those early disputes. Southern members predictably objected when the stories about white-on-Black violence in the South received national distribution, as was the case with the 1955 murder in Belzoni, Mississippi, of civil rights leader and minister George W. Lee three months before the Emmett Till lynching. The mounting complaints from southern members about story-handling led AP staff to second-guess their judgment about the play given to news about race and to ignore newsworthy stories that reflected badly on the South. As a result, the AP was sometimes scooped by the Black and northern presses. The murder of Lee, who had been registering Black voters, was covered extensively by the Black press, including an open-casket photo in *Jet* magazine of the disfigurement caused by a shotgun blast to the face.[30] In this case, northern AP members complained that the story was slow to circulate outside the South. In a memo to other southern bureau chiefs, Hawkins offered guidance for identifying stories that should be funneled from the South to the national wire:

> It may not have been AAA [national] caliber from the start. But whenever a Negro crusader for civil rights dies under violent and/or

mysterious circumstances, it should be S.O.P. to get the story on the trunk.

Not every case will lead to an intersectional hullaballoo as this one did. But the chance always is there and when we don't give trunk handling northward—GGG [southern wire] is not AAA—on such news we invite the criticism that we're suppressing the news. . . .

It's just a matter of varying news judgment. But we must be somewhat more bullish in our appraisal of such items, taking into account that a great many papers and readers in the North are interested in that sort of news.

This emphatically does not mean we should sensationalize such copy or try to build up the inter-racial angles in any degree. But we should be sure the record is complete from the time the story breaks.[31]

Hawkins's position on racial news values before the Till murder was far more circumspect and accommodating to northern members than it would be in the months to come, when news about white-on-Black violence in the South became a national story.

The murders of Lee and Lamar Smith, who also had registered Black voters in Mississippi in 1955, would soon be overshadowed by the Till lynching and trial, which consumed the national press in the late summer and fall of that year.[32] The fourteen-year-old's corpse was found in late August; a month later, a jury acquitted the two men who had been charged with the gruesome crime. In the meantime, despite the posturing of some white southern AP members, the story took on national and even international importance. Journalists converged on Mississippi for the trial, where the abject terror experienced by Black Mississippians riveted newspaper, magazine, and radio audiences and affirmed the news value of the unfolding civil rights story. A few months later, Rosa Parks was arrested, launching the Montgomery bus boycott, and the white northern press would remain fixated on the South for the next decade. Although white southern editors were already defensive about northern disapproval, the national press's focus on the Till murder and trial galvanized their paranoia. "The next left wing Northern newspaper man who shows up in my office is likely to get kicked down the stairs, one step at a time," James Kilpatrick of the *Richmond News Leader* complained in March 1956. Kilpatrick alerted Thomas Waring at the Charleston *News and Observer* to be wary of Jim Bishop, "a sort of cotton-mouthed son of a bitch" who had reported an eight-part series called "Dynamite in Dixie" for Hearst's *New York Journal American* and its King Features Syndicate.[33]

AP coverage of the Till murder trial in Sumner, Mississippi, was coordinated in detail by the New York General Office and the New Orleans bureau chief, Ken Davis. "The situation is extremely explosive and some normally level-headed people are talking about the chances of violence if Till's mother comes down from Chicago for the trial," Davis wrote Gould. "For that reason this is one we'll have to ride through to the finish."[34] It was unlikely that any AP coverage could have earned southern approval because the story focused on white-on-Black crime and appealed to a national audience. For Bill Leverty, news editor at the *Richmond Times-Dispatch*, the AP's reporting was too thorough. "Another overwritten [Dr. Sam] Sheppard case," Leverty complained, referring to the sensational media coverage in the 1954 Ohio murder trial. "Let's go for more news and less 'hearts, flowers and tears,' is my pitiful suggestion."[35] Despite some logistical hiccups in reporting during the four days of testimony, Gould defended his staff's performance to John Colburn, Leverty's boss. "This was a highly competitive story, of widespread interest, and if we had not given it comprehensive and fast coverage we would not have come near satisfying our members," Gould wrote. "Even as it was, we had requests for more."[36]

Witness testimony raised questions about how long the decomposed corpse had been submerged before it was retrieved from the Tallahatchie River and whether the body was indeed that of Emmett Till. Jurors cited the issue of identification in rationalizing their acquittal, stoking white southern speculation that Till's disappearance was staged by civil rights activists who had thrown someone else's body in the river. If the corpse had been in the river more than a week, as the coroner alleged, it could not have been Till's because he was missing just three days. After the trial, the AP quoted Sheriff H. C. Strider, in a story datelined Greenwood, Mississippi, as speculating that Till was alive in Detroit, based on a rumor whose source he did not know. "I definitely believe he's somewhere, but I don't know where," Strider said.[37] By uncritically reproducing implausible official statements from the sheriff and trial witnesses, the AP circulated the white supremacist claim that the Till lynching was a hoax. James Wechsler, white editor of the liberal *New York Post*, was chagrined by the AP's post-trial coverage and sent Gould nearly a thousand words of criticism, beginning with a telegram: "When will the AP start giving us decent coverage on aftermath of Till case in Mississippi? Copy so far, when we get any, is outrageous."[38] In his initial response to the telegram, Gould said he did "not think the file shows we have failed to report any actual news, from Mississippi, or elsewhere. This includes stories from Chicago and Detroit, in addition to a number from Greenwood and Jackson."[39]

In a more detailed complaint sent by letter, Wechsler attacked the AP's accuracy and thoroughness in reporting on the Till aftermath and civil rights generally. "The truth is that the A.P. covers Mississippi as if it were an Iron-Curtain country operating under strict censorship," Wechsler wrote, analyzing AP news copy he had seen that morning:

> It is a story from Charleston, Miss. which begins: "Circuit Clerk Charlie Cox answered NAACP claims that none of Tallahatchie County's 19,000 Negroes 'was allowed to vote' by saying that 'only four or five' applied and they were unqualified." Does the A.P. believe it fulfills its obligation to clients outside of Mississippi by carrying this quote? This is a clear issue of fact. Is the A.P. incapable of making an independent survey to determine how many Negroes actually applied and were found unqualified? Has it ever attempted to find out what kind of standards are applied to Negro applicants as opposed to whites?

Shifting attention to the AP's circulation of the Till hoax claim, Wechsler excoriated Gould for the news service's reporting of rumor and failure to do basic verification or enterprise reporting:

> The attached dispatch from Greenwood, Miss. . . . is the kind of story one might expect to get smuggled out of Czechoslovakia. Who was spreading the rumors that Till was still alive? Did they emanate from a local saloon? What was supposed to be the basis of the rumors? Sheriff Strider is quoted as saying, "I definitely believe he is somewhere, but I don't know where." Has Strider been looking for him? Has Strider been trying to find out the identity of the murdered body which he claims was not that of Emmett Till? Has the A.P.'s Mississippi organization made any effort to establish whether there's the slightest validity in the claim that this was not Emmett Till? How often are Negroes bumped off without subsequent identification or any semblance of police effort to find out who did it?

Wechsler also noted that, until civil rights leader A. Philip Randolph complained, the wire service did not report that two missing witnesses later were found out of state. "There is no evidence that the A.P. in Mississippi was even curious about the missing witnesses—who had been referred to often during and after the trial—until the story broke out of New York,"

Wechsler wrote. "Do key witnesses just vanish in Mississippi without any attempt by local A.P. men to find out what happened to them?"[40]

The *New York Post* was aggressively covering the civil rights movement, not just major events such as the Till trial. One of its white columnists, Murray Kempton, attended the Till trial, and much of the paper's high-profile reporting from the North was assigned to Ted Poston, who had been on the *Post*'s staff since 1936 and was one of the few Black journalists working at a metropolitan daily.[41] Because of the reciprocal agreement that required AP members to share their content with the wire service, the AP had access to Poston's enterprise reporting on racial issues, including a story published that day from an interview that he had obtained with Mose Wright, Till's uncle and a key prosecution witness who had fled to Chicago after the trial.[42] "As the story shows, he asserts that on the night of the acquittal three carloads of white men came after him," Wechsler wrote. ". . . Did the A.P. ever try to get the story of Mose Wright's departure from Mississippi? It becomes embarrassing as well as painful when we have to cover Mose Wright from New York while the A.P. misses it in both Mississippi and Chicago." Reminding Gould of the AP's access to the *Post*'s content, Wechsler was astonished that Poston's story had not been sent out on the wire. "I am sure that a fair number of A.P. clients would have been interested in this interview, even though it might have been spiked on a lot of Southern desks," Wechsler wrote. ". . . If the Chicago Sun-Times or the [St. Louis] Post-Dispatch had obtained this interview, I would certainly have expected the A.P. wire to give me a piece of it."[43]

Wechsler acknowledged the North-South divide within the news service and that such reporting would be unpopular with members below the Mason-Dixon Line. "Perhaps the A.P. will have to set up separate North and South wires to avoid offending some of the characters who run the Mississippi press," he wrote, noting that he could not afford to keep Kempton in the South and relied on the AP for most of the *Post*'s coverage from that region. Wechsler emphasized the gravity of the civil rights story and the humanity at stake. "I suspect that the most serious failure goes far beyond these examples. What is really happening in Mississippi in the aftermath of the trial? Is there increased terror against Negroes? What goes on in the Negro community? Do A.P. men ever visit those communities?" he asked. ". . . I am especially concerned about the problem because of indications that the situation may get worse before it gets better in Mississippi, and stories like that Greenwood dispatch destroy any confidence I have in the A.P.'s Mississippi operation."[44]

In his response to Wechsler, Gould stated that "steps have been taken which should result in more alert and consistent coverage of the legitimate news developments in this continuing story," and revealed that the wire service was tracking coverage in at least one Black newspaper, the *Chicago Defender*, which was not an AP member, for developments following the Till trial. "We are sure you do appreciate The Associated Press, unlike a newspaper, must avoid crusading for anything or anybody, no matter how worthy the cause or purpose," Gould wrote. "It is quite possible that we sometimes miss newsworthy developments by an over-eagerness to be fair and impartial, or by failing fully to size up the significance of them." He conceded that the AP should have transmitted the *Post*'s Mose Wright story the day of publication. "This was news and our failure to pick it up until the next day, in connection with the Chicago Defender's story on the two men sought for questioning as possible witnesses in the Till slaying, did not reflect good judgment." AP protocol called for quoting sources on opposing sides of a story and not making judgments about the truth or fiction of newsworthy claims; even with improbable statements, fairness was preserved by giving a news subject a chance to respond. Gould defended the handling of the voter registration story, which relied on an official source. He also noted uncritically that the Mississippi elections clerk had explained that "most Negroes 'don't even pay their poll tax.'" As for Wechsler's complaint about the AP reporting the sheriff's statements and the rumor that Till was alive, Gould argued that the hoax angle emerged during court proceedings and the story included a rebuttal by Till's mother.[45]

In deflecting Wechsler's criticisms, Gould suggested that the displeasure of members on both sides of the civil rights issue was an index of the AP's objectivity: "We have been under critical fire from both sections [regions], which is generally an indication that the coverage has been in reasonable balance." This old journalism chestnut about accuracy, also invoked by Harry Ashmore in chapter 3, is a logical fallacy that assumes truth is relative. Gould then cited objectivity and journalism standards as the reasons the AP would not engage in the kind of enterprise reporting Wechsler requested:

I cannot agree with your "iron curtain" premise, because I do not think it has application to our operations, north or south. This is the kind of story that has great emotional impact with feeling very high on both sides. It underscores clearly the fact we simply cannot crusade or go in for a lot of investigative reporting on our own, amounting to the same thing. This does not alter one bit my agreement with you that forthright, alert reporting of all actual news developments is called for and I agree with you that in some cases we have not done that.[46]

The correspondence between Wechsler and Gould circulated to pertinent staff in New York and elsewhere, with Gould's position articulating and emphasizing policy for the AP workforce. "James Wechsler's letter makes me feel like a sandwich, pressed equally by my southern constituents and my fellow northerners," responded Ken Davis, the New Orleans bureau chief.[47]

In his next letter, Wechsler directly engaged Gould's argument about journalism standards. "I think the heart of our difference is in your suggestion that there is a fatal conflict between objectivity and enterprise on a story like the Till case," he wrote. "I am not asking the A.P. to crusade; I suggested only that where there are issues of fact the A.P. has a responsibility to try to get the facts rather than simply accept communiques from the rival camps." Wechsler conceded that the issue was complex but added, "I honestly don't believe that the fact that you've been under criticism from both factions necessarily proves anything." He acknowledged that AP had been doing a bit more enterprise reporting since he first wrote, soon after the Till acquittals. Among stories the AP pursued in October 1955 was its own interview with Mose Wright.[48] That month, however, the AP offered an example of reporting based on a "communique" from segregationists when the wire service relayed the discovery that Emmett Till's father, who had served in the U.S. military during World War II, had been executed in 1945 in Italy after a court martial for rape and murder.[49]

Although the criminal charges against Till's father had no bearing on the guilt or innocence of Till's own murderers, the white Mississippi press seized on the story, which contradicted assumptions by the northern press, including *Life* magazine, that Till's father had been a hero who died "fighting for the American proposition that all men are created equal."[50] The *Jackson Daily News*, a white supremacist newspaper in Mississippi, published the information as a scoop in "a copyrighted story" on

October 14, 1955, and under the AP's reciprocal agreement, funneled it to the news service for distribution to other members.[51] As with all copy it transmitted, the AP made decisions about which wires would carry the story and then newsrooms could choose whether to publish it and how to edit it. When the AP story did not make a splash in the North, the Citizens' Councils of Mississippi issued a press release demanding answers about coverage and insinuating that the father's record was relevant to the provocative conduct attributed to his son:

> Mamie Bradley has admitted that this was her husband and the father of Emmett Till who was allegedly murdered in Mississippi for "wolf-whistling." . . .
>
> To our knowledge, not one single Northern newspaper carried this interesting development in the world famous Till case. Was the story killed in branch offices of the Associated Press or where? Who killed it? Why? Why should this vital fact, which can be verified by the War Department, be denied to the people, when the Northern press itself has made such a story out of the other side of the Till case.[52]

At least two southern AP members forwarded the Citizens' Council's press release to the wire service and demanded documentation of how and when the AP disseminated the story.[53] "The AP accounts of the Jackson Daily News story saying Emmett Till's father was executed for murder and rape were relayed in full to major Northern newspapers and bureaus—both the original 400-word story the night of Oct. 14 and the 300-word rewrite for PMS [the p.m. news cycle] of Oct 15," Gould responded to Waring, the segregationist editor in Charleston.[54] To answer another complaint, Davis, the New Orleans bureau chief, spent several days soliciting from Gould and the bureaus in Atlanta and Kansas City the precise dates and times they forwarded the story and to which wire.[55] A memo from the bureau chief in Kansas City, which was a hub for AP news to and from the West, provided times and reference codes to document that the AP bureaus did not kill or minimize the story: "The first story was received here Oct. 14 as B77 at 945ped [9:45 p.m. Eastern Daylight Time] and relayed west at 940pcs [9:40 p.m. Central Standard Time] as B84. The early story on October 15 was received here on the hookup direct from Atlanta (542AES) [5:42 a.m. Eastern Standard Time] and was relayed west as B58 at 609acs [6:09 a.m. Central Standard Time]."[56] Waring also asked for an accounting of how many northern papers had published the story, which Gould said he could not provide because the staff member who tracked story usage for the *AP Log*, an internal newsletter, looked only at newspapers' front pages.[57] The southern effort to monitor story usage by northern members would intensify in coming months and years.

Despite the misgivings about investigative reporting on southern racism that he articulated to Wechsler, Gould had no compunction about assigning enterprise stories to satisfy complaints of southern members. In the spring of 1956, when Hall at the *Montgomery Advertiser* and his allies complained about northern racial hypocrisy and lobbied the AP to run the "Askelon" series, Gould assigned AP Newsfeatures writer Bem Price to do in-depth reporting on racial discrimination in the North. Price's story, datelined Detroit, explored racial conditions in that city and Chicago, Baltimore, Los Angeles, and New York, focusing on housing, crime, schools, jobs, and Black access to accommodations and businesses. The story, which quoted both Black and white sources, asserted that "the problem of race relations is not confined to the South" but also surmised, "Despite all the troubles in the North with discrimination, there is no real comparison with segregation in the South, where the races are separated by law. The North is making steady moves toward equality."[58] In a Newsfeature, a long-form story that the AP moved for use generally on weekends, the reporter had more latitude and Price was even allowed to include first-person observation. Price incorporated multiple perspectives and the story appeared balanced while acknowledging that racial discrimination was a problem in the North.

Even so, AP personnel up and down the organization carefully anticipated negative southern reaction to this story. Two weeks before it was scheduled for release for use in Sunday morning papers, Hawkins, the Atlanta bureau chief, shared a concern with Davis in New Orleans about a reference to the Till murder in the next-to-last paragraph of the then-current version:

> If you haven't already done so, will you please read the penult paragraph of A157 in last Saturday night's report—it's the Bem Price blockbuster on discrimination in the North, for use in Sunday AMS [the a.m. news cycle] of May 13.
> You'll note it has AP saying Emmett Till was slain and that a murder was committed. As I recall it, the key maneuver of the defense was its effort to cast serious doubt on the identification of a body taken from a river. In effect, it contended the state never established that Till was slain and hence never proved a murder was committed.

> Since you are more familiar than I with this case, I'll leave it to you to mail a suggested sub paragraph to New York—if you think it worthwhile for the sake of avoiding later arguments. If you don't think it's necessary, that's okay by me, too.[59]

The archive does not include Davis's response or commentary from other AP personnel on Hawkins's concern; however, the story distributed to members did not contain the statement that Hawkins had seen in a previous penultimate paragraph. As expected with any story that moved on the wire, a sampling of newspapers shows that some members trimmed or condensed the story while others ran more or even all of it. The story distributed to members contained one reference to the Till case in a policeman's quoted reference: "After the Till murder case down in Mississippi, we must have investigated 40 beatings of whites by Negroes. They just wanted to take it out on somebody." This quote would have pleased segregationist editors who hoped to portray northern Black residents as antisocial and violent. The *Memphis [TN] Commercial Appeal*, a racially conservative paper that printed a long version of Price's story, let the reference stand without additional editing, while the *Birmingham [AL] News* inserted the following parenthetical qualifier following the policeman's mention of the Till case: "(Two white men were acquitted of a charge of murdering Emmett Till, the 14-year-old Negro boy, in Mississippi last Summer after he allegedly made an impertinent remark to a white woman. The defense contended that the body of a youth found in the river was not Till's.)"[60]

Despite its depth and candor regarding northern racial bias, Price's story did not satisfy Hall, who merely accelerated his agitation regarding northern hypocrisy and criticism of the northern press's journalism standards. A few weeks after Price's story ran, Rex Thomas, the AP's reporter in Montgomery, told Gould that Hall was "still sniping at us from time to time as part of his continuing campaign to show that Yankee newspapers suppress racial news. One of his more recent criticisms concerned Bem Price's piece on race relations in the North. He said it wasn't adequate; that the Advertiser had done more by telephone than the AP was able to do; that Price more or less apologized for the North."[61]

## Case Studies of "Riot" Complaints

During the 1950s Gould and other AP decision-makers became worn down by complaints, not only over AP handling of major news stories like the headline-grabbing Till trial or public confrontations over desegregation of public schools but also, and more routinely, by challenges to the AP's news judgment on stories about Black arrests and participation in disturbances. As white southern editors sifted through wire reports for evidence of bias in coverage of race in the North versus the South, they seized on incidents of racial conflict that implied Black Americans were incapable of functioning responsibly in society without segregation to hold their antisocial excesses in check. As the 1915 blockbuster film *Birth of a Nation* imagined, emancipated Black people, no longer restrained by the supposedly benign institution of slavery, would be prone to mayhem and violence.[62] The trope of the antisocial freedman retained its power when *Brown* effectively outlawed the social segregation of Jim Crow. White supremacists in the southern press insisted on receiving wire coverage of unruly and criminal Black behavior in the North and recirculated the stereotype as justification for their opposition to integration. For white southern editors who were leveraging journalism standards in this fight, it was easy to condemn stories that did not endorse the racial status quo, labeling them as inaccurate and unobjective.

As the primary U.S. conduit for racial news, the AP was clearly implicated in this ideological dispute. The following discussion samples five stories in 1956 and 1957 that drew criticism from white southern editors who perceived inadequate or biased AP coverage of racial disturbances in the North. The common threads in these complaints were a suspicion that Black Americans in the North, unconstrained by the de jure segregation that kept order in the South, were "rioting" or resorting to violence, demonstrating their unsuitability for inclusion in an integrated American society, and that the AP and northern members were suppressing this information or failing to give it appropriate play, out of bias and habit. In their complaints to the AP about missing or underplayed racial angles in reporting about Black crime, segregationist editors invoked journalism standards and accused the wire service of slanting the news to support civil rights.

## CHAPTER 4

### The Asbury Park "Riot"

In the summer of 1956 John Harper, white editor of the *Augusta Chronicle* in Georgia, accused the AP of ignoring a "race riot" in Asbury Park, New Jersey, that reportedly injured twenty-eight people and led to twenty-five arrests. In a letter to Hawkins, the Atlanta bureau chief, Harper wrote, "It impresses me, and several other Southern editors with whom I have talked, that AP is not playing the race question from two sides." Harper noted that the news from Asbury Park was a day old before southern members received a story. Then, in response to southern complaints about a racial angle they believed had gone unreported, AP staff had rewritten the top of the story to emphasize a racial element, even though a police source had said the brawl was not a racial incident. Harper was unsatisfied: "Only upon prodding of Southern members does it then get a second lead containing any reference to 'conflict,' 'whites,' 'Negroes' and 'riot.' I cannot see why the words are in good usage when applicable to the South, but opprobrious when applicable to an incident in the North."[63]

In his response, Hawkins noted that the Asbury Park police chief had said the incident was a fight, not a race riot.[64] Hawkins, who argued that regional context was important to racial news values, took a more nuanced approach than Gould had in his policy statement five months earlier, in response to the editorial in the Chattanooga newspaper. "The story of segregation in the South and discrimination in the North are different stories. Of course, both should be covered," Hawkins wrote. "But 'segregation' is state and local government policy, supported by law, and it is in opposition to federal law. . . . There is not nearly the deep, basic significance in 'discrimination' that there is in 'segregation.'"[65] This was a point Bem Price had made in his Newsfeature a few months earlier. Although Hawkins and some other AP staff were aware that white southern editors insisted on a false equivalence in their call for parallel coverage of racial issues in the North, theirs was an unpopular view, and one that became increasingly marginalized by incessant southern complaints and the AP executive leadership's acquiescence to southern demands.

### The Buffalo Cruise "Riot"

That same summer, AP executives fielded many complaints about coverage of interracial friction at a Canadian amusement park and on a party boat that ferried American teenagers back to Buffalo, New York. Nine

Buffalo teens—five Black and four white—were arrested in Ontario, and two white journalists, who happened to be passengers on the boat, provided eyewitness accounts. In its initial lede on May 30, datelined Buffalo, the AP reported, "Rioting by Negro teen-agers on a vessel plying between here and Crystal Lake Amusement Park, Ont., tonight turned the vessel into 'a nightmare of flashing knives and sobbing, frightened passengers.'" When the word "Negro" was deemphasized in updated versions, segregationist members complained of a coverup. In his review of AP's coverage, Paul Mickelson, the general news editor, wrote that "the New York General Desk promptly and properly called for a sub intro" that eliminated the word "Negro" from the lede: "The sub-intro was ordered through no prompting. It was ordered to give attribution to the statement, that negroes caused the trouble, to the two reporters, who saw it, and not to The Associated Press."[66] The controversy over the AP's handling of the story, which drew criticism from members in the North for playing up the racial angle, also was reported in *Editor and Publisher*.[67] Predictably, many white southern members approved of the emphasis on Black participation in the violent incident, which resulted in fines for three white and two Black teens, and of the AP's decision to move the story on the national wire. Notably, no one was hospitalized but southerners deemed the story of national significance.

After the AP scrambled to placate southern members, their criticism shifted from the AP's reporting to whether liberal northern newspapers used the story at all, and if so, how they played it. To find out, they queried the AP, whose bureaus had immediate access to local newsrooms, by sending messages on the wire. The *New York Daily News* and *New York Herald Tribune* then drew fire from southern newsrooms for not using the Buffalo story in their morning papers the day after the incident. Because coverage was first transmitted on the wire around midnight, some morning papers did not revise their news budgets but held the story to use a full day later. Alarmed that staff in the AP's New York bureau had provided the information about New York papers' use of the story, an editor of the *Herald Tribune* challenged the AP's participation in southern monitoring of northern news judgment.[68] Ultimately, Frank Starzel, the AP's general manager, determined that the information about members' use of AP content should not be transmitted on the wire in the future but that the AP was "bound to respond to such queries and members could easily get info elsewhere."⁶⁹ That he did not ask white southerners to use those other sources for that information, given concerns from northern members about AP complicity in the ideological surveillance of northern newsrooms, affirms the deference given to southern newspapers.

### *The Boston Dancehall "Riot"*

As school desegregation conflicts heated up in 1957, drawing unflattering national coverage of the South, white southern editors intensified their scrutiny of AP reporting on northern racial incidents. In October, a month after the historic confrontation at Central High School in Little Rock, southern members alleged that the AP had minimized its coverage of a race riot in Boston. Walter Grant, publisher of the *Danville Register* in Virginia, was among those who wrote to executives in New York or staff in bureaus. Grant lambasted the AP for moving a 170-word story on what he believed to be a mixed-race confrontation involving more than a thousand people and resulting in about two dozen arrests:

> The message was not listed on the [news] budget, was not identified as bulletin material but was handled as an ordinary minor news event.
> In accordance with the Associated Press's avowed policy of factual and unbiased reporting it is hard to reconcile your coverage of this "incident" with the coverage given happenings of lesser importance in the south. On many occasions incidents in the south which involved far fewer people than the one which happened last night in Boston required several thousand Associated Press words to cover.⁷⁰

Ironically, the story turned out to be inaccurate; the AP, mindful of segregationist demands for negative racial news from the North, had proactively moved the story on the national wire before it was fully reported and verified. The short item initially transmitted did indeed attract interest from members in the South, including a query from a Birmingham member to the Washington bureau, insisting that the AP seek comment from President Dwight D. Eisenhower. His opinion was deemed relevant because of his recent use of the military to enforce the *Brown* decision at Central High School in Little Rock.⁷¹

In a report to Starzel, Mickelson, the general news editor, noted that the police source described the incident as a brawl in a dance hall, not a riot; denied a crowd estimate of up to a thousand people; and said that whites were not attacked during the incident because few white people other than policemen were in attendance.[72] Starzel's subsequent reply to Grant is important for its assessment of the AP's overperformance in response to southern scrutiny of racial news in the North versus the South. "We were not satisfied with the Boston bureau's performance on this story but for reasons substantially different from those expressed in your letter. Rather than having minimized the scope and nature of the brawl, it is clear now that the original dispatch was overdrawn," Starzel wrote. He also took the position that fights in dancehalls did not merit extensive coverage without a more significant angle: "As a management problem, I am frankly much more concerned about the current tendency of the news reporting profession to overwrite such incidents, particularly when they occur in the north. This tendency has developed recently because of the sensitivity, at least in some quarters, over criticism by southern editors. I will be the first to grant that some of this criticism may have been justified in the past but my associates and I will exert our best efforts to insure that The Associated Press is not guilty of going to the other extreme."[73]

Although Starzel, AP's top executive, realized in 1957 that the wire service had overcompensated, changing direction would have been difficult since the personnel in AP bureaus across the North had been ordered to highlight racial news from the North and prioritize it on the national wire. Moreover, many white southern members did not concede any increase in balance and remained unrelenting in their criticism of AP coverage. In an editorial weeks after the initial inaccurate reporting on the Boston "riot," the segregationist *Chattanooga News-Free Press* excoriated the AP, drawing a strained journalistic equivalence between the dancehall melee and coverage of Central High School. "This was especially pitifully poor coverage in contrast with that of scores of reporters and photographers who had been providing thousands of words and hundreds of pictures during the Little Rock difficulties—where there was never a mob of 1,000 and where on no occasion were so many arrests made," the editorial stated, ignoring the presence of a thousand U.S. troops dispatched by Eisenhower. It continued, "It is not encouraging, or fair, however, at a time when the South is being victimized for cynical political purposes to see the South regularly pilloried in the press in the North—which seems to have even more and worse racial troubles—perfumed by censorship."[74]

## The Chicago Sunday Picnic "Riot"

Racial friction in the summer of 1957 in Chicago, a presumably liberal destination for Black emigration from the South, exacerbated scrutiny of the AP by white supremacist members. Fomented in part by Hall's editorials in the *Montgomery Advertiser*, southern papers criticized the AP and the *Chicago Tribune*, wrongly it turned out, for their reporting of a South Side disturbance during a Sunday picnic in late July at which forty-four people were injured and two automobiles burned.[75] As with all interracial conflicts, white southern editors were quick to term the interracial disturbance a "riot" and to assume that racial angles had not been reported thoroughly. In an editorial on August 15, Hall wrote that "the Associated Press has fallen on its face" in its coverage of racial friction in Chicago and instead played up the "pipsqueak story" of a Black boycott of white businesses in Tuskegee after the state of Alabama gerrymandered the town's Black majority out of its vote.[76] Hall's complaint was weakly sourced in an editorial that acknowledged he did not have all the facts and was forced to speculate because the AP had not given him the facts. By this point in the wrangling with southern members, AP staff were eager to counter the accusation that they had ignored or downplayed a story. Led by Rex Thomas, the AP reporter based in Montgomery who was the AP's primary liaison with Hall, the news service mobilized to counter the barrage. This episode demonstrated that the AP deferred even to member critiques that were not entirely accurate or well-reasoned and was willing to tailor wire service content to match those members' expectations. Ultimately, Hall would praise the wire service for its efforts to represent the white southern perspective.

The AP had in fact dispatched news copy about the Chicago situation, which the *Advertiser* staff ignored, Thomas reported to AP colleagues. "We have asked Hall time and again to check with us on matters like this—and a few times we've succeeded in stopping similar outbursts by showing him where the AP had moved stories his own paper threw away—but he seems obsessed with the idea of proving that northern papers hide their own racial problems and point instead to the south's," he wrote.[77] Two days after Thomas's personal ministrations, Hall published a follow-up editorial that doubled down on his criticism of the AP but also threw a bone to Thomas, who assured Gould in New York that he had "tried to reason with him that it wasn't fair to single out the AP instead of the wire services generally if he felt criticism was justified."[78] This opened up an interesting line of discussion within the AP: of course, wire service staff wanted members to believe their news product was superior to the "opposition's" but any measure of white southern approval was overtly ideological.

In the second piece, Hall acknowledged that he had repeatedly "given a hotfoot to the Associated Press for its news handling, usually because it dingdongs Southern racial strife and does not systematically or completely cover northern racial strife. But in making the AP the target, we assuredly did not mean that the United Press and the International News Service, or any of the other news services, cover northern race strife one whit better." He then paid the AP staff, whom he believed supported *Brown*, a backhanded compliment for improving coverage of race in the North. Despite its presumed bias against the South, "the AP no doubt puts out more news of yankees reacting like Southerners than the other services because it has a far stronger news network than the other services," Hall wrote. ". . . The AP is more faithfully relating the news of the Southern Way of Life in de Nawth than it was in 1956 and before. Its blurred vision is righting and its delusions unworking themselves." He cited examples of AP reporting that comported with white southern interests: "Its dispatches from the northern provinces are still attitudinalized; still somewhat the catspaw of stereotyped ideas begat in sin by Harriet Beecher Stowe. But the AP is gaining consciousness. It does not cover the northern scene like it and the dew cover Dixie, but it is more wary about taking the word of a police chief that a Buffalo race riot was just a 'hoodlum' workout without any relation to race, creed or color. All the major riots are now covered and even many of the bloodless disturbances." The AP is "vastly superior to the northern newspapers," he wrote, and postulated that the shortcomings of the northern press were an impediment for the wire service, which had to compensate when it picked up content from northern members who underreported the story of racial discrimination and strife in their communities. "The naive notion that there is something different in the ethics and morality of the northerner and Southerner will gradually dissolve as the Negro migration progresses," he concluded.[79]

The executive staff in New York was copied on most of Thomas's correspondence about Hall and monitored the situation closely, even though Hall and some of his southern peers were not credible critics. In response to intensifying complaints from southern members that summer, Mickelson, the AP's general news editor, had already assigned Chicago reporter Bernard Gavzer to do an overview story on the Chicago situation and to send his draft to New York for approval when it was done.[80] The article reported that "fast, firm police action has checked major racial violence in Chicago," though "fresh outbreaks" were still possible. In summarizing the summer's events, Gavzer wrote, "Disturbances range from sharp, brief fights involving a handful of persons to occasional demonstrations in which hundreds catcall and hurl brickbats."[81] In an editorial atoning in part for his erroneous claim that the AP had not covered the Chicago situation that summer, Hall praised Gavzer's reporting on "an appalling story of jungle life" but hoped for greater balance in coverage. "Generally, the national press has covered racial strife in Chicago when there was an outbreak of violence, whereas the South has been covered systematically and in rag-picking fashion. This is, of course, irksome to a Southerner," he wrote. "But the essential point we have striven to make is that this disproportion of coverage prevents the country from seeing the race problem as it really is."[82]

### The Philadelphia Children's "Riot"

In November 1957 AP executives in New York began investigating reports that Thomas Waring, editor of the Charleston *News and Courier*, was criticizing the AP's coverage of race in pro-segregation speeches on college campuses. A review of correspondence in the AP Corporate Archives suggests that Waring was likely the most frequent and strident single source of criticism about perceived anti-southern bias in AP coverage, and that he also incited other editors to complain.[83] As a result, Gould and his AP colleagues spent a good deal of time during the 1950s defending the wire service specifically against Waring's attacks and those instigated by him. After Waring published a candidly white supremacist article in *Harper's* defending segregation in 1956, he received speaking invitations from colleges and universities to offer the anti-integration perspective of the white South.[84] The speaking engagements also offered Waring fresh audiences for his complaints about the northern press and the AP.

In talks at Emory and Brandeis Universities, for which Waring had given the AP advance transcripts to encourage coverage of the speeches, Waring asserted that the wire service had not carried a story, published in the *Philadelphia Inquirer* that September, that "a thousand white and colored children rioted in a street in South Philadelphia. Can you imagine the display that would be given such a riot in Columbus, Miss., Macon, Ga., or Charleston, S.C.?" he asked his audiences.[85] AP staff investigated Waring's claim and found that the Philadelphia disturbance had ended by the time news photographers arrived at the scene. It began when children, who had just been let out of school, became concerned to see police cars at a nearby drugstore responding to a medical emergency and "stampeded." In a memo to Gould, Mickelson, the general news editor, reported that the *Inquirer* had misreported and overplayed the story. A publisher from Texas who was visiting Philadelphia in September had seen an article in the *Inquirer* and requested that it be moved on the wire for use in the South and West; however, the AP's story, which aligned with one published by the rival *Philadelphia Bulletin*, was brief and differed on significant details from the *Inquirer*'s. "It was a case of false alarm in a rather tense area of Philadelphia, and our story reported it that way. So did the Bulletin," Mickelson wrote.[86]

In his own letter to Waring the same day, Gould denied that news of a racial disturbance was being downplayed, asserted that the AP's "was a more accurate account," and provided a copy of the story that was moved South.[87] Unwilling to accept that representation on faith, Waring's staff tried to verify Gould's claim that a story had been transmitted on the southern wire but could not find one in the Charleston newspaper's meticulously maintained news service archive. Waring continued to press the issue and learned a few days later that the AP had indeed sent the story south but that it had not been relayed onto the South Carolina state wire by the bureau in Charlotte, North Carolina, because, the bureau chief said, of "the lateness of the hour the story was available and its obvious minor nature."[88] Waring's persistence had been rewarded as he caught the AP in a lapse in fulfilling segregationist demands, and he strongly objected to the bureau chief's characterization of the story's significance. "I hope the same news judgment will prevail in the handling by The Associated Press of racial discord, should it happen in the South," he wrote. "It is the opinion of several newspaper men whose judgment I respect that Southern race discord is given greater press play than Northern incidents."[89]

## Reigniting the Civil War

Later that month, November 1957, the southern charge of northern bias in news coverage of racial matters and its assumed impact on AP content erupted at the Associated Press Managing Editors national convention. Although AP staff had been fielding criticism from southern members for years, and Gould had acknowledged prickly discussions at smaller regional gatherings, this was the first time the debate was documented in the published minutes of the APME's annual meeting: "Someone said, 'We shouldn't try to re-fight the Civil War this morning.' And then the shooting started." The AP's recent coverage of the Central High School desegregation confrontation in Little Rock, which generally won praise from the membership, opened the door to the discussion.[90]

Sam Ragan of the *News and Observer* in Raleigh, North Carolina, had gathered comments from members for a Domestic News Committee report. "Many Southern editors . . . have been critical of the AP for not adequately reporting racial disturbances in the North," Ragan said, and then accused northern papers of lax journalism standards. "Some of the AP's difficulties in giving adequate coverage to the segregation-integration problem in the North can be traced directly to newspapers there. I understand that in many Northern cities there is an agreement among local news media to soft pedal news of racial disturbances—the theory being that the less written or said about it, the less chance of a serious outbreak."[91] The charge had gained traction in 1956 when Hall editorialized that a reporter visiting Montgomery from Detroit told him that "yankee papers think race news is news only if it occurs under a magnolia tree. . . . With disarming frankness, this reporter confirmed that race conflict in Detroit is a grievous problem and that the three Detroit dailies and the radio had 'some kind of agreement' to muffle race conflict in news in order not to add fuel to the flame." In the same editorial supposedly revealing a "covenant of silence" among Detroit media, Frank Angelo, managing editor of the *Detroit Free Press*, was quoted denying that any such agreement governed news judgment at his paper, though the editorial implied that his denial was not credible.[92]

During the 1957 meeting, when Ragan proffered the conspiracy theory again, APME members from Chicago, Detroit, and Minneapolis strongly denied that they intentionally skewed the news to hide information about racial conflict. Angelo was among them. "If there is anybody in this room who knows of such an agreement, I would like to have him step up and prove it," he said.[93] Mickelson, the AP's general news editor, read a letter from a bureau chief who had worked on both sides of the Mason-Dixon Line and been criticized by members from both regions for lapses in journalism standards: "If the newspapers in both sections would concentrate more on objectivity instead of making us—the AP—prove that the Negro is treated worse in a distant section than he is in their own backyards, all of us would be better off."[94]

## Conclusion

During the post-*Brown* years, with forced integration looming, many white southern editors assertively defended the honor of the South, hoping to persuade local and national audiences that segregation ensured social order and was a necessary institution that should be preserved. The Associated Press, as a wire service that bound southern and northern newspapers together in a common journalistic mission, framed the story of the civil rights movement and presented an easy target for southern anger and suspicion. The AP had a complex relationship with its ideologically diverse white membership, but the archive supports several conclusions.

First, although racism was indeed pervasive in the North, in the mid-1950s many white northern newsrooms were more racially liberal and were pursuing more race-neutral reporting that did not prioritize reporting on crime and discord involving Black Americans in their own communities. Without white southern intervention, the content of the AP wire reflected this perspective because much of the news on the wire was cultivated from northern members' daily news reports. Second, northern white audiences were fascinated by southern resistance to desegregation, and northern newspapers demanded thorough coverage of the unfolding civil rights story in the South. The southern members were not wrong on these points, nor were they mistaken about a third, namely that institutionalized racism in the North, which perpetuated housing segregation and other inequity, was going largely unreported there. If the southern faction of the AP membership performed any service for the common good, it was to highlight the need for reporting on racial injustice in the North. That was an incidental outcome, not an altruistic objective, however. Segregationist editors, who were engaged in an existential defense of the southern way of life, wanted the northern press to divert its focus from the former Confederacy. They expected AP wire content about inequity in the North to serve southern ends by portraying Black Americans as criminals and unruly deviants unfit for integrated society. Democracy, in their view, would be best served if Jim Crow endured.

The record also shows that AP executives in New York, who were shaping policy and practice for the wire service, bent their news judgment in response to advocacy by white southern editors during the 1950s. Confronted with unceasing complaints from segregationist editors who invoked journalism standards and accused the AP of bias against the South, AP decision-makers issued policies and made judgment calls on a case-by-case basis that embedded the southern white supremacist perspective into the formula for news judgment. Importantly, these decisions, at the behest of a strident and activist minority of the AP membership, altered wire content for all AP members across the country who had to edit the national wire to remove a pro-southern racial bias, or when time constraints prevented them from doing so, let national stories go into their papers as received. In addition, it would have been difficult for editors in northern newsrooms, even with ample time to read the wire closely, to recognize southern bias in every story. For example, the stereotype that unsegregated Black Americans were antisocial sometimes was inserted into the AP wire report, even after police sources denied that "riots" had occurred or that public disturbances had racial significance. Northern editors would not have known that southern editors had lobbied to have these stories written a certain way or elevated to the national wire.

The AP's capitulation to the southern membership required a perversion of enduring journalism standards, but the most astonishing was the implication that journalistic objectivity required a quantitative balance between news from the South about white racism and news from the North about Black crime and deviance. When Gould asked, "Would this be an AP story if it happened in Birmingham?" he removed context from news judgment. Lost in the conversation among AP executives and white southern editors was the concept that news values, under the rubric of objectivity, could not be determined by an ideological scorecard. Bewildering, for example, was the white southern insistence and AP agreement that saturation coverage of the Till trial or Little Rock confrontation meant that every racial incident in the North represented a national story about a threat to the white community. More perplexing was Gould's move in 1956 to incorporate the editorial position of a stridently white supremacist newspaper into an AP policy statement on coverage of race. Even in the midst of the rapidly developing civil rights story and unrelenting southern activism on the issue, which diverted organizational resources from the wire service's daily journalism, the implications of AP decision-making were striking.

In 1957, responding to a member complaint about the AP's coverage of the Boston dancehall "riot," which was moved on the wire before the story was verified, Frank Starzel, the AP's general manager, expressed concern about the AP's overcorrection for past underreporting on racial discord and discrimination in the North. Starzel characterized the overplaying of stories about race as "a management problem," but it was too late for him to intervene with Gould and others to make a case for moderation in this evolving national story. Although the AP's coverage gradually included more enterprise reporting, the civil rights story, which moved quickly from one moment of tension to the next, was driven by event coverage and spot news reporting. By the time Starzel formulated his concern, there was no turning back on concessions to the white southern membership, and by the end of the decade, when the civil rights movement often dominated the daily news budget, no one in AP bureaus and offices was engaging Starzel's reservations.

As the civil rights story accelerated beyond school desegregation to lunch counters and bus stations, a 1961 staff memo by Samuel Blackman, the AP's new general news editor, confirmed that lobbying by southern editors during the 1950s had anchored southern ideology on race directly and overtly into the daily news report and would guide AP protocol in the next decade. White southern activism had changed policy on whether and how stories about race, public disturbances, and crime were covered, as well as on which wire—state, regional, or national—a story moved and how many newspapers had access to it. As he steered the AP toward civil rights coverage in the 1960s, Blackman raised the specter of objectivity and aligned the wire service with the southern position. "Southern newspapers," he wrote, "quite naturally are critical of the Northern Press and news services when an incident of the type that gets headlines when it happens in the South is all but overlooked, or played down, when it happens in the North. . . . Our obligation is to cover the news everywhere, and to apply the same yardstick, no matter where." He pointed to two recent incidents, neither of them a "world-shaker," that had been circulated only on state wires until southern members demanded national distribution. The AP's reporting of the two incidents, one of them a protest over desegregation of a swimming pool in Cincinnati and the other a Wisconsin barkeep's removal of two Black patrons from his tavern, "left us with apologies to make for inadequate coverage," Blackman said. He then referenced Gould's 1956 memo, which compared the Till coverage to other stories of Black-on-white crime and instructed AP staff to compensate with additional reporting when stories generated by member newspapers in the North lacked racial detail important to white editors in the South. "It is NOT an excuse for failure to cover adequately and fairly," Blackman wrote.[95]

By framing their critique of race coverage as a professional imperative and defense of journalism standards, segregationist members forced the wire service to embrace a minority viewpoint within the AP network and make policy changes that impacted all member newsrooms, regardless of their position on desegregation. In complaining about objectivity and accuracy in stories that did not negatively stereotype Black Americans, white southern members weaponized journalism standards in defense of Jim Crow. Using objectivity to control the race story after *Brown* also was the mission of the Southern Education Reporting Service, whose early history coincided with and paralleled the debate within the Associated Press. The SERS is our next stop.

CHAPTER 5

# OBJECTIVITY THROUGH A DIXIE PRISM

WHITENESS AND THE SOUTHERN EDUCATION
REPORTING SERVICE

In one version of its history, the Southern Education Reporting Service (SERS) was a noble journalistic experiment that delivered objective news about racial conflict, just when the American South needed it most. In April 1954, as white southerners braced for the *Brown v. Board of Education* school desegregation ruling that arrived a month later, white southern newspaper editors met over drinks at a professional conference and agreed to manage the impending clash of civil rights and public education using neutral and nonpartisan journalism. According to white-press lore, the SERS was born from this gathering in the hotel room of Harry Ashmore, executive editor of the *Arkansas Gazette*.[1] By autumn, the reporting service had hired and trained nineteen white journalists across the South, the border states of the former Confederacy, and the District of Columbia, and was collating their reports into *Southern School News*, a monthly digest of developments on school desegregation. The SERS's white leaders were so certain of their own professional sanctity that they wanted the objectivity project nominated for a Pulitzer Prize, the highest honor in white journalism.[2] This chapter, which focuses on the SERS's first three years, is a counternarrative that documents the white editors' racial motive for founding the reporting service but emphasizes the Black editors and academics whose presence was minimized, distorted, or erased in the dominant version of the SERS story.

This analysis reunites professional acquaintances from previous chapters, most notably Dr. Charles Johnson, president of Fisk University, and P. B. Young Sr., publisher of the *Journal and Guide* in Norfolk, Virginia. They were the token Black members of the SERS board when the objectivity project was founded but were clearly pivotal actors in its early years.

Also reappearing in the narrative is Bonita Valien, a Fisk sociologist who would be dismissed from the SERS research staff for violating its objectivity policy, as well as Claude Barnett of the Associated Negro Press and Dr. Charles Thompson of Howard University, who both declined board membership when Johnson's and Young's seats became vacant. We first met these prominent Black scholars and editors in chapters 1 and 3, where their work in journalism and civil rights was dismissed and disparaged by members of the white press, some of whom later promoted the objectivity mission of the SERS. No matter the expertise of Black editors and scholars in the SERS orbit, journalistic objectivity was a white conversation in 1954, and white editors controlled the professional rules of the game. This tension was more pronounced in the South, where the *Brown* ruling threatened the laws and traditions of Jim Crow, but it afflicted journalism throughout the United States. After all, the American press at midcentury was a segregated institution that functioned to white advantage. By foregrounding Black academics and editors who were marginalized by the SERS, this chapter isolates the racial power differential inherent in an all-white reporting service. Moreover, as racial outsiders looking in, Black professionals also had critical distance from the project, and their interpretations of SERS history challenged the valorizing narrative constructed by white participants and observers.[3]

The SERS was a white southern agency with a board led by white southern editors. The chair was gradualist Virginius Dabney of the *Times-Dispatch* in Richmond, Virginia, whose attack on the Black press during World War II is chronicled in chapter 1. The vice chair was Thomas R. Waring Jr. of the *News and Courier* in Charleston, South Carolina, an intractable segregationist whose opposition to "racial mixing" preceded *Brown* but intensified after the rulings. Chapter 4 described Waring's activism to skew the news values of the Associated Press and legitimize the southern white news narrative on race. Also reappearing in our story of the SERS's early years are its first two executive directors, C. A. McKnight and Don Shoemaker, whose careers began in white southern newsrooms and whose views on (de)segregation defined them as white moderates or gradualists. As middle-roaders, they assumed an eventual end to strict Jim Crow laws and traditions but neither endorsed the federal intervention represented by the U.S. Supreme Court rulings in *Brown*. In their SERS role, they hired the all-white reporting staff, assigned and edited the content of *Southern School News*, and handled community relations and professional outreach for the SERS. Shoemaker opened the book with one of many speeches he made about the SERS and objectivity; McKnight's appearance in chapter 3 documented Ashmore's use of a racial slur.

As with the trajectory of this book, which traces a debate that became more reactionary after the military presence at Central High School in Little Rock in 1957, this chapter draws to a logical close a year later. McKnight, who was recruited to launch the SERS before the *Brown* decision was handed down in 1954, left after a year to edit the *Charlotte Observer*, and Shoemaker, his successor, joined the *Miami Herald* in 1958. In addition to turnover in the executive leadership, Dabney stepped aside as SERS board chair in 1957 to become president of the American Society of Newspaper Editors (ASNE), where the SERS had built a strong presence on convention programs and in the monthly publication.[4] Although the editors' group and the reporting service were not affiliated, Ashmore targeted southern members of the prestigious and all-white ASNE when he made his initial pitch for support of the SERS over cocktails at the 1954 convention. The implied endorsement of the ASNE, whose Canons of Journalism were the template for ethics in white journalism, placed the objectivity project squarely in the white journalism mainstream.[5]

When Ashmore attended the ASNE meeting in April 1954, he was awaiting publication of *The Negro and the Schools*, the data-driven report underwritten by the Fund for the Advancement of Education (FAE), an arm of the Ford Foundation. As noted in chapter 3, the "Ashmore Report" was the FAE's first experiment using objectivity to filter information about race and education, allowing the northern philanthropy, which was developing a liberal bent, to inform the post-*Brown* debate without appearing to intervene in southern politics.[6] Many, if not all, of the editors who met for drinks in Ashmore's hotel room had received advance copies of his book and would be writing reviews. It was too soon to declare the forthcoming Ashmore Report a success, but Ashmore and the FAE leadership in New York—whose board included columnist and objectivity advocate Walter Lippmann; Ralph McGill, moderate editor of the *Atlanta Constitution*; and Time Inc. executive Roy Larsen—endorsed formation of the Southern Education Reporting Service as the FAE's second objectivity project.[7] Following the ASNE gathering, the SERS held its organizational meeting in Nashville on May 11, positioning the objectivity project as a proactive response to the Supreme Court ruling, which would upend Jim Crow less than a week later. The FAE's initial grants totaling $133,022 in 1954 funded the startup of the headquarters in Nashville and the hiring of staff, including the all-white, all-southern reporting team; a two-year extension grant of $213,844 followed in 1955.[8]

Johnson and his colleagues at Fisk, some of whom had contributed research to *The Negro and the Schools*, also met with FAE representatives about an objective publication, but their vision of a fact-based report was usurped by white opponents of *Brown*.[9] In parallel conversations, Ashmore and other white southern editors persuaded the FAE that using objectivity to report on race and education would serve a public good at a time of social and political crisis by providing factual and nonpartisan information, in the mold of *The Negro and the Schools*, and that monthly updates would be necessary as the desegregation story unfolded.[10] Although producing books, collecting data, and maintaining a clipping library would be functions of the SERS, its main deliverable would be the monthly tabloid *Southern School News*, whose parameter was accurate, unbiased articles about the South's response to *Brown*, and whose target audience would be predominantly white. "SERS is not an advocate, is neither pro-segregation nor anti-integration, but simply reports the facts as it finds them, state by state," proclaimed the *Southern School News* masthead.[11] The primary function of the SERS, then, was to sift news accounts of white southern resistance to or compliance with the school desegregation ruling through a filter of objectivity, which Shoemaker defined as reporting "impartially, dispassionately, and without adjectives or adverbs."[12] By flattening news about the white South's response to *Brown*, the "objective" reports in *Southern School News* would, in theory, be palatable not only to white southerners like Dabney and Waring, who opposed expanding civil rights on the Supreme Court's timetable, if at all, but also to Black supporters of *Brown* like Johnson and Young. On the contrary, by neutralizing the injustice of segregation and making all positions morally equivalent in the news narrative, the SERS formula affirmed the racial status quo.

The publication Johnson and his Fisk colleagues had imagined also would have been fact-based. Indeed, they had published the *Southern School News* prototype, *Monthly Summary of Events and Trends in Race Relations*, which for five years had briefed President Franklin Roosevelt on racial developments.[13] In their approach, facts gathered and contextualized by a biracial staff would have ameliorated fear of desegregation, and from their vantage, more accurately defined the challenges facing both Black and white southerners. In contrast, the SERS's objectivity paradigm assumed that only white southern journalists were capable of unbiased reporting on civil rights, disqualifying Black and northern journalists as racial partisans. The SERS's objective reporting also emphasized desegregation's impact on southern whites.

Even so, when the Black press challenged the all-white composition of the SERS reporting staff, SERS leaders maintained that race had nothing to do with the objectivity of the journalism in *Southern School News*. A year after the launch of the objectivity project, Simeon Booker, associate editor of *Jet* magazine, wrote Shoemaker to question the exclusion of Black journalists from the SERS reporting staff. Booker, who had been the first Black journalist hired by the *Washington Post*, recommended three Black reporters working for Black newspapers in the South. "As a Negro newsman, I am interested in your service becoming an organ for full and complete coverage, and with conditions as they are in the South, I don't see how you can do much more than the daily newspapers under your present set-up," Booker wrote. "I believe that your organ should lead the way not only in coverage but in hiring practices as well."[14] Shoemaker's response is telling. "Since we do not regard a man's race as an index to his objectivity," he wrote, "and moreover since we are reporting facts and are not in any way expressing opinion, the only real measure of usefulness to us is a man's experience, contacts and general availability in a specific area. Needless to say, we would retain correspondents other than those now on the masthead if men obviously more competent that [sic] they are could be found." Shoemaker also took issue with Booker's assertion that *Southern School News* should "lead the way." "If you will consult our masthead," he continued, "you will see that *Southern School News* takes no position and is not devoted to leading the way to anything except full and fair coverage of the segregation-desegregation problem."[15]

SERS leaders consistently denied that their own white southern standpoint and their regulation of other perspectives on the SERS board and reporting staff impacted the objectivity of *Southern School News*. Shoemaker explained this position with an analogy between reporting on race and covering a football game. "At the Southern Education Reporting

Service in Nashville, the hired hands take no sides in the segregation-desegregation controversy," he said in a speech. "We rather like to think of our mission in terms of the sports editor who covers a Rose Bowl game between two teams he has never seen before and in whom he has not personal or pecuniary interest affecting himself, his heirs or assigns. He is there simply to tell what happened."[16] This oversimplification of the SERS's mission makes no accounting for either whiteness or regionalism as stakes in the outcome of desegregation. The SERS's definition of objectivity was elastic enough to accommodate the notion that race did not influence perspective when a journalist was white as well as the belief that race tainted perspective when a journalist was Black. The SERS's vision of objectivity valued social location in the decision to use southern reporters, whose knowledge of the region would give depth to reporting, but it also rejected the possibility that outsiders who had no sentimental attachment to southern social tradition might offer more balanced reporting of the desegregation story.

The white SERS founders ignored this contradiction in their concept of objectivity because they could not see that their own whiteness posed a conflict of interest. With the end of legal segregation, all white southerners would have their status in southern society redefined and, therefore, had a racial stake in the implementation of the *Brown* decision. Specifically, no white southerner was a disinterested party. Moreover, because journalism was a segregated profession, most white editors did not recognize that the racial composition of the reporting service undermined its accuracy and objectivity claims. This criticism is not a presentist intervention in historical analysis. As this chapter demonstrates, Black members of the press and academy recognized the incongruity in the SERS's position and registered their criticisms at the time, only to be dismissed by white southerners as illogical and self-interested—or, in the case of editor Young, "off his rocker."[17]

This chapter avoids direct content analysis to test the objectivity of *Southern School News*; the flat, deadpan approach to SERS reporting is not in dispute. Instead, this narrative emphasizes the relationships among SERS participants to foreground the white activism entailed in the reporting service, focusing specifically on the subversion of journalistic objectivity to advance political and racial ends. Previous scholarship on the SERS has documented the organization's history but has not fully engaged the ideological dimensions of objectivity within the reporting service.[18] Instead, this analysis examines the organization's racial mission through the lens of social construction, most particularly the theory set forth by Michael Omi and Howard Winant, who defined race as neither an essence nor an illusion but "an unstable and 'decentered' complex of social meanings constantly being transformed by political struggle."[19] In 1954 many participants in and observers of the SERS viewed race as an essence rooted in biological as well as cultural difference, and many white southerners did not view Black citizens as their equals. With the *Brown* decision, the most significant American racial milestone since emancipation, the "social meanings" associated with race came in for intense renegotiation. For white editors like Dabney, Waring, and Shoemaker, objectivity became a journalistic weapon in their struggle to defend a regional culture, as well as white rights and privileges, anchored in segregation.

The SERS could have documented and informed the expansion of educational opportunity for all southern children but that was not the white vision for the reporting service. Not only did the Black community see different possibilities for the objectivity project but it had its own version of the SERS creation story, one that had nothing to do with white editors sharing cocktails at the ASNE convention. Instead, their history starred scholars from historically Black Fisk University who practiced the scientific method and used objectivity in their study of race, joined by members of the Black press who saw through the SERS's racial double standard. For them, factual context and accuracy were a formula for social justice. Before we write them into the SERS's history, however, we will explore white editors' use of objectivity to control the news narrative about the post-*Brown* South.

## Bracing for Change

As they awaited the *Brown* decision and its impact, white southern editors anticipated that many of their white readers would not accept desegregation without incident. They also became increasingly concerned that the northern press, whose coverage of the South they often considered disparaging or condescending, would define the South's response to *Brown* in national discourse, largely by emphasizing conflicts over desegregation. In remarks to the ASNE in 1955, McKnight, the SERS's first executive director, said that newspapers "are published to be sold to other human beings and . . . quiet, constructive and unspectacular developments do not stimulate the same quick interest that conflict, controversy and disagreement will create."[20] An early mission of *Southern School News*, then, was to document cases in which schools were integrated peacefully, as well as those in which desegregation met with local resistance. In covering the South's response to *Brown*, *Southern School News* would offer a clear, dispassionate record of local reaction and would avoid incitement of white resentment, which might provoke white unrest and violence. As such, the SERS would be an arbiter of public perception both above and below the Mason-Dixon Line, a counterpoint to the sensationalized national coverage by the wire services and metropolitan papers in the North, which focused on resistance to desegregation and fed stereotypes of the South as a backward region. As time passed and white resistance to *Brown* hardened, peaceful transitions were few and even SERS reporting emphasized southern opposition to the ruling.[21]

The most active critic of the northern press's coverage of racial tension in the South was Grover C. Hall Jr. of the *Montgomery Advertiser*. Although he was not directly involved with the SERS, he influenced those who were. Hall, who corresponded with Dabney throughout the year and was his partner in Civil War reenactment tennis matches at yearly ASNE conventions, was particularly troubled that northern newspapers ignored racial inequality in their own communities, choosing instead to focus on desegregation conflicts in the South.[22] "What the national press has done so far is to turn out bubbly stereo plates about that part of the race problem under the magnolia," Hall wrote in the *ASNE Bulletin* in 1956.[23] A year later, the SERS's concern about misrepresentation of the South was a theme in the October 1957 *Bulletin*, published during Dabney's ASNE presidency. That issue examined news coverage of segregation and critiqued the northern press's focus on white mob protests. In a companion piece to Hall's article, Shoemaker, who had succeeded McKnight, offered the objectivity of *Southern School News* as an alternative to northern coverage and portrayed the northern journalists reporting the desegregation story as interlopers who invited the hostility they received from white southern protesters. "The record shows that many crowds regard strange newsmen as enemies. And why not?" Shoemaker asked. "The whole traumatic integration experience is strange itself."[24]

While the primary audience for *Southern School News* was white educators, journalists, and government officials in the South, it was mailed for free to thirty thousand readers by the end of its first year and also circulated to a national and multiracial audience.[25] It became clear, however, that the audience for detached reporting on school desegregation was limited. When the FAE insisted in 1955 that subscribers pay to receive the publication, the SERS mailing list shrank. In April 1956, after an aggressive subscription campaign, the SERS executive director reported 11,049 paid subscribers, at least one in every state. Five months later, the number had dropped to about 9,000, a level that held steady through 1957.[26] One of the practical realities of the SERS's clinical approach to journalism was that *Southern School News* made for dull reading. When he interpreted the objectivity mandate for the newly formed SERS board in 1954, McKnight said his emphasis would be on facts: "SERS should not, in my opinion, venture very far into the analysis and interpretation of events and trends, other than the essential backgrounding that any good news story contains."[27]

Although it positioned itself as above the fray, the FAE was not a neutral party and, like all philanthropies, awarded grants with an eye toward outcomes. In June 1954, following publication of the Ashmore Report and release of the *Brown* ruling, the Behavioral Sciences Division of the Ford Foundation apprised McKnight, then occupied with launching the SERS, that the philanthropy was formulating an agenda "to help in easing and facilitating the social transition that will be underway in the South in the next months and years." On short notice, the foundation summoned McKnight to New York for an idea session whose roster was a midcentury brain trust on race and southern schools. Charles Johnson and white scholar Gordon Blackwell of the University of North Carolina were the SERS board members on a list of experts that also included Kenneth Clark, the Black psychologist who assisted the NAACP Legal Defense Fund in the school litigation that led to *Brown*.[28]

As representatives of a northern philanthropy, the white FAE staff were more comfortable than many white southerners interacting with Black professionals and more appreciative of their contributions to biracial work. They endorsed Young's and Johnson's inclusion on the SERS board and treated Black participants in New York meetings equitably, but on matters of policy and operational decisions in the South, including staffing and content of *Southern School News*, they deferred to the SERS board, where the two Black directors had no power. Johnson was appointed to the SERS executive committee but was routinely excluded from operational decisions and denied professional courtesies, most notably in 1955 when white board members fired Valien, his former research assistant, behind his back. John Scanlon, the FAE program associate, articulated the philanthropy's policy on editorial matters this way: "We of the Fund staff have, from the very beginning of SERS, scrupulously avoided passing judgement on any prospective article for *Southern School News*, in order not to give anyone the slightest cause for asserting that we have any control whatever over the editorial content of the paper."[29] The FAE also took a hands-off approach to operational matters. When the FAE sponsored a project with headquarters in Nashville, which was still a segregated city in 1954, the philanthropy acquiesced to the racism embedded in local law and custom.[30]

The indignity imposed by Jim Crow, a persistent reminder that separate was not equal, had direct consequences for Black participation in the SERS. Because Valien, who had done graduate work in sociology, had conducted research for the Ashmore Report and had overseen publication of Fisk's *Monthly Summary of Events and Trends in Race Relations*, Philip Coombs, the FAE research director, admired her scholarship and assumed the SERS would hire her.[31] Despite her expertise, white SERS leaders did not allow Valien to work in the SERS headquarters, located in a building owned by the George Peabody College for Teachers, and required her to do SERS work from her home. In the mid-1950s, when documents were available only on paper or microfilm, this directly impeded her work. Moreover, the SERS made no provision for clerical support. In early 1955 Coombs questioned the arrangement but white board member Charles Moss, editor of the *Nashville Banner*, rebuffed his concern. Moss acknowledged that he and Coombs disagreed "on the propriety of having Mrs. Valien connected directly to the SERS headquarters, but to be fair and to keep the record straight, I must say that she did a remarkably fine job" on a recent project, which he described as "purely objective . . . and as good a piece of salesmanship as anything SERS has done for itself." Nonetheless, Moss continued, "I cannot relinquish my first reaction to the office relationship and do not wish to discuss it here for fear of doing her an injustice."[32]

Johnson lived on the Fisk campus in Nashville, so his lodging during board meetings was not a concern for the SERS; however, Young, who traveled to SERS events from Norfolk, was unable to stay at the Nashville hotel selected for white board members. This issue arose in July 1954 during arrangements for an early SERS seminar. "You are right," McKnight wrote Young. "The Andrew Jackson Hotel would not assign a room to you. I have asked Mrs. Valien to arrange hotel accommodations for you."[33] Instead, when Young traveled to Nashville for SERS business, he stayed in the Fisk University guesthouse.[34] As historian Benjamin Houston noted, even as some Jim Crow restrictions relaxed after World War II, interracial dining and lodging remained taboo in Nashville and elsewhere in the South.[35] Indeed, the problem of "mixed" dining arose as soon as the SERS set up shop in Nashville in 1954 and Johnson and Young attended the training seminar for the new reporting staff, the same event for which Young was denied a hotel room. A few days before the seminar, McKnight vaguely notified attendees of an adjustment to the schedule but disclosed privately to Ashmore that Jim Crow had necessitated the change. "We have cancelled the plans for the formal dinner because I have found it impossible to arrange satisfactory accommodations for a mixed group," he wrote. "There will be, however, drinks and a steak for everybody on a more informal basis."[36]

During the *Southern School News* training seminar, all board members who attended, including Johnson and Young, made remarks to the newly hired SERS reporters. In his handwritten notes from the seminar, William Workman, the South Carolina correspondent who also reported for Waring's *News and Courier*, identified Young inaccurately as Jr. instead of Sr.; his affiliation as "editor Norfolk Ledger and Guide," instead of *Journal and Guide*; and added the label "(Negro!)" next to his name.[37] Johnson, an expert on race and segregation, and Young, the only representative of the Black press affiliated with the SERS, certainly had perspective and information to contribute; however, they were not invited to subsequent training seminars. Two years later, Johnson realized during a meeting at the FAE offices in New York that he had been excluded and wrote to Shoemaker, who had taken over as executive director in 1955. "I was . . . somewhat embarrassed when I was asked if I had had a chance to attend any of the seminars of the Reporting Service, as a Board member," he reported. "Am I correct that Board members were not asked to share these discussions [sic]."³⁸ Shoemaker replied that "only the newspaper board members who would have a direct professional interest" had been invited to a recent "correspondents' roundtable." Given his record of scholarship on race and segregation, Johnson's "direct professional interest" in the work of the SERS was considerable.³⁹ As it happened, Young resigned before that meeting because he was no longer willing to tolerate the board's racism; without Johnson present, the correspondents received no input from a Black southerner and meal planning was less complicated.

Correspondence between the executive director and the board chair demonstrated a pattern of race consciousness and careful attention to maintaining Jim Crow for board functions, without concern for its impact on Black participation. Prior to the March 1956 board meeting, Dabney worried about a segregated party planned at a white board member's home and the awkwardness of Shoemaker's meeting Dabney's plane if Young arrived on the same flight. "We could simply say to Mr. Young that we had an engagement and would see him in the morning," Dabney wrote. "He won't be going to our hotel, anyway." Shoemaker then reported that the plan for the party had changed and Young would arrive at a different time. "I will have a room at the Andrew Jackson as sort of a headquarters and we will have an informal dinner around 8:30," Shoemaker wrote.⁴⁰ When Young resigned before the meeting, board networking was thus preserved as a whites-only opportunity.

At least one white representative of the FAE attended SERS meetings and would have experienced—and tacitly endorsed—the board's segregated hospitality. If the FAE had insisted on greater inclusivity, it is unlikely that all of the white southern board members would have attended or remained on the board.⁴¹ For example, in 1955 Waring's newspaper editorialized against Michigan's white governor, who canceled a speech to Alabama Democrats because the banquet would be segregated. "Here is a test that Southerners may welcome," the *News and Courier* opined. "One way to tell who our friends are may be to invite them to dinner. If they won't come, they don't want Southern votes."⁴²

Rather than ignoring Jim Crow as a social and legal anachronism over which the SERS had no control, this chapter views both the racial barriers within the SERS and the racist views of white board members as relevant to the objectivity mission because they structured inequity into the reporting service. None of the white editors on the SERS board supported integration; all were gradualists or devout segregationists who rejected the premise, argued by the plaintiffs in *Brown*, that separate can never be equal. In the years following the desegregation ruling, their newspapers were invested to varying degrees in defending a racial status quo that was now against the law. As such, their opposition to *Brown* on their editorial pages and in their communities was an act of political resistance that complicated the SERS's claim of journalistic neutrality. Johnson and Young were not copied on racially candid SERS correspondence, but they read the editorial pages of white southern newspapers and knew they were attending meetings with white supremacists. Even as white southern editors denied that their own views about separation of the races had bearing on the explicitly nonpartisan mission of SERS, their political engagement revealed objectivity to be an ideological weapon.

## Policing Objectivity

Of the white editors on the SERS board, Thomas Waring was most insistent that the reporting service define objectivity as political neutrality, particularly on the issue of segregation, and that the journalism in *Southern School News* in no way challenge white supremacy. On the editorial page of the *News and Courier* in Charleston and in correspondence on SERS matters, Waring decried the *Brown* decision as an encroachment on states' rights, an affront to white culture, and a step toward amalgamation.[43] Whereas the racial politics of gradualists like Ashmore and McKnight left some room for negotiation, Waring's views were concretely segregationist and he would eventually align himself with the White Citizens' Councils.[44] He understood that the ideological makeup of the SERS board shaped public perceptions of the reporting service's objectivity, and the audience he cared about was the conservative white South. His preoccupation with these issues during the early months of the reporting service, as it established its reporting protocols, formed an ideological vortex on the SERS board.

Waring was uneasy being associated with a northern philanthropy and communing with directors less fervent about separation of the races. After the first board meeting on May 11, 1954, Waring insisted that the founding directors universally embrace and document the objectivity commitment. On May 13, four days before the first *Brown* ruling, Waring wrote to everyone then involved in SERS leadership, outlining his understanding of the reporting service's objectivity mission and asking them to affirm agreement with his position, the responses functioning as a group pledge. "As I see it," Waring wrote to Dabney in a letter copied to nine other board members, "our purpose is to supply an impartial fact-gathering service, as unbiased as The Associated Press. We do not intend to single out either the good or the bad aspects of segregation, or the lack of it, but to report both the good and the bad impartially as they occur." He then emphasized the professional and political risks attached to his own involvement. "If anyone should get the idea that this is a propaganda agency for any viewpoint, or that the service is promoting some special line of thought, its usefulness would be lost," he continued. "In addition, embarrassment might be caused for individuals connected with the enterprise."[45] The commitment to objectivity allowed Waring to participate in the SERS without losing credibility with his South Carolina readers and fellow segregationists. "As you of course understand," he wrote Dabney a week later, "I cannot afford to be identified at any time with a group that is trying to 'sell' an idea which I am devoting most of my efforts to unselling in The News and Courier. We are only sniping editorially at this time, but if the going gets really rough we may be talking about civil disobedience, underground activity and bootleg segregation."[46] Just as Waring scrutinized the actions of other southern whites for their loyalty to the segregationist cause, he knew they also had him under surveillance.

That summer, as McKnight prepared the inaugural issue of *Southern School News*, Waring wrote to Roy V. Harris, a Georgia attorney and former Speaker of the Georgia House who edited a rabidly pro-segregation, anticommunist weekly with the lead headline often printed in red ink. Many of Harris's fellow editors shunned him—one referred to the *Augusta [GA] Courier* as a "political poop-sheet"—but Waring recognized Harris as a kindred spirit on racial matters, even if he thought less of his journalism.[47] Although they had never met, Waring cared that Harris knew he was a segregationist. In June, Harris attacked the Ford Foundation for "financing communization of the South and ultimate destruction of this country and her free enterprise system under which all of the Ford fortune was accumulated." In the third of four jumps in a long diatribe, Harris took brief aim at the newly formed SERS, which would "be staffed by liberal 'newsmen' . . . to coordinate activities of various groups and organizations which seek to end public school segregation."[48] Although the *Augusta Courier* had not named him, Waring wrote a letter to the editor, objecting that he would not be affiliated with an integrationist endeavor. "The News and Courier is carrying on a long term campaign, with all the vigor we possess, to prevent the end of segregation by whatever means may be deemed useful," Waring wrote. "I have personally informed all members of the board of the SERS that it is my understanding that it is non-partisan in this matter, will carry on no propaganda for either viewpoint and will serve as a strictly factual information service." He invited Harris and his readers to clarify their skepticism about the SERS: "Naturally I would not like to find myself hoodwinked and in the event you are correct, I want to know about it."[49]

Waring then engaged in a detailed, private exchange to assure Harris that he was not the only segregationist on the SERS board. "In my opinion, Frank Ahlgren of The Commercial Appeal [in Memphis] and Charles Moss of the Nashville Banner, to name two of the directors, have about the same determination that I do to fight for separation of the races," Waring wrote, affirming that his own SERS participation was part of a political strategy. "I went into this affair with my eyes open, on the theory that it was going to be done anyway, and that we reactionaries might as well have a seat on the board for spying purposes if for no other reason," he continued. "I told the group that first discussed this proposal last April in Washington that I would be the [Robert] Oppenheimer of the organization. If it gets too smelly at least I can tell what happened inside."[50]

Harris ignored Waring's reassurances and misconstrued the reporting service as a concession to *Brown*. "If we lose our fight we are going to lose it in the field of public opinion and we will lose it because the people will reach the conclusion that you have reached, that segregation is going anyway," Harris wrote.[51] In response, Waring vowed to go to jail to defend segregation. "When none of us is willing to take a risk, then we do not deserve to have segregation or any other kind of liberty," he stated, calling for political finesse. "In my opinion, a calm approach is better than extreme or threatening attitudes, which only serve to stir up the opposition and confuse those on the fence. We are outnumbered in the country as a whole. We should not let fly with the rebel yell every time somebody plays 'Yankee Doodle' on a piccolo." Waring also rejected

Harris's argument that SERS reporting about *Brown* would condition white people to accept integration and should be suppressed. "Being in the newspaper business I believe in shedding light on everything, including the things we don't like," he continued. "People put floodlights in their yards so they can aim better at prowlers. We have to be able to see our enemies." For Waring, then, the objectivity project was part of his political calculus. "If the Southern Education Reporting Service turns up Southern communities that accept mixing of schools, who are you and I to hide it?" he asked. ". . . If SERS covers that the South accepts an end of segregation meekly, that will be the story to print."[52]

Although Waring had promised Harris that the reporting service would not undermine segregation on his watch, a month later the *Augusta Courier* renewed its assault on *Southern School News*, which still had not published its first issue, and impugned Dabney as an integrationist and communist. Dabney was offended at the mischaracterization and considered suing Harris for libel. "I have never made any statement 'against segregated schools,'" he wrote to Waring. "On the contrary, every statement I have made has been in favor of them."[53] McKnight dismissed Harris's attacks, which reminded him of unpleasant reader correspondence at his previous newspaper. "If and when Brother Harris turns his attention to me I will promptly give it the same treatment I always give illiterate, uninformed and antagonistic communications to the Charlotte News, i.e., pitch it in the nearest wastebasket," he wrote.[54] Waring, however, did not want the SERS to rebuff Harris's concerns. "We small d Democrats are too timid to ignore the untutored mutterings of the mob. We sometimes tremble at receipt of rude diatribes and frequently print them too," he wrote. "Crude as Roy Harris may be, he represents a wide segment of Southern thinking—or feeling, if you prefer—and we have to reckon with it."[55]

White editors on the SERS board insisted they could editorialize about segregation in their own newspapers, taking overtly ideological stands on issues being covered by *Southern School News*, then abandon partisanship to lead the SERS within a framework of objectivity. On the contrary, the record is full of evidence that southern editors on the board were unable to maintain neutrality, that debates over the objectivity of SERS staffing and content were in fact ideological skirmishes. Not only did board members parse the language the SERS used but they also micromanaged selection of content for *Southern School News* to make a political point. In late August 1954, for example, as he was reassuring Harris of his own commitment to segregation, Waring challenged McKnight to prove in the inaugural issue that *Southern School News* was objective and not promoting integration. "In conversation with other South Carolina newspaper men I still find suspicion of SERS' impartiality," he wrote. "One editor said he thought a test of it would be the handling of the story from West Virginia about the protest (in Barbour County) against mixed schools."[56] Waring and his allies also flagged Associated Press coverage of an anti-integration protest in New Mexico: "I assume SERS' first issue will cover these stories fully and pass along the word that my colleagues will be watching for them."[57]

Dabney, who was copied on the letter to McKnight, was quick to validate Waring's request. "I can't doubt that Pete [McKnight] plans to include the West Virginia and New Mexico episodes—in the second issue, if they're too late to get in the first—and that they'll be played straight down the middle," Dabney wrote. ". . . If we aren't going to give full and unbiased accounts of such a development as that in Barbour County, West Virginia, then I'm out."[58] For McKnight, Waring's correspondence consumed considerable time and reminded him that the segregationists were monitoring his work. Although Waring had instructed McKnight to increase the amount and type of segregation coverage, his strategy was not entirely successful. The first issue of *Southern School News* mentioned the West Virginia protest, but ironically, McKnight planned to balance the story from Barbour County by covering in the next issue "some community in West Virginia yet to be selected where integration was successfully managed. This, I thought, would give both sides of the story in West Virginia." Similarly, the protest angle of the New Mexico story fizzled when integration proceeded without incident despite predictions of violence. "We will treat the Hobbs story in some detail in the next issue," he wrote to Waring.[59]

In separate communication to Dabney, McKnight reminded the chair that SERS would be reporting the two local responses to *Brown* as morally equivalent. "I think all of us are wasting a lot of time writing letters back and forth about the impartiality of the Reporting Service, and I propose to do no more of it," he argued. "It has been my understanding from the very first that the Reporting Service would be as factual, accurate and objective as it is humanly possible to make it. Under no other condition would I have undertaken this responsibility."[60] Although the SERS board offered McKnight a two-year extension, and he continued to support the objectivity project, he accepted another job a few months after *Southern School News* began publication and before the second *Brown* ruling in May 1955 ordered desegregation of schools "with all deliberate speed." Thereafter, white resistance throughout the South complicated the SERS's goal of editorial balance.

McKnight was no integrationist but he was certainly more racially moderate than any white editor on the board. Shoemaker, a North Carolina newspaperman who interviewed for the executive director job in March 1955, was more to Waring's liking. Waring asked Shoemaker "to state his own views on the segregation issue. His statement was satisfactory to me, though expressed in somewhat different terms from my own feelings."[61] In the summer of 1955, shortly after Shoemaker started the position, Waring encouraged him to give "due consideration" to a news tip from Robert B. Patterson, secretary of the White Citizens' Council (WCC), who wanted the SERS to report on speeches that Georgia governor Herman Talmadge and others had made at a WCC event.[62] When providing editorial guidance to Shoemaker, Waring copied Patterson on the correspondence, ensuring that members of the WCC knew Waring was advancing their interests with the new executive director. "In some quarters (not SERS) I have noted a tendency to belittle and to question all spokesmen for separation of the races, and to set up all spokesmen for integration as high-minded and authoritative," Waring wrote, arguing for journalistic equivalency. "As I view it, the function of SERS is more to report events and opinions as they occur and less to evaluate the motives and goodwill of the sources."[63] In his reply to Waring, Shoemaker said that "spokesmen for segregation . . . often say things that look just plain ridiculous between quotes. Too few thoughtful spokesmen for that point of view are as persuasive and comprehensible as yourself. I'll just do the best that I can."[64]

In summer 1955 Shoemaker reached out to Waring for support. "There has been some criticism within the board that we are 'dignifying the Citizens Councils and other groups' by reporting objectively on their activities," Shoemaker wrote. "I do not feel this is an editorial judgment (to report thusly) and I trust the others will support me in this."[65] He did not name the source of the criticism, but this was a concern raised by P. B. Young Sr., whose discomfort with the public racism of board members would culminate in his resignation from the board the following year. "Please do not let anyone stop you from telling the truth about Citizens Councils or any other phase of this issue," Waring replied. "I would be grateful if you'd keep me advised on the nature of the opposition to Citizens' Councils. . . . You must not be pressured into dishonest journalism."[66] After Shoemaker left the SERS in 1958, he confirmed why Waring found him so unthreatening: "There are those among us, namely me, who feel that the Brown decision came too soon; that some years, perhaps a generation, should have intervened before the stillson wrench was applied to a South which sticks devoutly to the belief that it can't happen here."[67]

Although Shoemaker might have been ambivalent about his employment with the FAE, it provided professional opportunities. In addition to the editorship of *Southern School News*, the FAE contracted Shoemaker to compile *With All Deliberate Speed*, a collection of essays about the *Brown* aftermath, published in 1957. That same year, Weldon James, associate editor of the *Louisville Courier-Journal* and a SERS correspondent covering Kentucky, coauthored another FAE-funded book, *The Louisville Story*, about the peaceful integration of that city's schools.[68] While preparing the manuscript, James wrote to Harry Ashmore on his newspaper's letterhead, thanking him for the opportunity to write *The Louisville Story* but admitting insecurity about comparisons of his book to *The Negro and the Schools*. "But maybe I'll survive," James wrote. "Come by for a drink session and improve the chances. Meantime, here's Don Shoemaker's subtitle for The Louisville Story: 'How I Became a Nigger-Lover for the Ford Foundation.'"[69]

## Objectivity's Racial Double Standard

White editors on the SERS board insisted their racial attitudes and activism had no bearing on the objectivity of the journalism in *Southern School News*. Even more implausible was the SERS policy that correspondents, the white reporters submitting monthly reports from the southern states in which they worked as journalists, were free to engage in politics. Waring had recommended William Workman, the *News and Courier*'s capital correspondent, to be the SERS's South Carolina reporter; however, Workman was at times directly involved with opposition to *Brown*. For example, in 1955 Workman helped organize an effort called the Committee of 52 and authored a position statement calling on the South Carolina legislature to defy the U.S. Supreme Court and thwart school integration.[70] Although he declined to join the states' rights movement, Workman affirmed his intention to support the cause. "I think I can probably accomplish more from without, as a writer and commentator and occasional speaker, than from within as an organizer or official," he wrote.[71] A few months later, he resigned from the Committee of 52 steering committee, finally acknowledging an ethical concern. "Whereas I was proud to be an initial subscriber to the statement of principles laid down by the Committee of 52, I am unwilling to be an active participant in an organization which engages in developments which I, as a newsman, must report," he wrote. "I do not consider it proper to be at once 'inside' an organization as a member and 'outside' as a reporter. . . . Be assured, however, that the sentiments expressed in the resolution of last August still reflect my personal views."[72] As historian Sid Bedingfield noted, Workman's byline appeared on relevant stories in the *News and Courier* before he resigned from the Committee of 52.[73] In addition, Workman was producing monthly South Carolina reports for *Southern School News*.

Without irony, Workman and Waring assailed sociologist Bonita Valien for public remarks supporting *Brown* and, just months after the launch of the SERS, set in motion her dismissal from the SERS staff for violating an objectivity policy that had consequences only for her, the sole Black employee. McKnight, who was executive director when Workman and Waring made their complaint, had to fire her; however, Shoemaker would affirm the hypocrisy of the objectivity policy when Workman was reputed in 1956 to be a member of the WCC and felt compelled to clarify that he was not directly involved in that organization. "My newspaper writings and radio-TV broadcasts leave little doubt as to my opposition to the Supreme Court's decision (more from a standpoint of political philosophy than anything else)," Workman wrote, "but I am not a combatant in the sense of being a member of an active organization. My stand is that of an individual South Carolinian, not as one of any group."[74] Coming from the SERS's objectivity standard bearer, Shoemaker's reply is informative: "As to Citizens Council membership, I care not one whit whether our correspondents belong to Council or NAACP, Republican or Democratic parties, Rotary or Kiwanis. Quite obviously, we do not own private opinions of the correspondents (which fairly bound the compass), and I hope that no one will ever gain any impression to the contrary."[75] Of course, it was unlikely that any SERS correspondent would affiliate with the NAACP.

The white editors who dominated the early SERS never intended to integrate either the reporting team or staff and ignored Johnson's advice that the SERS include Black perspectives. "It is conceivable that you might need a Negro correspondent, who can spend whatever time is required in particular communities to investigate and follow up situations pertinent to the objective of the Reporting Service," Johnson wrote to McKnight in June 1954.[76] In his letter to Shoemaker in 1955, Simeon Booker had suggested three Black journalists working for the Black press, and the *Nashville Banner* employed a Black reporter to do "Negro news," but there was no chance that Black journalists would be allowed to prepare SERS news copy. Irrespective of local Jim Crow laws, the white press persisted as a segregated institution because white editors questioned Black journalists' professional legitimacy, particularly when the subject was civil rights. Dabney had criticized the Black press's Double V campaign during World War II as reckless and unpatriotic and remained leery of the Black press during the 1950s.[77] For example, in a letter to a segregationist editor in 1957, Dabney wrote, "I was asked by *Ebony* and *Jet* to make a statement as ASNE president about the interference of the Little Rock mob with a Negro reporter from the *Amsterdam News*. I said I am against all mobs and that there is no excuse for any mob's interfering with legitimate newsgathering by a newspaperman. I suppose that's what the Harlem brother was doing, but I didn't go into that in the statement, and they seemed entirely satisfied with it at *Ebony*."[78]

In 1954 McKnight disingenuously promised to consider Johnson's suggestion of a biracial reporting staff and said he was "looking forward to working with Mrs. Valien. I hear good things about her from all sides."[79] Philip Coombs, the FAE's research director, and Johnson assumed that Valien, an accomplished, Nashville-based sociologist who had worked on the prototype for *Southern School News*, was the obvious choice to head SERS research, even before McKnight was hired as executive director.[80] Formal action at the second board meeting on June 6 set expectations for racial inclusion, though the white board members ignored them. Johnson's appointment to the executive committee did not guarantee his involvement in decision-making. "Editor members of the board" were tasked with "locating and appointing top quality correspondents, both regular and standby," who would be paid one hundred dollars per month, according to the minutes. Presumably, this would have included Young, who recommended the same Black correspondent as Johnson.

Although the recommendation to hire Valien had been made in New York, the minutes reported, "It was agreed that it would be desirable for the Executive Director to locate a mature Negro social scientist who could help on research and analysis on the central staff at Nashville." That brief notation and passive voice conceal the nature and extent of the board conversation, including what might define maturity in a Black social scientist, a distinction that would not have applied to a white academic and had nothing to do with age. The minutes also obscure whether white board members discussed the FAE's preference that Valien be on staff.[81] Whatever the conversation, McKnight immediately encountered resistance to Valien's hiring from white editors. Later that summer, he wrote Dabney, "I have given a great deal of thought and consideration to the problems involved in retaining Mrs. Valien, problems that I will discuss with you in more detail the next time we meet. I think I have finally worked out a solution which will enable us to use her great talents and experience without causing any concern among our board members or among other persons in the Deep South."[82] McKnight's solution was to have Valien work from home, under the pretext that her office was being remodeled.[83]

Even as Valien was hidden from sight in Nashville, she made an easy target for segregationists who opposed her association with the reporting service. In January 1955 board member Charles Moss of the *Nashville Banner* not only rejected Coombs's entreaty to allow Valien to work in the headquarters but went a step further, suggesting she be removed from the payroll. "If her ability could be used either by the Fund or SERS in a less binding association, without her feelings being hurt, I think it would be better," he wrote.[84] Workman supplied an ostensibly race-neutral pretext later that month, when he shared with Waring a clipping from the *Christian Science Monitor*, which reported that Valien had appeared on a panel at the National Association of Intergroup Relations Officials in November in Boston. The *Monitor* identified Valien as an employee of the SERS and said she criticized the *Brown* decision for noting only the adverse consequences of school segregation for Black children. The Court, she said, "might have addressed itself with advantage to the effect of segregation on the white child, creating in him the belief in inherent racial superiority."[85] Workman, who routinely advocated for segregation even as he wrote for *Southern School News*, split hairs in his criticism of the article. "Whereas all of us who profess any concern and knowledge of the situation speak out on our own views (in voice or in writing)," he said, "I know of no one down this side who has done so either in the name of the SERS or as a staff member of that organization." He threatened to quit the reporting service if Valien were speaking for the SERS and it had become "an agency with whose viewpoint I differ so completely."[86]

After Waring forwarded the *Christian Science Monitor* clipping to McKnight, the issue festered until March when the board fired Valien, effective June 30, 1955. In addition to the direct impact of the racial double standard on Valien, the process was disrespectful to Johnson and Young, who could not attend the meeting where the matter was handled and learned there was a problem three months after the board had acted. Waring had been most offended by Valien's comments and pushed the matter. "It is my understanding," he wrote McKnight, "that SERS is not proselyting for any viewpoint, but is what its name implies, a reporting service. Yet here a staff member appears as a partisan pleader." Waring argued that when he took editorial positions, he was not doing so as a representative of SERS: "Our editorials are not labeled as coming from the vice chairman of SERS."[87] This ignored the SERS's own descriptions of editors' views. To persuade the public of its objectivity, the SERS trumpeted the board's ideological diversity and drew attention to the racial politics of specific board members who could be categorized as moderate or pro-segregation.[88] When white editors espoused opinions about the *Brown* ruling, they claimed to enhance the organization's credibility; when a Black staff member did so, it was a breach of objectivity.

Dabney and McKnight seemed willing to let the matter go with a warning, but Waring was unrelenting.[89] Discovery of the clipping coincided with a *Time* magazine article about the SERS that said its mission was reporting "the progress of desegregation," a characterization that prompted a telegram of protest to the magazine.[90] The SERS also complained to King Features Syndicate the same week about a Westbrock Pegler column that described Ashmore's book as a project of the SERS and a "pleading for 'integration,' a new word in the sense of an alternative to 'segregation.'"[91] Waring was fuming. "These incidents are seriously disturbing to me personally," he wrote.[92] McKnight responded that in Boston Valien "stressed . . . that she was not appearing as a representative of SERS; that her work for SERS had no relationship to her past work in the field for Fisk University and the Ashmore Project; and that SERS was not in the opinion business. Incidentally, she paid her own way." He also ruminated on the challenge of doing analysis without opinion. In preparing for a recent talk himself, he "had the feeling that even the division of states into broad groups and the citing of yet-unidentified trends and observations encroached slightly, at least, into the field of opinion, as perhaps did the exposition of some of the administrative headaches in desegregation. . . . Any kind of interpretation or analysis of the facts, in a sense, becomes one man's opinion."[93] A week later McKnight informed Valien that pending a decision by the board when it met in March, no one on staff, including himself, was to make public appearances. Johnson, Young, and other board members were not copied on this correspondence.[94]

Valien's reply contains a detailed, thoughtful, and measured discussion of the SERS, the scientific method, her scholarship, and her duty as a citizen. Ironically, the white supremacists brandished objectivity to silence her, yet Valien was likely the only SERS employee who had been formally trained to use objectivity as a research method. Valien said she was attracted to the reporting service as "an opportunity to work in an area around which there is a good deal of fear, frustration, emotion and ignorance, where I could assist through my experience both in the field of sociology and research to not only uncover the facts around an admittedly difficult and complex area, but to assist in placing these facts in their total social complex and give them their proper perspective." She was comfortable with the SERS objectivity mission because objectivity was a component of social science research. "I gathered that this approach is rather new for a newspaper where the editorials occupy a respected and important role," she noted. *Southern School News* "was not, as the social scientist puts it, going to deal in value judgments." Valien used data to draw conclusions about *Brown* and civil rights. "This is, in my opinion, the proper role and I like to believe, responsibility, of a citizen actively interested in preserving our democratic way of life," she said, affirming her obligation to obey the law as set forth by the U.S. Supreme Court. "It is my further conviction that those of us who do believe in democracy must not remain silent; we must not fear—for fear and freedom cannot live in the same community on equal terms." In conclusion, she hoped "the Service, in its attempt to escape criticism, will not in the process destroy something which is in my opinion even more important and vital to our society, one of the fundamental tenets of our democracy—freedom of speech."[95]

Valien sent the letter just days before she addressed the Founder's Day celebration of the Nashville Chapter of the National Council of Negro Women (NCNW).[96] The title of her speech, "The Challenge of Desegregation," piqued interest among the SERS's white leadership because the reporting service archive contains a detailed, unsigned memo summarizing the NCNW program and Valien's remarks, paying particular attention to how Valien described her affiliation with the SERS and her opinions about civil rights. The memo reported that Valien was introduced as a "social science consultant" to the SERS and "chairman of the local [NCNW] chapter's citizenship education committee." Valien reportedly opened with "a declaration of independence," that "in no way was she representing SERS . . . that the organization deals in fact and never in forming opinions. At least two times, she said she was not representing SERS . . . but would be speaking as a citizen." The memo estimated the audience at 150 to 200 people.[97]

In summarizing her argument, the memo said Valien refuted the following claims, which often appeared in the anti-*Brown* arguments of white opponents of desegregation, including members of the SERS board: "(1) That civil rights cannot be legislated; (2) That we are making progress on civil rights front without laws (this wasn't so much a denial as it was a question of how much progress . . . or is it enough); (3) That any action of law in civil rights must be confined to the states; (4) That Negroes aren't ready for desegregation; (5) That Negroes are satisfied with things as they are." The memo summarized Valien's argument in this way: "Human behavior is subject to be controlled by laws . . . why not laws to hinder interference of human liberties; If we have progressed, it is not far enough . . . we still have much to do; States Righters don't want anybody to do anything about improving civil rights; Any Negro not wanting first class citizenship in America, is certainly not justified in the heritage set for him by his forefathers; We can't afford the luxury of gradualism." Despite Valien's support of *Brown*, the memo reassured gradualists like Dabney, who depicted themselves as "white friends of the Negro," that her tone was not ungrateful, "that she took careful note of the fact that amidst all of the unpleasantness . . . there have been and are people of goodwill."[98]

The memo was framed to address white supremacist talking points as well as Waring's and Workman's suspicions about Valien, but the reporter who gathered the information almost certainly was Black. Either W. H. Shackelford, the *Tennessean*'s Black stringer who received a byline for the column "Happenings among Colored People," or Robert Churchwell, a Black reporter who filed stories from home for the unintegrated *Nashville Banner* newsroom, could have inconspicuously scribbled notes during a speech on a Sunday afternoon in a Black church in Jim Crow Nashville.[99] The memo is a close match for the story published under Churchwell's byline in the *Banner*.[100] It is possible that Churchwell, a Fisk alumnus, was not the author of the memo, that it was prepared by a white employee of the *Banner* using his notes and Churchwell did not know he was conducting surveillance for the SERS. He also may have been following orders, given the memo's attention to how Valien was introduced at the meeting and whether she disassociated her views from the SERS. On that point, the memo stated that the president of the local NCNW chapter referred to Valien as "executive secretary" of the SERS, "a most important and progressive organization."[101] Importantly, Marie Johnson was the chapter president. Charles Johnson might have been less circumspect about the white supremacists on the SERS board if he had known they used a Black journalist to spy on his wife's club meeting.

## Silencing Bonita Valien

Valien flouted Waring's proscription against public comments by addressing the NCNW. When the SERS board convened a week later, Dabney, the white board chair, and Johnson and Young, the two Black directors, were among six members absent. With vice chair Waring presiding, the board took up the Valien matter as its last item of business: "It was agreed by the Board that no restrictions on public remarks could properly be applied to Board members, who draw no compensation, or to correspondents, who work for SERS on a part-time basis. It was also agreed that all persons on the central office payroll should conform to the same rigid yardstick of objectivity that the director has followed in his public remarks, and that the Director should be given final authority over this matter." The constraint on central office employees likely applied only to Valien; if white office workers received invitations to speak about civil rights, the SERS archive is silent. Then, according to minutes so cryptic that anyone not in the room would have had difficulty discerning what had taken place, the board authorized McKnight to remove Valien from the payroll: "There was also a discussion of the most effective manner in which SERS might use the services of research specialists after June 30, 1955. It was the opinion of the Director, concurred in by the Board, that SERS should not be limited to the professional consultation service of any one person but should be free to call upon specialists in all fields who may be available at Peabody College, Vanderbilt, Fisk and other universities in the Nashville area."[102]

Astonishingly, Johnson was not informed that SERS leadership had a problem with his former research associate, a courtesy that a white board member would have expected, and did not know that Valien's contract would not be renewed until he was copied on a letter to Valien three months after the board meeting.[103] In fact, Dabney neglected to mention this item of business when he briefed Johnson on action the board had taken in his absence in March.[104] Although Dabney also did not attend the quarterly meeting, he knew of Waring's displeasure with the Boston speech and the controversy about Valien working in the SERS headquarters. As chair he knew that action was taken against an employee and that Johnson had direct interest in Valien's work.

Upon learning in June that Valien had been dismissed, Johnson directed his first reaction, which was tempered but strong, to Coombs at the FAE in New York and followed with letters to Dabney and Shoemaker. Johnson reviewed the history of Valien's involvement in the project, noting that she was the second person hired, after McKnight. "For whatever reason of expediency, Mrs. Valien . . . who is a capable sociologist and worker with seven years of experience in handling the prototype of this journal and service, has not over the entire life of the program been permitted to work in the office of the organization," with her work "carried on—inconveniently and somewhat incongruously—in her home." Johnson noted that Fisk University's *Monthly Summary* targeted the same audience as *Southern School News* and achieved a higher circulation of fifteen thousand. "I have only recently learned that she has been receiving a salary less than her academic post would provide, and has none of the clerical or other facilities of the central office," he wrote.[105]

Johnson's central argument analyzed the impact of racial exclusion on the SERS's objectivity mission, a concept the white southerners were not willing to consider. "It would have been a logical expectation," he wrote, "in a regional situation such as ours involving dual racial orientations, to insure objectivity by using white and Negro reporters, with both subject to editorial balancing." Instead, Johnson noted the SERS's decision to use only white reporters from the daily press and described Valien's hiring as a "corrective mechanism." Although she was not a journalist, Valien's participation had provided "access to a world of Negro-white action, attitude, and opinion, which the average white reporter, however competent, has had no particular occasion and opportunity to develop." Johnson appealed directly to the SERS mission in tying Black participation to the objectivity of *Southern School News*' content and argued that "the provision of such a safeguard against oversights or limited views could give assurance of truly 'objective' intent." He signaled that the unintegrated reporting staff had compromised SERS credibility in the Black community. "As a member of the Board, I am finding it increasingly difficult to explain why and how it is possible to report accurately on bi-racial developments with only a uni-racial perspective," Johnson wrote. "Even the best of possible uni-racial reports are suspect and do an injustice to the fine work actually being done by the present reporters."[106]

Dabney ignored Johnson's detailed concerns about race and objectivity and denied responsibility for the board's action against Valien. "Like you, I was unable to get to the March meeting of the board," he replied. "It was then that the matter was discussed and a decision concerning it was reached." Dabney quoted from the March minutes and noted that Shoemaker planned to occasionally use Valien as a consultant and that the SERS would "retain other scholarly Negroes in similar capacities, and thus to benefit from their experience and wisdom," but Dabney left untouched the issues of the all-white staff and the fundamental obstacle of SERS's adherence to Jim Crow.[107] Johnson addressed similar concerns in his letter to Shoemaker, who had just stepped into the executive directorship, about the SERS moving forward without a Black perspective. "It is true there are two Negro members on the Board but their contact with actual operations is slight and infrequent," Johnson wrote. "The Board meetings, with obvious differences in personal orientation on the issue of school desegregation have operated in a spirit of broad tolerance and agreement, with 'objectivity' as the central control. Some semblance of this on the staff, it seems, would present no greater difficulties of operation."[108] Dabney and Shoemaker discussed the matter between themselves—on the phone and in a confidential letter that Shoemaker agreed to withhold from the SERS files.

That letter set down Shoemaker's impressions from a meeting with Johnson and conversations with white board members. "You are doubtless aware that the Valien business was a cross to Pete [McKnight]—as it may become to me," Shoemaker wrote, confirming that "the original request for this project came," not from Harry Ashmore, as the SERS had claimed, but "from a Negro group and that the group assumed Mrs. Valien would be a continuing part of the project." Shoemaker was impressed by Valien's work, offered her severance pay and a bonus, and reimbursed Fisk for her clerical support and supplies. Although Valien had "violated our strict injunction to all central office workers—that they take no sides in discussing this question and remain otherwise discreet," Shoemaker acknowledged that Valien had not been treated fairly. "Hindsight judgment suggests that if she had been able to work out of the central office as a staff member with quarters here the impulse to sound off might have been contained," he wrote. None of the white SERS leaders ever clarified why central office staff should be held to a higher standard of nonpartisanship than board members or correspondents.[109]

Shoemaker confirmed that the white editors of the two daily newspapers in Nashville, the *Tennessean* and the *Banner*, had insisted as board members that the SERS enforce Jim Crow. "Both Colie [Harwell] and Charlie [Moss] felt this was impossible from the start because of local opinion," Shoemaker wrote. "Dr. Johnson pointed out to me some groups here, notably Methodist Publishing House, which employ Negroes on administrative levels. But I defer to their judgment as the two persons best able to assay public opinion—and the two most to be affected by Nashville opinions if we erred." Jim Crow offered an easy rationalization for the SERS's racial double standard. "Personally, I would be quite amenable to a resident Negro assistant, though finding office space for one would be another problem," Shoemaker said. His candor documented that SERS leaders understood the request for racial equity in SERS operations and rejected it. "What is really at heart is the feeling of Negroes that this should be a bi-racial staff," he wrote. "Dr. Johnson is under some pressure to make it just that, I am sure. This pressure is emotional rather than logical. Dr. Johnson however argues the latter position," that a Black administrative employee would "give us an extra dimension in making assignments for our state reports and in other matters. He of course has a point. Such a Negro person obviously would not be Mrs. Valien."[110]

Shoemaker noted that the *Nashville Banner* would lend Robert Churchwell to the SERS as needed. "Of course, this isn't what the pressure people want—they want a bi-racial staff," he wrote. "I have not discussed this Negro reporter with Dr. Johnson. He seems content to let matters rock along for the immediate present." The blowback from the Valien firing was not over, however. "Dr. Johnson hinted that the Negro press might open up on us (which I do not fear) and he said it was his method not to resign from boards or groups abruptly upon some disagreement but to strive to make his point within the organization," Shoemaker wrote. "You can see from this that he will not let the matter drop. I rather think I put the burden on him, however, to introduce alternatives."[111]

Dabney described Johnson as "basically a reasonable person, and while he is doubtless under pressure from more extreme elements, he will be as cooperative as he can, under the circumstances." He cautioned Shoemaker "to proceed carefully and not get out on any limbs. . . . We can't let ourselves be bums rushed into putting in a bi-racial staff, if that seems contrary to the best interests of SERS. It might be particularly serious in the Deep South. I feel much as you do as to this, and wouldn't personally be at all upset if we had a qualified Negro or two in the central office. At the same time, it is important not to antagonize local sentiment." Dabney's opposition to an integrated SERS staff demonstrates that the organization's definition of objectivity was anything but ideologically neutral and in fact was bent to accommodate the social and legal requirements of Jim Crow. "I hope we can get by with our present policy without invoking the wrath of the Negro press," he wrote, naively. "I'd like to avoid any sort of open run-in with either the integrationists or the segregationists."[112]

## "The Wrath of the Negro Press"

In 1942, when Virginius Dabney lambasted the Black press in the *Atlantic Monthly*, he singled out P. B. Young Sr. as a moderate Black editor and his *Norfolk Journal and Guide* as "one of the sanest and best-edited newspapers in the United States."[113] At the time Young deflected Dabney's praise, comparing him to southern demagogues, "with the difference that their language is always coarse and their attitude brutal, while your language is always cultured and your attitude dignified. The result is the same."[114] Dabney had approved of Young and his newspaper in the 1940s because they followed the accommodationist racial approach inspired by Booker T. Washington and hesitated to align with racial progressives, for many years acquiescing to gradualism.[115] By 1954, when they found themselves serving on the SERS board, Dabney as chair and Young as a relatively powerless token Black director, the civil rights movement had advanced, clarifying the stakes for white and Black southerners and narrowing the field for compromise. Young was now among southern Black moderates who believed they had waited long enough.

The Valien controversy alarmed Johnson, but he was committed to the civil rights long game, and as a social scientist and university president, he chose to navigate the overt and subtle racism on display in the SERS in hopes of producing change within a prominent organization.[116] He also believed in objectivity as a component of the scientific method. Young, however, grew more and more troubled by the white South's hardening response to *Brown*, including the white editorial voices who portrayed Black civil rights as an existential threat and the *Brown* decision as unconstitutional. He struggled to collaborate with white members of the SERS board whose racism was now on full display. For Young, the Valien dismissal was a breach of faith, a violation of the rules of fair play even within the construct of Jim Crow. When Johnson forwarded his correspondence about the Valien situation, it was Young's first intimation of what had transpired and seemed to crystallize his disillusionment with the SERS, if not with white institutions generally. Over the next eight months Young wrestled with his conscience and sense of duty, resigning from the board twice in the autumn of 1955 before finalizing his departure in March 1956. Young's rejection of the SERS's objectivity premise is a profound yet underappreciated moment in the organization's history.[117]

Young wrote Dabney to protest Valien's dismissal and the news that during her brief tenure with the SERS she had been required to work from home. Young tied this slight to the ideological orientation of the SERS leadership and its failure to honor its objectivity mission. Young did not expect participation in the SERS to change the racial politics of white board members, "but knowing that there is such a thing as restraint in light of one's association with something that is supposed to be impartial and objective, I felt that this body would be influenced by that circumstance," he wrote. "I am aware that the Service was not set up to end segregation, but neither was it set up to practice it or to promote segregation." With Valien's departure, "there is now no Negro in a position to make any contribution to the purposes of the service," noting that for "the two minority members on the board . . . there is slight opportunity for them to have anything to do with policy making or the actual operations of the body."[118] Young incorporated these points into a frank, private letter to Johnson, which expounded on his disillusionment. He acknowledged being lobbied to resign from the board by Black citizens who read the editorial pages of white board members and were surprised that Young associated with them. "The questions flowing from the Supreme Court's decision have not been treated objectively by either the chairman or vice-chairman," Young wrote. "It has been difficult to reconcile the stated purpose of the Southern Education Reporting Service, to give the country an objective analysis of developments, when it has been so obvious that important members of the board were biased."[119]

Young first resigned on September 1, 1955, but withdrew the letter after a telephone call from Dabney. Young had objected to the southern white press's defiance of the *Brown* ruling, "encouraged to a very large degree by a considerable majority of the members of the board who have daily newspaper connections." He believed he was obligated to abide by the Supreme Court ruling. "I am, therefore, so much out of line with a large majority of the board that the association has ceased to be pleasant." When white board members fomented "open revolt against the government's highest judicial tribunal, I do not think this can be dissociated in the public mind from the board itself." He also noted that "in many influential quarters my identification with the board has been misunderstood, to my detriment."[120] In withdrawing his resignation two days later at Dabney's urging, Young explained that "my resignation at this time might cause some misunderstandings, and although my mind is right much disturbed about the matters I discussed with you, I would not like to take any step that would injure the cause."[121]

Johnson was relieved to learn that Young had withdrawn his resignation. Acknowledging that the white board members' views were opposed to theirs, Johnson explained that he still believed in the SERS mission because of "the possibility and the reality of keeping the Reporting Service itself objective and unbiased in either direction. I have had confidence enough in the underlying direction of public conscience and morality to rest the case of objectivity with the transcendency of our constitutional principles." Countering Young's concern for the editorial positions of segregationists on the board, Johnson wrote that those members "have a right to their private views so long as they do not attempt to impose them on the public through this medium and in opposition to what is now the supreme law of the land. It would be far better for both of us to stay on the board and meet these issues at the source of policy making." Johnson said he did not detect bias in *Southern School News*: ". . . The facts have been reported without slanting and prejudicial coloration. My faith is in the facts themselves."[122]

In October, Young reinstated his resignation but the following month withdrew it after Dabney and Shoemaker visited him in Norfolk. As white resistance to *Brown* intensified and it became clear that Dabney was no longer a moderate on desegregation, Young took the editorial stands of the *Richmond Times-Dispatch* personally.[123] When Young mailed Dabney his second resignation, detailed in two letters sent the same day, he was distraught that Dabney's paper, wielding influence from Virginia's capital, was solidifying white resistance in Young's home state. The immediate sources of his distress were a pro-segregation column that, among other complaints, stereotyped Black Virginians as promiscuous and a lengthy *Times-Dispatch* editorial that opposed the *Brown* ruling as an unconstitutional encroachment on states' rights and local autonomy.[124] "You indicated clearly that you do not respect either the dignity or legal rights of Negroes," Young wrote.[125] He sent a stronger letter of resignation that same day, drawing attention to the nonpartisan mission of the SERS, which was "negated by the violent support of segregation and all that it stands for by some members of the board." He then expanded his criticism of the *Times-Dispatch* editorial, which he described as "the most deliberate and calculated distortion of the Supreme Court's decision, and the strongest appeal to race prejudice, that I have seen in many a year." Young underscored the incongruity between the objectivity mission of the SERS and the racism he saw in Dabney's newspaper: "When the chairman of the board takes the extreme position expressed in your editorial of the 25th, it raises serious questions in the minds of people who are unable, for the most part, to draw the fine distinction between Mr. Dabney, the chairman, and Mr. Dabney, the editor."[126]

Shoemaker, still new in his job, was alarmed when he saw the letters. "At this very critical stage, the success of the project in Nashville depends heavily upon the unity of our board," he responded and arranged to meet Young in Norfolk.[127] Dabney also wrote to Young that he had "seriously misinterpreted the Times-Dispatch editorial and column to which you refer in your letter. Furthermore, if I may say so, it appears to me that you have confused two entirely separate and unrelated issues." The racial attitudes of board members had no bearing on the objectivity of the SERS and *Southern School News*, Dabney wrote, condescendingly suggesting that Young had overreacted: "Is it possible that you still see these two matters in the same light as when you wrote me on October 25?"[128]

After the visit in Norfolk, Dabney thanked Young for again rescinding his resignation: "Had you not done so, I am frank to say that the whole future of the enterprise would have been jeopardized."[129] Young in turn acknowledged his intention to remain on the board and noted that the *Times-Dispatch* quoted the advice of Percy Greene, Black editor of the *Jackson Advocate* in Mississippi: "No solution can be found to the race problem . . . in an atmosphere of vituperation, vindictiveness, finger-pointing, name-calling and the threat of retaliation."[130] Dabney and Shoemaker agreed to keep Young's resignation letters and their correspondence about him in their private files. In briefing McKnight, Dabney dismissed Young's concern about the ideological makeup of the board and blamed other factors. "He not only withdrew it, but promised not to do it again," Dabney wrote. "The old gentleman is discouraged and upset over the course of events in the South, and specifically in Virginia and North Carolina. He feels that he has put in fifty years trying to bring about better relations, and that he and those like him seem to have accomplished very little." In Virginia decisions about schools were now made entirely by whites and Young was no longer being consulted: "He is quite emotional over the issue of segregation, although his emotion does not often appear on the surface. He exploded in the two letters of resignation, and was obviously emotionally moved at certain points in our conversation."[131] Dabney's insight into Young's anguish and disillusionment produced no empathy for how Young felt sitting in meetings with white supremacists.

Having dispensed with Young's complaints, Dabney was blindsided four months later when Young again withdrew from the board.[132] This time, Young resigned by telegram and Dabney was in no mood to cajole after the time and energy he had devoted to securing Young's promise "not to do it again."[133] Young declined to attend the board's March 1956 meeting. "After reading the hysterical and grossly unfair editorial in the March 13th issue of the Nashville Banner and similar editorials in other papers whose editors are on the board I believe that the spirit of moderation in the consideration of Negroes' constitutional guarantees has departed and a majority of the board reflects the mind of the nullificationists and discriminationists," Young's telegram stated. "The references in these editorials to the NAACP are false and vicious and reflect both a lack of fairness and sportsmanship. The objectivity which characterizes the Southern School News . . . is polluted in part with racists with antebellum ideas who would drive the nation into another civil war."[134] The referenced *Banner* editorial applauded southern congressmen who had signed the Declaration of Constitutional Principles, known as the Southern Manifesto, in opposition to desegregation.[135]

Dabney responded with a strident telegram of his own, asserting that Young had "severed [his] relationship with organization which seems to be hitting peak of usefulness." Noting that coverage in the white press had been favorable, including a feature in *Look* magazine, Dabney emphasized that the SERS had just received one of the 1956 Russwurm Awards from the National Newspaper Publishers Association, a Black organization, for its contribution to democracy. Dabney also noted that Young's son Thomas was a member of the association's board and rejected Young's concern about the racial ideology of SERS board members. "You will recall board was chosen deliberately to represent varying and contrasting points of view on segregation," Dabney replied. "Hence it does not seem valid to say, as you do, that some board members have taken a position on this question which you find highly distasteful." Dabney made no allowance for the increased stridency on many white editorial pages since *Brown*. He also emphasized that Johnson continued to support the SERS, though he overstated Johnson's position by characterizing him as an "enthusiastic member of the board." In the draft of his telegram, Dabney crossed out "Sincerely yours" in the closing.[136] Young wrote Dabney once more, noting that he had not disputed the objectivity of *Southern School News*. "I do not relish being a member of a group which places me in a hostile climate," he wrote, noting that McKnight was the only white editor who had seemed willing to let the courts identify solutions. "All of them deliberately misrepresent the NAACP," portraying it among "lawless, subversive groups, uninvited and unauthorized to legally represent Negroes in the courts."[137]

This time Dabney and Shoemaker moved on quickly, deleting Young's name from the *Southern School News* masthead lest he "get upset all over again," and naively endeavored to fill Young's token seat on the board with another Black editor.[138] The Black press, meanwhile, took offense on Young's behalf. Dabney's archive contains clippings from the *Baltimore Afro-American*, quoting Young's resignation telegram, and from Young's own paper, quoting NAACP leader Roy Wilkins, who praised Young for resigning: "This marks one of the few significant times in America when one of our men in a key position refused to remain as window dressing for something that he couldn't stomach." In a clipping from *Jet*, Simeon Booker said Johnson also was being encouraged to resign.[139] Young's career as a competent editor and moderate conservative would stymie the effort to replace him with a representative of the Black press. "The *Journal & Guide* is far and away the best and most reputable paper in the South," Shoemaker wrote Dabney, noting that Johnson had discouraged him from pursuing a stunningly insensitive proposal to invite one of Young's family remembers to replace him on the SERS board. Although Johnson was being consulted, this was a white decision. "It seems to me that the board members attending ASNE could caucus over a highball somewhere and pretty well settle the thing," Shoemaker suggested.[140]

First to decline the SERS's invitation to fill Young's seat was Dr. Charles Thompson of Howard University, editor of the *Journal of Negro Education*. Thompson had been Harry Ashmore's host at the predominantly Black conference at Howard in 1952, when Ashmore was less than gracious.[141] After receiving Dabney's inquiry about board membership, Thompson posed several questions about the ideological composition of the board with regard to the issue of segregation and questioned the objectivity of an organization with such strong representation from anti-integration editors. Thompson said Young had always taken "a middle-of-the-road position in general and in interracial matters in particular." As a result, Thompson found it disturbing that Young "felt it necessary to resign from the Board . . . because he thinks the present composition of the Board is so heavily and actively pro-segregation in its attitude that it must inevitably affect policy. I do not know all of the facts, but I do know Mr. Young. He would not take such a step inconsiderately." Thompson asked for Dabney's version of events and sought clarification of Dabney's assertion that the board was "set up to represent various points of view on the segregation issue."[142]

In reporting to Waring that Thompson would not accept nomination to the board, Dabney portrayed Thompson as a bad fit for the SERS: "His reason, he says, is the Southern School News 'gives as much space to the sinners as it does to the saints.' I gather that he means we give full attention to the doings of the Citizens Councils and other anti-integrationists agencies [sic]. He seems to think we ought to play them down and play up the pro-integrationists. This, of course, is journalistically impossible, given the basis on which we are operating. So, he is out of the picture."[143] Waring wondered, however, whether an integrated board benefited SERS beyond impressing its contacts at the Fund for the Advancement of Education. "What if the SERS board should become segregated?" he wrote to Dabney. "Would we lose our source of income? Otherwise I would not weep. Journalistic integrity means more to me than representation of the rainbow."[144] Thompson's concerns were in line with criticism of the SERS that circulated in the Black press. Indeed, in an editorial titled "Our Answer Is No," the *Baltimore Afro-American* urged prominent Black men to decline service on the SERS board:

> If you were asked to accept appointment to the board of the Southern School News, what would be your answer?
> Our answer would be no.
> The Southern School News is the official publication of the Southern Education Reporting Service, which professes to be "an objective, fact-finding agency," designed to provide "accurate, unbiased information" on developments arising from the Supreme Court's decision.
> Dominating its board are some of the most rabid, inflammatory and bitter end racists of Southern journalism.

> Many of them pay open homage to the White Citizens Councils and are firmly dedicated to an unyielding attitude toward equality.
> No self-respecting and decent person would want to sit on the board or associate with them.
> The very fact that P.B. Young, president of the Norfolk Journal and Guide, resigned his position because he simply couldn't stomach their company, is reason enough for us to answer in the negative.[145]

Johnson suggested the SERS next pursue Claude Barnett, editor of the Associated Negro Press, with whom Johnson had proposed the "Minority View" column project at the end of World War II. Dabney and other southern white editors had declined to publish those columns then, and now Dabney wanted Barnett's cooperation. Barnett also declined to serve, citing time constraints, but not before consulting privately with Johnson.[146] "I read P.B. Young's letter of resignation and protest," Barnett wrote. "I must live with newspaper people as well as a section of the public." He worried that "if one as conservative as P.B. felt impelled to resign and assail the group, the taking of his place would find little favor." Barnett distinguished his own position from Johnson's: "It is far better to have someone like yourself working with these people where you have a chance to help mold their thinking, but . . . I doubt whether I should poke my head into an apparently highly controversial situation."[147]

In his reply to Barnett, Johnson said he respected Young's decision but explained why he was not bowing to pressure from the *Baltimore Afro-American* and other critics to resign as well. Johnson had known Barnett was unlikely to accept. "In a sense, it would be as difficult for you to come on the governing board as it would be in good conscience for me to get off," Johnson wrote, explaining that his SERS involvement allowed him to influence white opinion. "If anything at all, I am a sociologist with a conscience about factual rectitude and a conscience about keeping the channels of communication open in an increasingly tense situation, that normally would result only in a wide breach and ineffectual counter argument." The SERS board gave him access to segregationists: "I felt it important to do my fighting in the council chamber where policy is made, and where, if I cannot affect the most extreme member of the council, I can at least influence, with incontrovertible fact, the opinions of others." Johnson also believed *Southern School News* enlightened thousands of people in its audience and said it would be "something approaching the desertion of an ideal to withdraw from this opportunity." Johnson wished "a distinction could be made in this historic struggle for integration between strategy and tactics," and said he would not resign unless the situation became hopeless. For the time being, there was "room enough within our grand strategy of complete integration and democracy to require, in fact, demand more than one local strategy."[148]

Shoemaker valued Johnson's reasoned influence and reminded Dabney that SERS "would really be in a pickle if he should pull out."[149] After the Black press attacked Johnson for remaining with the SERS, Dabney sought to bolster his commitment and assure him that his "presence on the board is a virtual guarantee to fair-minded persons of both races that the Southern Education Reporting Service and Southern School News are still objective and factual."[150] This was an interesting argument for the SERS chair to make, given Shoemaker's insistence to Booker that "we do not regard a man's race as an index to his objectivity." In worrying about replacing Young, Shoemaker spun the issue as "a personality dilemma—Mr. Young's own standing within his group," not the result of the white board members' overt ideology, and claimed Young had misunderstood objectivity.[151] When Waring weighed in on the lingering issue of Young's vacant seat, he declined to see a problem. "Maybe SERS will have to worry along with white people in charge. I can think of a worse fate," he wrote.[152]

Dabney and Shoemaker explained away Young's criticisms as unreasonable and even racist. "I'm afraid he just up and hates white folks," Shoemaker wrote to Waring.[153] When Young editorialized against the *Richmond Times-Dispatch* and mentioned that Dabney was chairman of the SERS, "which is supposed to be objective, but which is not because of its officials' association with active nullificationists and interpositionists," Shoemaker dismissed Young as "feeding on his own bitterness."[154] In describing the *Journal and Guide* editorial to Waring, Dabney concluded that "P.B. Young has gone off his rocker still further."[155] As Shoemaker wondered whether to ask Young to desist, an odd idea given their dismissal of Young's objections to editorials in white newspapers, Dabney said writing Young would not be effective. "I'm afraid I've given up PBY as a bad job," Dabney said. "It seems to me that he has thought this over carefully and deliberately, and has decided to do us the maximum amount of damage that he possibly can."[156]

When Johnson died unexpectedly in October 1956, both seats designated for Black members were then vacant. Shoemaker and white board member Coleman Harwell of the *Nashville Tennessean* attended Johnson's funeral, which Shoemaker described as "the kind of funeral accorded a statesman, which of course he was—and this impresses one more and more." Shoemaker was already anticipating a replacement for Johnson and scouted the memorial service, which was attended by prominent Black professionals.[157] Within a month of Johnson's death, the SERS board had secured a commitment from George Redd, a dean at Fisk.[158] Waring, who was engaged in a fierce editorial campaign to link desegregation and communism, said he hoped "his name has no political significance."[159] The following spring, Redd was joined on the SERS board by Dr. Luther Foster, president of Tuskegee Institute.[160]

## Conclusion

The claim to objectivity offered white southern editors a professionally sanctioned means of controlling the race story, primarily by restricting who was allowed to tell it. In the moment, white SERS leaders ignored this criticism, made clearly and repeatedly by Black observers, because it contradicted the racial commonsense of white southern journalism. By declaring that reporting in *Southern School News* would be nonpartisan, even if it followed the most simplistic and rudimentary definition of objectivity, the SERS shrouded itself in a myth of racial and regional neutrality, a mere observer on the sidelines of a historic moment. Clearly, however, the SERS had been designed precisely to shape the journalistic narrative. In founding the SERS, white southerners persuaded themselves that objectivity made the reporting service professionally virtuous, but coming as a response to *Brown*, the SERS embodied both political engagement and political resistance. And it was successful in at least one respect: the absence of public controversy over *Southern School News* content suggests that it left the status quo unchallenged. Ironically, the white founders imagined the SERS as an antidote for alarmist and sensational reporting by the northern press, but as the civil rights movement wore on and the daily papers of the South grew more racially intransigent, their own news and editorial pages begged for the SERS's factual counterpoint. Editor Young certainly thought so.

At midcentury, the segregation of American journalism was taken for granted, a norm that the SERS's white founders did not expect to defend. They knew Black journalists would tell a different story, which is why it was important to discredit and exclude them; however, as Johnson, Young, Valien, Booker, and others argued, accurate and objective reporting about *Brown* and the civil rights movement could not be achieved by a monoracial staff. Historian Douglas O. Cumming noted the paradox that the SERS "managed to denature one of the most dramatic news stories of the century. Part of what its 'objectivity' filtered out was the passion of the black experience, black perspective, and black anger that the mainstream press had so long misread."[161] Cumming saw this as incidental to the objectivity process, but this counternarrative, which ascribes political motive to the white leaders of the SERS, argues that using objectivity to erase the Black perspective was precisely the point. Dabney, Waring, and Shoemaker shrank from the South's most significant moral challenge since the Civil War and aligned their journalism with the segregationist cause.

Dabney's attacks on the Black press in World War II set a baseline of sorts, when he held up the accommodationist *Norfolk Journal and Guide* as an exemplar for other Black newspapers to follow. After the *Brown* decision, when it was clear that Young viewed the Supreme Court ruling as a legal mandate and the payoff for his life's work, Dabney invoked the SERS objectivity framework to discredit Young as doddering, confused, and emotionally unstable. Dabney's callous treatment of Young, after Young disclosed his anguish over white southern resistance to the *Brown* decision, proved Young's point, that SERS board service placed him in a racially hostile environment. Moreover, Dabney was disingenuous in arguing that the professional standard of objectivity required Young to tolerate the flagrant white supremacy then apparent on the editorial pages of white board members. When Young and Johnson agreed to serve in 1954, most white editorial pages were taking a wait-and-see approach, as Harry Ashmore documented following publication of *The Negro and the Schools*. Young and Johnson did not sign on to commune with editors who expressed the unvarnished racism that a year later dominated the editorial pages of the *Nashville Banner*, *Richmond Times-Dispatch*, and Charleston *News and Courier*.

When Young decided that "he simply couldn't stomach" serving alongside "some of the most rabid, inflammatory and bitter end racists of Southern journalism," the *Baltimore Afro-American* honored Young's resignation and drew a boundary that would discourage other prominent Black men from taking his place: "No self-respecting and decent person would want to sit on the board or associate with them."[162] That summer Shoemaker doubled down on the objectivity claim. In dismissing Young's criticisms as racial self-interest, Shoemaker said mixed audiences for his own speeches had questioned the SERS's neutrality claim: "On several occasions recently I have taken a pounding during the question period from people—Negroes, almost without exception—who can't understand why we are not advocates. That, I think, really sums up Mr. Young's situation."[163]

Young's resignation exposed the structural racism of the SERS, but the real hero was Valien, who was in her early thirties when the *Brown* ruling arrived. Her letter to McKnight and speech to the Nashville women's club, both of which had professional consequences, were acts of courage. As a young sociologist enacting her democratic convictions with confidence in her academic training, Valien did not equivocate when the SERS moved to silence her. Conversely, Coombs, McKnight, and Shoemaker all valued her work, but all acquiesced to her mistreatment by white supremacists Waring, Workman, and Moss.

Johnson, who had a standing relationship with the Ford Foundation, had a clear reason to be involved with SERS but he may have idealized his own participation. He was a busy college president who often missed board meetings. Wielding the influence he imagined for himself would have required being present and continually pressing the case for *Brown*'s implementation and integration of the SERS staff. When he theorized the value of his SERS board service in letters to Young and Barnett, he did so as a passive director whose other obligations prevented him from being routinely engaged, creating a vacuum in oversight of the white supremacists running the SERS across town in Nashville. Although Dabney and McKnight took steps to conceal Waring's and Moss's campaign against Valien in 1955, it seems curious that Johnson was blindsided by Valien's firing. When he learned of the decision in June, he thought the board had acted at the quarterly meeting he missed earlier that month, when in fact the firing had occurred three months earlier.[164] It was old news when McKnight sent Valien the dismissal letter, copied to Johnson as McKnight was wrapping up loose ends at the end of his contract.

The white SERS leaders misunderstood Johnson, who approached the SERS as a world-renowned sociologist and university president. He strongly opposed segregation yet white board members mistook him for an accommodationist; his detachment was a professional pose, which they misread as acquiescence to the racial inequity that defined the SERS. Letters between Dabney and Shoemaker document that they valued Johnson's logical approach, which was far easier to engage than Young's visceral reactions to the content of segregationist newspapers. They minimized Johnson's concerns about the biracial staff and assumed his views reflected pressure from "extremists" in the Black press, not a reasoned position Johnson arrived at himself. Although they feared a backlash in the Black community if he should resign, they ignored his objections to the Valien situation, which also was a professional snub that no white director would have confronted. In their dealings with Johnson, Shoemaker and Dabney repeatedly affirmed their commitment to the racial status quo and the SERS's role in that racial project. They also declined to see a moral dimension to the segregation question.

When Johnson died in 1956, Massive Resistance had gained momentum, affirming the civil rights movement as a broad contest between good and evil. The lingering issue of the SERS's monoracial reporting staff was important to Johnson, but he was not likely to divert his focus to a local, micro issue, given the stakes. Six months after Young's final resignation from the SERS board and a month before his death, Johnson published an opinion piece in the *New York Times Magazine* describing the national crisis over segregation as a moral contest that threatened an American creed based on "voluntary cooperation in a democratic process that respects the dignity and rights of individuals." Aligning with Valien and Young, Johnson acknowledged *Brown* as a legal mandate and asserted his faith in court-ordered reform. "The really critical problem of the present . . . is the confusion of the moral imperatives of this issue with the tired policy of moderation, our middle-of-the-road philosophy," he wrote. "Whatever the personal sentiment, there can be no middle-of-the-road attitude toward morality or legality, if the fabric of our society is to remain inviolate."[165] Dabney and the other editor board members should have seen themselves in this argument, but Johnson's death relieved them of the obligation to respond.

AFTERWORD

# "THE BIRTH OF A NOTION"

This history of weaponized journalism standards ends where it began, with Don Shoemaker proselytizing that the white southern rubric of objectivity produced neutral, nonpartisan reporting on race, that moral equivalency on two sides of the segregation question ensured the integrity of the civil rights–era news report. The archive of Shoemaker's career in journalism preserves speeches he made in the 1950s as executive director of the Southern Education Reporting Service (SERS), a Jim Crow organization that excluded Black journalists and researchers even after the U.S. Supreme Court, in *Brown v. Board of Education*, declared compulsory segregation unconstitutional.[1] Brandishing objectivity, Shoemaker and many of his contemporaries in the white southern press discredited northern and Black reporting as biased while valorizing their own journalism as the professional standard. For these editors and many white southern readers of the 1940s and 1950s, civil rights gains in the federal courts and by executive order portended a racial apocalypse that would dismantle the Black subordination that defined white rights and privileges. White southerners like Shoemaker, who did not see a moral imperative in the *Brown* decision, or white resistance as illogical or undemocratic, wielded journalism standards to control the news narrative on race and defend the status quo.

Although shrouded in journalism principles, their primary loyalties were to pigment and the southern way of life, an ethos grounded in the history of white supremacy and imbricated into popular culture by social practice and the mass media. In remarks to the Georgia Press Institute in 1956, promoting SERS coverage of school desegregation, Shoemaker inadvertently dropped his pretense of neutrality by activating one of the twentieth century's most poignantly racist discourses about Negrophobia. In an intentional and revealing pun, Shoemaker described the founding of the SERS two years earlier, with its objectivity mission and claim to racial impartiality, as "the birth of a notion," a reference to D. W. Griffith's *The Birth of a Nation,* the 1915 silent film based on Thomas Dixon Jr.'s stunningly racist novel *The Clansman*—works that portrayed emancipation as a threat to white civilization, particularly to white womanhood, and sought to justify Jim Crow segregation and lynching as social control and patriotic expressions of states' rights.[2] Emphasizing the political context, scholar George M. Fredrickson described Dixon's narratives as "intensified . . . efforts to demonstrate the bestial propensities of the blacks," portraying them as "bad enough to deserve what they got."[3] *The Birth of a Nation* glorified the Ku Klux Klan, whose on-screen terrorism of the film's Blackface characters protected white feminine virtue and restored social order. Indeed, historians have linked the film's release to race riots instigated by whites, a wave of lynchings, and a resurgence of the Klan—what John Egerton called "the torch that lit the cross."[4] The film's racism registered as so vile and outlandish even in the second decade of the twentieth century that the early NAACP protested the film's disparagement of Black Americans and encouraged theater boycotts.[5]

The audience at a white-press gathering in the mid-1950s tolerated the racial humor in Shoemaker's comment, although they might have been less comfortable with it a decade later, after the civil rights movement had made jokes about racism less acceptable. Even in 1956, however, an editor of Shoemaker's ken would have known that the NAACP, the Black press, and white progressives had opposed Griffith's film and other racist entertainment, such as the popular but controversial *Amos 'n' Andy* radio and television programs.[6] Moreover, in 1950 the silent *Birth of a Nation* was re-released with audio, reigniting protest by the NAACP.[7] White southern newspapermen of Shoemaker's generation also may have known that in response to *Brown,* some of the most strident opponents of desegregation were again offering the film as a cautionary tale about civil rights and "racial mixing." Historian Pete Daniel found that the Ku Klux Klan used *Birth* to recruit new members in the 1950s.[8] And when Shoemaker addressed the Georgia Press Institute in 1956, he knew that young Emmett Till had been lynched six months earlier, allegedly for "wolf-whistling," itself a racially freighted term, at a white woman.[9] Yet in preparing scripted remarks, Shoemaker chose "the birth of a notion" to frame the objectivity initiative's founding.

Although unremarkable during a public talk to a white southern audience in 1956, Shoemaker's choice of pun shows that the politics of racial identity were not truly absent from his discussion of civil rights–era objectivity, even one that was ostensibly race-neutral and whose topic was journalistic neutrality about race. Because of the shared experience of being white in America, the prevalence of racialized public memory, and the timelessness of media products like Dixon's films and novels, Shoemaker could count on a white southern audience in 1956 to understand his reference to *The Birth of a Nation,* even four decades after the film's debut in theaters—or whenever his script for that speech would be discovered in his archive.

This public address and others like it were affirmations of the white prerogative. In the context of the freedom struggle, when the question of who had the authority to speak was often contested, the act of speechmaking was politically significant. As professional writers, Shoemaker, Thomas Waring, Harry Ashmore, and other white southern editors had routine access to the pages of the white press, where they could publish opinion and manage news reporting on the desegregation conflict; however, their scripted remarks to professional and community organizations constituted sidebar conversations with primarily white audiences in which they framed and contextualized their own journalism and commented on the state of the profession—what scholar Matt Carlson termed "metajournalistic discourse."[10] In the 1950s speeches by white southern editors were both an assertion of journalism norms and a racialized intervention into the white audience's reception of news about civil rights. The racial double standard undergirding the SERS provides evidence that segregationist editors understood public addresses about *Brown* to be racialized performances of authority and professional autonomy. After all, the white speechmakers running the reporting service, who freely discussed their views about Jim Crow in public comments, fired Black sociologist Bonita Valien for sharing her expertise. To silence her, they contrived a defense of objectivity to brand her public remarks and her audiences as subversive. In this context, Shoemaker's pun cannot be dismissed as an innocent aside.

As this analysis has shown, no racial project is a random occurrence or an aberration; a racial project cannot be extracted from the cultural, social, and political conditions that produced it.[11] For that reason,

American journalism's persistence as a segregated institution and the enduring claim that whiteness protected journalism standards have foundational relevance for this book. The American press was, until the later twentieth century at least, bifurcated into a white press and a Black press, serving distinct audiences, supported by racially exclusive wire services and professional associations, and, with few exceptions, employing monoracial newsrooms. The Black press emerged in opposition to racism in the early nineteenth century, coalescing around the abolition movement, but segregation was so baked into American journalism by the twentieth century—so much a matter of commonsense—that few in the white press, always attentive to their own constitutionally protected freedoms and democratic entitlements, recognized the ethical contradiction in journalism's racial exclusions.[12]

In *The Mind of the South*, W. J. Cash was able to see the historical peril in the white southern racial orthodoxy, but most white southern editors of this period lacked the democratic imagination that responding to the freedom struggle required.[13] They could not see, and might not have cared, that their intransigence on the issue of desegregation would once again place the white southern press on the wrong side of history, just as it had a century earlier.[14] Their own normative white supremacy, their dismissal of the Black press as partisan and substandard, and their fixation on the hypocrisy of the northern white press blinded many white southern editors to their own stakes in the inequity and injustice that defined the political moment.[15] For example, the Black press had been documenting northern racism for more than a century, but the logic of white supremacy foreclosed an alliance between the white southern press and Black journalism on this issue of mutual concern. White southern insistence on Black inferiority meant that the white southern press could not regard the Black press as a credible source of information, even when their assessments of northern racism aligned.

Significantly, every historical episode examined in this book finds white southern editors on the defensive over civil rights and deploying journalism standards in a counteroffensive to protect their own racial self-interest. This is a consistent theme running through Virginius Dabney's and Westbrook Pegler's attacks on the Black press during World War II, white southerners' agitation within the Associated Press over racial labeling and news values, and the feigned racial neutrality of the Ashmore Report and the SERS, the two objectivity projects underwritten by the Fund for the Advancement of Education. For segregationists, midcentury journalism was predicated on a belief that Black Americans were unequal to whites and that civil rights gains, rather than moving American society toward the ideal of equality, would come at whites' expense.

Few opponents of *Brown* within the white press ever imagined that separate would or should be equal; their activism was always about maintaining a racial status quo defined by skin color.[16] Their white supremacy marginalized even accomplished Black professionals like editor P. B. Young Sr. of the *Norfolk Journal and Guide*; Claude Barnett, founder of the Associate Negro Press; and Charles S. Johnson, the renowned sociologist who was appointed Fisk University's president in 1946. Despite their education and achievement, decades of moderate biracial work, and gradualist civil rights activism, these Black leaders did not win authentic respect from southern whites. Their pigment disqualified their expertise. Perhaps one of the most compelling moments in this counternarrative comes in chapter 5, when Dabney, the white editor of the *Richmond Times-Dispatch*, scoffed at Young's anguish over the defiantly segregationist editorial positions taken by white members of the SERS board of directors after *Brown*. Dabney insisted that Young's discomfort with the racism in white southern newspapers was irrational, and because all SERS board members had taken an objectivity pledge, Young was professionally obligated to serve with white editors who labored daily to deny him his civil rights.

White southern vexation about the hypocrisy of the northern white press also was a diversionary tactic. Although northern white newspapers were indeed fixated on southern racism instead of discrimination in their own communities, white southern editors pointed to this double standard to deflect attention from the southern response to Brown, not to ameliorate racial injustice on the other side of the Mason-Dixon Line. White southern claims that a paper curtain censored southern views from appearing in the northern press, an ironic complaint often expressed in articles published in northern newspapers and magazines, was another obfuscation. So was the argument that objectivity ensured accuracy in reporting on race. Within a profession that still practiced Jim Crow, white southern editors easily and effectively invoked journalism standards in their resistance to integration. By continually insisting that news stories were inaccurate and biased when they portrayed Black people as nonviolent contributors to society and worthy of full citizenship, white southerners shifted the focus of debate from southern racism to journalistic objectivity and forced editors and news service personnel who disagreed to entertain these arguments anyway. Within the normative Associated Press news cooperative, where white supremacists were a minority but had outsized clout as member-owners, the unrelenting agitation of the white southern faction altered news judgment in the national daily news report. Northern editors and AP staff who disagreed had to engage and accommodate racist views in AP meetings, and when time allowed, remove segregationist news frames and unnecessary racial detail before publishing AP news reports in their own newspapers.

A thorough complaint by James Wechsler of the *New York Post*, one of the most racially liberal white editors during the 1950s, illustrated this forced northern acquiescence to white supremacist activism within the AP. Wechsler wrote Alan Gould, the news service's executive editor, more than a thousand words about the inadequacy of AP reporting after the Till lynching trial and suggested angles for improved follow-up coverage. Having attended contentious meetings of the Associated Press Managing Editors, Wechsler knew that white southern members who opposed civil rights objected to wire stories highlighting white-on-Black crime. Although Wechsler sharply criticized AP reporting on the trial's aftermath, he knew the AP would prioritize southerners' free-speech rights over the ethical position on race that he himself had taken. With the Till coverage, Wechsler could see how white southern racism shaped news values in the daily wire report and that he, as a northern editor, held far less sway than the vocal white supremacists in AP member newsrooms. "Perhaps the A.P. will have to set up separate North and South wires to avoid offending some of the characters who run the Mississippi press," Wechsler wrote.[17] Instead, in the years after the Till trial, the AP appeased the strident segregationist minority in its membership.

## Foregrounding Whiteness

This analysis inverts the familiar white-press history of the 1940s and 1950s and intentionally foregrounds the racial identities of both the Black and white editors and academics who appear in this account. Too often whiteness is assumed to be the norm, the taken-for-granted standard against which its racial "others" are judged. We qualify a reference to "the Black press" but assume that "the press" without a racial label refers to the white press. Similarly, when Black subjects enter a historical narrative, we typically introduce them as such while the race of their white contemporaries often goes unmentioned.[18] Just as the AP debate over racial labeling had implications for the daily news report, so does the historian's decision about representation in a biracial context. The reasons here are different, of course. The white southern editors who agitated for the "Negro" label in news copy wanted to ensure that a Black news subject did not pass as white on the newspaper page and, like Charles Logan, father of triplets, be portrayed as an upstanding citizen and family man—a characterization that white southern newspapers did not apply to a Black person at midcentury. This book tags both white and Black subjects to ensure that both white and Black identities are visible. To expose and analyze the power imbalance in media representations, no one is unraced in this historical account.[19]

In the mid-1950s Shoemaker and his contemporaries were enveloped in Massive Resistance to *Brown*, and the white South had not made its last stand in defense of segregation. Ahead lay a decade of confrontation over integration of lunch counters and public transportation, punctuated by dramatic encounters between brutal white police and peaceful southern Black citizens seeking the right to vote and claiming their share of the American good life. Historian Sid Bedingfield noted that televised images of police violence propelled the Civil Rights Act of 1964 and the Voting Rights Act of 1965, legislation that formalized the end of Jim Crow, but instead of realigning its politics with racial justice, the segregationist bulwark in the South mutated into a socially acceptable brand of racism called "colorblind conservatism": If "all men are created equal," according to the American creed, then race occasions no special pleading. Alienated by the Democratic Party's leftward slide since the New Deal, South Carolina senator Strom Thurmond led fellow segregationists into the Republican tent as part of the "Great White Switch."[20]

By the mid-1960s the white press would begin to move, unevenly and imperfectly, toward new assessments of both objectivity and race and their role in journalism. As racial tensions smoldered and combusted in the 1960s, producing violent unrest that paralyzed northern cities, white news organizations heard the first rumblings that comprehensive reporting on race would require integrated newsrooms. This perspective crystallized in *The Kerner Report*, a 1968 study on the causes of racial disorders. In its critique of segregated journalism, the biracial presidential commission focused on both race and objectivity:

> The media report and write from the standpoint of a white man's world. The ills of the ghetto, the difficulties of life there, the Negro's burning sense of grievance, are seldom conveyed. Slights and indignities are part of the Negro's daily life, and many of them come from what he now calls the "white press"—a press that repeatedly, if unconsciously, reflects the biases, the paternalism, the indifference of white America. This may be understandable, but it is not excusable in an institution that has the mission to inform and educate the whole of our society.[21]

In the decades after, the white press—including print, broadcast, and online media—would move in fits and starts toward diversified newsrooms, as advocates for racial equity confronted a recurring white backlash. Although multiracial news staffs with integrated management lost their novelty over time, they were far from universal at the turn of the twenty-first century, when economic pressures on the media industries diverted focus from diversity initiatives.[22]

In the 1960s and 1970s the concept of objectivity in journalism also came in for renegotiation after Senator Joseph McCarthy's obsession with communism had exposed the inadequacy of just-the-facts, both-sides reporting. In addition, competitive pressure from television and magazines prompted daily newspapers to introduce more interpretation and analysis into their reporting.[23] The 1960s saw both a rise in press criticism, with the founding of the *Columbia Journalism Review* and other professional publications, and a new awareness that journalists had an ethical obligation to the public. In many newsrooms white journalists rebelled against objectivity, viewing its framework as a constraint on their reporting.[24] Still, despite renewed scrutiny of the concept, the white journalism profession was not ready to abandon objectivity as its North Star. In 1973, for example, when the Society of Professional Journalists developed its first ethics code, the organization elevated objectivity as a guiding aspiration.[25] Subsequent codes would reframe the journalist's duty, emphasizing such concepts as impartiality and transparency. Eventually, the predominance of the internet in the news ecosystem, where algorithms replaced editors, made objectivity as a professional standard seem quaint and naive. Even so, objectivity retained considerable traction through the decades and still had its qualified defenders. In her analysis of fake news in American history, Andie Tucher wrote that "for all its flaws, when it's carried out correctly, genuine professional objectivity still offers news consumers an alternative increasingly rare in the chaotic, hyperpartisan scrum that is today's media landscape: a declaration that the truth is contingent not on emotion or individual whim or partisan mandate but on evidence tested through the use of dedicated processes and tools."[26]

## Race and Reckoning

A central concern of this book, which challenges received narratives about race and American journalism, is how the white southern press of the 1940s and 1950s stoked and validated defensive white fear about the consequences of integration. From a remove of many decades and with civil rights for all Americans long codified into law, we might reasonably expect American society to have evolved beyond concerns about white backlash; however, this book's focus on the politics of objectivity during the civil rights years places it in conversation with the reenergized interrogation of race and objectivity that paralleled the Black Lives Matter (BLM) movement, which followed the 2012 murder of Trayvon Martin and 2014 police killing of Michael Brown.[27] Through its construction of counternarratives, BLM refocused attention on the relationship between racial standpoint and power. For example, Black eyewitness accounts now hold greater authority with the legacy media than they did in the 1950s, when terrorism against Black people was routinely unprosecuted or exonerated. Although the credibility of Black testimony is now contingent on visual evidence provided by cellphones or police body cameras, Black observation is entered into the historical record.[28] Importantly, objectivity's critics now openly theorize the inequity produced when journalism privileges one viewpoint as objective, marginalizing differing perspectives as not objective.[29] Notable contributions to the recent literature have extended the discussion beyond the Black-white and two-gender binaries to foreground other identities marginalized by objectivity and to legitimate social justice as an ethical precept of journalism.[30]

This book also joins the call for a reckoning by the legacy white press, whose news coverage for generations presented white supremacy as the norm. Accountability for white newspapers requires not only an assessment of their past racism but also atonement and a commitment to reconsider their ongoing relationship to the broader community.[31] Significantly, the Associated Press in 2020 amended its venerable stylebook, the normative template for news copy, to capitalize the "B" in "Black." John Daniszewski, AP's vice president of standards, said the policy acknowledged "an essential and shared sense of history, identity and community among people who identify as Black, including those in the African diaspora and within Africa. The lowercase black is a color, not a person." AP left the style on "white" intact as "capitalizing the term white, as is done by white supremacists, risks subtly conveying legitimacy to such beliefs."[32] Importantly, the AP's policy on racial identification has for some time strictly limited the contexts in which identification by race is even necessary. It is hard to imagine a more striking comparison to Alan Gould's 1956 memo, which quoted a segregationist editorial and commanded that all "Negroes" be identified as such when "pertinent," which for most white southern editors was every time they were mentioned.

Despite generations of activism and a canon of scholarship focused on newsroom diversity and the need for inclusive journalism, Black journalists and academics still find the playing field tilted by whiteness and cite the objectivity standard as an obstacle to their full and equitable participation in the profession.[33] A lightning rod for this conversation was Black journalist Wesley Lowery's 2020 *New York Times* opinion piece, which posited the racial history of the white mainstream press as a democratic concern following the May 2020 murder of George Floyd by a white policeman in Minneapolis, Minnesota. Lowery linked the continuing marginalization of Black news workers to the framework of journalistic objectivity:

> Black journalists are publicly airing years of accumulated grievances, demanding an overdue reckoning for a profession whose mainstream repeatedly brushes off their concerns; in many newsrooms, writers and editors are now also openly pushing for a paradigm shift in how our outlets define their operations and ideals.
>
> While these two battles may seem superficially separate, in reality, the failure of the mainstream press to accurately cover black communities is intrinsically linked with its failure to employ, retain and listen to black people.[34]

Lowery pointed to the enduring, systemic racism that is structured into journalism, a profession that still drafts history and still imposes representation upon news subjects.

When reviewing the southern white press's candid resistance to the civil rights movement in the 1940s and 1950s, with Jim Crow segregation and the southern way of life hanging in the balance, racism in journalism discourse is comparatively easy to identify. In the twenty-first century, even after generations of contestation over racial politics, white supremacy is still conspicuous and objectivity remains a weapon of racialized power in journalism. During a forum on journalistic objectivity in 2022, Lowery cited the "continued backlash to integration" in newsrooms, which "are still essentially apartheid institutions. These are all-white institutions with a sprinkling of other people who've managed to make their way in over time." Objectivity, he said, is still used as a method of ideological control when white editors and journalists decide which stories not to cover and how to report those that are assigned. "Objectivity has always been wielded to silence people who do not fit with the politics of the people who own and operate the newspaper," Lowery said. "It has always been a censorious force, never an expansive force."[35]

This was a stunning observation for a Black journalist to make so long after the central moral and legal questions about racial justice were officially resolved. But whiteness is resilient, always shape-shifting in response to new threats to its dominance while remaining consistent and predictable.[36] Recent efforts to resecure white supremacy exploit white anxiety about a loss of control over the racial narrative, just as the white southern editors feared in the 1940s and 1950s. The white backlash against BLM and other calls for reckoning was exacerbated by political confrontations over Confederate iconography throughout the American South. As southerners of all races grappled with the legacy of Jim Crow, many challenged the myth of the Lost Cause, which valorized the South's unsuccessful defense of slavery in the Civil War and animated white southern opposition to integration after *Brown*. When reformers questioned the enduring presence of Confederate flags and statuary in public spaces in the twenty-first century, they lured flagrant white supremacy away from the fringes and into public view. For example, the violent and deadly protest in Charlottesville, Virginia, in 2017 attracted hundreds of antisemites and white supremacists who, according to their chants, construed removal of a Robert E. Lee statue from a city park as an effort to "replace" white Christians.[37]

The battle over the racial narrative, over who gets to tell the story of race in America, has moved well beyond the civil rights decades, but more recent struggles also bear traces of historical exclusions. In a broad attack on the movement for social justice, racially conservative politicians condemn a range of narratives—including journalism, entertainment, and school curricula—that critique American racial history as something other than heroic or well-intentioned. Just as their white supremacist forebears claimed integration would end white civilization and fought for control of the news narrative, these new defenders of the white status quo have contrived a nonwhite threat to their version of the national story. Drawing on media images of BLM protests and appropriating a Black descriptor of social awareness, contemporary white supremacists have posited the "woke mob" as anathema to white culture and placed themselves on a historical continuum with D. W. Griffith, Don Shoemaker, and the Charlottesville protesters. Their stereotype of nonwhites and their allies, looming as an uncontrollable racial enemy, is a dog-whistle that plays on fear and prejudice, ignores advantages that accrue to whiteness, and manipulates standpoint for political purposes. It also demonstrates that for them, like the white southern editors of the 1940s and 1950s, the claim to objectivity still defends the racial status quo.

# NOTES

## PREFACE AND ACKNOWLEDGMENTS

1. *Brown v. Board of Education of Topeka, Kansas*, 347 U.S. 483 (1954). The court combined five cases in its landmark ruling.
2. White, who had editorialized against the Ku Klux Klan's activity in the 1920s, was a prominent white editor in his day. M. Sue Kendall, *Rethinking Regionalism: John Steuart Curry and the Kansas Mural Controversy* (Washington, DC: Smithsonian Institution Press, 1986), 19–20. The mural also depicts the explorer Francisco Vasquez de Coronado, the missionary Fray Juan de Padilla, and wagon trains of white settlers heading west but fails to paint Indigenous people into Kansas history. The only visible Black subjects are small figures cowering beneath a Confederate flag.
3. The irony of the *Brown* case arising in the town that is home to the Curry mural of John Brown may not be my original observation, but I do not recall the first time I thought, read, or heard it. This illustrates the trickiness of cultural memory about race: how did we learn what we've always known?
4. James J. Kilpatrick, "Landmark School Case Closed at Last," *The Record* (Hackensack, NJ), May 11, 1987.
5. I made this decision before the Associated Press changed its style rules on race in 2020. The AP explained its use of the capital "B" on Black and the lowercase "w" on white, noting that white supremacists prefer the capital 'W.' "AP Changes Writing Style to Capitalize 'B' in Black," Associated Press, June 19, 2020, https://apnews.com, and "Explaining AP Style on Black and White," Associated Press, June 20, 2020, https://apnews.com. On this point, Martha Biondi wrote that "Black" "reflects the self-naming and self-identification of a people whose national or ethnic origins have been obscured by a history of capture and enslavement." In her scholarship, "'white' is not capitalized because historically it has been deployed as a signifier of social domination and privilege, rather than as an indicator of ethnic or national origin." Biondi, *To Stand and Fight: The Struggle for Civil Rights in Postwar New York City* (Cambridge, MA: Harvard University Press, 2003), front matter.
6. *Davis v. County School Board of Prince Edward County, Virginia*, 103 F. Supp. 337 (1952); *Loving v. Virginia*, 388 U.S. 1 (1967).

## INTRODUCTION

1. In *Brown v. Board of Education of Topeka*, 347 U.S. 483 (1954), the U.S. Supreme Court held that the equal protection clause of the Fourteenth Amendment made segregated schools unconstitutional. This ruling overturned the separate-but-equal provision of *Plessy v. Ferguson*, 163 U.S. 537 (1896). The second *Brown* ruling in 1955, 349 U.S. 294, offered guidance for implementing school desegregation "with all deliberate speed." See also Michael J. Klarman, *From Jim Crow to Civil Rights: The Supreme Court and the Struggle for Racial Equality* (New York: Oxford University Press, 2004), chapter 6.
    Shoemaker, who had worked for the *Asheville Times* and *Asheville Citizen*, was the SERS executive director from 1955 to 1958. He retired in 1978 as editor of the *Miami Herald* but wrote a column for the newspaper until his death. Arnold Markowitz, "Don Shoemaker, Herald's Voice for Decades, Dies at 85," *Miami Herald*, Nov. 7, 1998.
2. C. A. McKnight, "Approaching Ten and Definitely in Long Pants," *ASNE Bulletin*, Oct. 1963, 10.
3. Don Shoemaker, remarks to an unspecified audience in Kinston, NC, Feb. 21, 1956, Don Shoemaker Papers, folder 42, Southern Historical Collection, University of North Carolina at Chapel Hill.
4. Don Shoemaker, remarks to the 20th Anniversary Conference of the Public Affairs Committee, New York City, June 20, 1956, Shoemaker Papers, folder 42.
5. On the function of discourse as practice, see Gwyneth Mellinger, *Chasing Newsroom Diversity: From Jim Crow to Affirmative Action* (Champaign: University of Illinois Press, 2013), 11, which applies the theoretical approach from Michel Foucault, *The Archaeology of Knowledge* (New York: Pantheon Books, 1972), 49, and Foucault, *The History of Sexuality*, vol. 1, *An Introduction* (New York: Vintage, 1990), 27.
6. On the segregation of the newspaper industry, see Kimberley Mangun and Earnest L. Perry Jr., "The Negro/National Publishers Association and Its Dual Roles as a Trade and Advocacy Organization," *Journalism and Communication Monographs* 22, no. 4 (Winter 2020): 268, and Lawrence D. Hogan, *A Black National News Service: The Associated Negro Press and Claude Barnett* (Haworth, NJ: St. Johann Press, 2002), especially chapters 1 and 2. According to a Lincoln University study, between 1948 and 1955 the number of Black journalists working in daily newspaper newsrooms ranged from twelve to twenty-one. Armistead Scott Pride, "Low Man on the Totem Pole," Nieman Reports, April 1955, 21, quoted in David R. Davies, "An Industry in Transition: Major Trends in American Daily Newspapers, 1945–1965" (PhD diss., University of Alabama, 1997), chapter 6.
7. Kathy Roberts Forde, "Ida B. Wells-Barnett and the 'Racist Cover-Up,'" in *Political Pioneer of the Press: Ida B. Wells-Barnett and Her Transnational Crusade for Social Justice*, ed. Lori Amber Roessner and Jodi L. Rightler-McDaniels (Langham, MD: Lexington Books, 2018), 180. Useful histories of the Black press include Bernell Tripp, *Origins of the Black Press: New York, 1827–1847* (Northport, AL: Vision Press, 1992); Henry Lewis Suggs, "Origins of the Black Press in the South," in *The Black Press in the South, 1865–1979*, ed. Henry Lewis Suggs (Westport, CT: Greenwood Press, 1983), 3–31; Brian Shott, *Mediating America: Black and Irish Press and the Struggle for Citizenship, 1870–1914* (Philadelphia: Temple University Press, 2019), 89–158; Todd Vogel, ed., *The Black Press: New Literary and Historical Essays* (New Brunswick, NJ: Rutgers University Press, 2001); Patrick S. Washburn, *The African*

*American Newspaper: Voice of Freedom* (Evanston, IL: Northwestern University Press, 2006); Fred Carroll, *Race News: Black Journalists and the Fight for Racial Justice* (Champaign: University of Illinois Press, 2017); and D'Weston Haywood, *Let Us Make Men: The Twentieth-Century Black Press and a Manly Vision for Racial Advancement* (Chapel Hill: University of North Carolina Press, 2018).
8. Mellinger, *Chasing Newsroom Diversity*, 174–77.
9. This understanding of the concept of whiteness is synthesized from and most strongly influenced by scholarship that views whiteness both as a social construction and as an organizing force in social and political relationships and institutions. This work includes Ruth Frankenberg, *White Women, Race Matters: The Social Construction of Whiteness* (Minneapolis: University of Minnesota Press, 1993); David Roediger, *The Wages of Whiteness: Race and the Making of the American Working Class* (London: Verso, 1991), and George Lipsitz, *The Possessive Investment in Whiteness: How White People Profit from Identity Politics* (Philadelphia: Temple University Press, 1998). My application of whiteness as an analytical tool follows from the historical and cultural analyses contained in the work of Roediger and others: Theodore Allen, *The Invention of the White Race*, vol. 1, *Racial Oppression and Social Control* (London: Verso, 1994); Matthew Frye Jacobson, *Whiteness of a Different Color: European Immigrants and the Alchemy of Race* (Cambridge, MA: Harvard University Press, 1998); Ian Haney Lopez, *White by Law: The Legal Construction of Race* (New York: New York University Press, 1996); Richard Dyer, *White* (London: Routledge, 1997); and Tomas Almaguer, *Racial Fault Lines: The Historical Origins of White Supremacy in California* (Berkeley: University of California Press, 1994).
10. Michael Omi and Howard Winant, *Racial Formation in the United States: From the 1960s to the 1990s*, 2nd ed. (1986; New York: Routledge, 1994), 60.
11. Defining essentialism as "belief in real, true human essences, existing outside or impervious to social and historical context," Omi and Winant explained, "A racial project can be defined as *racist* if and only if it *creates or reproduces structures of domination based on essentialist categories of race*. Such a definition recognizes the importance of locating racism within a fluid and contested history of racially based social structures and discourses. Thus there can be no timeless and absolute standard for what constitutes racism, for social structures change and discourses are subject to rearticulation. Our definition, therefore, focuses on the 'work' essentialism does for domination, and the 'need' domination displays to essentialize the subordinated." Omi and Winant, *Racial Formation in the United States*, 71.
12. Most helpful in the vast canon on this subject are W. Fitzhugh Brundage, *The Southern Past: A Clash of Race and Memory* (Cambridge, MA: Belknap Press of Harvard University Press, 2005); David W. Blight, *Race and Reunion: The Civil War in American Memory* (Cambridge, MA: Belknap Press of Harvard University Press, 2001); James C. Cobb, *Away Down South: A History of Southern Identity* (New York: Oxford University Press, 2005); and C. Vann Woodward, *The Burden of Southern History*, 3rd ed. (1960; Baton Rouge: Louisiana State University Press, 2008).
13. David Goldfield, *Still Fighting the Civil War: The American South and Southern History* (Baton Rouge: Louisiana State University Press, 2002), 27.
14. Stuart Hall, "The Whites of Their Eyes: Racist Ideologies and the Media," in *The Media Reader*, ed. Manuel Alvarado and John O. Thompson (London: British Film Institute, 1990), 9–11. On the legacy of Negrophobia, see George M. Fredrickson, *The*

*Black Image in the White Mind: The Debate on Afro-American Character and Destiny, 1817–1914* (New York: Harper and Row, 1971), chapter 9.
15. Jason Sokol, *There Goes My Everything: White Southerners in the Age of Civil Rights, 1945–1975* (New York: Vintage, 2007), 37.
16. See chapter 1.
17. Don Shoemaker to Simeon Booker, July 12, 1955, Virginius Dabney Papers, MSS 7690h, box 6, folder Don Shoemaker, Albert and Shirley Small Special Collections Library, University of Virginia, Charlottesville; C. A. McKnight, "How Is the Press Reporting School Desegregation?" *Problems of Journalism: Proceedings of the American Society of Newspaper Editors*, April 21–23, 1955, 83.
18. George Tindall, *The Emergence of the New South, 1913–1945* (Baton Rouge: Louisiana State University Press, 1967), 208–10. See also Angie Maxwell, *The Indicted South: Public Criticism, Southern Inferiority, and the Politics of Whiteness* (Chapel Hill: University of North Carolina Press, 2014), 3.
19. Fred C. Hobson Jr., *Serpent in Eden: H. L. Mencken and the South* (Chapel Hill: University of North Carolina Press, 1974), 24.
20. H. L. Mencken, "The Sahara of the Bozart," *New York Evening Mail*, Nov. 13, 1917. This early denunciation is mild by comparison to later Mencken comments. After the Scopes trial, he reportedly characterized the South as "the bunghole of the United States, a cesspool of Baptists, a miasma of Methodism, snake-charmers, phony real estate operators, and syphilitic evangelists." Charles P. Roland, "The South of the Agrarians," in *A Band of Prophets: The Vanderbilt Agrarians after Fifty Years*, ed. William C. Harvard and Walter Sullivan (Baton Rouge: Louisiana State University Press, 1982), 37–38, quoted in Maxwell, *The Indicted South*, 87.
21. Mencken arranged for Clarence Darrow to defend John Thomas Scopes, the teacher, and Mencken's employer, the *Baltimore Evening Sun*, put up Scopes's bail and nicknamed the proceedings the "monkey trial." Hobson, *Serpent in Eden*, 147–48.
22. Maxwell, *The Indicted South*, 22. See also Maxwell's detailed treatment of the Scopes trial, chapters 1–3.
23. Cash was given to melancholy and died by suicide five months after the book appeared. Fred Hobson, *Tell about the South: The Southern Rage to Explain* (Baton Rouge: Louisiana State University Press, 1983), 245. Two biographers minimized Cash's anxiety about the book's reception in the South, detailing symptoms of mental illness prior to the suicide: Joseph L. Morrison, *W. J. Cash: Southern Prophet* (New York: Knopf, 1967), 127–35, and Bruce Clayton, *W. J. Cash: A Life* (Baton Rouge: Louisiana State University Press, 1991), 184–91.
24. W. J. Cash, *The Mind of the South* (1941; reprint New York: Vintage, 1991), 98, 296, 299.
25. Gunnar Myrdal, *An American Dilemma: The Negro Problem and Modern Democracy*, 2 vols. (1944; reprint New Brunswick, NJ: Transaction, 1996), 1:462. On the impact of *An American Dilemma* on the press and civil rights movement, see Gene Roberts and Hank Klibanoff, *The Race Beat: The Press, the Civil Rights Struggle, and the Awakening of a Nation* (New York: Vintage, 2007), 3–13. On white southern editors' reception of Myrdal's work, see John Egerton, *Speak Now against the Day: The Generation before the Civil Rights Movement in the South* (Chapel Hill: University of North Carolina Press, 1995), 274–76.
26. Roberts and Klibanoff, *The Race Beat*, 86.

27. Thomas R. Waring, "The Southern Case against Desegregation," *Harper's*, Jan. 1956, 39–43.
28. Ironically, Waring's complaint about the "paper curtain" was published in a northern magazine despite its editors' objection to the article's content. See Sid Bedingfield, *Newspaper Wars: Civil Rights and White Resistance in South Carolina, 1935–1965* (Champaign: University of Illinois Press, 2017), 175–82, and Maxwell, *The Indicted South*, 207–10.
29. Numan V. Bartley, *The Rise of Massive Resistance: Race and Politics in the South during the 1950s* (Baton Rouge: Louisiana State University Press, 1969), 177–79.
30. On the impact of World War II on defenses of racism, C. Vann Woodward noted, "American war propaganda stressed above all else the abhorrence of the West for Hitler's brand of racism and its utter incompatibility with the democratic faith for which we fought. The relevance of this deep stirring of the American conscience for the position of the Negro was not lost upon him and his champions. Awareness of the inconsistency between practice at home and propaganda abroad placed a powerful lever in their hands." Woodward, *The Strange Career of Jim Crow* (1955; reprint Oxford: Oxford University Press, 2002), 131.
31. The cases were, respectively, *Missouri ex rel. Gaines v. Canada*, 305 U.S. 337 (1938); *Smith v. Allwright*, 321 U.S. 649 (1944); *Morgan v. Virginia*, 328 U.S. 373 (1946); and *Shelly v. Kraemer*, 334 U.S. 1 (1948). On July 26, 1948, Truman signed Executive Order 9981, fully desegregating the U.S. military. This was one of the recommendations in "To Secure These Rights: The Report of the President's Committee on Civil Rights," Dec. 1947, Truman Presidential Library, Independence, MO, https://www.trumanlibrary.gov.
32. Bartley, *The Rise of Massive Resistance*, 32.
33. Quoted in Roberts and Klibanoff, *The Race Beat*, 64.
34. James J. Kilpatrick, editorial, *Richmond News Leader*, Nov. 23, 1955, quoted in William P. Hustwit, *James J. Kilpatrick: Salesman for Segregation* (Chapel Hill: University of North Carolina Press, 2013), 53.
35. Elizabeth Gillespie McRae, *Mothers of Massive Resistance: White Women and the Politics of White Supremacy* (New York: Oxford University Press, 2018), 185. On state actions against the NAACP, see Bartley, *The Rise of Massive Resistance*, 186–89, 221–24.
36. Bartley offered a thorough discussion of the legal concept of interposition in *The Rise of Massive Resistance*, chapter 8.
37. McRae, *Mothers of Massive Resistance*, 188.
38. Rodger Streitmatter identified the civil rights movement as "the first great TV news story" and the confrontation at Central High School in Little Rock as its "first chapter." Streitmatter, *Mightier Than the Sword: How the News Media Have Shaped American History*, 4th ed. (2016; New York: Routledge, 2018), 147–48. For a comprehensive history of broadcast news coverage of civil rights, see Aniko Bodroghkozy, *Equal Time: Television and the Civil Rights Movement* (Champaign: University of Illinois Press, 2012).
39. Michael J. Klarman, "How *Brown* Changed Race Relations: The Backlash Thesis," *Journal of American History* 81, no. 1 (June 1994): 81–118.
40. Matthew D. Lassiter and Andrew B. Lewis, "Massive Resistance Revisited: Virginia's White Moderates and the Byrd Organization," in *The Moderates' Dilemma: Massive Resistance to School Desegregation in Virginia*, ed. Matthew D. Lassiter and Andrew B.

Lewis (Charlottesville: University Press of Virginia, 1998), 4–5; Anders Walker, *The Ghost of Jim Crow: How Southern Moderates Used* Brown v. Board of Education *to Stall Civil Rights* (New York: Oxford University Press, 2009), 9.

41. Jason Morgan Ward framed this perspective as "The White South's 'Double V'" and "southernizing freedom." Ward, *Defending White Democracy: The Making of a Segregationist Movement and the Remaking of Racial Politics, 1936–1965* (Chapel Hill: University of North Carolina Press, 2011), chapters 2, 4.
42. Sokol, *There Goes My Everything*, 37.
43. Fred Hobson wrote of the South's "literature of shame and guilt": "The need to defend and to explain the American South began almost as soon as the inhabitants of that region below the Potomac realized they *were* Southern, even before they fully realized they were American." Hobson, *Tell about the South*, 11, 19.
44. See chapters 2 and 4.
45. This followed from the white supremacist theory that Black degeneracy presumably followed emancipation. Fredrickson, *The Black Image in the White Mind*, 249–62.
46. Anne Waldron, *Hodding Carter: The Reconstruction of a Racist* (Chapel Hill, NC: Algonquin Books, 1993), 283. See also Egerton, *Speak Now against the Day*, 548–49. Another white southerner who was awarded a Pulitzer Prize for opinion in the 1950s was Buford Boone of the *Tuscaloosa [AL] News*, who remained a low-key moderate and opposed extremism.
47. Egerton, *Speak Now against the Day*, 11.
48. Jeanne Theoharis noted that the righteousness of northern white journalists was often constructed over and against their southern counterparts, even as northern newspapers minimized racial disparities in their own communities. The northern white press also dismissed issues raised by the Black press. Theoharis took aim at Roberts and Klibanoff's framing of the northern press in their Pulitzer Prize–winning history *The Race Beat*, which "painstakingly detailed the process by which many Northern journalists came to see the importance of the Southern struggle and summoned the courage and resources to cover it. . . . History as *ABC Afternoon Special*, their story of the scrappy journalists who help push their news outlets to expose the South's intransigence is ultimately a feel-good one—of good people who do the right thing. To have examined how their colleagues disregarded and legitimated racism in their own cities and regions raises more disturbing questions." Theoharis, *A More Beautiful and Terrible History: The Uses and Misuses of Civil Rights History* (Boston: Beacon Press, 2018), 102–5.
49. Ward, *Defending White Democracy*, 6–7.
50. The political and cultural significance of white southern identity undergirds much of the scholarship cited in this book. Of particular note are Sokol, *There Goes My Everything*; Egerton, *Speak Now against the Day*; Maxwell, *The Indicted South*; and Ward, *Defending White Democracy*. So distinctive was the southern identity at the end of the 1960s, when the sociology of race was intent on assigning people to categories, that white southerners merited their own volume in a series on comparative ethnic groups. Peter I. Rose, "Foreword," in Lewis Killian, *White Southerners* (New York: Random House, 1970), x.
51. Matthew D. Lassiter and Joseph Crespino, "Introduction: The End of Southern History," in *The Myth of Southern Exceptionalism*, ed. Matthew D. Lassiter and Joseph Crespino (Oxford: Oxford University Press, 2010), 5.

52. Theoharis, *A More Beautiful and Terrible History,* 34. See also Jacquelyn Dowd Hall, "The Long Civil Rights Movement and the Political Uses of the Past," *Journal of American History* 91, no. 4 (March 2005): 1233–63; Matthew J. Countryman, *Up South: Civil Rights and Black Power in Philadelphia* (Philadelphia: University of Pennsylvania Press, 2006); and Martha Biondi, *To Stand and Fight: The Struggle for Civil Rights in Postwar New York City* (Cambridge, MA: Harvard University Press, 2003).
53. Houston A. Baker Jr., "Critical Memory and the Black Public Sphere," *Public Culture* 7 (1994): 3–33.
54. Gwyneth Mellinger, "Journalism's Ethical Progression," in *Journalism's Ethical Progression: A Twentieth-Century Journey,* ed. Gwyneth Mellinger and John Ferré (Lanham, MD: Lexington Books, 2021), xiv–xv.
55. Michael Schudson, *Discovering the News: A Social History of American Newspapers* (New York: Basic Books, 1978), 154–57. For context and discussion of interpretive journalism, see Kathy Roberts Forde, *Literary Journalism on Trial: Masson v. New Yorker and the First Amendment* (Amherst: University of Massachusetts Press, 2008), 48–49, and Matthew Pressman, *On Press: The Liberal Values That Shaped the News* (Cambridge, MA: Harvard University Press, 2018), 23–30. In the 1950s Walter Lippmann was on the board of the Ford Foundation's Fund for the Advancement of Education, which underwrote the journalism objectivity projects discussed in chapters 3 and 5 of this book.
56. Tim P. Vos, "'Homo Journalisticus': Journalism Education's Role in Articulating the Objectivity Norm," *Journalism* 13, no. 4 (2011): 445.
57. Michael Schudson, "The Objectivity Norm in American Journalism," *Journalism* 2, no. 2 (Aug. 2001): 149. See also Hazel Dicken-Garcia, *Journalistic Standards in Nineteenth-Century America* (Madison: University of Wisconsin Press, 1989), 98.
58. Schudson, *Discovering the News,* 155–56.
59. Commission on Freedom of the Press, *A Free and Responsible Press* (Chicago: University of Chicago Press, 1947), 22. In addition to its discussion in the Hutchins Report, the concept of the press's obligation to abandon neutrality gained traction with the publication in 1956 of Theodore Peterson's important essay "The Social Responsibility Theory of the Press," in *Four Theories of the Press,* ed. Fred Siebert, Theodore Peterson, and Wilbur Schramm (Urbana: University of Illinois Press, 1956), 73–103.
60. Gaye Tuchman, *Making News: A Study in the Construction of Reality* (New York: Free Press, 1978), 88.
61. Schudson, "The Objectivity Norm in American Journalism," 163.
62. Steven J. A. Ward, *The Invention of Journalism Ethics: The Path to Objectivity and Beyond* (Montreal: McGill-Queen's University Press, 2004), 215, 217. Barbara M. Kelly argues that objectivity had become the professional standard by the 1920s: Kelly, "Objectivity and the Trappings of Professionalism, 1900–1950," in *Fair and Balanced: A History of Journalistic Objectivity,* ed. Steven R. Knowlton and Karel L. Freeman (Northport, AL: Vision Press, 2005), 152.
63. David T. Z. Mindich, *Just the Facts: How "Objectivity" Came to Define American Journalism* (New York: New York University Press, 1998), 48–49. In addition to detachment, Mindich identified nonpartisanship, facticity, balance, and the inverted pyramid as elements in the application of objectivity in the nineteenth century.

Mindich drew on Daniel C. Hallin's theoretical construct of the Spheres of Consensus, Legitimate Controversy, and Deviance outlined in *The "Uncensored War": The Media and Vietnam* (Berkeley: University of California Press, 1986), 116–18.

64. David R. Davies, "The Challenges of Civil Rights and Joseph McCarthy," in Knowlton and Freeman, eds., *Fair and Balanced*, 216.
65. Schudson, *Discovering the News*, 155.
66. See, for example, Oxie Reichler, "Does 'Deadpan' Reporting Do the Job?" *ASNE Bulletin*, Aug. 1, 1952, 7, and Carl Lindstrom, "By What Right Do We Interpret or Explain?" *ASNE Bulletin*, Jan. 1, 1953, 2–3. In 1933 the ASNE had passed a resolution clearing the way to interpretive or explanatory reporting within the framework of conventional, objective journalism. Schudson described the move as the editors' "response to a world grown suddenly very complex" and in need of contextualized reporting following World War I. *Discovering the News*, 148.
67. Thomas R. Waring, "Race Relations and Objectivity," *ASNE Bulletin*, June 1, 1955, 2.
68. Michael Ryan, "Journalistic Ethics, Objectivity, Standpoint Epistemology and Public Journalism," *Journal of Mass Media Ethics* 16, no. 1 (2001): 3.
69. As part of the professional routine in journalism, this would align with the ideal state that John Rawls imagined in his theory of the Veil of Ignorance. Rawls argued that socially just outcomes could be determined if individuals abstracted themselves from their personal identities and self-interest to contemplate an inequity and its solution. However, the white southern editors in this historical analysis subverted objectivity to further racial self-interest, not to achieve redistributive justice. Gwyneth Mellinger and Erin Coyle, "'Blackening Up Journalism': An Ethical Imperative for Newsroom Diversity," in Mellinger and Ferré, eds., *Journalism's Ethical Progression*, 194.
70. The canonical scholarship in this area includes Thomas Nagel, *The View from Nowhere* (Oxford: Oxford University Press, 1986); Peter Novick, *That Noble Dream: The "Objectivity Question" and the American Historical Profession* (Cambridge: Cambridge University Press, 1988); and Thomas L. Haskell, *Objectivity Is Not Neutrality: Explanatory Schemes in History* (Baltimore: Johns Hopkins University Press, 1998). See also Douglas O. Cumming's explication of the scholarship on journalistic objectivity in "Facing Facts, Facing South: The Southern Education Reporting Service and the Effort to Inform the South after *Brown V. Board*, 1954–1960" (PhD diss., University of North Carolina at Chapel Hill, 2002), 55–63.
71. Mindich, *Just the Facts*, 8, 14.
72. Richard L. Kaplan, *Politics and the American Press: The Rise of Objectivity, 1865–1920* (Cambridge: Cambridge University Press, 2002), 184–85.
73. Michael Schudson, "The Sociology of News Production Revisited (Again)," in *Mass Media and Society*, 3rd ed., ed. James Curran and Michael Gurevitch (1991; London: Arnold, 2000), 191.
74. This analysis is informed by Stuart Hall's application of Gramscian common sense to study of the media: "What passes for 'common sense' in our society—the residue of absolutely basic and commonly-agreed consensual wisdoms—helps us to classify out the world in simple but meaningful terms. Precisely, common sense does not require reasoning, argument, logic, thought: it is spontaneously available, thoroughly recognizable, widely shared. It feels, indeed, as if it has always been there, the sedimented, bedrock wisdom of 'the race,' a form of natural wisdom, the content of

which has changed hardly at all with time. However, common sense does have a content as well as a history." Hall, "Culture, Media and the 'Ideological Effect,'" in *Mass Communication and Society,* ed. James Curran et al. (Beverly Hills, CA: Sage, 1979), 325. See also these useful analyses by Hall: "The Rediscovery of 'Ideology': Return of the Repressed in Media Studies," in *Culture, Society and the Media,* ed. Michael Gurevitch et al. (London: Routledge, 1982), 56–90, and "Gramsci's Relevance for the Study of Race and Ethnicity," in *Stuart Hall: Critical Dialogues in Cultural Studies,* ed. David Morley and Kuan-Hsing Chen (London: Routledge, 1996), 411–40.
75. Klarman, "How *Brown* Changed Race Relations," 110–16.
76. Jeff Woods, *Black Struggle, Red Scare: Segregation and Anti-Communism in the South, 1948-1968* (Baton Rouge: Louisiana State University Press, 2004), 5. See also George Lewis, *The White South and the Red Menace: Segregationists, Anticommunism, and Massive Resistance, 1945-1965* (Gainesville: University Press of Florida, 2004); Mary Dudziak, *Cold War Civil Rights: Race and the Image of American Democracy* (Princeton, NJ: Princeton University Press, 2000); and Thomas Borstelmann, *The Cold War and the Color Line: American Race Relations in the Global Arena* (Cambridge, MA: Harvard University Press, 2001). On anticommunist attacks on the press, see Edward Alwood, *Dark Days in the Newsroom: McCarthyism Aimed at the Press* (Philadelphia: Temple University Press, 2007). Alwood noted the impact of journalists' reliance on objectivity: "Ironically, the press played an important role in promoting McCarthyism by reporting questionable committee procedures in an uncritical manner, thereby legitimizing them" (6).
77. Egerton, *Speak Now against the Day,* 560–61.
78. The editorial page of the Charleston *News and Courier* was staunchly anticommunist and editor Waring accused the NAACP and other racially progressive organizations of being "fellow travelers." Although the Highlander Folk School (which trained Rosa Parks and other civil rights activists in integrated classes) was in Tennessee, not South Carolina, Waring took an interest because it was located near his alma mater, the University of the South at Sewanee. He deployed the news columns of his newspaper in a campaign to put Highlander out of business. Gwyneth Mellinger, "Saving the Republic: An Editor's Crusade against Integration," *Journalism History* 42, no. 4 (Jan. 2017): 212–24.
79. Aimee Edmondson, *In Sullivan's Shadow: The Use and Abuse of Libel Law during the Long Civil Rights Struggle* (Amherst: University of Massachusetts Press, 2019), 5.

## CHAPTER 1

1. P. L. Prattis, "The Role of the Negro Press in Race Relations,' *Phylon* 7, no. 3 (1946): 278.
2. On the relationship of economic and political trends to Black rights, see Doxey A. Wilkerson, "Freedom through Victory in War and Peace," in *What the Negro Wants,* ed. Rayford W. Logan (Chapel Hill: University of North Carolina Press, 1944), 194. Wilkerson, a former faculty member at Howard University, was executive editor of the Black newspaper *People's Voice*. On the historical and political significance of *What the Negro Wants,* see John Egerton, *Speak Now against the Day: The Generation before the Civil Rights Movement* (Chapel Hill: University of North Carolina Press, 1994), 271–74.

3. Lee Finkle, *Forum for Protest* (Cranberry, NJ: Associated University Presses, 1975), 65. Finkle offered a comprehensive discussion of the Pegler matter on pages 64–68.
4. Westbrook Pegler, "Fair Enough," *Binghamton [NY] Press-Bulletin*, May 11, 1942.
5. Finkle, *Forum for Protest*, 63–64; Virginius Dabney, "Press and Morale," *Saturday Review of Literature*, July 4, 1942, 25. On the "Negro Problem," see Gunnar Myrdal, *An American Dilemma: The Negro Problem and Modern Democracy*, 2 vols. (1944; New Brunswick, NJ: Transaction, 1996), 1:26–49. In the 1940s white southerners referenced the "Negro problem" as a cultural fact of life. See, for example, Virginius Dabney, *Below the Potomac: A Book about the New South* (New York: D-Appleton-Century, 1942), 235, reprinted as "The Negro and His Schooling," *Atlantic Monthly*, April 1941, 459.
6. Myrdal, *An American Dilemma*, 2:660.
7. Regarding the normative function of the press, Clifford G. Christians and colleagues posited, "Not only is freedom of belief defended but also the right to persuasively project one's beliefs into the sphere of public debate. This guarantee rules out all external, public criteria of truthfulness as long as the expression is not a threat to the rights of others." Christians et al., *Normative Theories of the Media: Journalism in Democratic Societies* (Urbana: University of Illinois Press, 2009), 49. In the 1940s most members of the southern white press recognized the Black press's constitutional right to publish but did not acknowledge Black individuals' entitlement to other civil rights. This was an ethical tension in the white southern press's relationship to the Black press in the 1940s and 1950s.
8. Gwyneth Mellinger, *Chasing Newsroom Diversity: From Jim Crow to Affirmative Action* (Champaign: University of Illinois Press, 2013), chapter 1.
9. Gwyneth Mellinger, "An Idea before Its Time: Charles S. Johnson, Negro Columnist," *Journal of Human and Civil Rights* 4, no. 2 (Fall 2018): 62–89.
10. A 1955 Lincoln University study reported that twenty-one Black journalists were employed at white-owned daily newspapers, while earlier studies placed the number at twelve in 1952 and fifteen in 1948. Armistead Scott Pride, "Low Man on the Totem Pole," *Nieman Reports*, April 1955, 21, quoted in David R. Davies, "An Industry in Transition: Major Trends in American Daily Newspapers, 1945–1965" (PhD diss., University of Alabama, 1997), chapter 6.
11. Armistead S. Pride and Clint C. Wilson II, *A History of the Black Press* (Washington, DC: Howard University Press, 1997), 9.
12. Regarding the *Pittsburgh Courier*'s Double V Campaign, see Patrick S. Washburn, "Pittsburgh Courier's Double V Campaign in 1942," *American Journalism* 3, no. 2 (1986): 73–86; Patrick S. Washburn, *The African American Newspaper: Voice of Freedom* (Evanston, IL: Medill University Press, 2006), 143–53; Jinx Coleman Broussard, *African American Foreign Correspondents: A History* (Baton Rouge: Louisiana State University Press, 2013), 112; Patrick S. Washburn, *A Question of Sedition: The Federal Government's Investigation of the Black Press during World War II* (New York: Oxford University Press, 1986), 100–103; and Harvard Sitkoff, "African American Militancy in the World War II South: Another Perspective," in *Remaking Dixie: The Impact of World War II on the American South*, ed. Neil R. McMillen (Jackson: University Press of Mississippi, 1997), 74–75.
13. The relevant scholarship on Pegler includes Oliver Pilat, *Angry Man of the People* (Boston: Beacon Press, 1963); Finis Farr, *Fair Enough: The Life of Westbrook Pegler*

(New York: Arlington House, 1975); Philip Glende, "Westbrook Pegler and the Rise of the Syndicated Columnist," *American Journalism* 36, no. 3 (2019): 322–47; and David Witwer, "Westbrook Pegler and the Anti-Union Movement," *Journal of American History* 92, no. 2 (Sept. 2005): 527–52. Two authoritative sources on Dabney are Morton Sosna, *In Search of the Silent South: Southern Liberals and the Race Issue* (New York: Columbia University Press, 1977), and John T. Kneebone, *Southern Liberal Journalists and the Issue of Race, 1920-1944* (Chapel Hill: University of North Carolina Press, 1985). Two pointedly useful analyses of Dabney's views on race in the early 1940s are Alexander Leidholdt, "Virginius Dabney and Lenoir Chambers: Two Southern Liberal Editors Face Virginia's Massive Resistance to Public School Integration," *American Journalism* 15, no. 4 (Fall 1998): esp. 35–52, and J. Douglas Smith, "'The Ordeal of Virginius Dabney': A Southern Liberal, the Southern Regional Council, and the Limits of Managed Race Relations," paper presented to the Southern Regional Council and the Civil Rights Movement conference, University of Florida, Gainesville, Oct. 23–26, 2003. That paper informs J. Douglas Smith, *Managing White Supremacy: Race, Politics, and Citizenship in Jim Crow Virginia* (Chapel Hill: University of North Carolina Press, 2002).

14. Rayford W. Logan, "The Negro Wants First-Class Citizenship," in Logan, ed., *What the Negro Wants*, 14. Logan was a Black historian who joined the Howard University faculty in 1938. His contributions to the canon on nineteenth- and twentieth-century Black history are often overlooked by white scholars.

15. Kimberley Mangun and Earnest L. Perry Jr., "The Negro/National Newspaper Publishers Association and Its Dual Roles as a Trade and Advocacy Organization, 1940–2020," *Journalism and Communication Monographs* 22, no. 4 (Winter 2020): 269.

16. Washburn, "Pittsburgh Courier's Double V Campaign in 1942," 81–84. When America entered World War II, it adopted the V for Victory campaign launched by British prime minister Winston Churchill in 1941. The patriotic slogan encouraged Americans to support the war effort by, for example, rationing, buying war bonds, and planting "victory" gardens.

17. Egerton, *Speak Now against the Day*, 213–17. Egerton described in detail Randolph's negotiation with Franklin Roosevelt, who signed Executive Order 8802 on June 25, 1941, appointing the Fair Employment Practice Committee in exchange for Randolph's cancellation of a March on Washington.

18. A. Philip Randolph, "March on Washington Movement Presents Program for the Negro," in Logan, ed., *What the Negro Wants*, 153–55; E. Franklin Frazier, "Ethnic and Minority Groups in Wartime, with Special Reference to the Negro," *American Journal of Sociology* 48, no. 3 (Nov. 1942): 376. Frazier joined the Howard University faculty in 1934; he became the first Black president of the American Sociological Association in 1948.

19. Frazier, "Ethnic and Minority Groups in Wartime," 377. His reference to the racial "caste system" preceded publication of Myrdal's groundbreaking study of American race, which popularized that terminology. Myrdal, *An American Dilemma*, 2:667–88.

20. Frazier, "Ethnic and Minority Groups in Wartime," 375.

21. Washburn, *The African American Newspaper*, 172–73. The Negro Newspaper Publishers Association also was involved in the change in 1944, which was followed by admission of a Black reporter to a presidential press conference. Mangun and Perry, "The Negro/National Newspaper Publishers Association," 270.

22. Egerton offered a narrative account of preparation for the meeting and white reaction to the Durham Manifesto in *Speak Now against the Day*, 305-8.
23. Gordon B. Hancock, "Race Relations in the United States: A Summary," in Logan, ed., *What the Negro Wants*, 237. Hancock was a sociologist at Virginia Union University in Richmond. Neither Blacks nor whites were monolithic in their views of the Durham conference. Henry Lewis Suggs, *P. B. Young, Newspaperman: Race, Politics, and Journalism in the New South, 1910-62* (Charlottesville: University Press of Virginia, 1988), 122-23.
24. The Black leaders' Durham meeting was followed by an all-white meeting in Richmond, Virginia, in June 1943, then by a biracial meeting in Atlanta in August. The Atlanta meeting led to the formation of the Southern Regional Council, initially headed by Johnson and Howard Odum, a prominent white sociologist at the University of North Carolina. Egerton, *Speak Now against the Day*, 305-12.
25. Quoted in Harold H. Martin, *Atlanta and Environs: A Chronicle of Its People and Events, 1940s-1970s* (Athens: University of Georgia Press, 2011), 86. The column was published on Dec. 18, 1942.
26. John Temple Graves, "The Southern Negro and the War Crisis," *Virginia Quarterly Review* 18, no. 4 (Autumn 1942), http://www.vqronline.org.
27. Washburn, *A Question of Sedition*, 84-85.
28. See Jeff Woods, *Black Struggle Red Scare: Segregation and Anti-Communism in the South, 1948-1968* (Baton Rouge: Louisiana State University Press, 2004); Mary L. Dudziak, *Cold War Civil Rights: Race and the Image of American Democracy* (Princeton, NJ: Princeton University Press, 2000); George Lewis, *The White South and the Red Menace: Segregationists, Anticommunism, and Massive Resistance, 1945-1965* (Gainesville: University Press of Florida, 2004); and Thomas Borstelmann, *The Cold War and the Color Line: American Race Relations in the Global Arena* (Cambridge, MA: Harvard University Press, 2001).
29. See, for example, Westbrook Pegler, "Fair Enough," *Dothan [AL] Eagle*, April 29, 1942.
30. Finkle, *Forum for Protest*, 65.
31. Stated another way, Pegler's *daily* opinion column had an audience perhaps nine times as large as the combined circulation of the Black *weeklies* publishing in 1942. Mangun and Perry, "The Negro/National Newspaper Publishers Association," 269; Glende, "Westbrook Pegler and the Rise of the Syndicated Columnist," 322-23, 336. Pegler's column was distributed by United Feature and later King Features.
32. Pegler, "Fair Enough," April 29, 1942.
33. "The Press: Crackdown on Coughlin," *Time*, April 27, 1942, https://content.time.com.
34. Glende, "Westbrook Pegler and the Rise of the Syndicated Columnist," 337-38.
35. For decades in the twentieth century, the American Society of Newspaper Editors restricted membership to top editors of daily newspapers, marginalizing the editors of weekly newspapers. Mellinger, *Chasing Newsroom Diversity*, 7.
36. "The Press: Crackdown on Coughlin"; Pegler, "Fair Enough," April 29, 1942.
37. Pride and Wilson, *A History of the Black Press*, 261-62. Thomas Young was the son of P. B. Young Sr., who appears in this chapter and elsewhere in the book.
38. Pegler, "Fair Enough," May 11, 1942.
39. Pegler, "Fair Enough," May 11, 1942
40. Westbrook Pegler, "Fair Enough," *Scranton [PA] Tribune*, June 17, 1942.

41. "The Press: Negro Publishers," *Time*, June 15, 1942, https://time.com.
42. Mangun and Perry, "The Negro/National Newspaper Publishers Association," 269.
43. Westbrook Pegler, "Fair Enough," *Dothan Eagle*, June 18, 1942.
44. Westbrook Pegler, "Fair Enough," *Binghamton Press and Sun-Bulletin*, July 16, 1942.
45. Robert Durr, "The Negro Press: Its Character, Development, and Function," Mississippi Division of the Southern Regional Council (1948), 3, General Education Board Archive, series 1, subseries 3, box 473, folder 5041, Rockefeller Archive Center, Sleepy Hollow, NY.
46. Finkle, *Forum for Protest*, 67.
47. Westbrook Pegler, "Fair Enough," *Binghamton Press and Sun-Bulletin*, Nov. 15, 1943. Marshall Field's inclusion in the "frictioneers" discussion may have referenced his financial support for the *People's Voice*, a Harlem publication started that year by Adam Clayton Powell Jr. "The Press: Negro Publishers."
48. Westbrook Pegler, "Ashmore's Article Reviewed by Carter," *Greenwood [SC] Index Journal*, Jan. 17, 1958.
49. Westbrook Pegler to the Counsel for Roy Bryant and J. W. Milam, Sept. 10, 1955, William Bradford Huie Papers, box 38, folder 353a, Ohio State University Special Collections, Columbus.
50. Virginius Dabney, "Nearer and Nearer the Precipice," *Atlantic Monthly*, Jan. 1943, 94–100.
51. On the FEPC, see Egerton, *Speak Now against the Day*, 213–17. *Gaines v. Canada*, 305 U.S. 337, was a 1938 U.S. Supreme Court ruling that required the state of Missouri to provide graduate school education to a Black student. It was an early victory by the NAACP in the legal journey to desegregate public education. Finkle noted that Dabney first editorialized against the Black press in an editorial in the *Richmond [VA] Times-Dispatch* on April 26, 1942. Finkle, *Forum for Protest*, 63–64.
52. Leidholdt, "Virginius Dabney and Lenoir Chambers," 51.
53. Egerton, *Speak Now against the Day*, 616.
54. Dabney, "Press and Morale," 5–6, 24–25; Warren Brown, "A Negro Looks at the Negro Press," *Saturday Review of Literature*, Dec. 19, 1942, 5–6; V. V. Oak, "What About the Negro Press?" *Saturday Review of Literature*, March 13, 1943, 4–5.
55. Mellinger, *Chasing Newsroom Diversity*, 10.
56. Dabney, "Press and Morale," 25.
57. Kneebone attached the label of southern liberal in *Southern Liberal Journalists*.
58. On the limits of southern liberalism, see Smith, *Managing White Supremacy*, 274–75.
59. Dabney, "Nearer and Nearer the Precipice," 94, 95.
60. Although the incident received wide coverage in the Black press, it also was carried by the AP wire service and reported in white newspapers. "Beaten in Georgia, Says Roland Hayes," *New York Times*, July 17, 1942.
61. Dabney, "Nearer and Nearer the Precipice," 96, 97, 99.
62. Quoted in Sosna, *In Search of the Silent South*, 133, 132. Young's reference is to three outspoken racists: Mississippi congressman John E. Rankin, Georgia governor Eugene Talmage, and Mississippi senator and governor Theodore Bilbo.
63. Virginius Dabney, "Newspapers and the Negro," *Quill*, Nov.–Dec. 1943, 3, 14, was a reprint of "The Press and the Interracial Crisis," *ASNE Bulletin*, Sept. 1, 1943, 1–2, 3.
64. Jackson Davis, Interview Report: Virginius Dabney, Jan. 7, 1944, General Education Board Archives, series 1, subseries 3, box 427, folder 5037. Davis, a native Virginian

then based in New York, routinely visited the South to gather information for the Rockefeller philanthropy. He called on Dabney in Richmond.

65. Public transportation ridership had increased during the war. Smith wrote, "Forced to sit or stand in the rear of common carriers, African American riders had to push their way through aisles packed with whites. Instead of keeping the races apart, as intended, Dabney explained, this particular segregation statute actually had the opposite effect and had become a 'constant source of trouble, irritation, and bad feeling.'" Smith, "'The Ordeal of Virginius Dabney,'" 16.
66. Finkle, *Forum for Protest*, 75
67. Brown, "A Negro Looks at the Negro Press," 5–6; Oak, "What About the Negro Press?" 4–5. Oak's article has received little attention in scholarship on the wartime Black press. Although Finkle provided a detailed account of the Warren Brown fiasco, he did not address V. V. Oak's *Saturday Review of Literature* article. Finkle, *Forum for Protest*, 73–77. In *The African American Newspaper*, Washburn cites Oak's scholarship on the business side of the Black press but does not engage either of the *Saturday Review* articles.
68. Finkle, *Forum for Protest*, 73, 75. Finkle's sourcing for his detailed discussion of the Brown fiasco comes from articles in eight Black newspapers, which covered it widely.
69. Jackson Davis, Interview Report: Claude Barnett, March 1, 1944, General Education Board Archives, series 1, subseries 3, box 390, folder 4084. Davis's background information on Brown and the *Saturday Review* article came from Claude Barnett of the Associated Negro Press. A few weeks later, Davis memorialized conversations with Brown and others affiliated with the CFD, who sought GEB funding for a news agency that would compete with Barnett's. Jackson Davis, Interview Report: Charles S. Johnson, March 13, 1944, General Education Board Archives, series 1, subseries 3, box 390, folder 4084. The GEB did not fund the request.
70. Warren H. Brown, "A Negro Warns the Negro Press," *Richmond Times-Dispatch*, Dec. 27, 1942.
71. Brown, "A Negro Looks at the Negro Press," 5, 6.
72. Oak, "What About the Negro Press?" 4.
73. Oak, "What About the Negro Press?" 4–5.
74. Myrdal, *An American Dilemma*, 2:910.
75. Oak's history is unclear and he may not have published any discussion about race and journalism after 1950. In 1948 he authored a book on the Black press and then dropped out of the canon. V. V. Oak, *The Negro Press* (Yellow Springs, OH: Antioch Press, 1948).
76. Ethan Michaeli, *The Defender: How the Legendary Black Newspaper Changed America* (Boston: Mariner Books, 2016), 245.
77. Jackson Davis, Interview Report: Claude Barnett, Jan. 25, 1943, General Education Board Archives, series 1, subseries 3, box 390, folder 4084.
78. Washburn, *A Question of Sedition*, chapters 4–6.
79. Mellinger, "An Idea before Its Time," 62–89.
80. The number of columns is estimated from extant drafts and supporting correspondence in the Charles S. Johnson Papers at Fisk University, Nashville, and the digitized records of the Associated Negro Press, including the Claude A. Barnett Papers, Black Freedom Struggle in the Twentieth Century, History Vault Collection, ProQuest.

81. Claude A. Barnett to Bonita Valien, April 20, 1946, Charles S. Johnson Papers, box 9, folder 10, Fisk University, Nashville.
82. Despite a broad archive documenting the careers of both men, Johnson's and Barnett's collaboration is not mentioned in the literature on their contributions to civil rights generally and to the Black press specifically. Two histories of the ANP provide the most detailed treatment of Barnett's career: Lawrence D. Hogan's updated and expanded history of the ANP, *A Black National News Service: The Associated Negro Press and Claude Barnett* (Haworth, NJ: St. Johann Press, 2002), and Gerald Horne, *The Rise and Fall of the Associated Negro Press: Claude Barnett's Pan-African News and the Jim Crow Paradox* (Champaign: University of Illinois Press, 2017). Of the large volume of scholarship on Johnson, the definitive histories are Patrick J. Gilpin and Marybeth Gasman, *Charles S. Johnson: Leadership beyond the Veil in the Age of Jim Crow* (Albany: SUNY Press, 2003), and Richard Robbins, *Sidelines Activist: Charles Johnson and the Struggle for Civil Rights* (Jackson: University of Mississippi Press, 1996).
83. The same month that Johnson added a college presidency to his curriculum vitae, Barnett reported that Walter White, executive secretary of the NAACP, had also started writing a column for the daily press. "Looks as though we paved the way for Walter White, doesn't it?" Barnett wrote. "Evidently one of the New York syndicates attempted to sell his stuff." Claude Barnett to Charles Johnson, Oct. 30, 1946, Johnson Papers, box 9, folder 10. Graphic Syndicate would distribute White's column to daily newspapers until 1950, when the *New York Herald Tribune,* the only daily paper publishing it routinely, dropped it and the syndicate in turn dropped White as a client. Kenneth Robert Janken, *Walter White: Mr. NAACP* (Chapel Hill: University of North Carolina Press, 2006), 348. Because White's column very pointedly contributed to the public relations function of the NAACP, its significance for breaking barriers in daily journalism is negligible. The column's byline identified White as an officer of the NAACP, his topic often was the NAACP itself, and his argument generally advanced the positions of the organization, blurring the line between an opinion column and a press release. See, for example, Walter White, "Red Threat to 'Take Over' NAACP No Cause for Alarm," *Akron [OH] Beacon Journal,* Dec. 19, 1947, and Walter White, "Negro Petition to U.N.," *Detroit Free Press,* Oct. 26, 1947. Notably, White also wrote a column for the Black press, which was published widely for many years.
84. For a comprehensive history of the role of the white press in the civil rights movement, see Gene Roberts and Hank Klibanoff, *The Race Beat: The Press, the Civil Rights Struggle, and the Awakening of a Nation* (New York: Vintage, 2007).
85. Hogan, *A Black National News Service,* 250. Roberts and Klibanoff's description of the ANP emphasizes the limitations of content distributed by mail. Roberts and Klibanoff, *The Race Beat,* 16. Barnett suspended the ANP's operations in 1964, when the fortunes of the Black press, which had set circulation records during the 1940s, declined and the business model could not be sustained. Hogan, *A Black National News Service,* 246–48. Washburn's *The African American Newspaper* mentions Barnett and the ANP only in passing and defers to Hogan.
86. Charles S. Johnson, "A Minority View: Voting Appeal, North and South," n.d., Johnson Papers, box 166, folder 1.

87. Charles S. Johnson, "A Minority View: Race and Economics," Aug. 25, 1946, Johnson Papers, box 166, folder 3.
88. Charles S. Johnson, "A Minority View: The Passing Show," n.d., Johnson Papers, box 166, folder 3.
89. Gilpin and Gasman, *Charles S. Johnson*, 29.
90. Gilpin and Gasman, *Charles S. Johnson*, 19–25. During the 1920s, Johnson also was among the Black contributors to *The Messenger*, a prominent publication on culture and politics that provided an outlet during the Harlem Renaissance. In particular, Johnson wrote an installment in a series called "These 'Colored' United States." Adam McKible, "Our(?) Country: Mapping 'These "Colored" United States' in *The Messenger*," in *The Black Press: New Literary and Historical Essays*, ed. Todd Vogel (New Brunswick, NJ: Rutgers University Press, 2001), 124–26.
91. Marybeth Gasman, "The Presidency of Charles S. Johnson at Fisk University as a Model of Collaboration between Philanthropy and Black Higher Education, 1946–1956," *Research Reports*, Spring 1999, 6, Rockefeller Archive Center. On GEB support for Fisk University, see Raymond B. Fosdick, *Adventure in Giving: The Story of the General Education Board* (New York: Harper and Row, 1962), 193.
92. Charles Johnson to Claude Barnett, Dec. 17, 1942; Jan. 13, 1943, Johnson Papers, box 9, folder 9.
93. Claude Barnett to Charles Johnson, July 13, 1943, Johnson Papers, box 9, folder 9.
94. Jackson Davis, interoffice memo, May 10, 1945, General Education Board Archives, series 1, subseries 3, box 390, folder 4084.
95. Jackson Davis, report of interview with Arthur Hays Sulzberger, April 14, 1944, General Education Board Archives, series 1, subseries 3, box 420, folder 4405.
96. Channing H. Tobias to Claude Barnett, April 17, 1944, Johnson Papers, box 9, folder 9. Tobias, who was affiliated with the Young Men's Christian Association (YMCA) and was on temporary assignment to the GEB, was a director of the NAACP. He would be appointed to the President's Committee on Civil Rights in 1946 and would serve as chair of the NAACP from 1953 to 1960.
97. Charles Johnson to Jackson Davis, May 23, 1945; General Education Board, "Grant in Aid to Fisk University," May 30, 1945; General Education Board, "Grant in Aid to Fisk University," March 7, 1946, General Education Board Archives, series 1, subseries 3, box 420, folder 4405.
98. In 1944 Johnson compiled for Barnett a list of ten white southern daily newspaper editors whose racial dispositions hinted at some degree of moderation, and who Johnson thought should receive an initial solicitation: Mark Ethridge, *Louisville [KY] Courier-Journal*; Harry Ayers, *Anniston [AL] Star*; Jennings Perry, *Nashville Tennessean*; Virginius Dabney, *Richmond Times-Dispatch*; C. M. Stanley, *Montgomery [AL] Advertiser & Journal*; Ralph McGill, *Atlanta Constitution*; Ted Dealey, *Dallas Morning News*; Jack Carley, *Memphis Commercial Appeal*; Josephus Daniels, *Raleigh [NC] News and Observer*; and Louis Jaffe, *Norfolk Virginian-Pilot*. Charles Johnson to Harry M. Ayers, undated draft, and H. M. Perry to Claude Barnett, Jan. 8, 1944, Johnson Papers, box 9, folder 9; Johnson to Barnett, Jan. 23, 1945, Johnson Papers, box 9, folder 10.
99. Charles Johnson to Harry M. Ayers, n.d., Johnson Papers, box 9, folder 9.
100. Charles Johnson to Harry M. Ayers, n.d., Johnson Papers, box 9, folder 9.
101. Claude Barnett to Charles Johnson, Nov. 7, 1944, Johnson Papers, box 9, folder 9.
102. Claude Barnett to Alma Forrest, Dec. 9, 1944, Johnson Papers, box 9, folder 9.

103. Claude Barnett to Charles Johnson, Jan. 23, 1945; Johnson to Barnett, Jan. 27, 1945, Johnson Papers, box 9, folder 10.
104. Virginius Dabney to Claude Barnett, Jan. 27, 1945, Johnson Papers, box 9, folder 10.
105. R. L. McGrath to Claude Barnett, Feb. 8, 1945, Johnson Papers, box 9, folder 10.
106. Erwin D. Canham to Claude Barnett, Feb. 19, 1945, Johnson Papers, box 9, folder 10.
107. David R. Davies, *The Postwar Decline of American Newspapers, 1945–1965* (Westport, CT: Praeger, 2006), 6–7. Davies notes that even though the federal rationing order ended in 1945, newsprint remained in short supply and prices were inflated after the war.
108. Ted Dealey to Charles Johnson, Jan. 26, 1945, Claude Barnett Papers, box 234, folder 1.
109. In 1941 President Franklin Roosevelt appointed Ethridge as the first director of the FEPC, created by executive order to eliminate discrimination in defense-industry employment. Ethridge resigned three years later in frustration over the FEPC's lack of enforcement power. Egerton, *Speak Now against the Day*, 216–17.
110. Mark Ethridge to Claude Barnett, Jan. 26, 1946, Johnson Papers, box 9, folder 10.
111. Claude Barnett to Charles Johnson, Feb. 22., May 12, 1944, Johnson Papers, box 9, folder 9. As it happened, Johnson had assisted Myrdal with data collection for the project. Gilpin and Gasman, *Charles S. Johnson*, 71–77.
112. Charles Johnson to Claude Barnett, Dec. 28, 1945, Johnson Papers, box 9, folder 10.
113. Bonita Valien to Claude Barnett, Feb. 19, 1946; Barnett to Valien, Feb. 23, 1946, Johnson Papers, box 9, folder 10.
114. Bonita Valien to Claude Barnett, March 26, 1946, Johnson Papers, box 9, folder 10, and all in Claude Barnett Papers, box 234, folder 1: Claude Barnett to Bonita Valien, Dec. 7, 1946; April 22, 1947; Valien to Barnett, June 6, 1947; and Barnett to Valien, June 13, 1947.
115. Charles S. Johnson, "Opinion Poll on Race Question Shows Sway of Ignorance and Bias," *Kansas City [MO] Star*, Feb. 2, 1945; Johnson, "And Segregation Came: Negro Educator Tells Childhood Experience," *Des Moines [IA] Register*, Feb. 10, 1945.
116. Charles S. Johnson, "Cotton Picking Device Perils Millions in South," *Milwaukee Journal*, Feb. 17, 1946.
117. Carroll Binder to Claude Barnett, Jan. 29, 1946, Claude Barnett Papers, box 234, folder 1; Binder to Barnett, March 12, April 4, May 21, 1946, Johnson Papers, box 9, folder 10.
118. Bonita Valien to Claude Barnett, March 26, 1946; Barnett to Valien, March 30, April 20, 1946, Johnson Papers, box 9, folder 10.
119. All to the ANP and found in the Claude Barnett Papers, box 234, folder 1: N. J. Minor, March 1, 1947; Hilda E. Winns, March 2, 1947; Mildred R. Mell, March 3, 1947; William W. Sibley, March 7, 1947; Joseph Stepansky, March 25, 1947; and L. B. Langes, n.d. Also, Claude Barnett to Fred Schechter, March 2, 1947, and to Mary Arakelian, March 25, 1947.
120. George L. Gardiner to Claude Barnett, July 1, 1959, Claude Barnett Papers, box 234, folder 1.
121. Claude Barnett to George L. Gardiner, July 1, 1959, Claude Barnett Papers, box 233, folder 5.
122. Mellinger, *Chasing Newsroom Diversity*, 52–57.
123. Carl T. Rowan, *Breaking Barriers* (New York: Harper Perennial, 1991), 278. In fact, Rowan was not the first Black columnist to receive a contract for regular national

distribution with a newspaper syndicate. A year earlier Roy Wilkins had secured a contract with the Register and Tribune Service of the Cowles Newspaper Company. His columns appeared weekly in more than a hundred newspapers. Sid Bedingfield, "The Journalism of Roy Wilkins and the Rise of Law and Order Rhetoric, 1964–1968," *Journalism History* 45, no. 3 (2019): 250–69n7.

124. Pamela Newkirk, *Within the Veil: Black Journalists, White Media* (New York: New York University Press, 2000), 191.
125. Charles Johnson to Jackson Davis, Feb. 21, 1946, General Education Board Archives, series 1, subseries 3, box 420, folder 4405.
126. General Education Board, "Grant in Aid to Fisk University," March 7, 1946, General Education Board Archives, series 1, subseries 3, box 420, folder 4405.
127. Charles Johnson to Jackson Davis, Feb. 21, 1946, General Education Board Archives, series 1, subseries 3, box 420, folder 4405.

## CHAPTER 2

1. See, for example, Associated Press: "Startled Nurse Handed Basket Full of Babies," *Post-Register* (Idaho Falls, ID), Dec. 7, 1948; "Wife Has Triplets; He Brings Them to Hospital in Basket," *Chicago Tribune*, Dec. 8, 1948; and "Triplets Born, Dad Is 'Stork,'" *Baltimore Sun*, Dec. 8, 1948.
2. A series of U.S. Supreme Court rulings began the integration of graduate schools, outlawed the white primary, banned segregation on interstate transportation, and found race-based real estate covenants to be unconstitutional. The cases were, respectively, *Missouri ex rel. Gaines v. Canada*, 305 U.S. 337 (1938); *Smith v. Allwright*, 321 U.S. 649 (1944); *Morgan v. Virginia*, 328 U.S. 373 (1946); and *Shelly v. Kraemer*, 334 U.S. 1 (1948).
3. See, for example, "Objectivity Is Called Screen for 'Phonies,'" *Editor and Publisher*, Nov. 17, 1951, 26. In addition, Michael Schudson referenced a 1933 resolution by the American Society of Newspaper Editors calling for a greater emphasis on interpretive reporting. Schudson, *Discovering the News: A Social History of American Newspapers* (New York: Basic Books, 1978), 148. In the five years preceding the *Brown v. Board of Education* desegregation decision, the ASNE's monthly *Bulletin* published more than a dozen articles and letters debating the merits of reporting that employed the conventions of objectivity. See, for example, Oxie Reichler, "Does 'Deadpan' Reporting Do the Job?" *ASNE Bulletin*, Aug. 1, 1952, 7, and Carl Lindstrom, "By What Right Do We Interpret or Explain?" *ASNE Bulletin*, Jan. 1, 1953, 2–3.
4. Reese also reportedly rejected a suggestion by his publisher, Joseph Pulitzer, in 1941 to hire a Black reporter. "Pulitzer of the St. Louis Post Dispatch," *American Journalism Review*, Nov. 1991, http://ajrarchive.org.
5. H. T. Meek to Alan J. Gould, Oct. 1, 1948, 1948 Subject Files, box 80, Negro file, Associated Press Corporate Archives (hereafter APCA), New York.
6. W. S. Kirkpatrick to Alan J. Gould, Dec. 27, 1948, APCA, Subject Files, box 80, Negro file.
7. *The APME Red Book 1948* (New York: Associated Press, 1948), 35.
8. Alan J. Gould to W. S. Kirkpatrick, Dec. 29, 1948, APCA, Subject Files, box 80, Negro file. Gould had an important AP career before taking the executive editor's position in 1941. His varied resume included development of the AP college football rankings

and oversight of the wire service's World War II coverage. Wolfgang Saxon, "Alan J. Gould, 95, Editor and Innovator at Associated Press," *New York Times*, June 22, 1993.
9. "Triplets Born, Dad Is 'Stork,'" *Baltimore Sun*, Dec. 8, 1948.
10. David R. Davies, *The Postwar Decline of American Newspapers, 1945–1965* (Westport, CT: Praeger, 2006), 64. For an analysis of anti-crime rhetoric in midcentury news reporting, see Sid Bedingfield, "The Journalism of Roy Wilkins and the Rise of Law and Order Rhetoric," *Journalism History* 45, no. 3 (2019): 250–69.
11. The dysfunctional-family stereotype would be validated in the mid-1960s by the "The Negro Family: The Case for National Action," published by the Office of Policy Planning and Research, U.S. Department of Labor, and commonly referred to as the "Moynihan Report." Although intended to benefit Black Americans, the report has been widely criticized as pathologizing the Black family. Daniel Geary, "The Moynihan Report: An Annotated Edition," *Atlantic*, Sept. 14, 2015, https://www.theatlantic.com.
12. This sample shows how AP members edited the story differently for use on their front pages: The *Baltimore Sun* ran a version that described Logan as "a Negro cement worker" and the *Chicago Tribune* referred to Logan as "a young Negro," while the Idaho Falls paper identified him as "a young man." "Startled Nurse Handed Basket Full of Babies," *Post-Register*, Dec. 7, 1948; "Wife Has Triplets; He Brings Them to Hospital in Basket," *Chicago Tribune*, Dec. 8, 1948; "Triplets Born, Dad Is 'Stork,'" *Baltimore Sun*, Dec. 8, 1948.
13. Alvin Orton, memo to New York AP office, Dec. 8, 1948, APCA, Subject Files, box 80, Negro file. Whalen's comment echoed Ira Harkey, who edited the *Pascagoula [MS] Chronicle* from 1949 to 1963 and was one of the few white southern editors who condemned the racism in attaching the Negro adjective to every noun associated with a Black news subject or Black culture. "The fetish produces foolish journalism," he wrote. Ira Harkey, *The Smell of Burning Crosses* (N.p.: Xlibris, 1967), 42.
14. Michael J. Klarman, *From Jim Crow to Civil Rights: The Supreme Court and the Struggle for Racial Equality* (New York: Oxford University Press, 2004), 385–442.
15. During the 1920s, the NAACP compiled and updated a list of publications that capitalized the "N" in Negro. Walter White to Herbert Seligman, Oct. 15, 1929, NAACP Papers, part 15, series B, group 2, box A-430, reel 8, Library of Congress, Washington, DC.
16. In his biography of Louis Jaffe, editor of the *Norfolk Virginian-Pilot* from 1919 to 1950, Alexander Leidholdt describes Jaffe's leadership in coverage of Black Americans. Jaffe was using the capital "N" on his editorial page by 1927, eleven years before editor Ralph McGill adopted the policy for the *Atlanta Constitution*. Leidholdt, *The Life of Louis Jaffe: Editor for Justice* (Baton Rouge: Louisiana State University Press, 2002), 213.
17. Virginius Dabney, "Newspapers and the Negro," *Quill*, November–December 1943, 14. Dabney also said the honorifics Dr. and Professor should precede Blacks' names and that such courtesy titles as Mr., Mrs., and Miss should be used on a case-by-case basis, as with whites: "Educated men and women, perhaps with college degrees and achievements in the arts and sciences, cannot be handled as illiterate swineherds."
18. Edna Freeman to Mrs. Donald Siskind, April 30, 1952; James Egert Allen to Henry L. Moon, March 27, 1953, NAACP Papers, part 15, series B, group 2, box A-453, reel 9.

19. Westbrook Pegler, "Fair Enough," *Dothan [AL] Eagle*, June 18, 1942. Singer Marian Anderson and boxer Joe Louis were celebrities at the time.
20. "Race in the News," *New York Times*, Aug. 11, 1946.
21. Edna Freeman to Mrs. Donald Siskind, April 30, 1952; James Egert Allen to Henry L. Moon, March 27, 1953, NAACP Papers, part 15, series B, group 2, box A-453, reel 9. It was logical for the NAACP to focus its direct advocacy on northern newspapers as many southern editors expressed contempt for the NAACP, which they suspected of communist affiliation. By the mid-1950s some states used the allegation of a communist tie as an excuse for restricting NAACP operations. See, for example, George Lewis, *The White South and the Red Menace: Segregationists, Anticommunism, and Massive Resistance, 1945–1965* (Gainesville: University Press of Florida, 2004); Yashuhiro Katagiri, *Black Freedom, White Resistance, and Red Menace: Civil Rights and Anticommunism in the Jim Crow South* (Baton Rouge: Louisiana State University Press, 2014); and Jeff Woods, *Black Struggle, Red Scare: Segregation and Anti-Communism in the South, 1948–1968* (Baton Rouge: Louisiana State University Press, 2004).
22. Race Relations Committee, City Club of Chicago, "John Smith, Negro, in the Tribune," Sept. 12, 1950, 4, 7, 3, in APCA, 1951 Subject Files, box 95, Negro file. The 1947 report of the Commission on Freedom of the Press headed by Robert Hutchins, president of the University of Chicago from 1945 to 1951, echoes here. Robert D. Leigh, ed., *A Free and Responsible Press* (Chicago: University of Chicago Press, 1974).
23. City Club of Chicago, "John Smith, Negro, in the Tribune," 4.
24. David R. Davies offers a detailed discussion of the debate over racial identification and representation in news about Black Americans in "An Industry in Transition: Major Trends in American Daily Newspapers, 1945–1965" (PhD diss., University of Alabama, 1997), chapter 6. Typically, historical treatment of the issue is mentioned in passing, tied to an editor's decision to change newsroom policy. See, for example, Gene Roberts and Hank Klibanoff, *The Race Beat: The Press, the Civil Rights Struggle, and the Awakening of a Nation* (New York: Vintage, 2007), 55–56. Roberts and Klibanoff, who discuss representation decisions at the *Arkansas Gazette*, refer to the identifier issue as "racial tagging." The research of Roy Carter Jr. also informs this area of scholarship: "Segregation and the News: A Regional Content Study," *Journalism Quarterly* 34 (Winter 1957): 3–18, and "Racial Identification Effects upon the News Story Writer," *Journalism Quarterly* 36 (Summer 1959): 284–90.
25. This characterization does not imply that the AP was politically neutral in this role. See Gene Allen, *Mr. Associated Press: Kent Cooper and the Twentieth-Century World of News* (Champaign: University of Illinois Press, 2023), chapter 8, and Larry Heinzerling and Randy Herschaft, *Newshawks in Berlin: The Associated Press and Nazi Germany* (New York: Columbia University Press, 2024), 39–40.
26. Gwyneth Mellinger and Erin K. Coyle, "'Blackening Up Journalism': An Ethical Imperative for Newsroom Diversity," in *Journalism's Ethical Progression: A Twentieth-Century Journey*, ed. Gwyneth Mellinger and John Ferré (Lanham, MD: Lexington Books, 2020), 190.
27. According to various studies, twenty-one Black journalists were employed at white-owned daily newspapers in 1955, twelve in 1952, and fifteen in 1948. Armistead Scott Pride, "Low Man on the Totem," *Nieman Reports*, April 1955, 21, cited in Davies, *The Postwar Decline of American Newspapers*, 66.

28. The segregated content was often designated by a black star on the nameplate of a newspaper's edition. Gunnar Myrdal, *An American Dilemma: The Negro Problem and Modern Democracy*, 2 vols. (1944; reprint New Brunswick, NJ: Transaction, 1996), 29. See also Davies, *The Postwar Decline of American Newspapers*, 64–65.
29. The list of publications, speeches, and radio and television appearances is long. See, for example, Thomas R. Waring, "The Southern Case against Desegregation," *Harper's*, Jan. 1956, 39–45; James Kilpatrick, *Sovereign States: Notes of a Citizen of Virginia* (Chicago: Regnery, 1957); and William D. Workman, *The Case for the South* (New York: Devin-Adair, 1960).
30. Roberts and Klibanoff, *The Race Beat*, 215–21.
31. Thomas Waring, "Highlander School's Influence Felt among Charleston County Negroes," *News and Courier* (Charleston, SC), March 12, 1959.
32. On interpellation, see Louis Althusser, "Ideology and Ideological State Apparatuses (Notes towards an Investigation)," in *Lenin and Philosophy and Other Essays* (New York: Monthly Review Press, 1971), 175. A number of scholars have theorized the power that whiteness derives from invisibility. They include Toni Morrison, bell hooks, Ruth Frankenberg, David Roediger, Howard Winant, George Lipsitz, and Ian Haney-Lopez. However, in the context of objectivity in the media, Stuart Hall's work is directly on point. Hall defined the power of whiteness as "the 'absent' but imperializing 'white eye'; the unmarked position from which all these 'observations are made and from which, alone, they make sense." Hall, "The Whites of Their Eyes," in *The Media Reader*, ed. Manuel Alvarado and John O. Thompson (London: British Film Institute, 1990), 14.
33. On the legal and ideological significance of racial "passing," which entailed a person with Black ancestry circulating undetected in white society, see Cheryl Harris, "Whiteness as Property," in *Critical Race Theory: The Key Writings That Formed the Movement*, ed. Kimberle Crenshaw et al. (New York: New Press, 1995), 276–91. The "one-drop rule" and white fear that Blacks would pass for white was salient as white Americans defended the racial status quo. From 1929 to 1955 the NAACP was led by the blonde, blue-eyed Walter White, who chose to embrace his Black ancestry. His biographer wrote, "His appearance gave him the option—which he did not exercise—to pass for white, but it nevertheless stamped the way he looked at the world and the way the world looked at him." Kenneth Robert Janken, *Walter White: Mr. NAACP* (Chapel Hill: University of North Carolina Press, 2003), 2.
34. In his autobiography, Kent Cooper, former AP executive director, marveled that "an imponderable, indefinable feeling akin to devotion for The Associated Press came into the hearts of some of" the members. Cooper, *Kent Cooper and the Associated Press* (New York: Random House, 1959), 201.
35. John Herbers, *Deep South Dispatch: Memoir of a Civil Rights Journalist* (Jackson: University Press of Mississippi, 2018), 47, 51–52.
36. Tanner Hunt to Alan J. Gould, Oct. 29, 1956, APCA, 1956 Subject Files, box 118, Negro file.
37. Calvin Monroe to Alan J. Gould, Dec. 8, 1955, APCA, 1955 Subject Files, box 113, Negro file.
38. *Associated Press Stylebook* (New York: Associated Press, 1953), 8. Despite the stylebook's prescription for capitalization, members of the AP staff applied the rule inconsistently in their own correspondence.

39. *Associated Press Stylebook*, 1960, 6. Regarding changes that commenced with the 1977 AP stylebook, Fred Vultee described the 1960 edition as "a slender 50 pages, devoted to such matters as typography and spelling." The 1977 edition was "the first incarnation of the dictionary-like guide known today." Vultee, "A Paleontology of Style: The Evolution of the Middle East in the AP Stylebook, 1977–2010," *Journalism Practice* 6, no. 4 (2012): 452.
40. Misidentifying a white person as Black constituted libel per se—libel on its face—into the 1950s. See Aimee Edmondson, "'Pure Caucasian Blood': Libel by Racial Misidentification in American Newspapers (1900–1957)," *American Journalism* 38, no. 1 (2021): 54–80, and Samuel L. Brenner, "Negro Blood in His Veins: The Development and Disappearance of the Doctrine of Defamation Per Se by Racial Misidentification in the American South," Samuel L. Brenner blog, Feb. 2009, 54–62, http://works.bepress.com.
41. Byron Price to News Editors, Bureau Chiefs and Correspondents, Nov. 1, 1940, News Department Circular Letters, series 2, APCA, AP Collections Online, AP15.3, box 1, folder 1.
42. Alan J. Gould, "Note to File re: AP Reference Book, page 40A," n.d., APCA, 1954 Subject Files, box 107, Negro file.
43. Alan J. Gould, "Note to File re: APME Session in Washington, April 14, 1954," APCA, 1954 Subject Files, box 107, Negro file.
44. *The APME Red Book 1955* (New York: Associated Press, 1955), 34.
45. The organization of correspondence in the Associated Press Corporate Archive complicates a precise count of letters expressing editor sentiment on the issue. AP executives judiciously filed their correspondence, but letters appear not only in corporate subject files on racial issues but also in member files and bureau records. In addition, members often addressed multiple issues related to the news report in a single letter, which means some letters may not have been cross-referenced to files about racial identification.
46. Alan J. Gould to Bob Choate, April 7, 1954, APCA, 1954 Subject Files, box 107, Negro file.
47. David Tenant Bryan to Frank Starzel, Sept. 7, 1956, APCA, 1956 Subject Files, box 118, Negro file.
48. Paul R. Mickelson to David Tenant Bryan, Sept. 10, 1956, APCA, 1956 Subject Files, box 118, Negro file.
49. Harmon Phillips to Alan J. Gould, Sept. 17, 1955, APCA, 1955 Subject Files, box 113, Negro file.
50. Alan J. Gould to Harmon Phillips, Sept. 21, 1955, APCA, 1955 Subject Files, box 113, Negro file.
51. Tippen Davidson to Noland Norgaard, Jan. 1, 1954, APCA, 1954 Subject Files, box 107, Negro file.
52. Noland Norgaard to Tippen Davidson, Jan. 12, 1954, APCA, 1954 Subject Files, box 107, Negro file.
53. Malcolm B. Johnson to Tippen Davidson, Jan. 18, 1954, APCA, 1954 Subject Files, box 107, Negro file.
54. Ben Leuchter to Samuel Blackman, Feb. 22, 1955, APCA, 1955 Subject Files, box 113, Negro file.

55. Samuel Blackman to Ben Leuchter, Feb. 25, 1955, APCA, 1955 Subject Files, box 113, Negro file.
56. Lew Hawkins, memo to staff of AP Atlanta Bureau, Nov. 11, 1954, APCA, 1954 Subject Files, box 107, Negro file.
57. Lew Hawkins to Alan J. Gould, Nov. 11, 1954, APCA, 1954 Subject Files, box 107, Negro file.
58. Alan J. Gould to Lew Hawkins, Nov. 12, 1954, APCA, 1954 Subject Files, box 107, Negro file.
59. Stan Atkins to Alan J. Gould, April 23, 1956, APCA, 1956 Subject Files, box, 118, Negro file.
60. Paul R. Mickelson to Michael J. Ogden, June 29, 1955, APCA, 1955 Subject Files, box 113, Negro file.
61. Samuel G. Blackman to Nelson Bryant, March 27, 1959, APCA, Subject Files 1961, box137, Negro file.
62. Cy Douglass to Paul Mickelson, Jan. 28, 1956, APCA, Subject Files 1956, box 118, Negro file.
63. Miles A Smith to Lew Hawkins, May 31, 1956, APCA, Subject Files 1956: box 118, Negro file.
64. Lewis Hawkins to Miles A. Smith, June 2, 1956, APCA, 1956 Subject Files, box 118, Negro file.
65. Miles A Smith to Lew Hawkins, May 31, 1956, APCA, 1956 Subject Files: box 118, Negro file.
66. Waring's newspaper relented on courtesy titles as well as the capital N. Thomas R. Waring to William D. Workman, Nov. 18, 1955, William D. Workman Papers, box 10, folder: CN&C, General, 1955, University of South Carolina, Columbia.
67. Angie Maxwell offers extensive treatment of the southern inferiority complex in terms of the North, as well as southern editors' perception of a "paper curtain" that separated northern and southern journalism during the civil rights movement. Maxwell, *The Indicted South: Public Criticism, Southern Inferiority, and the Politics of Whiteness* (Chapel Hill: University of North Carolina Press, 2014), 204–10.
68. Quoted in Miles Wolff to Oscar Morris, March 12, 1954, APCA, 1954 Subject Files, box 107, Negro file.
69. "Censorship," *Chattanooga [TN] News-Free Press*, Jan. 21, 1956.
70. Alan J. Gould, Memo to Domestic Chiefs of Bureau and Correspondents, Feb. 2, 1956, APCA, 1956 Subject Files, box 118, Negro file.
71. Roberts and Klibanoff, *The Race Beat*, 85–106. For a detailed analysis of regional self-interest in media coverage of the Emmett Till murder and trial, see Darryl Mace, *In Remembrance of Emmett Till: Regional Stories and Media Responses to the Black Freedom Struggle* (Lexington: University of Kentucky Press, 2014).
72. Alan J. Gould to Tanner T. Hunt, Nov. 2, 1956, APCA, 1956 Subject Files, box 118, Negro file.
73. Quoted in Lew Hawkins to Alan J. Gould, April 25, 1956, APCA, 1956 Subject Files, box 118, Negro file.
74. The Kerner Report would make this point: "The media report and write from the standpoint of a white man's world." *Report of the National Advisory Commission on Civil Disorders* (Princeton, NJ: Princeton University Press, 2016), 368.

## CHAPTER 3

1. Harry S. Ashmore, *An Epitaph for Dixie* (New York: Norton, 1957), 160.
2. Harry Ashmore to Walter White, Dec. 1, 1948, Harry S. Ashmore Collection, box 1, folder 3, Center for Arkansas History and Culture, University of Arkansas–Little Rock. Ashmore used the "man in the middle" device differently in a collection of lectures delivered at the University of Missouri in the mid-1960s. There, Ashmore's "man in the middle," who belongs to "democracy's controlling majority," is "complacent and intellectually inert." Harry S. Ashmore, *The Man in the Middle* (Columbia: University of Missouri Press, 1966), 42.
3. Most notably Harry S. Ashmore, *Hearts and Minds: The Anatomy of Racism from Roosevelt to Reagan* (New York: McGraw-Hill, 1982), and Ashmore, *Civil Rights and Wrongs: A Memoir of Race and Politics, 1944–1996* (Columbia: University of South Carolina Press, 1997).
4. Ashmore, *An Epitaph for Dixie*, 78.
5. Elizabeth Jacoway, *Turn Away Thy Son: Little Rock, the Crisis That Shocked the Nation* (New York: Free Press, 2007), 23, 26. Jacoway argued that Ashmore was caught off guard by the Little Rock school desegregation crisis because of his disengagement from Little Rock and the distraction of writing *An Epitaph for Dixie*, published earlier that year.
6. Gene Roberts and Hank Klibanoff, *The Race Beat: The Press, the Civil Rights Struggle, and the Awakening of a Nation* (New York: Vintage, 2007), 143–45.
7. Porter McKeever to H. Rowan Gaither Jr., internal FAE memos, Jan. 6, 25, 1954, McPeak Collection, Program Area 4, series 2, box 6, folder 177, Ford Foundation Archives, Rockefeller Archives Center hereafter RAC), Sleepy Hollow, NY. Ashmore, *An Epitaph for Dixie*, 160–61, dates the FAE decision to fund the research in 1954, but the project was underway in 1953. In addition, Ashmore claimed the book was "published coincidentally with the Court's ruling," but internal FAE memos affirm that the timing was partially by design, after the FAE considered holding the book until the summer of 1954. The report was first published in a limited run by the University of North Carolina Press for free distribution. FAE directors with a special interest in the white press—Time Inc. executive Roy Larsen, syndicated columnist Walter Lippmann, and Louisville newspaper editor Barry Bingham Sr.—were consulted on this and other aspects of the project. The board agreed to publish the book when the manuscript was finished, and knowing that the book would appear in April or May, declined to intervene in the publication schedule to avoid a release concurrent with the anticipated Supreme Court ruling. The Jan. 6, 1954, memo cited here acknowledged that "a decision to postpone is in itself a political judgement in relation to a study which is wholly non-political in concept and execution."
8. Roberts and Klibanoff, *The Race Beat*, 56. Jacoway is among those who misconstrued the decision. She assumed Ashmore's racial politics, postwar and in later decades, were liberal, that his proposing the change to publisher J. N. Heiskell signaled something more than basic courtesy to Black readers, and that he wanted the newspaper to be more progressive on race. She wrote, "Although Harry Ashmore was not yet an advocate of complete social equality, he must have chafed under these constraints." Jacoway, *Turn Away Thy Son*, 12–13. She cited Ashmore, *Hearts and Minds*, 149, as a

9. Ashmore, *Hearts and Minds*, 272. The subscriber boycott cost the *Gazette* $2 million, $14 million in 2006 dollars. David Folkenflick, "Little Rock Editor Faced Down Segregationists," "All Things Considered," National Public Radio, Nov. 30, 2006, https://www.npr.org.
10. Michael J. Klarman, Brown v. Board of Education *and the Civil Rights Movement* (New York: Oxford University Press, 2007), 82.
11. Harry Ashmore, "Reflections in a Hurricane's Eye," *Arkansas Gazette* (Little Rock), Sept. 9, 1957, in *Pulitzer Prize Editorials: America's Best Writing, 1917–2003*, 3rd ed., ed. William David Sloan and Laird B. Anderson (1980; Ames: Iowa State University Press, 2003), 142.
12. Roberts and Klibanoff, *The Race Beat*, 165.
13. Roberts and Klibanoff, *The Race Beat*, also drew on four of Ashmore's books, two speeches, and three magazine articles. John Egerton interviewed Ashmore for *Speak Now against the Day: The Generation before the Civil Rights Movement* (Chapel Hill: University of North Carolina Press, 1994); for *Turn Away Thy Son*, Jacoway cited three interviews plus Egerton's.
14. Roberts and Klibanoff, *The Race Beat*, 14, 28.
15. Patricia Sullivan, *Days of Hope: Race and Democracy in the New Deal Era* (Chapel Hill: University of North Carolina Press, 1996), 269.
16. Folkenflick, "Little Rock Editor Faced Down Segregationists."
17. Raymond Arsenault, "The News from Little Rock," *New York Times*, Jan. 21, 2007, https://www.nytimes.com. Interest in Ashmore was rekindled by *The Race Beat*'s publication in 2006. Among Arsenault's books is *Freedom Riders: 1961 and the Struggle for Racial Justice* (New York: Oxford University Press, 2006). See also Roy Reed, "The Lives They Lived: Harry S. Ashmore, the Laughing Liberal," *New York Times*, Jan. 3, 1999.
18. Harry Ashmore to Louis C. Cohen, Dec. 6, 1950, Harry S. Ashmore Papers (hereafter HAP), box 1, correspondence, folder 17, University of Arkansas–Little Rock.
19. 163 U.S. 537 (1896); Ashmore, *An Epitaph for Dixie*, 160.
20. Ashmore, *An Epitaph for Dixie*, 160–61. This view was shared by FAE leadership before a decision was made about the timing of the book's distribution: "The question had been discussed by [the FAE] Board and the general disposition was that the report was so thoroughly objective that it most likely could be published whether or not the Supreme Court had reached a decision on the segregation issue." Porter McKeever to Rowan Gaither, Report on Ashmore Project, Nov. 10, 1953, McPeak Collection, Program Area 4, series 2, box 6, folder 63.
21. Ashmore, *An Epitaph for Dixie*, 161.
22. Harry S. Ashmore, *The Negro and the Schools* (Chapel Hill: University of North Carolina Press, 1954), xiv–xv.
23. Ashmore, *An Epitaph for Dixie*, 162.
24. Kathy Roberts Forde, *Literary Journalism on Trial: Masson v. New Yorker and the First Amendment* (Amherst: University of Massachusetts Press, 2008), 15–16; Daniel C. Hallin, *The 'Uncensored War': The Media and Vietnam* (Berkeley: University of California Press, 1989), 65–66.

25. A summary of the FAE board's discussion reported, "It was urged by [Ray] Larsen, [Barry] Bingham and [Walter] Lippmann that copies be sent well in advance of publication date to newspaper editors as distinguished from news desks so there would be a maximum opportunity for thoughtful comment." Porter McKeever to H. Rowan Gaither Jr., Ashmore Project Report, Jan. 25, 1954, McPeak Collection, Program Area 4, series 2, box 6, folder 177.
26. Philip H. Coombs, "Reactions to The Negro and the Schools—Report Number I," May 24, 1954, Gaither Collection, records group 21, series 4, box 6, folder 65, RAC.
27. Ashmore referenced the 1857 decision in *Dred Scott v. Sandford*, 60 U.S. (19 How.) 393 (1856), in which the U.S. Supreme Court held that Black Americans were not citizens. After the Civil War, the decision was reversed by passage of the Thirteenth and Fourteenth Amendments, which abolished slavery and extended citizenship to all persons born in the United States.
28. Coombs, "Reactions to The Negro and the Schools—Report Number I."
29. "Excerpts from Informal Memorandum from Harry Ashmore, May 18, 1954," attached to Philip H. Coombs, "Reactions to The Negro and the Schools—Report Number I," May 24, 1954, Gaither Collection, records group 21, series 4, box 6, folder 65.
30. 349 U.S. 294 (1955).
31. Harry Ashmore to Chief Justice of the United States, May 31, 1955, HAP, box 5, correspondence, folder 7. Owen Roberts, retired U.S. Supreme Court justice, chaired the FAE and wrote the foreword to *The Negro and the Schools*.
32. Ed McQuiston to Harry Ashmore, Dec. 14, 1951, HAP, box 2, correspondence, folder 12.
33. The best contemporary history of the Ford Foundation in the postwar years is Dwight MacDonald, *Ford Foundation: The Men and the Millions* (New Brunswick, NJ: Transaction, 1956). Important recent scholarship describes the role of the "Ashmore Project" in the Ford Foundation's argument "that American racism was a Southern problem, and that racial inequality was a product of social retardation that would be dissolved by the wholesale modernization and rationalization of American society, particularly in the 'backward' South." Karen Ferguson, *Top Down: The Ford Foundation, Black Power, and the Reinvention of Racial Liberalism* (Philadelphia: University of Pennsylvania Press, 2013), 43.
34. Public relations concerns about the Ashmore Project appeared in correspondence to and from Rowan Gaither Jr., president of the Ford Foundation. Porter McKeever to Rowan Gaither, Nov. 10, 1953; Gaither to James Cummings, Dec. 14, 1953, McPeak Collection, Program Area 4, series 2, box 6, folder 63. In addition, Ira Harkey, editor of the *Pascagoula [MS] Chronicle*, described image problems for the Ford brand after it became associated in the South with Black consumers: "Falstaff beer became known in Mississippi as 'nigger' beer in the mid-1950s after much statewide publicity was given to donations made by the brewing company to the National Association for the Advancement of Colored People. Ford automobile products came under the same shadow because of humane activities by the Ford Foundation." *The Smell of Burning Crosses* (N.p.: Xlibris, 1967), 43.
35. Richard Kluger, *Simple Justice: The History of* Brown v. Board of Education *and Black America's Struggle for Equality* (New York: Vintage, 2004), 536–37, quotes from Ashmore, *The Negro and the Schools*, 81–82.
36. Kluger, *Simple Justice*, 720–21. The plaintiffs in the *Brown* cases used research assem-

bled by Dr. Kenneth Clark, who approached the issue differently; however, Kluger wrote, "most of the findings in the Ashmore book were no surprise at Thurgood Marshall's NAACP Legal Defense Fund office."

37. The U.S. Supreme Court consolidated five parallel cases from Kansas, South Carolina, Virginia, Delaware, and the District of Columbia and ruled on them under the umbrella of the Kansas case.

38. "An Address by Harry S. Ashmore, Executive Editor of the *Arkansas Gazette*, before the Southern Governors Conference, at Hot Springs, Arkansas, Nov. 12, 1951," HAP, box 9, folder 3.

39. Ashmore, *Hearts and Minds*, 170–73. President Harry S. Truman's 1948 package of civil rights legislation, which proposed a federal antilynching law and bans on the poll tax, employment discrimination, and some forms of segregation, fueled the Dixiecrat movement, formally known as the States' Rights Party. For a thorough discussion of the Dixiecrat phenomenon, see Sid Bedingfield, *Newspaper Wars: Civil Rights and White Resistance in South Carolina, 1935–1963* (Urbana: University of Illinois Press, 2017), 97–107, and Glenn Feldman, *The Great Melding: War, the Dixiecrat Rebellion, and the Southern Model for America's New Conservatism* (Tuscaloosa: University of Alabama Press, 2015), especially chapter 12.

40. Ashmore's speech to the Southern Governors' Conference is not obscure but its significance as an ideological baseline in Ashmore's career, and as an attempt to control the news narrative on race, has been overlooked. A few historians mention it in discussion of the pre–civil rights period though none has analyzed the speech itself or the press coverage and its presentation of Ashmore's argument. Indeed, none considers Ashmore's responses to either his segregationist critics or the integrationists who initially inferred from news reports that they had found a white southern ally. Egerton, *Speak Now against the Day*, 577–78; Jacoway, *Turn Away Thy Son*, 14–15; Nathania K. Sawyer, "Harry S. Ashmore: On the Way to Everywhere" (MA thesis, University of Arkansas–Little Rock, 2001), 38–39. Ashmore recounted the episode in at least three books across the decades—omitting the ideological skirmish over his intended message, which is clearly documented in his archived correspondence. See, specifically, Ashmore, *Civil Rights and Wrongs*, 89–91; Ashmore, *Hearts and Minds*, 170–73; and Ashmore, *An Epitaph for Dixie*, 179–82.

41. Ashmore, *Hearts and Minds*, 172.

42. Harry Ashmore to Herbert Thomas, Dec. 15, 1948, HAP, box 1, correspondence, folder 3. In the *Arkansas Gazette*, see, in particular, "The Area of Compromise," Dec. 29, 1948, and "Hays Opens Bid to Compromise on Civil Rights," Feb. 3, 1949.

43. Begun by Roosevelt as the Fair Employment Practices Committee, the body was later renamed the Fair Employment Practices Commission. In 1947 the 178-page report of the President's Committee on Civil Rights proposed that President Harry Truman make the FEPC permanent. Egerton, *Speak Now against the Day*, 216, 413–16; "To Secure These Rights: The Report of the President's Committee on Civil Rights," 1947, Harry S. Truman Library, Independence, MO, https://www.trumanlibrary.gov.

44. Ashmore, *Hearts and Minds*, 120–23.

45. Ashmore, *Civil Rights and Wrongs*, 89.

46. William Workman to Frank Bane, Oct. 30, 1951, William Workman Papers, box 41, folder Southern Governors' Conference 1951, South Carolina Political Collection, University of South Carolina, Columbia. Workman, a states' rights advocate, was

alerted to the newsworthiness of the conference by the office of South Carolina governor James Byrnes.

47. Owing to the event's significance, the Chicago-based Council of State Governments coordinated press credentials and hotel accommodations for journalists who traveled to Arkansas for the meeting. Southern Governors' Conference, "For Your Information," undated registration list, Ashmore Collection, box 2, folder 14.

48. All quotations from Ashmore's speech are drawn from "An Address by Harry S. Ashmore, Executive Editor of the *Arkansas Gazette*, before the Southern Governors Conference, at Hot Springs, Arkansas, Nov. 12, 1951."

49. Gunnar Myrdal, *An American Dilemma: The Negro Problem and Modern Democracy*, 2 vols. (1944; reprint New Brunswick, NJ: Transaction, 1996).

50. Harry Ashmore to J. Montgomery Curtis, Nov. 21, 1951, HAP, box 2, folder 12. Ashmore might have referenced a sidebar published by his own newspaper that collated reactions to the speech by various governors. "Speech Draws Varied Reaction," *Arkansas Gazette*, Nov. 13, 1951.

51. Ashmore, *Civil Rights and Wrongs*, 91. Analysis of the conference's impact is complicated by many factors at play. Controversy over House Speaker Sam Rayburn's speech that evening eclipsed Ashmore's luncheon address. Rayburn, a Texan, angered the most conservative Democratic governors, who already felt betrayed by Truman on the issues of states' rights and segregation, by warning that dissension in the party ranks, whether through an unpatriotic third-party run for the presidency, similar to the 1948 Dixiecrat rebellion, or defection to the Republicans would give the 1952 election and control of Congress to the Republicans. The political calculus would shift when Truman declined to seek reelection in 1952 and removed himself as a lightning rod for southern dissatisfaction with the national Democratic Party, making Ashmore's address more significant for what it said about a white southern editor's own views on race and journalism, and his concern for others' perceptions, than for its impact on national politics. Larry Wayne Blomstedt, "Truman, Congress, and the Struggle for War and Peace in Korea" (PhD diss., Texas State University, 2008), 74.

52. Harry S. Ashmore, "April 1948: The South and the South's Problem," *Nieman Reports*, Winter 1999–Spring 2000, 135.

53. Peter Edson, "Single Party Held Doomed," *Tuscaloosa [AL] News*, Nov. 10, 1948.

54. Harry S. Ashmore, "The South's Year of Decision," *Southern Packet* 4, no. 11 (Nov. 1948): 3. The *Southern Packet* article was reprinted widely, including, according to Ashmore, in the *Des Moines [IA] Register, St. Louis Post-Dispatch, Montgomery [AL] Advertiser, St. Petersburg [FL] Times*, and *Birmingham [AL] News*. Harry Ashmore to George Stephens, Dec. 14, 1948, HAP, box 1, correspondence, folder 3. In addition, the *Arkansas Gazette*'s gradualist position was clearly documented in, for example, the newspaper's editorial endorsement of "The Arkansas Plan," a proposed compromise to the Truman civil rights package that was developed by Congressman Hays and Governor McMath in collaboration with Ashmore. The Arkansas response acquiesced to abolition of the poll tax and making lynching a federal crime but strongly opposed strengthening the oversight and enforcement power of the FEPC. See, for example, "The Area of Compromise," *Arkansas Gazette*, Dec. 29, 1948, and "Hays Opens Bid to Compromise on Civil Rights," *Arkansas Gazette*, Feb. 3, 1949.

55. The speech has been glossed by some historians sympathetic to Ashmore, who down-

played its defense of segregation. In his account, for example, John Egerton described Ashmore's address to the southern governors as "a most remarkable thing" because Ashmore dared broach the subject of civil rights, while biographer Elizabeth Jacoway emphasized the publicity's impact on Ashmore's professional ambition. Egerton, *Speak Now against the Day*, 577; Jacoway, *Turn Away Thy Son*, 14. Even Ashmore, in his later reflections on the conference, underscored the boldness of talking about race to southern governors. Ashmore, *Hearts and Minds*, 172; Ashmore, *Civil Rights and Wrongs*, 89.

56. This conclusion is documented by the unwavering accuracy of most of the direct quotations in published news stories and the presence of a full text of the speech in the archive of a journalist who covered the conference. Workman Papers, box 41, folder Southern Governors' Conference, 1951.
57. Don Whitehead, "South's Governors Turn to Civil Rights Issues," *Blytheville [AR] Courier*, Nov. 12, 1951.
58. "Byrnes Says South Owes No Loyalty," *Kingston [NY] Daily Freeman*, Nov. 12, 1951.
59. Leon Hatch, "Realistic Race Policy Urged; Reaction Varies," *Arkansas Gazette*, Nov. 13, 1951.
60. "Governors Talking Segregation First," *Delta Democrat-Times* (Greenville, MS), Nov. 12, 1951.
61. John Howard, "Dixie Governors Attend Unsegregated Confab," *Pittsburgh Courier*, Nov. 24, 1951.
62. "Dixie Governors Seek Key to Rights Issue," *Chicago Defender*, Nov. 24, 1951.
63. "Revolt in Dixie," *Chicago Defender*, Nov. 24, 1951.
64. James B. Lafourche, "Arkansas Gazette Takes Bold Stand against Segregation at Southern Governors' Parley," *Black Dispatch* (Oklahoma City, OK), Nov. 24, 1951.
65. Walter White to Harry Ashmore, Dec. 4, 1951, HAP, box 2, correspondence, folder 13.
66. Walter White, untitled column embargoed for Nov. 22, 1951, HAP, box 2, correspondence, folder 13.
67. Thomas L. Stokes, "Dixie Governors Are Cool to Civil Rights," *El Paso [TX] Herald-Post*, Nov. 13, 1951.
68. Harry Ashmore to John Temple Graves II, Nov. 29, 1951, HAP, box 2, correspondence, folder 12.
69. Howard, "Dixie Governors Attend Unsegregated Confab."
70. Bill Farley, "Negroes Join Governors in Talk," *Arkansas Gazette*, Nov. 13, 1951.
71. Nicholas P. Mitchell, "Byrnes Cites Need of More Medically Trained Negroes," *Greenville [SC] News*, Nov. 13, 1951.
72. Jonathan Daniels to Harry Ashmore, Nov. 13, 1951; Ralph McGill to Ashmore, Nov. 13, 1951, HAP, box 2, correspondence, folder 11; Nelson Poynter to Ashmore, Nov. 21, 1951, HAP, box 2, correspondence, folder 12.
73. John N. Popham, "Dissidents Reject Rayburn's Appeal," *New York Times*, Nov. 14, 1951; John N. Popham to Harry Ashmore, Nov. 17, 1951, HAP, box 2, correspondence, folder 11. Popham also explained that a telegraph problem resulted in the loss of Popham's copy related to Ashmore's speech and that his story was not published.
74. William Workman to Harry Ashmore, Dec. 16, 1951, Workman Papers, box 41, folder Southern Governors' Conference, 1951.
75. Harry Ashmore to Fielding Wright; Harry Ashmore to Johnston Murray, both Nov. 29. 1951, HAP, box 2, correspondence, folder 12.

76. Fielding Wright to Harry Ashmore, Dec. 5, 1951, HAP, box 2, correspondence, folder 13.
77. Harry Ashmore to John Temple Graves II, Nov. 29, 1951, HAP, box 2, correspondence, folder 12.
78. John Temple Graves II to Harry Ashmore, Dec. 6, 1951, HAP, box 2, correspondence, folder 13.
79. James Dombrowski to Harry Ashmore, Nov. 28, 1951, HAP, box 2, correspondence, folder 12.
80. Harry Ashmore to James Dombrowski, Dec. 15, 1951, HAP, box 2, correspondence, folder 14.
81. Fleur Cowles to Harry Ashmore, Dec. 5, 1951, HAP, box 2, correspondence, folder, 13.
82. Harry Ashmore to Fleur Cowles, Dec. 15, 1951, HAP, box 2, correspondence, folder 14.
83. Lawrence A. Davis to Harry Ashmore, Dec. 4, 1951, HAP, box 2, correspondence, folder 13.
84. Harry Ashmore to Lawrence A. Davis, Dec. 6, 1951, HAP, box 2, correspondence, folder 13.
85. Charles H. Thompson to Harry Ashmore, Nov. 28, 1951, HAP, box 2, correspondence, folder 12.
86. Harry Ashmore to Charles H. Thompson, Dec. 15, 1951, HAP, box 2, correspondence, folder 14.
87. Fred McCuiston to Harry Ashmore, Jan. 16, 1952, HAP, box 2, correspondence, folder 15.
88. Louis Ray, *Charles H. Thompson: Policy Entrepreneur of the Civil Rights Movement, 1932–1954* (Lanham, MD: Fairleigh Dickinson University Press, 2012), 159–60. Ashmore was one of two white gradualists on the program. Also speaking was Ward I. Miller, Wilmington, Delaware, school superintendent.
89. Harry Ashmore to Charles Thompson, April 12, 1952, HAP, box 3, correspondence, folder 3.
90. Howard University, "A Conference on the Courts and Racial Integration in Education, April 16–18, 1952," HAP, box 2, correspondence, folder 15. Improbably, Ashmore suggested that the NAACP step aside and allow the white South to implement separate-but-equal, the mandate it had ignored for more than five decades. Patricia Sullivan, *Lift Every Voice: The NAACP and the Making of the Civil Rights Movement* (New York: New Press, 2009), 415.
91. Harry S. Ashmore, "Racial Integration with Special Reference to Education in the South," *Journal of Negro Education* 21, no. 3 (Summer 1952): 252.
92. U.S. Supreme Court rulings on the unconstitutionality of segregated graduate schools included *Sweat v. Painter* (339 U.S. 629) and *McLaurin v. Oklahoma State Regents* (339 U.S. 637).
93. Ashmore, "Racial Integration with Special Reference to Education in the South," 252.
94. Ashmore, "Racial Integration with Special Reference to Education in the South," 255.
95. Simeon Booker, "Negroes Should 'Sue and Sue' for Integration, Educator Says," *Washington Post*, April 17, 1952. Booker left the *Post* after less than two years, citing a racist work environment. Pamela Newkirk, *Within the Veil: Black Journalists, White Media* (New York: New York University Press, 2000), 59. Booker also was the author of *Black Man's America* (Englewood Cliffs, NJ: Prentice-Hall, 1964).

96. "Howard U. Delegates Debate Court Fight on Race Segregation," *Washington Evening Star*, April 17, 1952.
97. "Equal Education Favored by Dixie," *Pittsburgh Courier*, April 26, 1952.
98. "So. Editor Warns against Elimination of Separate Schools in Howard Talk," *Alabama Tribune* (Montgomery), April 25, 1952.
99. Harry Ashmore to Charles H. Thompson, May 20, 1952, HAP, box 3, correspondence, folder 4.
100. Ashmore, *Hearts and Minds*, 189–90.
101. Kluger, *Simple Justice*, 536, 539.
102. Ashmore, *Hearts and Minds*, 189–90.
103. Harry Ashmore to Virginius Dabney, Aug. 7, 1952, HAP, box 3, correspondence, folder 7.
104. Horace Mann Bond, "The Present Status of Racial Integration in the United States, with Especial Reference to Education," *Journal of Negro Education* 21, no. 3 (Summer 1952): 249.
105. Virginius Dabney to Harry Ashmore, Aug. 12, 1952, HAP, box 3, correspondence, folder 7.
106. Ashmore, *The Negro and the Schools*, xv.
107. "Desegregated Schools," University of Chicago *Roundtable*, no. 862. Oct. 17, 1954, HAP, box 9, folder 3.
108. Harry Ashmore to Walter White, June 9, 1954, HAP, box 4, correspondence, folder 9.
109. Myles Horton to Harry Ashmore, June 11, 1954; Ashmore to Myles Horton, June 17, 1954, HAP, box 4, correspondence, folder 9.
110. Gwyneth Mellinger, "Saving the Republic: An Editor's Crusade against Integration." *Journalism History* 42, no. 4 (Jan. 2017): 212–24.
111. Ashmore, *An Epitaph for Dixie*, 46, 44, 162–63.
112. Ashmore, *An Epitaph for Dixie*, 87; Hodding Carter Jr., "The South as It Was, Is and Will Be," *New York Times Book Review*, Jan. 12, 1958.
113. Westbrook Pegler, "Ashmore's Article Reviewed by Carter," *Greenwood [SC] Index Journal*, Jan. 17, 1958.
114. George Sokolsky, "Negro-Booster Opposes Integrated Obituaries," *Monroe [LA] Morning World*, July 13, 1958.
115. Ashmore, *Hearts and Minds*, 289.
116. William P. Hustwit, *James J. Kilpatrick: Salesman for Segregation* (Chapel Hill: University of North Carolina Press, 2013), 216–23; Elizabeth Atwood, "Reaching the Pinnacle of the 'Punditocracy': James J. Kilpatrick's Journey from Segregationist Editor to National Opinion Shaper," *American Journalism* 31, no. 3 (2014): 358–77.
117. Harry Ashmore to C. A. McKnight, Oct. 23, 1980, C. A. McKnight Papers, box 4, folder 11, University of North Carolina at Charlotte.
118. Harry Ashmore to C. A. McKnight, Jan. 9, 1980; McKnight to Ashmore, Jan. 16, 1980, McKnight Papers, box 4, folder 11.
119. Ashmore, *Civil Rights and Wrongs*, 109–10.

## CHAPTER 4

1. Angie Maxwell offers extensive treatment of the southern inferiority complex in terms of northern perceptions, including disparagement by H. L. Mencken and others.

Maxwell, *The Indicted South: Public Criticism, Southern Inferiority, and the Politics of Whiteness* (Chapel Hill: University of North Carolina Press, 2014), 204–10.
2. This is not Daniel C. Hallin's concept of political deviance, which describes news stories "unworthy of being heard." Here, the deviance of "the benighted South" is inherently newsworthy, at least in the North. Hallin, *The "Uncensored War": The Media and Vietnam* (Berkeley: University of California Press, 1989), 117.
3. Joe Parham to Lew Hawkins, April 12, 1956, Subject Files, new box 129, Negro segregation file, Associated Press Corporate Archive (hereafter APCA), New York.
4. Paul R. Mickelson to Rex Thomas, Aug. 20, 1957, APCA, Subject Files 1957: Negro file, box 123.
5. Edgar Arnold Jr. to Alvin Orton, March 29, 1957, APCA, Subject Files 1957: Negro file, box 123.
6. Edgar Arnold Jr. to Alan J. Gould, March 21, 1957, APCA, Subject Files 1957: Negro file, box 123.
7. Alan J. Gould to Edgar Arnold Jr., March 27, 1957, APCA, Subject Files 1957: Negro file, box 123.
8. Alvin Orton to Edgar Arnold Jr., March 26, 1957, APCA, Subject Files 1957: Negro file, box 123.
9. Alan J. Gould to Edgar Arnold Jr., March 27, 1957, APCA, Subject Files 1957: Negro file, box 123.
10. Edgar Arnold Jr. to Alvin Orton, March 29, 1957, APCA, Subject Files 1957: Negro file, box 123.
11. AP staff correspondence references discussions at AP meetings for which there is no formal record, and the APME's accounts of floor discussions at its annual meetings were often cursory and incomplete. The APME's most detailed, documented discussion of the North-South news divide occurred in conjunction with the Domestic News Committee's report at the 1957 meeting, which was held in New Orleans on Nov. 20–23, two months after the confrontation at Central High School in Little Rock, and included the committee's analysis of AP coverage of that story. *The APME Red Book 1957* (New York: Associated Press, 1957), 76–84. This is discussed later in this chapter.
12. For United Press history and a discussion of its midcentury financial challenges, see Gregory Gordon and Ronald E. Cohen, *Down to the Wire: UPI's Fight for Survival* (New York: McGraw-Hill, 1990), 16–20. On the history of the AP stylebook leading to its pivotal edition in 1977, see Fred Vultee, "A Paleontology of Style: The Evolution of the Middle East in the AP Stylebook, 1977–2020," *Journalism Practice* 6, no. 4 (2012): 451–53.
13. James W. Carey resonates here. Carey, *Communication as Culture: Essays on Media and Society* (New York: Routledge, 2009), 155–77.
14. George M. Fredrickson traced the image of the "Negro as a brute and a savage" through the nineteenth and early twentieth centuries. As Black Americans sought civil rights after Reconstruction, white fear of the degeneracy of free Blacks justified lynching and Jim Crow laws, providing "a convenient rationale for new and more overtly oppressive racial policies," including "the need to segregate or quarantine a race liable to be a source of contamination and social danger to the white community, as it sank ever deeper into the slough of disease, vice, and criminality." Fredrickson, *The Black Image in the White Mind: The Debate on Afro-American Character and Destiny,*

*1817–1914* (New York: Harper and Row, 1971), 255. This stereotype has deep roots in twentieth-century media narratives. For example, D. W. Griffith's 1915 feature film *Birth of a Nation* suggested that Black crime and mayhem followed emancipation. Mimi White, "*The Birth of a Nation*: History as Pretext," in *The Birth of a Nation*, ed. Robert Lang (New Brunswick, NJ: Rutgers University Press, 1994), 214–24.

15. "When Negroes Move North: Many Problems of the South—and Others, Too—Come with Them," *U.S. News and World Report*, April 10, 1956.
16. Hall and his staff primarily advanced this argument in a series of 1956 articles and editorials called "Published in Askelon," which are discussed later in this chapter. Numan V. Bartley wrote, "The Askelon campaign was very likely the most successful of all deliberative southern efforts to influence northern opinion." Bartley *The Rise of Massive Resistance: Race and Politics in the South during the 1950s* (Baton Rouge: Louisiana State University Press, 2004), 179. See also Gene Roberts and Hank Klibanoff, *The Race Beat: The Press, the Civil Rights Struggle, and the Awakening of a Nation* (New York: Vintage, 2007), 211–12, and Douglas Cumming, "Building Resentment: How the Alabama Press Prepared the Way for *New York Times v. Sullivan*," *American Journalism* 22, no. 3 (Summer 2005): 7–32.
17. William P. Hustwit, *James J. Kilpatrick: Salesman for Segregation* (Chapel Hill: University of North Carolina Press, 2013), 110; Maxwell, *The Indicted South*, 204–10.
18. "The Paper Curtain around the South," *Macon [GA] News*, April 2, 1956.
19. Sid Bedingfield, *Newspaper Wars: Civil Rights and White Resistance in South Carolina, 1935–1965* (Urbana: University of Illinois Press, 2017), 175.
20. Douglas O. Cumming, "Facing Facts, Facing South: The Southern Education Reporting Service and the Effort to Inform the South after *Brown v. Board*, 1954–1960" (PhD diss., University of North Carolina at Chapel Hill, 2002), 320.
21. Lew Hawkins to Alan Gould, April 25, 1956, APCA, Subject Files 1956, box 118, Negro file.
22. Cumming, "Facing Facts, Facing South," 329–31, 330 (quotation). Examples of news pegs for the series included "a movie theater in Canton, Ohio, boycotted by blacks after a black man had been asked to leave the white section; a Chicago housing project where 150 police were on long-term assignment to protect new black residents from attack: a Detroit suburb with policies to ensure that only whites move in; white students from the University of Wisconsin who showed up at the Advertiser's office at the end of a Florida vacation to explain their opposition to interracial dating; a hoax of a bomb threat sent to a Long Island college with an anti-black note."
23. The redundancy of a "project" on race in the North by AP journalist Bem Price was also the reason Hawkins gave to Rex Thomas, the AP correspondent in Montgomery, Alabama, for not running a story that Thomas had written about Hall and his crusade. Lew Hawkins to Rex Thomas, April 3, 1956, APCA, Subject Files 1956, new box 129, Negro segregation file.
24. Lew Hawkins to Joe Parham, April 11, 1956, APCA, Subject Files 1956, new box 129, Negro segregation file.
25. Joe Parham to Lew Hawkins, April 12, 1956, APCA, Subject Files 1956, new box 129, Negro segregation file.
26. "Censorship," *Chattanooga [TN] News-Free Press*, Jan. 21, 1956.

27. Alan J. Gould, Memo to Domestic Chiefs of Bureau and Correspondents, Feb. 2, 1956, APCA, 1956 Subject Files, box 118, Negro Identification file.
28. As noted in chapter 2, the *St. Louis Post-Dispatch*, under editor Ben Reese in the 1940s, demanded that the AP supply racial identification on all stories about Black news subjects. After his retirement in 1951, the newspaper became more egalitarian in its outlook and was less likely to supply, much less demand, racial detail. Interestingly, Reese served for two decades as a leader of the American Press Institute. "Ben Reese of Press-Dispatch, Pulitzer-Winning Editor, Dies," *New York Times*, June 1, 1974.
29. Alan J. Gould to bureau chiefs, 24 April 1956, APCA, Subject Files 1956, box 118, Negro file.
30. "Mississippi Gunmen Take Life of Militant Negro Minister," *Jet*, May 26, 1955, 8–11.
31. Lew Hawkins, memo to bureau chiefs, May 23, 1955, APCA, 1955 Subject Files, box 113, Negro file.
32. On press coverage of the Till murder and trial, see Roberts and Klibanoff, *The Race Beat*, chapter 7; John N. Herbers, *Deep South Dispatch: Memoir of a Civil Rights Journalist* (Jackson: University Press of Mississippi, 2018), chapters 8–9; Darryl Mace, *In Remembrance of Emmett Till: Regional Stories and Media Responses to the Black Freedom Struggle* (Lexington: University Press of Kentucky, 2014), chapter 5; Davis W. Houck and Matthew A. Grindy, *Emmett Till and the Mississippi Press* (Jackson: University Press of Mississippi, 2008); and Timothy B. Tyson, *The Blood of Emmett Till* (New York: Simon and Schuster, 2017), chapter 16.
33. James J. Kilpatrick to Thomas R. Waring, March 27, 1956, James J. Kilpatrick Papers, box 53, University of Virginia, Charlottesville.
34. The New Orleans bureau filed stories as they were phoned in during the trial. The AP assigned two reporters, Sam Johnson from Jackson, Mississippi, and Arthur Everett of the New York bureau, to provide "running coverage," supported by two photographers, Gene Herrick and Harold Valentine, who had access to an AP-member darkroom at the *Clarksdale [MS] Press Register*, half an hour away from the courthouse. Ken Davis to Alan Gould, Sept. 12, 1955; Gould to Davis, Sept. 14, 1955, APCA, 1958 Subject File, box 127, Till murder file.
35. John Colburn to Alan Gould, Sept. 23, 1955, APCA, 1958 Subject File, box 127, Till murder file. In his complaint to the AP, Colburn included comments from Leverty, who worked for him, and referenced the 1954 murder trial of Dr. Sam Sheppard. The U.S. Supreme Court would set aside Sheppard's conviction, ruling that excessive news coverage interfered with his right to a fair trial. *Sheppard v. Maxwell*, 384 U.S. 333 (1966).
36. Alan Gould to John Colburn, Sept. 23, 1955, APCA, 1958 Subject File, box 127, Till murder file.
37. "Rumors Say Till Boy Is Still Alive," undated clipping, APCA, 1958 Subject File, box 127, Till murder file.
38. James Wechsler to Alan Gould, Oct. 1, 1955, APCA, 1958 Subject File, box 127, Till murder file. Wechsler, who had disavowed communist affiliation in his early years, was targeted by Senator Joseph McCarthy in 1953. This episode in journalism history is recounted succinctly in Edward Alwood, *Dark Days in the Newsroom: McCarthyism Aimed at the Press* (Philadelphia: Temple University Press, 2002),

69–72, and in greater detail in James Wechsler, *The Age of Suspicion* (New York: Random House, 1953).
39. Alan Gould to James Wechsler, Oct. 3, 1955, APCA, 1958 Subject File, box 127, Till murder file.
40. James Wechsler to Alan Gould, Oct. 1, 1955, APCA, 1958 Subject File, box 127, Till murder file.
41. On Poston's careers at the *Amsterdam News* and *New York Post*, see Pamela Newkirk, *Within the Veil: Black Journalist, White Media* (New York: New York University Press, 2000), 57–59. Historian Douglas O. Cumming related an anecdote about plans that Kempton and Grover Hall Jr., editor of the *Montgomery Advertiser*, developed in March 1956 for Kempton to serve as Hall's guide on a tour of New York City, allowing Hall to report on race in the North. Wechsler had already assigned Poston to do a series on discrimination in the North and invited Hall to work with Poston, but Hall wanted to work with Kempton. The *Advertiser* hosted Poston during a lengthy visit to report on race in the South. Cumming, "Facing Facts, Facing South," 329–30. On Poston's visit to Montgomery, see "New Negro Report Fans Hall-Wechsler Feud," *Editor and Publisher,* June 16, 1956, 72.
42. Ted Poston, "Mose Wright Left Everything to Flee for Life," *New York Post*, Oct. 3, 1955.
43. James Wechsler to Alan Gould, Oct. 1, 1955, APCA, 1958 Subject File, box 127, Till murder file.
44. James Wechsler to Alan Gould, Oct. 1, 1955, APCA, 1958 Subject File, box 127, Till murder file.
45. Alan Gould to James Wechsler, Oct. 5, 1955, APCA, 1958 Subject File, box 127, Till murder file.
46. Alan Gould to James Wechsler, Oct. 5, 1955, APCA, 1958 Subject File, box 127, Till murder file.
47. Ken Davis to Alan Gould, Oct. 10, 1955, APCA, 1958 Subject File, box 127, Till murder file.
48. James Wechsler to Alan Gould, Nov. 3, 1955; Gould to Lou Kramp, Oct. 18, 1955, APCA, 1958 Subject File, box 127, Till murder file.
49. Poet Ezra Pound was imprisoned with Louis Till and briefly described the execution in *The Pisan Cantos*, new ed., ed. Richard Sieburth (1948; Cambridge, MA: New Directions, 2003), 51.
50. On the controversy surrounding the Oct. 10, 1955, issue of *Life* magazine, see Houck and Grindy, *Emmett Till and the Mississippi Press*, 135–37.
51. Senator James Eastland, a Mississippi segregationist, procured government documents for the story. "Till's Dad Raped 2 Women, Murdered a Third in Italy," *Jackson [MS] Daily News*, Oct. 14, 1955.
52. Citizens' Council of Mississippi, undated press release, APCA, 1958 Subject File, box 127, Till murder file.
53. Thomas R. Waring to Alan Gould, Oct. 22, 1955; William Henry Harris to Ken Davis, Oct. 24, 1955, APCA, 1958 Subject File, box 127, Till murder file.
54. Alan Gould to Thomas Waring, Oct. 25, 1955, APCA, 1958 Subject File, box 127, Till murder file.
55. Ken Davis to W. Henry Harris, Oct. 26, 1955; Lew Hawkins to Davis, Oct. 28, 1955; Alan

Gould to Davis, Oct. 31, 1955; Frank Gorrie to Davis, Oct. 31, 1955, APCA, 1958 Subject File, box 127, Till murder file.
56. Frank Gorrie to Ken Davis, Oct. 31, 1955, APCA, 1958 Subject File, box 127, Till murder file.
57. Alan Gould to Thomas Waring, Oct. 25, 1955, APCA, 1958 Subject File, box 127, Till murder file.
58. Bem Price, "The Negro in the North: As Population Increases, So Does Problem," *Birmingham [AL] News*, May 13, 1956.
59. Lew Hawkins to Ken Davis, April 30, 1956, APCA, 1958 Subject File, box 127, Till murder file.
60. Bem Price, "Negros Moving to North Still Find Discrimination—Housing Major Sore Spot," *Memphis Commercial Appeal*, May 13, 1956; Price, "The Negro in the North."
61. Rex Thomas to Alan Gould, June 1, 1956, APCA, Subject Files 1956, new box 129, Negro segregation folder.
62. White, "*The Birth of a Nation*: History as Pretext," 214–24; Melvyn Stokes, *D. W. Griffith's* The Birth of a Nation: *A History of "the Most Controversial Motion Picture of All Time"* (New York: Oxford University Press, 2007), 22–24. See also Fredrickson, *The Black Image in the White Mind*, chapter 9.
63. John Harper to Lew Hawkins, July 1, 1956, APCA, Subject Files 1956, box 118, Negro file.
64. Lew Hawkins to John Harper, July 3, 1956, APCA, Subject Files 1956, box 118, Negro file.
65. Lew Hawkins to John Harper, July 3, 1956, APCA, Subject Files 1956, box 118, Negro filer.
66. Paul R. Mickelson to John Colt, June 25, 1956, APCA, Subject Files 1957, box 123, Negro file.
67. Robert U. Brown, "Shop Talk at 30," *Editor and Publisher*, June 16, 1956, 80.
68. Samuel Blackman to Luke Carroll, June 12, 1956, APCA, Subject Files 1957, box 123, Negro file.
69. Paul R. Mickelson to Frank Starzel, June 12, 1956, APCA, Subject Files 1957, box 123, Negro file.
70. Walter L. Grant to Frank Starzel, Oct. 5, 1957, APCA, Subject Files 1957, box 123, Negro file.
71. Paul R. Mickelson to Frank J. Starzel, Oct. 7, 1957, APCA, Subject Files 1957, box 123, Negro file.
72. Paul R. Mickelson to Frank J. Starzel, Oct. 7, 1957, APCA, Subject Files 1957, box 123, Negro file.
73. Frank J. Starzel to Walter Grant, Oct. 9, 1957, APCA, Subject Files 1957, box 123, Negro file.
74. "North Perfumed by Censorship," *Chattanooga News-Free Press*, Oct. 22, 1957.
75. "Editor Defends Handling of Chicago Race Story," *Editor and Publisher*, Aug. 17, 1957, 15.
76. "The Sick and Dangerous City of Chicago," *Montgomery [AL] Advertiser*, Aug. 15, 1957.
77. Rex Thomas to Alvin Orton, Aug. 15, 1957, APCA, Subject Files 1957, box 123, Negro file.

78. Rex Thomas to Alan Gould, Aug. 17, 1957, APCA, Subject Files 1957, box 123, Negro file.
79. "We Neglected to Mention," *Montgomery Advertiser*, Aug. 17, 1957.
80. Paul Mickelson to James Pope, Aug. 9, 1957, APCA, Subject Files 1957, box 123, Negro file.
81. Bernard Gavzer, "Police Move Fast to Curb Violence," *Greenville [NC] News*, Aug. 25, 1957.
82. "Erratum," *Montgomery Advertiser*, Aug. 25, 1957.
83. In 1955 Waring floated the idea among segregationist southern editors to organize a pool of reporters that would venture "singly or in teams, into several Northern cities to check on race conditions. . . . So many Northern journalists are 'Doing the South' that a reverse stunt should make good copy for ourselves. It might attract comment in Northern newspapers and magazines. Even if we were ignored, we could inform and bolster the morale of our own subscribers." "Dear Editor" form letter, Aug. 25, 1955, William D. Workman Papers, box 31, folder: Integration/Civil Rights General, 1946–1956, University of South Carolina, Columbia. Gene Roberts and Hank Klibanoff offered a detailed account of Waring's collaboration with Citizens' Council leader Robert Patterson and his role in organizing southern editors in a 1959 protest against perceived disparities and imbalance in AP coverage of race in the North and South. Waring even attempted to organize a public relations effort on behalf of the South. Roberts and Klibanoff, *The Race Beat*, 214–21.
84. Thomas R. Waring, "The Southern Case against Desegregation," *Harper's*, Jan. 1956, 39–45.
85. An additional dimension of this correspondence focused on Waring's inquiries about the play his speeches received. Waring learned, for example, that his Brandeis speech moved on the eastern and southern regional wires, as well as the New York state wire. Waring also wrote Ben McKelway, president of the AP board of directors, about the way coverage of his speeches was framed. Such correspondence reminded AP officials that he was surveilling the wire, and even if he had a clear conflict of interest regarding coverage of himself, demanded reporting that met southern standards of objectivity. L. A. Brophy to Thomas Waring, Nov. 20, 1957; Waring to Benjamin M. McKelway, Nov. 8, 1957, APCA, Subject Files 1957, box 124, Negro School Segregation–General file.
86. Paul R. Mickelson to Alan J. Gould and Victor Hackler, Nov. 14, 1957, APCA, Subject Files 1957, box 124, Negro School Segregation–General file.
87. Alan J. Gould to Thomas Waring, Nov. 14, 1957, APCA, Subject Files 1957, box 124, Negro School Segregation–General file.
88. Paul Hansell to Thomas Waring, Nov. 18, 1957, APCA, Subject Files 1957, box 124, Negro School Segregation–General file.
89. Thomas Waring to Paul Hansell, Nov. 20, 1957, APCA, Subject Files 1957, box 124, Negro School Segregation–General file.
90. Associated Press Managing Editors, "Segregation-Integration: Domestic News," in *APME Red Book 1957*, 76. The convention took place Nov. 20–23 in New Orleans.
91. Associated Press Managing Editors, "Segregation-Integration," 76.
92. "Montgomery Calling Detroit," *Montgomery Advertiser*, March 10, 1956.
93. Associated Press Managing Editors, "Segregation-Integration," 77.
94. Associated Press Managing Editors, "Segregation-Integration," 82.

95. Samuel Blackman, "Memo to the Staff, Subject: The General News Report," June 22, 1961, APCA, Circular Letters, box 1, file 19.

## CHAPTER 5

1. Gene Roberts and Hank Klibanoff described the SERS as "a unique experiment in the history of American journalism." Roberts and Klibanoff, *The Race Beat: The Press, the Civil Rights Struggle, and the Awakening of a Nation* (New York: Vintage, 2007), 57. Their extensive discussion of the SERS (pp. 57–60, 67–71) relied on interviews with Harry Ashmore and did not mention the project's conceptualization by Black scholars before the white editors gathered during the 1954 American Society of Newspaper Editors convention. The most comprehensive SERS history is Douglas O. Cumming, "Facing Facts, Facing South: The Southern Education Reporting Service and the Effort to Inform the South after *Brown v. Board*, 1954–1960" (PhD diss., University of North Carolina at Chapel Hill, 2002).
2. Barry Bingham to Don Shoemaker, Nov. 23, 1955; Virginius Dabney to Shoemaker, Dec. 28, 1955; SERS board minutes, March 18, 1956, Don Shoemaker Papers, Correspondence 1955–1956, folder 18, Southern Historical Collection, University of North Carolina at Chapel Hill.
3. This discussion does not presume to speak for Black subjects, only to adjust the focus of analysis to encompass and emphasize their documented perspectives. Of course, Black opinion was not monolithic.
4. See, for example, C. A. McKnight, "How Is the Press Reporting School Desegregation?" *Problems of Journalism: Proceedings of American Society of Newspaper Editors*, April 21–23, 1955, 80–88.
5. Gwyneth Mellinger, *Chasing Newsroom Diversity: From Jim Crow to Affirmative Action* (Champaign: University of Illinois Press, 2013), 5.
6. Karen Ferguson, *Top Down: The Ford Foundation, Black Power, and the Reinvention of Racial Liberalism* (Philadelphia: University of Pennsylvania Press, 2013), 40–48.
7. The Ford Foundation created the Fund for the Advancement of Education in 1951 to pursue five outcomes, one of them "to reduce inequalities of educational opportunities." In February 1954 the FAE received a $25 million infusion from the Ford Foundation to fund a decade of work. Since the Ashmore Project was authorized (see chapter 3), Barry Bingham Sr., publisher of the Louisville, Kentucky, newspapers, had left the FAE board and McGill had joined. Ford Foundation, "The Ford Foundation Report 1954: To Advance Human Welfare," Dec. 31, 1954, 11, www.fordfoundation.org.
8. Virginius Dabney to Clarence H. Faust, July 5, 1954, Race Relations Information Center, Southern Education Reporting Service Archive (hereafter RRIC-SERS Archive), box 78, folder 1, Amistad Center, Tulane University, New Orleans; SERS press releases, July 29, May 5, 1955, RRIC-SERS Archive, box 70, folder 18. The SERS would remain active until the 1970s. The *Race Relations Law Reporter* was added in 1959, *Southern School News* was replaced in 1975 by the magazine *Southern Education Reporter*, and the SERS clipping and data libraries were made available to libraries as *Facts on File*. During the 1960s the reporting staff was racially integrated and in 1969 the SERS was replaced by the Race Relations Information Center (RRIC). In 1972 the RRIC, which lost its Ford funding, won a two-year reprieve with a new underwriter. Cumming, "Facing Facts, Facing South," 345–57.

9. Scholar Patrick Gilpin situated Johnson as a central player in the FAE conversations that produced the SERS, the decision to model the *Southern School News* after the *Monthly Summary of Events and Trends in Race Relations*, and the expectation that Bonita Valien would be directly involved. Importantly, Gilpin, who believed Johnson had been denied credit for conceptualizing the SERS, argued that these decisions were made in early April 1954, before the white editors gathered at the ASNE convention. Patrick J. Gilpin, "Charles S. Johnson and the Southern Educational Reporting Service," *Journal of Negro History* 63, no. 8 (July 1978): 201–2. Gilpin's account is plausible. To establish the date of Johnson's understanding of the plan for the SERS, Gilpin relied on a letter in possession of the Johnson family, which Johnson wrote to his wife on April 6, 1954. Gilpin also interviewed Philip Coombs, FAE research director, whose recollections did not fully confirm Johnson's account, and Bonita Valien and her husband, Preston, a Fisk faculty member, who recalled meeting with Coombs at Fisk. For SERS documentation, Gilpin used only the Johnson Papers at Fisk and did not compare that correspondence with the archives of Dabney, Shoemaker, Waring, or the RRIC. Therefore, he missed confirmation in the SERS director correspondence discussed later in this chapter. Although Gilpin substantiated his overall claim, his article contained minor inaccuracies. Douglas Cumming, who interviewed Bonita Valien, was less persuaded by Gilpin's argument. Cumming, "Facing Facts, Facing South," 93.
10. Minutes of the First Meeting of the Board of Directors of the Southern Education Reporting Service, May 11, 1954, RRIC-SERS Archive, box 6, folder 15; C. A McKnight, Story for IPI Report, 1954, RRIC-SERS Archive, box 1, folder 6.
11. Don Shoemaker, remarks to the Georgia Press Institute, Athens, GA, Feb. 24, 1956, Shoemaker Papers, folder 42.
12. Don Shoemaker, "A New Dimension in Journalism," remarks to Nashville Rotary Club, 1956, Shoemaker Papers, folder 49.
13. Gilpin, "Charles S. Johnson and the Southern Education Reporting Service," 199. Gilpin said Franklin Roosevelt requested a confidential report on race relations that became a monthly update and was produced at Fisk, influencing local, regional, national, and international policymakers.
14. Simeon Booker to Don Shoemaker, June 30, 1955, Virginius Dabney Papers, MSS 7690-n, box 6, folder Shoemaker, Don, Albert and Shirley Smalls Special Collections Library, University of Virginia, Charlottesville. On Booker's history, see Pamela Newkirk, *Within the Veil: Black Journalists, White Media* (New York: New York University Press, 2000), 59. The three journalists he recommended were Alec Riviea of the *Pittsburg Courier* and William Gordon and A. A. Morrisey of the *Atlanta Daily World*. Gordon was a former Nieman Fellow. Douglas Cumming noted that Booker also applied for an SERS correspondent position. Cumming, "Facing Facts, Facing South," 176.
15. Don Shoemaker to Simeon Booker, July 12, 1955, Dabney Papers, MSS 7690-n, box 6, folder Shoemaker, Don. Two white women reporters, from Oklahoma and Washington, DC, were on the SERS roster.
16. Shoemaker repeated the Rose Bowl/football game analogy in a series of speeches he delivered on behalf of the SERS. This excerpt is from the prepared text he used in addresses to unspecified audiences in Durham, North Carolina, and Portland, Oregon, in 1955. Don Shoemaker, "Remarks," n.d., Shoemaker Papers, folder 41.

17. On presentism and the history of journalism and race, see Kathy Roberts Forde and Sid Bedingfield, *Journalism and Jim Crow: White Supremacy and the Black Struggle for a New America* (Urbana: University of Illinois Press, 2021), 17. On the characterization of P. B. Young Sr., see Virginius Dabney to Thomas Waring, Aug. 14, 1956, Dabney Papers, MSS 7690-h, box 6, folder Don Shoemaker.
18. In his comprehensive history of the SERS, Douglas Cumming acknowledged the frameworks for social construction, audience reception, and framing, then staked out different parameters for his scholarship. "This study avoids the entanglements of these theories," Cumming wrote. "Instead, it looks at how the SERS performed on its own terms and its historical context." Cumming, "Facing Facts, Facing South," 57.
19. Michael Omi and Howard Winant, *Racial Formation in the United States: From the 1960s to the 1990s*, 2nd ed. (1986; New York: Routledge, 1994), 55.
20. McKnight, "How Is the Press Reporting School Desegregation?" 85. While mass communication scholars had not yet articulated the concept of media framing, editors in the 1950s well understood that with every edition, a newspaper published a first draft of history. The genealogy of framing theory has been traced to sociologist Erving Goffman, who introduced the concept in his 1974 book *Frame Analysis: An Essay on the Organization of Experience*. Denis McQuail, *McQuail's Mass Communication Theory*, 4th ed. (1983; London: Sage, 2000), 343.
21. The SERS tracked the number of desegregated southern schools, and in addition to reporting the information in *Southern School News*, announced the data in press releases. For example, an untitled press release of Jan. 5, 1957, announced that 672 districts had at least begun desegregation with more than 3,000 remaining segregated. RRIC-SERS Archive, box 70, folder 22.
22. Gwyneth Mellinger, "The ASNE and Desegregation: Maintaining the White Prerogative in the Face of Change," *Journalism History* 34, no. 3 (Fall 2008): 135–44.
23. Grover C. Hall Jr., "To: Northern Editors of ASNE," *ASNE Bulletin*, Aug. 1, 1956, 5. For a detailed account of Hall's obsession with the hypocrisy of the northern press, see Doug Cumming, "Building Resentment: How the Alabama Press Prepared the Ground for *New York Times v. Sullivan*," *American Journalism* 22, no. 3 (2005): 7–32.
24. Don Shoemaker, "1,000 Per Cent Improvement in General Press Reports," *ASNE Bulletin*, Oct. 1, 1957, 1.
25. McKnight, "How Is the Press Reporting School Desegregation?" 80.
26. "Report from the Director," Southern Education Reporting Service, April 9, Aug. 6, 1956; May 9, 1957, Thomas Waring Papers, box 427, folders 1–2, South Carolina Historical Society, Columbia.
27. C. A. McKnight, "Memorandum for Members of the Board of the Southern Education Reporting Service," May 23, 1954, RRIC-SERS Archive, box 78, folder 1.
28. Bernard Berelson to C. A. McKnight, June 2, 1954, RRIC-SERS Archive, box 1, folder 2. Following the death of founder Howard Odum in 1954, Gordon Blackwell became director of the University of North Carolina's Institute for Research in the Social Sciences. The Ford meeting was not given "any public notice," according to Berelson, the foundation's director of behavioral sciences. In addition to Kenneth Clark, who was on the faculty of the City College of New York, the other attendees included Donald Young, director of the Russell Sage Foundation; Robin Williams and Edward Suchman, Department of Sociology, Cornell University; Albert Reiss, Department of Sociology, Vanderbilt University; Truman Pierce, George Peabody

College for Teachers; Edward McCuiston, director, Arkansas Division of Negro Education; Logan Wilson, president, University of Texas; Harold Fleming, deputy director, Southern Regional Council; Philip H. Coombs, FAE's director of research; and David Freeman, secretary, Fund for the Republic. The FAE grant for the SERS was made to Peabody College in Nashville; Pierce was the author of one of the FAE books spun off from the Ashmore Project.

29. John J. Scanlon to Edward D. Ball, May 1, 1959, Ford Foundation Collection, Grant Files, series 2, box 35, folder Eq Ed: BiRacial, SERS General Correspondence, 1955–1962, Rockefeller Archive Center, Sleepy Hollow, NY.

30. This included white and Black restrooms, waiting rooms in bus stations, playgrounds and beaches, and drinking fountains, as well as the backs of buses and movie theaters and owner preference on hotels and restaurants. From the 1930s to the 1960s, Black travelers in the Jim Crow South relied on *The Negro Motorist Green Book* for information about where to find accommodations and hospitality.

31. Gilpin, "Charles S. Johnson and the Southern Education Reporting Service," 199; Charles Johnson to Philip Coombs, June 20, 1955; Coombs to Johnson, July 9, 1955, Charles Spurgeon Johnson Papers, box 109, folder 18, Fisk University, Nashville; Don Shoemaker to Virginius Dabney, July 25, 1955, Shoemaker Papers, folder 18.

32. Charles Moss to Philip Coombs, Jan. 6, 1955, RRIC-SERS Archive, box 78, folder 4.

33. P. B. Young Sr. to C. A. McKnight, July 14, 1954; McKnight to Young, July 19, 1954, RRIC-SERS Archive, box 78, folder 2.

34. A biography noted that Johnson acquiesced to Jim Crow when, as president of the Southern Sociological Society in 1946, he and other Black members of the prominent academic group were not allowed to stay in the convention hotel in Atlanta: "Johnson chose to ignore publicly the humiliation and to serve as president in hopes of future gains." Patrick J. Gilpin and Marybeth Gasman, *Charles S. Johnson: Leadership beyond the Veil in the Age of Jim Crow* (Albany: State University of New York Press, 2003), 156.

35. Benjamin Houston, *The Nashville Way: Racial Etiquette and the Struggle for Social Justice in a Southern City* (Athens: University of Georgia Press, 2012), 15–16.

36. C. A. McKnight to SERS Board of Directors, July 21, 1954, Johnson Papers, box 9, folder 17; McKnight to Harry Ashmore, July 21, 1954, Harry Ashmore Papers, box 4, folder 10, University of Arkansas–Little Rock.

37. William D. Workman, SERS seminar notes, July 24, 1954, Workman Papers, box 13, folder SERS general, 1954, South Carolina Political Collections, University of South Carolina, Columbia.

38. Charles S. Johnson to Don Shoemaker, June 15, 1956, RRIC-SERS Archive, box 78, folder 8.

39. Don Shoemaker to Charles S. Johnson, June 16, 1956, RRIC-SERS Archive, box 78, folder 8. Although the FAE had suggested to Johnson that he attend the seminars, Shoemaker wrote Vanderbilt University president Harvie Branscomb to see whether he believed directors should have been invited. As a white board member who was not an expert on race, Branscomb reassured Shoemaker that he had confidence in the executive director and did not need to be included in every meeting. Harvie Branscomb to Don Shoemaker, June 22, 1956, RRIC-SERS Archive, box 78, folder 8.

40. Virginius Dabney to Don Shoemaker, March 10, 1956; Shoemaker to Dabney, March 12, 1956, RRIC-SERS Archive, box 78, folder 7.

41. Benjamin Houston noted that "the white southern psyche refused to accept blacks and whites eating together. Partaking in food together was an intimacy presuming equal status." However, he observed that "some hotels permitted . . . the use of banquet facilities for interracial groups, even when the same hotels refused rooms to black patrons." Houston, *The Nashville Way*, 16.
42. "The Men Who Came to Dinner," *News and Courier* (Charleston, SC), Oct. 20, 1955. According to the editorial, a city ordinance in Birmingham "prevents Negros from dining in public with white people."
43. Thomas R. Waring, "The Southern Case against Segregation," *Harper's*, Jan. 1956, 39–45, summarizes the *News and Courier*'s editorial campaign against desegregation. In reporting that Waring had toned down his rhetoric by the mid-1960s, even if he had not abated his basic views about segregation, Roger M. Williams noted that "almost anything would have been an improvement. It [*News and Courier*] had been one of the fiercest resisters in all of Dixie, with an editorial page described by a *Time* magazine correspondent as 'one long, continuous, high-fidelity rebel yell.' For years, the paper derided Negroes, Northerners and federal agents as ingrates and interlopers. Tom Waring speaks more moderately today. Now he laments the civil-rights movement not so much as an invasion of the South as of individual freedom." Roger M. Williams, "Newspapers of the South," *Columbia Journalism Review*, Summer 1967, 26–35.
44. Sid Bedingfield, *Newspaper Wars: Civil Rights and White Resistance in South Carolina, 1935–1965* (Urbana: University of Illinois Press, 2017), 158–59.
45. Thomas Waring to Virginius Dabney, May 13, 1954, Waring Papers, box 426, folder 5.
46. Thomas Waring to Virginius Dabney, May 22, 1954, Waring Papers, box 426, folder 5.
47. Joe Parham, "A Dead Cat Is Thrown by a Peanut Politician," *Macon [GA] News*, Aug. 25, 1954. See also John Egerton, *Speak Now against the Day: The Generation before the Civil Rights Movement* (Chapel Hill: University of North Carolina Press, 1994), 374, on Harris's role in 1946 in formation of the Cracker Party, "a Nazi-like cadre of brown-shirted bullies preaching hatred of blacks, Jews, and Communists."
48. Harris's primary vexation was the Southern Regional Council, an agency supported by the Fund for the Republic, another Ford philanthropy, but he often conflated the Ford charities in his editorializing. Roy V. Harris, "Southern Regional Council Financed by Ford Exposed as Haven for Commies," *Augusta [GA] Courier*, June 28, 1954.
49. Thomas R. Waring to the Editor of the *Augusta Courier*, June 28, 1954, Waring Papers, box 426, folder 6.
50. Thomas R. Waring to Roy V. Harris, July 22, 1954, Waring Papers, box 426, folder 6. Physicist J. Robert Oppenheimer worked on the Manhattan Project, which developed the atomic bomb.
51. Roy V. Harris to Thomas R. Waring, July 27, 1954, Waring Papers, box 426, folder 6.
52. Thomas R. Waring to Roy V. Harris, July 28, 1954, Waring Papers, box 426, folder 6.
53. Virginius Dabney to Thomas R. Waring, Aug. 23, 1954, Waring Papers, box 426, folder 6.
54. C. A. McKnight to Thomas R. Waring, Aug. 27, 1954, Waring Papers, box 426, folder 6.
55. Thomas R. Waring to C. A. McKnight, Aug. 30, 1954, Waring Papers, box 426, folder 6.
56. Thomas Waring to C. A. McKnight, Aug. 28, 1954, Waring Papers, box 426, folder 6; "Desegregation Step Keys Mass Protest," *Fort Worth [TX] Star-Telegram*, Aug. 19, 1954.
57. Thomas Waring to C. A. McKnight, Aug. 28, 1954, Waring Papers, box 426, folder 6.

58. Virginius Dabney to Thomas Waring, Aug. 31, 1954, RRIC-SERS Archive, box 78, folder 2.
59. C. A. McKnight to Thomas Waring, Sept. 1, 1956, RRIC-SERS Archive, box 78, folder 2; "Desegregation of Hobbs' Schools Works without Violence, Disturbance," *Binghamton [NY] Press*, Aug. 31, 1954.
60. C. A. McKnight to Virginius Dabney, Sept. 2, 1954, RRIC-SERS Archive, box 78, folder 2.
61. Thomas Waring to Virginius Dabney, March 24, 1955, Waring Papers, box 426, folder 7.
62. Robert B. Patterson to Don Shoemaker, June 29, 1954, Waring Papers, box 426, folder 7.
63. Thomas Waring to Don Shoemaker, July 2, 1955, Waring Papers, box 426, folder 7. In addition to Patterson, others copied on the letter were Dabney and the more racially moderate editors Harry Ashmore of the *Arkansas Gazette* in Little Rock and Hodding Carter Jr. of the *Delta Democrat-Times* in Greenville, Miss.
64. Don Shoemaker to Thomas Waring, July 5, 1955, Waring Papers, box 426, folder 7.
65. Don Shoemaker to Thomas Waring, Nov. 17, 1955, Waring Papers, box 426, folder 7.
66. Thomas Waring to Don Shoemaker, Nov. 21, 1955, Waring Papers, box 426, folder 7.
67. Don Shoemaker, remarks at the University of Chicago, Dec. 9, 1958, Shoemaker Papers, folder 52. A stillson is an adjustable plumbing wrench.
68. Don Shoemaker, *With All Deliberate Speed* (New York: Harper and Brothers, 1957); Omer Carmichael and Weldon James, *The Louisville Story* (New York: Simon and Schuster, 1957).
69. Weldon James to Harry Ashmore, Jan. 14, 1956, Ashmore Papers, box 5, folder 12.
70. On Workman's activism and the conflict of interest, see Bedingfield, *Newspaper Wars*, 155–57. As Bedingfield noted, Waring showed keener awareness of the optics of his activism and declined to sign the Committee of 52 declaration while vowing to continue his editorial support.
71. William D. Workman to Osta L. Warr, Aug. 28, 1955, Workman Papers, box 32, folder Integration/Civil Rights, Committee of 52.
72. William D. Workman to Ellison D. Smith Jr., Nov. 1, 1955, Workman Papers, box 32, folder Integration/Civil Rights, Committee of 52.
73. Bedingfield, *Newspaper Wars*, 156. Waring gave Workman leave from his reporting duties to write a book defending segregation; see William D. Workman Jr., *The Case for the South* (New York: Devin-Adair, 1960).
74. William D. Workman to Don Shoemaker, March 30, 1956, Workman Papers, box 14, folder SERS, Correspondence, 1956.
75. Don Shoemaker to William Workman, April 3, 1956, Workman Papers, box 14, folder SERS, Correspondence, 1956.
76. Charles Johnson to C. A. McKnight, June 19, 1954, Johnson Papers, box 9, folder 17. Johnson and P. B. Young Sr. both endorsed Jess O. Thomas, who had written McKnight to apply. McKnight to Thomas, June 16, 1954, Johnson Papers, box 9, folder 17.
77. Virginius Dabney, "Nearer and Nearer the Precipice," *Atlantic Monthly*, Jan. 1943, 94–100.
78. Virginius Dabney to Jake Mahaffey, Sept. 13, 1957, Dabney Papers, MSS 7990-h, box 3, folder ASNE Committees.
79. C. A. McKnight to Charles Johnson, June 24, 1954, Johnson Papers, box 9, folder 17.
80. Charles S. Johnson to Philip Coombs, June 20, 1955; Coombs to Johnson, July 8, 1955,

Johnson Papers, box 109, folder 18. Coombs did not disclose to Johnson that the board had resisted Valien's hiring because of her race.
81. SERS, Minutes of the Second Meeting of the Board of Directors, June 6, 1954, Waring Papers, box 426, folder 6.
82. C. A. McKnight to Virginius Dabney, Aug. 12, 1954, Waring Papers 23, box 426, folder 6.
83. Houston, *The Nashville Way*, 50–51; Cumming, "Facing Facts, Facing South," 181.
84. Charles Moss to Philip Coombs, Jan. 6, 1955, RRIC-SERS Archive, box 78, folder 4.
85. Emilie Tavel, "Desegregation Seen Aid to All," *Christian Science Monitor*, Nov. 18, 1954, Waring Papers, box 426, folder 7.
86. William Workman to Thomas Waring, Jan. 14, 1955, RRIC-SERS Archive, box 78, folder 4.
87. Thomas Waring to C.A. McKnight, Jan. 15, 1955, RRIC-SERS Archive, box 78, folder 4.
88. At the SERS board's organizational meeting on May 11, 1954, the minutes report, "The question was raised as to whether the Board had a sufficiently diversified membership and it was unanimously agreed that the group should be broadened to include a prominent editor of a Negro newspaper and a leading public school administrator. To implement this decision, the group agreed to extend an invitation to Mr. P.B. Young, Sr., Editor of the Norfolk Journal and Guide, and Dr. Henry Willett, Superintendent of Schools in Richmond, Virginia, to join the group." Willett was white; no board member represented Black education. Minutes of the SERS Board, May 11, 1954, Waring Papers, box 426, folder 6.
89. Valien had told McKnight she was traveling to Boston for the event and he had reminded her to "limit her remarks to describing the objectives and the functions of the Reporting Service." Virginius Dabney to C. A. McKnight, Jan. 17, 1955; McKnight to Thomas Waring, Jan. 17, 1955, RRIC-SERS Archive, box 78, folder 4.
90. C. A. McKnight to Virginius Dabney and Thomas R. Waring, Feb. 2, 1955, RRIC-SERS Archive, box 78, folder 4; "The No. 1 Story," *Time*, Jan. 17, 1955, 67.
91. Coleman A. Harwell to Virginius Dabney, Jan. 17, 1955, RRIC-SERS Archive, box 78, folder 4.
92. Waring instructed McKnight that Valien was "to refrain from giving out partisan statements" and that compliance was "mandatory rather than optional." Thomas Waring to C. A. McKnight, Feb. 3, 1955; Waring to Virginius Dabney, Jan. 19, 1955, RRIC-SERS Archive, box 78, folder 4.
93. C. A. McKnight to Thomas R. Waring, Feb. 4, 1955, RRIC-SERS Archive, box 78, folder 4.
94. C. A. McKnight to Bonita Valien, Feb. 10, 1955, RRIC-SERS Archive, box 78, folder 4. Waring informed Frank Ahlgren at the *Memphis Commercial Appeal*, a fellow segregationist on the SERS board, of his displeasure with Valien. Thomas Waring to Frank Ahlgren, Jan. 20, 1955, Waring Papers, box 426, folder 7.
95. Bonita Valien to C. A. McKnight, Feb. 21, 1955, RRIC-SERS Archive, box 78, folder 4.
96. The NCNW, a prominent women's organization founded in 1935 by Mary McLeod Bethune, announced its celebration of Black history in a press release that generated at least three mentions in the Nashville white press during the week before the event. Two of them were in the *Tennessean*'s column "Happenings among Colored People," while a third appeared in the news section of the *Banner*. W. H. Shackelford, "Happenings among Colored People: Segregation Talk Slated," *Nashville Tennessean*, Feb.

20, 1955; Shackelford, "Happenings among Colored People: NCNW Chapter to Give Program," *Nashville Tennessean*, Feb. 27, 1955. The *Nashville Banner* also ran a short item from the press release: "Negro Women's Council to Meet," *Nashville Banner*, Feb. 23, 1955.

97. "Founder's Day Program of Nashville Chapter of National Council of Negro Women, Feb. 27, 1955, at First Baptist Church, Eighth Ave., North. Principal Speaker, Mrs. Preston Valien. Subject: 'The Challenge of Desegregation,'" memo, Feb. 28, 1955, RRIC-SERS Archive, box 78, folder 4 (hereafter Founder's Day Program Memo), ellipses in original, here and in all subsequent quotations from this document.
98. Founder's Day Program Memo.
99. *Banner* editor Charles Moss also told the SERS leadership that he had "a Negro reporter who would be available to us in any capacity," though that of course would not entail work as a regular SERS correspondent. Don Shoemaker to Virginius Dabney, July 25, 1955, Shoemaker Papers, folder 18.
100. Robert Churchwell, "Laws Help Gain Civil Rights, Declares Fisk U. Scientist," *Nashville Banner*, Feb. 28, 1955. On Churchwell's history at the *Nashville Banner*, see David Halberstam, *The Children* (New York: Random House, 1998), 180–86.
101. Founder's Day Program Memo.
102. SERS, Minutes of the Fourth Meeting of the Board of Directors, March 6, 1955, Waring Papers, box 426, folder 7.
103. Although Valien knew the Boston speech had created problems, McKnight did not mention it in the letter, which focused instead on the board's action in March and a plan to focus less on research and more on reporting. In addition, McKnight waited to send the letter until he was leaving for vacation before the end of his own contract with the SERS. C.A. McKnight to Bonita Valien, June 12, 1955, Johnson Papers, box 109, folder 18; Charles Johnson to Don Shoemaker, June 22, 1955, RRIC-SERS Archive, box 78, folder 5.
104. Virginius Dabney to Charles Johnson, March 29, 1955, Johnson Papers, box 109, folder 18.
105. Charles S. Johnson to Philip Coombs, June 20, 1955; Coombs to Johnson, July 8, 1955, Johnson Papers, box 109, folder 18. Interestingly, racial etiquette allowed Johnson to be on a first-name basis with the FAE representative in the North but not with Dabney, whom he had known much longer.
106. Charles S. Johnson to Virginius Dabney, July 13, 1955, Dabney Papers, MSS 7690-h, box 6, folder Southern School News. That summer, Simeon Booker would write Shoemaker, making essentially the same point and recommending three journalists working for the Black press in the South. Booker to Shoemaker, June 30, 1955, Johnson Papers, box 109, folder 18.
107. Virginius Dabney to Charles Johnson, July 21, 1955, Johnson Papers, box 109, folder 18.
108. Charles Johnson to Don Shoemaker, June 22, 1955, Johnson Papers, box 109, folder 18. Shoemaker, who said he was "in theoretical agreement" with Johnson's position, described the issue as "a policy matter that must be hammered out by the board." Shoemaker to Johnson, June 29, 1955, Johnson Papers, box 109, folder 18.
109. Don Shoemaker to Virginius Dabney, July 25, 1955, Shoemaker Papers, folder 18. Shoemaker wondered "whether [Johnson] is aware that Mrs. Valien was retained by the Fund (in a manner of speaking) and not by Pete [McKnight]." Johnson was. Gilpin, who did not have access to this letter, reached the same conclusion from

documents in the Johnson Papers at Fisk and interviews with living participants, including Coombs and Valien. Gilpin, "Charles Johnson and the Southern Education Reporting Service," 201.
110. Don Shoemaker to Virginius Dabney, July 25, 1955.
111. Don Shoemaker to Virginius Dabney, July 25, 1955.
112. Virginius Dabney, letter to Don Shoemaker, July 28, 1955, Dabney Papers, MSS 7690-h, box 6, folder Shoemaker, Don.
113. Dabney, "Nearer and Nearer the Precipice," 99. During the war years, Dabney also complimented Johnson as "preeminent" among "distinguished younger Negro scholars in the South." Virginius Dabney, *Below the Potomac: A Book about the New South* (New York: D. Appleton-Century, 1942), 235.
114. Quoted in Morton Sosna, *In Search of the Silent South: Southern Liberals and the Race Issue* (New York: Columbia University Press, 1977), 133.
115. Henry Lewis Suggs, *P. B. Young, Newspaperman: Race, Politics, and Journalism in the New South, 1910–62* (Charlottesville: University Press of Virginia, 1988), 25, 100, 126. Suggs also described Dabney's effort to nominate Young's paper and staff for the inaugural Wendell Wilkie Awards for Distinguished Writing by Negro Journalists in 1946. The awards, Suggs wrote, were meant for "the conservative black press and were designed to solidify support for the Democratic party." Young delivered the keynote on "The Negro Press in a Changing World" (140–41).
116. Two biographies emphasize Johnson's long-term strategy within the civil rights movement and describe the SERS's role: Richard Robbins, *Sidelines Activist: Charles S. Johnson and the Struggle for Civil Rights* (Jackson: University Press of Mississippi, 1996), 158–60, and Gilpin and Gasman, *Charles S. Johnson*, 158–68.
117. "Publisher Quits Education Group," *Baltimore Afro-American*, April 7, 1956. Young's resignation received only brief mention in the two most prominent histories of the SERS: Roberts and Klibanoff, *The Race Beat*, 192, and Cumming, "Facing Facts, Facing South," 217.
118. P. B. Young Sr. to Virginius Dabney, July 18, 1955, Johnson Papers, box 109, folder 18. A Dabney reply to this letter was not found in the RRIC-SERS Archive or the Johnson, Dabney, or Shoemaker Papers. Young's papers are privately held and not publicly accessible. The letter itself, which was copied to Johnson, appears in his SERS papers and the Dabney collection.
119. P. B. Young Sr. to Charles Johnson, July 18, 1955, Johnson Papers, box 109, folder 18.
120. P. B. Young Sr. to Virginius Dabney, Sept. 1, 1955, Johnson Papers, box 109, folder 18.
121. P. B. Young Sr. to Virginius Dabney, Sept. 3, 1955, Johnson Papers, box 109, folder 18.
122. Charles S. Johnson to P. B. Young Sr., Sept. 12, 1955, Johnson Papers, box 109, folder 18.
123. Young did not misinterpret Dabney's position. In 1961 Dabney would be among the white southern editors who endorsed Carleton Putnam's *Race and Reason: A Yankee View*, the pseudo-scientific defense of racist essentialism, what Neil McMillen described as "a veritable white supremacist's catechism." McMillen, *The Citizens' Council: Organized Resistance to the Second Reconstruction, 1954–1964* (Urbana: University of Illinois Press, 1971), 167.
124. Ross Valentine, "A Liberal Looks at Farmville, Va.," *Richmond [VA] Times-Dispatch*, Oct. 17, 1955; Valentine, "'Unhappy Subjects' or Free Citizens," *Richmond Times-Dispatch*, Oct. 25, 1955.

125. P. B. Young Sr. to Virginius Dabney, Oct. 25, 1955, 1st letter, Shoemaker Papers, folder 18.
126. P. B. Young Sr. to Virginius Dabney, Oct. 25, 1955, 2nd letter, Shoemaker Papers, folder 18.
127. Don Shoemaker to P. B. Young Sr., Oct. 28, 1955, Shoemaker Papers, folder 18.
128. Virginius Dabney to P. B. Young Sr., Nov. 8, 1955, Dabney Papers, MSS 7690-h, folder Don Shoemaker.
129. Virginius Dabney to P. B. Young Sr., Nov. 14, 1955, Dabney Papers, MSS 7690-h, folder Don Shoemaker.
130. P.B. Young Sr. to Virginius Dabney, Nov. 17, 1955, Shoemaker Papers, folder 18; "A Middle-of-the-Road Program," *Richmond Times-Dispatch*, Nov. 15, 1955.
131. Virginius Dabney to C. A. McKnight, Nov. 15, 1955, Dabney Papers, MSS 7690-h, box 6, folder Don Shoemaker.
132. In correspondence with Dabney about the March 1956 board meeting, Johnson mentioned in passing that Young had resigned; Dabney thought Johnson was referring to the October–November 1955 resignation. Young sent Dabney a telegram of resignation after this exchange between Dabney and Johnson. Charles Johnson to Virginius Dabney, March 12, 1956; Dabney to Johnson, March 14, 1956, Johnson Papers, box 109, folder 19.
133. Virginius Dabney to Don Shoemaker, Nov. 21, 1955, Shoemaker Papers, folder 18.
134. P. B. Young Sr. to Virginius Dabney, telegram, March 17, 1956, RRIC-SERS Archive, box 84, folder 16.
135. "Manifesto States Case: South's Men of Conviction Stand Up to Be Counted," *Nashville Banner*, March 13, 1956. This editorial took only a passing swipe at the NAACP. Earlier in the month, the *Banner* had opened fire on the NAACP for its handling of the Autherine Lucy case to integrate the University of Alabama. The *Banner* supported her expulsion from the university. "Insolence Rebuked: Expulsion Was in Order," *Nashville Banner*, March 2, 1956.
136. Virginius Dabney to P. B. Young Sr., March 19, 1956, telegram, RRIC-SERS Archive, box 84, folder 16. The National Newspaper Publishers Association was a Black professional organization formed to represent the Black press in response to segregation of the newspaper industry.
137. P. B. Young Sr. to Virginius Dabney, March 20, 1956, Dabney Papers, MSS 7690-h, box 6, folder Board Members. On Young's long history of involvement with the NAACP, see Suggs, *P.B. Young, Newspaperman*.
138. Virginius Dabney to Don Shoemaker, April 11, 1956, Shoemaker Papers, folder 18.
139. Assorted press clippings, Dabney Papers, MSS 7690-h, box 6, folder Board Members; "Publisher Quits Education Group," *Baltimore Afro-American*, April 7, 1956; Simeon Booker, "Ticker Tape USA," *Jet*, April 26, 1956, 15; "Wilkins Tells of NAACP Role in Battle for Rights," *Norfolk [VA] Journal and Guide*, April 28, 1956.
140. Don Shoemaker to Virginius Dabney, April 13, 1956, RRIC-SERS Archive, box 78, folder 7.
141. See chapter 3 of this book.
142. Virginius Dabney to Charles Thompson, April 25, 1956; Thompson to Dabney, April 30, 1956, RRIC-SERS Archive, box 78, folder 7. Dabney wondered how to respond and whether to telephone Thompson. Virginius Dabney to Don Shoemaker, May 1, 1956, Dabney Papers, MSS 7690-h, box 6, folder Don Shoemaker.

143. Virginius Dabney to Thomas Waring, May 19, 1956, Dabney Papers, MSS 7690-h, box 6, folder Shoemaker, Don. Dabney's accounting does not accurately reflect the existing correspondence with Thompson. The source of the quotation about "the sinners" and "the saints" is not in the archive and may have derived from a telephone call or letter than was not filed.
144. Thomas Waring to Virginius Dabney, May 21, 1956, Dabney Papers, MSS 7690-h, box 6, folder Shoemaker, Don.
145. "Our Answer Is No," *Baltimore Afro-American*, June 2, 1956, Waring Papers, box 427, folder 1.
146. Virginius Dabney to Claude Barnett, May 28, 1956; Barnett to Dabney, June 12, 1956, RRIC-SERS Archive, box 78, folder 7; Chapter 1 of this book.
147. Claude Barnett to Charles Johnson, June 4, 1956, Johnson Papers, box 109, folder 19.
148. Charles Johnson to Claude Barnett, June 15, 1956, Johnson Papers, box 109, folder 19.
149. Virginius Dabney to Don Shoemaker, July 11, 1956, RRIC-SERS Archive, box 78, folder 8.
150. Virginius Dabney to Charles Johnson, July 11, 1956, Dabney Papers, MSS 7690-h, box 6, folder Shoemaker, Don; Booker, "Ticker Tape USA."
151. Don Shoemaker to Virginius Dabney, July 18, 1956, RRIC-SERS Archive, box 78, folder 8.
152. Thomas Waring to Virginius Dabney, June 19, 1955, Dabney Papers, MSS 7690-h, box 6, folder Shoemaker, Don.
153. Don Shoemaker to Thomas Waring, July 18, 1956, RRIC-SERS Archive, box 78, folder 8.
154. "The Negro Exodus and Why," *Norfolk Journal and Guide*, Aug. 11, 1956; Don Shoemaker to Virginius Dabney, Aug. 10, 1956, RRIC-SERS Archive, box 78, folder 8.
155. Virginius Dabney to Thomas Waring, Aug. 14, 1956, Dabney Papers, MSS 7690-h, box 6, folder Don Shoemaker.
156. Don Shoemaker to Virginius Dabney, Aug. 10, 1956; Dabney to Shoemaker, Aug. 14, 1956, Dabney Papers, MSS 7690-h, box 6, folder Don Shoemaker.
157. Among those initially considered were Benjamin Mays, president of Morehouse College, and William Gordon of the *Atlanta Daily World*, whom Simeon Booker had suggested for the reporting staff. Don Shoemaker to Virginius Dabney, Nov. 1, 1956, RRIC-SERS Archive, box 78, folder 8.
158. Virginius Dabney to the SERS board, Nov. 23, 1956, RRIC-SERS Archive, box 78, folder 8.
159. Thomas Waring to Don Shoemaker, Nov. 26, 1956, Waring Papers, box 427, folder 1; Gwyneth Mellinger, "Saving the Republic: An Editor's Crusade against Integration." *Journalism History* 42, no. 4 (Jan. 2017): 212–24.
160. Coleman Harwell to Luther Foster, April 17, 1957, RRIC-SERS Archive, box 78, folder 9; Don Shoemaker to Foster, May 21, 1957, RRIC-SERS Archive, box 78, folder 10.
161. Cumming, "Facing Facts, Facing South," 55.
162. "Our Answer Is No," *Baltimore Afro-American*, June 2, 1956, Waring Papers, box 427, folder 1.
163. Don Shoemaker to Thomas Waring, July 18, 1956, Waring Papers, box 427, folder 1.
164. Charles Johnson to Virginius Dabney; Johnson to P. B. Young Sr., July 13, 1955, Johnson Papers, box 109, folder 18.

165. Charles S. Johnson, "A Southern Negro's View of the South," *New York Times Magazine*, Sept. 23, 1956, 66.

## AFTERWORD

1. In the 1960s, the SERS integrated its reporting staff and changed its name to the Race Relations Information Center. By the time it ceased operations in the early 1970s, it described itself as "a biracial agency." Patrick J. Gilpin, "Charles S. Johnson and the Southern Education Reporting Service," *Journal of Negro History* 63, no. 3 (July 1978): 197.
2. Don Shoemaker, remarks to the Georgia Press Institute, Feb. 24, 1956, Don Shoemaker Papers, folder 42, Southern Historical Collection, University of North Carolina at Chapel Hill.
3. George M. Fredrickson, *The Black Image in the White Mind: The Debate on Afro-American Character and Destiny: 1817–1914* (New York: Harper and Row, 1971), 280, 282.
4. John Egerton, *Speak Now against the Day: The Generation before the Civil Rights Movement in the South* (Chapel Hill: University of North Carolina Press, 1994), 48.
5. The NAACP secured statewide bans in Kansas and Ohio. Melvyn Stokes, *D. W. Griffith's* The Birth of a Nation: *A History of "the Most Controversial Motion Picture of All Time"* (New York: Oxford University Press, 2007), 227. For more on the film's impact on race in the twentieth century, see Robert Lang, ed., *The Birth of a Nation* (New Brunswick, NJ: Rutgers University Press, 1994), and Dick Lehr, The Birth of a Nation: *How a Legendary Filmmaker and a Crusading Editor Reignited America's Civil War* (New York: Public Affairs, 2014).
6. For example, after the film's release in 1915, renowned social reformer Jane Addams described *The Birth of a Nation* as a "pernicious caricature of the Negro race." Lang, *The Birth of a Nation*, 159. See also Bart Andrews and Ahrgus Juillard, *Holy Mackerel! The Amos 'n' Andy Story* (New York: Dutton, 1986), 12–13; Melvin Patrick Ely, *The Adventures of Amos 'n' Andy: A Social History of an American Phenomenon* (New York: Free Press, 1991), 150; and Ibram X. Kendi, *Stamped from the Beginning: The Definitive History of Racist Ideas in America* (New York: Bold Type Books, 2016), 334.
7. Martha Biondi, *To Stand and Fight: The Struggle for Civil Rights in Postwar New York City* (Cambridge, MA: Harvard University Press, 2003), 95–97.
8. Pete Daniel, *Lost Revolutions: The South of the 1950s* (Chapel Hill: University of North Carolina Press, 2000), 242; Allison Graham, *Framing the South: Hollywood, Television, and Race during the Civil Rights Struggle* (Baltimore: Johns Hopkins University Press, 2001), 85. Melvyn Stokes reported that the film "would continue to be screened by Klan audiences at least until the 1970s." Stokes, *D. W. Griffith's* The Birth of a Nation, 9.
9. For many white southerners grappling with the 1954 *Brown* ruling, the "wolf-whistling" allegation against Till, a signal of sexual impropriety, seemed to affirm the evils of race-mixing. Elizabeth Gillespie McRae, *Mothers of Massive Resistance: White Women and the Politics of White Supremacy* (New York: Oxford University Press, 2018), 181.
10. Matt Carlson, "Metajournalistic Discourse and the Meanings of Journalism:

Definitional Control, Boundary Work, and Legitimation," *Communication Theory* 26 (2016): 350.

11. Michael Omi and Howard Winant, *Racial Formation in the United States: From the 1960s to the 1990s*, 2nd ed. (1986; New York: Routledge, 1994), 71.
12. Stuart Hall, "Culture, Media and the 'Ideological Effect,'" in *Mass Communication and Society*, ed. James Curran et al. (Beverly Hills, CA: Sage, 1979), 325; Gwyneth Mellinger and Erin K. Coyle, "'Blackening Up Journalism': An Ethical Imperative for Newsroom Diversity," in *Journalism's Ethical Progression: A Twentieth Century Journey*, ed. Gwyneth Mellinger and John Ferré (Lanham, MD: Lexington Books, 2021), 185–203; Gwyneth Mellinger, *Chasing Newsroom Diversity: From Jim Crow to Affirmative Action* (Champaign: University of Illinois Press, 2013), 34–42.
13. W. J. Cash, *The Mind of the South* (1941; reprint New York: Vintage, 1991).
14. Donald E. Reynolds, *Editors Make War: Southern Newspapers in the Secession Crisis* (1970; reprint Carbondale: Southern Illinois Press, 2006).
15. The term "white supremacy" first appeared in the Black and white presses after the Civil War. Kathy Roberts Forde and Sid Bedingfield, *Journalism and Jim Crow: White Supremacy and the Black Struggle for a New America* (Champaign: University of Illinois Press, 2021), 17. Although the southern white press was directly implicated in the resistance to *Brown v. Board of Education*, Jeanne Theoharis reminds us that the indifference of many in the northern white press miscast segregation as a peculiarly southern evil and facilitated the "redneckification of racism." Theoharis, *A More Beautiful and Terrible History: The Uses and Misuses of Civil Rights History* (Boston: Beacon Press, 2018), 85.
16. By the 1970s Jacques Derrida would share his theoretical understanding that the two sides of a binary can never be equal, but it also was the *Brown v. Board* plaintiffs' key argument in 1954 (347 U.S. 483) to overturn the 1896 ruling in *Plessy v. Ferguson* (163 U.S. 537). Derrida made this point throughout his work on deconstruction; see, for example, Derrida, *Dissemination* (Chicago: University of Chicago Press, 1981), 22.
17. James Wechsler to Alan Gould, Oct. 3, 1955, Subject file 1958, new box 127, folder "Till murder," Associated Press Corporate Archive, New York.
18. Mellinger, *Chasing Newsroom Diversity*, 10.
19. In this vein, Gary Younge noted that "so much of Black History Month takes place in the passive voice. Leaders 'get assassinated,' patrons 'are refused' service, women 'are ejected' from public transport. So the objects of racism are many but the subjects are few. In removing the instigators, the historians remove the agency and, in the final reckoning, the historical responsibility." "White History 101," *Nation*, Feb. 21, 2007, quoted in Theoharis, *A More Beautiful and Terrible History*, 83.
20. Sid Bedingfield, *Newspaper Wars: Civil Rights and White Resistance in South Carolina, 1935–1965* (Urbana: University of Illinois Press, 2017), 200–12. On colorblind conservatism, see also McRae, *Mothers of Massive Resistance*, 215. On the southern history of the civil and voting rights acts, see Jason Sokol, *There Goes My Everything: White Southerners in the Age of Civil Rights, 1945–1975* (New York: Vintage, 2007), chapters 4–5. On the American creed, see Declaration of Independence (1776).
21. National Advisory Commission on Civil Disorders, *The Kerner Report* (Princeton, NJ: Princeton University Press, 2016), 338.
22. Mellinger, *Chasing Newsroom Diversity*, 120–25, 167–78.

23. Matthew Pressman, *On Press: The Liberal Values That Shaped the News* (Cambridge, MA: Harvard University Press, 2018), 25–44.
24. Kevin Lerner, *Provoking the Press: [MORE] Magazine and the Crisis of Confidence in American Journalism* (Columbia: University of Missouri Press, 2019), 29; Gwyneth Mellinger, "Conflicts of Interest in Journalism: Debating a Post-Hutchins Ethical Self-Consciousness," *American Journalism* 34, no. 4 (2017): 9–11.
25. Until 1973 the Society of Professional Journalists, formerly known as Sigma Delta Chi, borrowed the American Society of Newspaper Editors' Canons of Journalism. The new code said "objectivity in reporting the news is another goal which serves as the mark of an experienced professional. It is a standard of performance toward which we strive. We honor those who achieve it." Society of Professional Journalists, Code of Ethics, adopted Nov. 16, 1973, in Casey Bukro, "The SPJ Code's Double-Edged Sword: Accountability, Credibility," *Journal of Mass Media Ethics* 1, no. 1 (1985): 10–13.
26. Andie Tucher, *Not Exactly Lying: Fake News and Fake Journalism in American History* (New York: Columbia University Press, 2022), 289. The renegotiation of objectivity's role and significance also has generated important scholarship among journalism paradigm theorists. See, for example, the discussion of paradigm reconsideration in Tim P. Vos and Joseph Moore, "Building the Journalism Paradigm: Beyond Paradigm Repair," *Journalism* 21, no. 1 (Jan. 2020): 25–27. The article surveys the literature on paradigm theory and journalism.
27. Barbara Ransby, *Making All Black Lives Matter: Reimagining Freedom in the 21st Century* (Oakland: University of California Press, 2018), 1.
28. Sheryl Kennedy Haydel suggested this line of analysis during a panel on "Moving Beyond Official Frames: Evaluating Unreliable Sources," American Journalism Historians Association Annual Conference, online, Oct. 8, 2021.
29. Nikole Hannah-Jones, speaking on NPR's 1A podcast: "So when white Americans say to me, 'I just want factual reporting,' what they're saying to me is they want reporting from a white perspective . . . with a white normative view, and that simply has never been objective." "The Debate over Objectivity in Journalism," 1A Podcast, June 9, 2020, National Public Radio, https://www.npr.org. See also John Drescher, "Nikole Hannah-Jones, a Mega-Donor, and the Future of Journalism," *The Assembly*, May 30, 2021, https://quirky-cray-af5aca.netlify.app.
30. See, for example, Candis Callison and Mary Lynn Young, *Reckoning: Journalism's Limits and Possibilities* (New York: Oxford University Press, 2020), and Lewis Raven Wallace, *The View from Somewhere: Undoing the Myth of Journalistic Objectivity* (Chicago: University of Chicago Press, 2019). See also Nikki Usher's analysis of race, place, and audience: Usher, *News for the Rich, White, and Blue: How Place and Power Distort American Journalism* (New York: Columbia University Press, 2021), 61.
31. See, for example, Mike Fannin, "The Truth in Black and White: An Apology from the *Kansas City Star*," Dec. 22, 2020, https://www.kansascity.com, and "Editorial: An Examination of the *Times*' Failures on Race, Our Apology and a Path Forward," *Los Angeles Times*, Sept. 27, 2020, https://www.latimes.com. Other newspapers that have undertaken self-reflective examinations of their past include the *Philadelphia Inquirer*, *Baltimore Sun*, *Boston Globe*, *Cleveland Plain Dealer*, and *Seattle Times*. "Coming Clean: Truth, Reconciliation, and Reparation in Journalism," Association

for Education in Journalism and Mass Communication, panel discussion, Washington, DC, Aug. 8, 2023.

32. "AP Changes Writing Style to Capitalize 'b' in Black," Associated Press, June 19, 2020, https://apnews.com, and "Explaining AP Style on Black and white," Associated Press, June 20, 2020, https://apnews.com.

33. For example, this was the topic of the panel "Newsroom Reckoning: Objectivity, Belonging, and Beyond," Racialisation and the Media: From Television to Twitter, an online conference hosted by the Rothermere American Institute, April 20, 2021, https://www.youtube.com. Of particular interest were comments by scholar Jane Rhodes, *Framing the Black Panthers: The Spectacular Rise of a Black Power Icon* (Champaign: University of Illinois Press, 2007).

34. Wesley Lowery, "A Reckoning over Objectivity, Led by Black Journalists," *New York Times*, July 23, 2020. Lowery's op-ed and the response from his professional peers quickly inspired peer-reviewed scholarship: Thomas R. Schmidt, "Challenging Journalistic Objectivity: How Journalists of Color Call for a Reckoning," *Journalism* 25, no. 3 (2023): 1–18. Lowery's *New York Times* piece appeared about six months after he resigned from the *Washington Post*. At issue was a dispute with management over the *Post*'s social media policy.

In his memoir, former editor Martin Baron, who is white, discussed at length his position on Lowery's time at the *Post* and the circumstances of Lowery's resignation. Baron, *Collision of Power: Trump, Bezos, and the* Washington Post (New York: Flatiron Books, 2023), 365–74. Baron described Lowery's "intemperate" use of social media and defended the *Post*'s policy, which then applied to 850 news department employees. "If each of them acted as newsperson and commentator, it would be a cacophonous, unprofessional mess" (373–74). Baron also defended the professional standard of objectivity: "In Wes's words, news organizations' 'core value needs to be truth, not the perception of objectivity.'" Baron described the *Post*'s process for objective reporting, a diligent fact-finding effort that harkened to the scientific method, and said, "No one had abandoned the idea of truth as was cartoonishly portrayed" (374). Notably, Baron's discussion of objectivity does not address the implications of standpoint and journalism's history as a segregated institution. Lowery's public criticism of the *Post* had clearly struck a nerve as Baron devoted eleven pages of his memoir to his response.

35. "The Objectivity Wars," Columbia University Journalism School, Sept. 13, 2022, https://www.youtube.com.

36. Ruth Frankenburg described it this way: "Whiteness is in a continual state of being dressed and undressed, of marking and cloaking." Frankenburg, "The Mirage of an Unmarked Whiteness," in *The Making and Unmaking of Whiteness*, ed. Birgit Brander Rasmussen et al. (Durham, NC: Duke University Press, 2001), 74.

37. Yair Rosenberg, "'Jews Will Not Replace Us': Why White Supremacists Go after Jews," *Washington Post*, Aug. 14, 2017, https://www.washingtonpost.com. See also Wesley Lowery, *American Whitelash: A Changing Nation and the Cost of Progress* (New York: Mariner Books, 2023), 204–24, and Aniko Bodroghkozy, *Making #Charlottesville: Media from Civil Rights to Unite the Right* (Charlottesville: University of Virginia Press, 2023), chapter 2.

# INDEX

NOTE: Page references in *italics* reference figures.

"A Basis for Interracial Cooperation and Development in the South: A Statement by Southern Negroes" (Durham Manifesto), 34
Addams, Jane, 265n6
Ahlgren, Frank, 175
*Alabama Tribune*, and racial gradualism, 118
Alwood, Edward, 225n76
"American dilemma," Myrdal on, 105
*American Mercury*, and Mencken, 6
American Society of Newspaper Editors (ASNE): *Bulletin* of, 19, 46, 168, 224n66, 234n3; Canons of Journalism, 267n25; membership, 228n35; and racial gradualism, 116; and SERS, 163, 167, 168, 181, 196
*Amos 'n' Andy* programs, 205
*Amsterdam News* (New York): and Black press as indicted/othered, 47; and SERS, 181
*An American Dilemma: The Negro Problem and Modern Democracy* (Myrdal), 7–8, 49
Angelo, Frank, 156–57
*Anniston Star* (Alabama), and Black press as indicted/othered, 54
antisemitism: and "replacement theory," 214–15; *Social Justice* and Coughlin, 37–38
*Arkansas Gazette*: and Ashmore, 13; and journalistic objectivity, 25; misinterpretation of Ashmore's statements, 25, 93, 94, 96, 107, 112, 124; and SERS, 161. *See also* Ashmore, Harry S.
Arkansas Teacher Education Program, 100
Arnold, Edgar, Jr., 129–30
Asbury Park "riot," 148
Ashmore, Harry S.: career path of, 94–95, 124; *An Epitaph for Dixie*, 93, 94, 122–23, 240n7; *Hearts and Minds: The Anatomy of Racism from Roosevelt to Reagan*, 125; and journalistic objectivity, 13; on "man in the middle," 94, 98, 240n2; misinterpreted positions of, 93–98, 120–25, 240–41n8; *The Negro and the Schools* (a.k.a. "Ashmore Report"), 25, 95–102, 121–24, 163–64, 170, 179, 208, 240n7, 241n20, 242n25; and North-South press divide, 142; racial slurs of, 125; and SERS, 161, 163, 173, 179, 184, 189, 196, 201; "Some Major Problems Involved in Racial Integration with Especial Reference to Education in the South," 115–21; Southern Governors'

Ashmore, Harry S. (*continued*)
Conference address by, 102–15, 243n40, 244n47; Southern Political Science Association address by, 107; University of Chicago *Roundtable* NBC broadcast by, 121–22
Associated Negro Press (ANP), 24, 49–51, 53–56, 58–60, 109–10
Associated Press (AP): *AP Log*, 145; *The APME Red Book*, 78–79; AP Reference Book (for personnel), 77–78; on Ashmore's statements, 107, 108; Associated Press Managing Editors (APME), 65, 75, 78–79, 84, 130, 156, 248n11; *Associated Press Stylebook*, 27, 77, 87, 237–38nn38–39; Blackman and North-South press divide, 159–60; on capitalization of "B" in "Black," 213; Corporate Archives of, 71, 127, 238n45; framework of, 13, 75–79, 131–33; and McKelway's role, 253n85; Newsfeatures, 145, 148; and SERS, 162, 173, 177; southern editors' protest (1959), 253n83; Wirephoto, 64–67, 66, 76, 86, 89. *See also* Associated Press (AP) and racial identifier issue; North-South press divide
Associated Press (AP) and racial identifier issue, 64–92; and AP framework, 75–79; and AP's pertinence policy, 67, 77–89, 213; and gradualist stance, 92; NAACP on racial identifier issue, 69–70; Reese *(St. Louis Post-Dispatch)* on racial identification, 250n28; and regional bias allegations, 87–90, 91–92; segregation and stereotyping, 70–75, 90–91; Ypsilanti triplets example, 64–67, 66, 72, 75, 86, 89
Atkins, Stan, 83
*Atlanta Constitution*: Ashmore misinterpreted by, 113; and Black press as indicted/othered, 34; and journalistic objectivity, 13; and racial identification, 82; and SERS, 163
*Atlanta Journal*, and racial identification, 65, 67
*Atlantic Monthly*: and Black press as indicted/othered, 29, 43, 44; and SERS, 191
*Augusta Chronicle* (Georgia), and North-South press divide, 148
*Augusta Courier* (Georgia), and SERS, 174–75, 176
Ayers, Harry, 54

*Baltimore Afro-American*, and SERS, 196, 197–98, 201–2
*Baltimore Evening Sun*, and Scopes trial, 6, 220n20
*Baltimore Sun*, and racial identification, 67, 235n12
Barnett, Claude: Associated Negro Press founded by, 24; on Brown, 230n69; marginalization of, 208; "A Minority View," plans for, 31, 49–56; "A Minority View," response of northern dailies, 32, 56–62; and SERS, 162, 198, 202; on Walter White, 231n83
Baron, Martin, 268n34
Bartley, Numan V., 10
Bedingfield, Sid, 180, 210
Bethune, Mary McLeod, 260n96
Bilbo, Theodore, 45, 51
"Billions for Science, Pennies for People" (*PM* newspaper), 60
Binder, Carroll, 59
Bingham, Barry, Sr., 254n7
*Birmingham News* (Alabama), and North-South press divide, 146
*Birmingham Post-Herald* (Alabama), 113
*The Birth of a Nation* (film), 147, 205–6, 249n14, 265n6
"the birth of a notion," Shoemaker on, 204–6
Bishop, Jim, 138
Black History Month, 266n19
Black Lives Matter (BLM), 212–15
Blackman, Samuel, 81–82, 84, 159–60
Black press: on Ashmore's statements, 107, 109–10; inception of, and opposition to racism, 207; newsroom integration efforts/resistance, 60, 117–18, 218n6, 226n10, 234n4, 236n27, 246n95; number of weeklies and circulation, 33; at

# INDEX

presidential briefings, 34, 227n21; on Emmett Till's murder, 142. *See also* Black press, indicting and othering of; *individual names of publications*
Black press, indicting and othering of, 28–63; Black freedom struggle of 1940s, 32–36; Blackness and Black press as "other," 30; and Brown-Oak debate, 47–49; Dabney's national magazine articles about "extremists" in Black press, 42–47, 61–62; and Double V campaign, 6, 24, 31–36, 42, 44, 61, 227n16; and "A Minority View" column, 31, 49–62; Pegler's demonization of Black press, 36–42, 61–62; World War II and critiques of Black press, overview, 28–32
"black star" editions of newspapers, 72, 237n28
"Black," terminology for, xii, 213, 217n5. *See also* terminology
Blackwell, Gordon, 168, 256n28
"Bleeding Kansas," x
Bond, Horace Mann, 118, 120
Bond, Julian, 120
Booker, Simeon, 117–18, 120, 165, 181, 196, 199, 201, 246n95, 261n106
Boston dancehall "riot," 150–51, 159
*Boston Herald*, and racial identification, 79
Bradley, Mamie (Emmett Till's mother), 144
Brandeis University, 154, 253n85
Branscomb, Harvie, 257n39
Brown, John, x, xii
Brown, Linda, x
Brown, Michael, 212
Brown, Robert, 89
Brown, Warren H., 32, 42, 43, 47–48, 230n69
*Brown v. Board of Education of Topeka* (1954): Central High School (Little Rock) enforcement of, 9, 11, 95–97, 140, 150, 156, 163, 221n38; journalistic objectivity and racial politics of segregation, 1–5; and postwar criticism of Black press, 29–31; and racial gradualism by Ashmore, 99–103, 118–22, 124; ruling, ix–x, 218n1; second *Brown* ruling

(1955), 86, 101, 137; SERS and response to *Brown* decision, 26, 161–64, 166–69, 173, 175–80, 182–86, 191–93, 196, 200; southern editors' reaction to, 132–33. *See also* Associated Press (AP) and racial identifier issue; Black press, indicting and othering of; North-South press divide; racial gradualism
Bryan, David Tenant, 80
Buffalo cruise "riot," 148–50
*Bulletin* (American Society of Newspaper Editors, ASNE): and Black press as indicted/othered, 46; on objectivity in reporting, 19, 224n66, 234n3; and SERS, 168
Byrnes, James, 101, 102, 112

Canham, Erwin, 56
Canons of Journalism (ASNE), 267n25
Carlson, Matt, 206
Carter, Hodding, Jr., 10, 13, 123
Cash, W. J., 7, 122–23, 207
Central High School (Little Rock), 9, 11, 95–97, 140, 150, 156, 163, 221n38
"The Challenge of Desegregation" (speech, Bonita Valien), 182–87
*Charleston News and Observer* (South Carolina): and North-South press divide, 138; and racial gradualism, 123
*Charlotte News* (North Carolina), and SERS, 176
*Charlotte Observer* (North Carolina): and racial gradualism, 125; and SERS, 163
*Chattanooga News-Free Press* (Tennessee): and North-South press divide, 135, 151; and racial identification, 88–89
*Chicago Daily News*, and Black press as indicted/othered, 60
*Chicago Defender*: and Black press as indicted/othered, 31, 33, 36, 38, 45, 47, 49; and North-South press divide, 142; and racial gradualism, 109
*Chicago Sun*, and Black press as indicted/othered, 41
Chicago Sunday picnic "riot," 152–54
*Chicago Tribune*: and Black press as indicted/othered, 43; and North-South

*Chicago Tribune (continued)*
  press divide, 152; and racial identification, 70, 235n12
Christians, Clifford G., 226n7
*Christian Science Monitor*: and Black press as indicted/othered, 56–57; and SERS, 182–83
Churchill, Winston, 51
Churchwell, Robert, 186, 190
Citizens' Councils of Mississippi, 144
City Club of Chicago, 70
Civil Rights Act (1964), 210
civil rights movement: and AP's pertinence policy, 84–85; Black freedom struggle of 1940s, 32–36; Black press criticized as precursor to, 29; George Lee's murder, 137; Massive Resistance movement, 124, 203, 210; Montgomery bus boycott, 138; and Randolph, 140; Streitmatter on, 221n38; and Truman, 105; Truman on civil rights, 244n54
Civil War, legacy of, 4–5, 214. *See also* journalistic objectivity; North-South press divide
*The Clansman* (Dixon), 205
Clark, Kenneth, 121–22, 168
*Clarksdale Press Register* (Mississippi), on Till trial, 250n34
Colburn, John, 139
*Collision of Power: Trump, Bezos, and the Washington Post* (Baron), 268n34
*Columbia Journalism Review*, inception of, 211
*Columbus Ledger* (Georgia), and racial identification, 89
*The Commercial Appeal* (Memphis), and SERS, 175
Commission on Freedom of the Press (Hutchins Commission), 124
Committee of 52, 180, 259n70
common sense, Stuart Hall on, 224–25n74
communism: *Daily Worker* (Communist Party), Pegler's criticism of, 37, 38; and McCarthy, 20n38, 22, 211; Waring on, 226n78
Coombs, Philip, 170, 181, 182, 187, 202, 255n9

Cooper, Kent, 237n34
Coughlin, Charles, 37, 38
Council for Democracy (CFD), 47, 49
Cowles, Fleur, 114
Cracker Party, 258n47
Crespino, Joseph, 16
crime stories in press: and deviance concept, 126, 248n2; racial identification in press and stereotyping, 69–70, 74–75, 80, 85–86, 88–90. *See also* North-South press divide; Till, Emmett
criticism of Black press (1940s). *See* Black press, indicting and othering of
Cumming, Douglas O., 134, 201, 256n18
Curry, John Steuart, x
Curry mural (Topeka), x, 217n3
Cutter, John, 108

Dabney, Virginius: *Below the Potomac: A Book about the New South*, 42; Black press as indicted/othered by, 24, 29, 30–32, 42–49, 56, 61–63; on courtesy titles, 235n17; and journalistic objectivity, 5–6, 13; on "N" capitalization, 68–69; "Nearer and Nearer the Precipice," 43, 44–45, 49; "Newspapers and the Negro," 45–46; "Press and Morale," 42–44, 47; on *Race and Reason* (Putnam), 262n123; and racial gradualism, 120–21; racial self-interest of, 207, 208; and SERS, 27, 162–64, 168, 172, 174, 176–78, 181, 183, 186–97, 199, 201–3
*Daily Republic* (Mitchell, South Dakota), and racial identification, 67
*Daily Worker* (Communist Party), Pegler's criticism of, 37, 38
*Dallas Morning News*, and Black press as indicted/othered, 57
Daniel, Pete, 205
Daniels, Jonathan, 113
Daniszewski, John, 213
*Danville Register* (Virginia), and North-South press divide, 150
Darrow, Clarence, 220n21
Davidson, Tippen, 81
Davies, David R., 18
Davis, Jackson, 53, 54, 62, 229–30n64

INDEX 273

Davis, Ken, 139, 143–46
Davis, Lawrence A., 114
*Daytona Beach Morning Journal*, and racial identification, 81
Dealey, Ted, 57
*Delta Democrat-Times* (Greenville, Mississippi): and Carter, 13–14; and racial gradualism, 123
Democratic Party, Dixiecrat rebellion of 1948, 104
*Des Moines Register* (Iowa): and Black press as indicted/othered, 59; and racial gradualism, 114
Detroit, and North-South press divide, 156. *See also individual names of publications*
*Detroit Free Press*, and North-South press divide, 156
deviance concept, 126, 248n2
Dixiecrat rebellion of 1948, 104
Dixon, Thomas, Jr., 205
Dombrowski, James, 114
Double V campaign, 6, 24, 31–36, 42, 44, 61, 227n16
Douglass, Cy, 84–85
Durham Manifesto ("A Basis for Interracial Cooperation and Development in the South: A Statement by Southern Negroes"), 34, 51
"Dynamite in Dixie" (Bishop), 138

*Ebony*, and SERS, 181
*Editor and Publisher*, and North-South press divide, 149
Edmondson, Aimee, 22–23
Edson, Peter, 107
education, rulings on. *See Brown v. Board of Education of Topeka* (1954); *Plessy v. Ferguson* (1896)
education (higher), graduate school integration: Howard University conference on, 115; at University of Arkansas, 106. *See also* racial gradualism
Egerton, John, 14, 205
Eisenhower, Dwight: *Brown* decision enforced by, 150, 151; school integration by, 11

Emory University, 154
essentialism, defined, 219n11
Ethridge, Mark, 35, 43, 57–58, 59, 233n109
evolution, Scopes trial on, 6, 132, 220nn20–21

Fair Employment Practice Committee (FEPC, later Fair Employment Practice Commission): and Black press treatment by white press, 33, 35, 42, 57; first director of, 233n109; implementation of, 10; and racial gradualism, 104, 106, 243n43
Faubus, Orval, 95
Federal Bureau of Investigation (FBI), 35–36, 40
Field, Marshall, 41, 229n47
Fisk University: and housing for Black members of SERS, 171; Institute for Race Relations, 52, 63; *Monthly Summary of Events and Trends in Race Relations*, 63, 164–65, 187–88; and Redd, 200; on SERS and objectivity importance, 167. *See also* Johnson, Charles S.
Fleeson, Doris, 104
Floyd, George, 213
Ford, Henry, II, 201
Forde, Kathy Roberts, 3
Ford Foundation: Behavioral Sciences Division, 169; Fund for the Republic, 124, 258n48. *See also* Fund for the Advancement of Education (FAE)
Foster, Luther, 200
framing theory, 256n20
Frazier, E. Franklin, 33–34
Fredrickson, George M., 205, 248–49n14
"A Free and Responsible Press" ("Hutchins Report," Commission on Freedom of the Press), 124
Fulbright, J. William, 103
Fund for the Advancement of Education (FAE, Ford Foundation): inception of, 254n7; and *The Negro and the Schools* (Ashmore, ed.), 25, 95–101, 121–24, 240n7, 241n20, 242n25; and SERS, 101, 118, 163–64, 254n7, 257n28
Fund for the Republic (Ford Foundation), 124, 258n48

Gavzer, Bernard, 154
General Education Board (GEB, Rockefeller philanthropy), 47, 52–54, 59, 62
Georgia Press Institute, 204, 205
Gilpin, Patrick, 255n9
Goffman, Erving, 256n20
Goldfield, David, 4
Gordon, William, 255n14
Gould, Alan: AP roles of, 66, 234–35n8; and North-South press divide, 129–30, 134–37, 139–46, 148, 152, 154, 155, 158, 159, 160; on pertinence policy, 213; and racial identification, 66, 76, 78–80, 82–83, 85, 88–89, 91; Wechsler's complaint to, 209. *See also* Associated Press (AP)
gradualist stance. *See* racial gradualism
Gramscian common sense, Stuart Hall on, 224–25n74
Granger, Lester, 115
Grant, Walter, 150–51
Graves, John Temple, II, 35, 113–14, 121
Greene, Percy, 194
*Greenville News* (South Carolina), and racial gradualism, 112
Griffith, D. W., 147, 205–6, 215, 249n14. *See also The Birth of a Nation* (film)

Hall, Grover, Jr.: and journalistic objectivity, 9; on northern press and racial hypocrisy, 133–35, 145–46, 152–54, 156–57, 249n16, 249n53, 251n41; and SERS, 168
Hall, Stuart, 224–25n74, 237n32
Hallin, Daniel C., 248n2
Hancock, Gordon B., 34
"Happenings among Colored People" (Shackelford), 186
Harkey, Ira, 235n13, 242n34
Harper, John, 148
*Harper's*: and journalistic objectivity, 8, 19; and North-South press divide, 154
Harris, George, 104
Harris, Roy V., 174–76, 258nn47–48
Harwell, Coleman "Colie," 189, 200
Hawkins, Lew: and North-South press divide, 134–35, 137–38, 145–46, 148, 249n23; and racial identification, 82–83, 85–86, 89
Hayes, Roland, 45
Hays, Brooks, 103
Hearst International News Service, and United Press (UP)/United Press International (UPI), 75–76
Hearst newspapers: and criticism of Black press, 36–37, 43; King Features Syndicate, 123, 138, 183; and North-South press divide, 138
*Hearts and Minds: The Anatomy of Racism from Roosevelt to Reagan* (Ashmore), 125
Heath, Dorothy, 66, 66
Heiskell, J. N., 94
Henry Holt and Company, 62
Herbers, John, 76
Herbert, Bob, 61
Herrick, Gene, 250n34
Highlander Folk School (Tennessee), 122, 225n78
hoax claim, about Emmett Till's death, 139–40, 142
Hobson, Fred C., Jr., 12
Horton, Myles, 122
Houston, Benjamin, 171, 258n41
Howard University: Ashmore's speech, 95, 115–21, 246n90; "A Conference on the Courts and Racial Integration in Education" (April 1952), 115–21; Pegler's criticism of, 38; and Rayford Logan, 227n14
Hughes, Langston, 45
Hunt, Tanner, 76
Hutchins, Robert M., 17, 124
"Hutchins Report" ("A Free and Responsible Press," Commission on Freedom of the Press/Hutchins Commission), 124

Institute for Race Relations, Fisk University, 63. *See also* Johnson, Charles S.
International News Service, 131
interpretive reporting, 54, 234n3
"Is the Negro Newspaper Here to Live or Die?" (symposium, Lincoln University School of Journalism), 37–38

# INDEX

*Jackson Advocate* (Mississippi), and SERS, 194
*Jackson Daily News* (Mississippi), and North-South press divide, 143–44
Jaffe, Louis, 235n16
James, Weldon, 179
*Jet*: and North-South press divide, 137; and SERS, 165, 181, 196
Jim Crow. *See* segregation
"John Smith, Negro, in the Tribune" (City Club of Chicago), 70
Johnson, Charles S.: "Billions for Science, Pennies for People," 60; and Black press as indicted/othered, 24; death of, 199–200, 203; Gilpin on, 255n9; marginalization of, 208; *The Messenger* and articles by, 232n90; "A Minority View," plans for, 31, 49–56; "A Minority View," response of northern dailies, 32, 56–62; *New York Times Magazine* opinion piece by, 203; SERS role of, 27, 161–64, 169–73, 181–84, 186–93, 196, 198–99, 201–3, 261–62n109; and Southern Regional Council, 228n24; and Southern Sociological Society, 257n34
Johnson, Malcolm, 81
Johnson, Marie, 186
*Journal and Guide* (Norfolk, Virginia): and Black press as indicted/othered, 37–38, 41, 45; and SERS, 161, 171, 196, 199
journalism, practice of: AP's style influence on, 27, 72, 77, 87, 131, 237–38nn38–39; interpretive reporting, 54, 234n3; and newsprint rationing during World War II, 57, 61, 62, 233n107; newsroom integration efforts/resistance, 60, 117–18, 218n6, 226n10, 234n4, 236n27, 246n95; normative function of press, 226n7; reporter pools, 253n83. *See also* Associated Press (AP); Black press; journalistic objectivity; North-South press divide
journalistic objectivity: Gould on journalistic accuracy, 142; and ideology of segregation, 9–14; as journalism standard, Ashmore on, 98; and *The Kerner Report*, 211; "metajournalistic discourse," Carlson on, 206; objectivity, constructing and conferring, 16–19, 214; racial and regional divides, 5–9; and racial politics of segregation, overview, 1–5; reframing history for understanding of, 14–16, 22–23; theorizing of, 19–21. *See also* Associated Press (AP) and racial identifier issue; Black press, indicting and othering of; North-South press divide; racial gradualism; Southern Education Reporting Service (SERS); terminology
*Journal of Negro Education*: and school desegregation, 115, 120; and SERS, 196
Julius Rosenwald Fund, 52

Kansas: "Bleeding Kansas," x; Topeka School Board, x. *See also Brown v. Board of Education of Topeka* (1954)
*Kansas City Star*: and Black press as indicted/othered, 59; and racial identification, 76
Kaplan, Richard L., 21
Kempton, Murray, 141, 251n41
*The Kerner Report (Report of the National Advisory Commission on Civil Disorders)*, 211, 235n74
Kilpatrick, James J., 10, 11, 13, 123, 124, 133, 134, 138
King, Martin Luther, Jr., 122
King Features Syndicate (Hearst), 123, 138, 183
Kirkpatrick, W. S., 65–67
Klibanoff, Hank, 8, 97, 253n83, 254n1
Kluger, Richard, 101–2, 119
Ku Klux Klan, 205, 205n2, 217n2

labor: Pegler on, 32, 37; Randolph and March on Washington Movement, 33–34, 38, 42, 44
Larsen, Roy, 163
Lassiter, Matthew D., 16
Laura Spelman Rockefeller Memorial, 52
Lee, George W., 137
Lee, Robert E., 215
Legal Defense Fund (NAACP), 95, 102, 115, 169

Leidholdt, Alexander, 235n16
Leuchter, Ben, 81–82
Leverty, Bill, 139
*Life*, and North-South press divide, 143
Lincoln University, 37–38, 118, 218n6, 226n10
Lippmann, Walter, 16–17, 59, 99, 163, 223n55
"Little Rock Editor Faced Down Segregationists" (NPR), 97
Logan, Charles, 64, 66, 66, 75, 210, 235n12
Logan, Rayford W., 32, 227n14
*Look*, and SERS, 195
*Los Angeles Tribune*, and Black press as indicted/othered, 39
*Louisville Courier-Journal* (Kentucky): and Black press as indicted/othered, 57; and SERS, 179
*The Louisville Story* (James), 179
*Loving v. Virginia* (1967), xii
Lowery, Wesley, 213, 214, 268n34
lynchings: and Dabney's rhetoric, 45; Oak on, 48. *See also* Till, Emmett

*Macon News* (Georgia), and North-South press divide, 127, 134
*Madisonville Messenger* (Kentucky), and North-South press divide, 129
Mahaffey, J. Q., 88
"man in the middle," and Ashmore, 94, 98, 240n2
March on Washington Movement, 33–34, 38, 42, 44
Marshall, Thurgood, 95, 115, 119–20, 125, 246n90
Martin, Trayvon, 212
Massive Resistance movement, 124, 203, 210
Maxwell, Angie, 7, 239n67
McCarthy, Joseph, 22, 211, 250n38
McCormick, Robert, 70
McDonald, Roy, 135
McGill, Ralph, 13, 34, 113, 163, 254n7
McGrath, R. L., 56
McKelway, Ben, 253n85
McKnight, C. A.: and racial gradualism, 125; and SERS, 162–63, 167–69, 171, 173, 176–78, 180–84, 187, 189, 196, 202, 260n89, 261–62n109, 261n103
McMath, Sid, 103–4, 106, 110–11
meaning, politics of. *See* racial gradualism
media framing theory, 256n20
Meek, H. T., 65
*Memphis Commercial Appeal*, and North-South press divide, 146
Mencken, H. L., 6–8, 220nn20–21
*The Messenger*, Charles Johnson's contributions to, 232n90
"metajournalistic discourse," Carlson on, 206
Methodist Publishing House, 189
*Miami Herald*, and SERS, 163
Mickelson, Paul, 80, 83–84, 128, 149, 154, 155, 157
military: Dabney on, 46; Pegler on, 40–41; Truman's integration of, 10, 64
Miller, Doris, 46
*Milwaukee Journal*, and Black press as indicted/othered, 59
Mindich, David T. Z., 18, 20, 223–24n63
*The Mind of the South* (Cash), 7, 122–23, 207
*Minneapolis Star-Journal and Tribune*, and Black press as indicted/othered, 59
"A Minority View" column: Barnett's and Charles Johnson's plans for, 31, 49–56; response of northern dailies to, 32, 56–62
*Montgomery Advertiser* (Alabama): "Askelon" series, 134–35, 145, 249n16; and journalistic objectivity, 9; and North-South press divide, 133–35, 145, 152; and SERS, 168
Montgomery bus boycott, 138
*A Monthly Summary of Events and Trends in Race Relations* (Institute for Race Relations, Fisk University), 63, 164–65, 187–88, 255n13
Morrisey, A. A., 255n14
Moss, Charles, 170, 175, 182, 189, 202, 261n99
"Moynihan Report" (U.S. Department of Labor), and dysfunctional-family stereotype, 235n11

mural (Topeka), x, 217n3
Myrdal, Gunnar, 7–8, 49, 58, 105

*Nashville Banner*, and SERS, 170, 175, 181, 182, 186, 189, 190, 195, 201, 260–61n96, 263n135
National Association for the Advancement of Colored People (NAACP): advocacy focus of, 236n21; on *Birth of a Nation* (film), 205; criticism of, by white southerners, 12; Legal Defense Fund, 95, 102, 115, 169; *Nashville Banner* on, 263n135; and North-South press divide, 140; on racial identifier issue, 69–70; and Walter White, 94, 110, 115, 122, 231n83, 237n33; and white criticism of Black press, 36, 42, 44; and Young's resignation from SERS, 196
National Association of Intergroup Relations Officials, 182–83
National Council of Negro Women (NCNW), 185–86, 260–61n96
National Negro Publishers Association (NNPA), 39, 227n21
National Newspaper Publishers Association, 195, 263n136
National Urban League, 52
*Native Son* (Wright), 48
NBC Radio, and racial gradualism, 121–22
"N" capitalized in "Negro," 68–69, 87, 235n16, 237–38nn38–39
*The Negro and the Schools* ("Ashmore Report," Ashmore, ed.), 25, 95–102, 121–24, 163–64, 170, 179, 240n7, 241n20, 242n25
Negro identifier practice. *See* Associated Press (AP) and racial identifier issue
"A Negro Looks at the Negro Press"/"A Negro Warns the Negro Press" (Brown), 47–48
"Negro problem," 226n5
Newkirk, Bill, 86
*News and Courier* (Charleston, South Carolina): on communism, 226n78; and journalistic objectivity, 8, 13, 19; and North-South press divide, 134, 154; and racial gradualism, 113; and racial identification, 74, 87; and SERS, 162, 171, 172, 179–80, 201; and "The Southern Case against Segregation" (Waring), 258n43
Newsfeatures (AP), 145, 148
newsroom integration, 60, 117–18, 218n6, 226n10, 234n4, 236n27, 246n95. *See also* journalism, practice of
New York City Council, on racial identification in crime stories, 69
*New York Daily News*: and Black press as indicted/othered, 43; and North-South press divide, 149
*New York Herald Tribune*: and North-South press divide, 149; and racial gradualism, 125
*New York Journal American*: and Black press as indicted/othered, 37; and North-South press divide, 138
*New York Post*: and North-South press divide, 139, 141, 142; and Poston, 141, 251n41; and Wechsler, 209
*New York Times*: and Black press as indicted/othered, 61; Lowery's opinion piece in, 213; and racial gradualism, 97, 104, 113, 123; and racial identification, 69, 70
*New York Times Magazine*, Johnson's opinion piece in, 203
*New York World-Telegram*, and Black press as indicted/othered, 32, 37
*Nieman Reports*, and racial gradualism, 106
"Nigger-Loving Boogie" (song), 125
*Norfolk Journal and Guide* (Virginia): and journalistic objectivity, 27; and SERS, 191, 201. *See also* Young, P. B., Sr.
*Norfolk Virginian-Pilot*, "N" capitalized in "Negro," 68–69, 87, 235n16
normative function of press, 226n7
North-South press divide, 126–60; and AP framework, 131–33; and Ashmore's career ambition, 94–95; and Associated Press (AP) and racial identifier issue, 87–90, 91–92, 239n67; Blackman on, 159–60; Grover Hall on northern racial hypocrisy, 133–35, 145–46, 152–54,

North-South press divide (*continued*) 156–57, 249n16, 249n53, 251n41; and hypocrisy of northern white press accusation as diversionary tactic, 208–9; "A Minority View," 31, 32, 49–62; as "paper curtain," 9, 26, 134, 208, 221n28, 239n67; racial barriers of, xi; and "riot" complaints, 147–55; segregationist AP members on news judgment and policy, overview, 26, 126–30, 157–60; Theoharis on, 222n48; and Emmett Till murder and trial, 126, 133, 135, 138–46, 250n34; white press (southern), segregated text/images and "black star" editions, 72, 237n28

NPR, "Little Rock Editor Faced Down Segregationists," 97

Oak, V. V., 32, 43, 47, 48–49
objectivity in journalism. *See* journalistic objectivity
Odum, Howard, 228n24
Omi, Michael, 4, 167, 219n11
"one-drop rule," 237n33
*Opportunity* (National Urban League), and Black press as indicted/othered, 52
Orton, Alvin, 129
"othering": AP and racial identification debate, 74, 237n32; Blackness and Black press as "other," 30; by white southerners, 7. *See also* Associated Press (AP) and racial identifier issue; Black press, indicting and othering of
"Our Answer Is No" *(Baltimore Afro-American)*, 197–98, 201–2

"paper curtain," 9, 26, 134, 208, 221n28, 239n67
Parham, Joe, 127, 134–35
Park, Robert E., 52
Parks, Rosa, 122, 138
*Pascagoula (Mississippi) Chronicle*, racism condemned by, 235n13, 242n34
Patterson, Robert B., 178, 253n83
Pegler, Westbrook: AP and racial identification, 69; and Black press as indicted/othered, 24; Black press as indicted/othered by, 29, 30–32, 43, 47–49, 61; "Fair Enough" syndicated column, 36–42; and journalistic objectivity, 6; and racial gradualism, 123; racial self-interest of, 207; and SERS, 183–84

*People's Voice*, funding of, 229n47
pertinence policy, Associated Press (AP), 67, 77–89, 213
*Philadelphia Bulletin*, and North-South press divide, 155
Philadelphia children's "riot," 154–55
*Philadelphia Inquirer*, and North-South press divide, 155
Philander Smith College, 110
Phillips, Harmon, 80
*Pittsburgh Courier*: and Black press as indicted/othered, 28, 31–34, 36, 38, 48, 49; Double V campaign of, 6, 24, 31–36, 42, 44, 61, 227n16; and racial gradualism, 109, 111–12, 118
*Plessy v. Ferguson* (1896), 10, 44, 98, 102, 106, 115, 116, 218n1, 266n16
*PM* newspaper, "Billions for Science, Pennies for People," 60
Popham, Johnny, 104, 113
Poston, Ted, 141, 251n41
*Post-Register* (Idaho Falls, Idaho), and racial identification, 235n12
postwar criticism of Black press. *See* Black press, indicting and othering of
Pound, Ezra, 251n49
Powell, Adam Clayton, Jr., 229n47
Poynter, Nelson, 113
Prattis, P. L., 28
President's Committee on Civil Rights (Truman administration), 104
Price, Bem, 145–46, 148
Price, Byron, 77, 83, 91
Publishers Newspaper Syndicate, 60–61
Pulitzer, Joseph, 234n4
Pulitzer Prize, 32, 95
Putnam, Carleton, 262n123

*Quill*, and Black press as indicted/othered, 46

race, racism, and race relations, 204–15; citizenship of Black Americans as conditional, 29–31, 40, 49, 50, 61, 62; essentialism, defined, 219n11; "evolutionary processes" to raise standard of living, 43–44; foregrounding whiteness to reframe history of, 209–12; and hypocrisy of northern white press accusation as diversionary tactic, 208–9; "inter-racial cooperation," 34; *Loving v. Virginia* (1967), xii; "Negro problem," 226n5; "one-drop rule," 237n33; racial "passing," 75, 237n33; reckoning of, 212–15; and "replacement theory," 214–15; and Shoemaker on "the birth of a notion," 204–6; whiteness concept, 219n9; and white prerogative, 206–8; white southern identity, significance of, 222n50; white supremacy, terminology for, 266n15; World War II and impact of, 221n30. *See also* Associated Press (AP) and racial identifier issue; Black press, indicting and othering of; journalistic objectivity; North-South press divide; racial gradualism; segregation; Southern Education Reporting Service (SERS); stereotyping in the white press; terminology

*Race and Reason: A Yankee View* (Putnam), 262n123

*The Race Beat: The Press, the Civil Rights Struggle, and the Awakening of a Nation* (Roberts and Klibanoff), 97

Race Relations Information Center (RRIC), 254n8, 265n1

racial gradualism, 93–125; and Ashmore's Howard University speech, 95, 115–21, 246n90; Ashmore's positions, misinterpretation of, 93–98, 120–25, 240–41n8; and Ashmore's Southern Governors' Conference speech, 102–15, 243n40, 244n47; and Associated Press (AP) and racial identifier issue, 92; gradualism, defined, 94; misinterpretation of Ashmore's statements, 25; and *The Negro and the Schools* (a.k.a. "Ashmore Report," Ashmore), 25, 95–102, 121–24, 240n7, 241n20, 242n25

racial identifier issue. *See* Associated Press (AP) and racial identifier issue

Ragan, Sam, 156

*Raleigh News and Observer* (North Carolina): and North-South press divide, 156; and racial gradualism, 113

Randolph, A. Philip, 33–34, 140. *See also* March on Washington Movement

Rankin, John, 45, 51

Rawls, John, 224n69

Rayburn, Sam, 104, 107, 108

*Reader's Digest*, and Black press as indicted/othered, 47

Redd, George, 200

Reese, Ben, 65, 234n4, 250n28

regional bias allegations. *See* North-South press divide

Reid, Mrs. Ogden, 125

"replacement theory," 214–15

*Report of the National Advisory Commission on Civil Disorders (The Kerner Report)*, 211, 239n74

*Richmond News-Leader* (Virginia): and journalistic objectivity, 10, 13; and North-South press divide, 133, 138; and racial gradualism, 123

*Richmond Times-Dispatch* (Virginia): and Black press as indicted/othered, 42, 47, 56; and journalistic objectivity, 6, 13; and North-South press divide, 139; and racial gradualism, 120; and racial identification, 68, 80; and SERS, 162, 193–94, 199, 201. *See also* Dabney, Virginius

"riot" complaints and North-South press divide: Asbury Park "riot," 148; Boston dancehall "riot," 150–51, 159; Buffalo cruise "riot," 148–50; Chicago Sunday picnic "riot," 152–54; Philadelphia children's "riot," 154–55; and "rioting" term, 147

Riviea, Alec, 255n14

Roberts, Gene, 8, 97, 253n83, 254n1

Robeson Paul, 59

Rockefeller Foundation: and Jackson Davis, 229–30n64; General Education Board (GEB), 47, 52–54, 59, 62; and Sulzberger, 53

Roosevelt, Franklin: and Black journalists

Roosevelt, Franklin (*continued*)
  at presidential briefings, 34; Fair Employment Practices Committee, 10, 33, 37, 233n109; *Monthly Summary of Events and Trends in Race Relations*, 63, 164–65, 255n13
Rose Bowl/football analogy, 166, 255n16
*Roundtable* (NBC Radio), and racial gradualism, 121–22
Rowan, Carl T., 60–61
Russwurm Awards (National Newspaper Publishers Association), 195
Ryan, Michael, 20

"The Sahara of the Bozart" (Mencken, *Baltimore Evening Sun*), 6
*Saturday Review of Literature*, and Black press as indicted/othered, 29, 32, 42–43, 47, 48, 230n69
Scanlon, John, 170
Schudson, Michael, 17, 21, 234n2
Scopes trial, 6, 132, 220nn20–21
Scripps-Howard newspapers: on Ashmore's statements, 107; and criticism of Black press, 36–37; and United Press (UP)/United Press International (UPI), 75–76
*Seattle Times*, and Black press as indicted/othered, 56
segregation: Ethridge on southern retrenchment of, 34–35; examples of, 171, 257n30, 258n41; identity and "othering," 7, 30, 74, 237n32; Pegler on "segregated circulation," 37; *Plessy v. Ferguson* (1896) on "separate-but-equal public education," 10, 44, 98, 102, 106, 115, 116, 218n1, 266n16; Shoemaker on "segregation" and "desegregation," 2; and stereotyping in the white press, 70–75, 90–91. *See also* Associated Press (AP) and racial identifier issue; Black press, indicting and othering of; *Brown v. Board of Education of Topeka* (1954); North-South press divide; *Plessy v. Ferguson* (1896); racial gradualism; Southern Education Reporting Service (SERS)

Shackelford, W. H., 186
Sheppard, Sam, 139
Shoemaker, Don: *With All Deliberate Speed*, 179; on "birth of a notion," 204–6; and Branscomb, 257n39; career of, 218n1; and journalistic objectivity, 1–3; and Massive Resistance, 210; Rose Bowl/football analogy of, 166, 255n16; and SERS, 25, 26, 162–68, 171–72, 178–81, 187–90, 193, 194, 196, 199–203, 261–62n109, 261n108; on "the birth of a notion," 204–6
Sigma Delta Chi (Society of Professional Journalists), 46, 211, 267n25
*Simple Justice* (Kluger), 101–2
Smith, J. Douglas, 46
Smith, Lamar, 138
Smith, Lillian, 1
Smith, Miles, 85, 86
*Social Justice* (Coughlin's publication), and antisemitism, 37–38
Society of Professional Journalists (Sigma Delta Chi), 46, 211, 267n25
Sokol, Jason, 4–5, 12
Sokolsky, George, 123
"Some Major Problems Involved in Racial Integration with Especial Reference to Education in the South" (speech, Ashmore), 95, 115, 119–20, 125, 246n90
Southern Conference Educational Fund (SCEF), 114
Southern Education Reporting Service (SERS), 161–203; biracial makeup and uneven power of, 161–62, 165–67, 169–73, 179–80, 260n88; and *Brown* decision, 26, 161–64, 166–69, 173, 175–80, 183–86, 191–93, 196, 200; and Charles Johnson's death, 199–200, 203; Committee of 52, 180, 259n70; and FAE's role in, 101, 118, 163–64, 254n7, 257n28; inception of, 26, 161; mission of, 26–27, 63, 164–67; objectivity as debated by, 173–79, 186–89, 200–203; P. B. Young, Sr.'s resignation from, 191–99, 263n132; as Race Relations Information Center (RRIC) precursor, 254n8, 265n1; and racial gradualism, 118; Bonita

Valien fired by, 27, 180–92, 201–3, 260n89, 260n92, 261–62n109, 261n103. *See also* Dabney, Virginius; Fund for the Advancement of Education (FAE, Ford Foundation); Johnson, Charles S.; McKnight, C. A.; *Southern School News* (SERS); Valien, Bonita; Young, P. B., Sr.
Southern Governors' Conference (speech, Ashmore): content/context of, 102–7, 243n40, 244n47; misinterpretation of, 112–15; press coverage of, 107–12
*Southern Packet*, and racial gradualism, 107
Southern Political Science Association, 107
Southern Regional Council, 228n24
*Southern School News* (SERS): audience of, 167–69, 188; and Black press as indicted/othered, 63; content of, 161, 163–67, 170–73, 180, 181; mission of, 1–2; objectivity of, as debated by SERS, 173–79, 186–89, 200–203; SERS board, biracial makeup and uneven power of, 161–62, 165–67, 169–73, 179–80; SERS board, P. B. Young, Sr.'s resignation, 191–99, 263n132; Bonita Valien's speech about, 182–87
Southern Sociological Society, 257n34
*St. Louis Post-Dispatch*, and racial identification, 65, 67, 250n28
*St. Petersburg Times* (Florida), and racial gradualism, 113
Starzel, Frank, 149, 150–51, 159
stereotyping in the white press: crime stories and racial identification, 69–70, 74–75; dysfunctional-family stereotype, 67, 235n11; identifying white people as Black as libelous, 77, 83, 86, 91, 238n40; pertinence policy of AP, 67, 77–89, 213; and segregation practices, 70–75, 90–91. *See also* Associated Press (AP) and racial identifier issue; crime stories in press; North-South press divide
Stevenson, Adlai, 95
Stokes, Thomas L., 104, 107–8, 110–11
Streitmatter, Rodger, 221n38
Strider, H. C., 139, 140

Suggs, Henry Lewis, 262n115
Sulzberger, Arthur Hays, 53–54

Talmadge, Eugene, 45
Talmadge, Herman, 1, 112, 178
"Tell It Not in Gath, Publish It Not in the Streets of Askelon" ("Askelon" series, *Montgomery Advertiser*), 134–35, 145, 249n16
*Tennessean* (Nashville), and SERS, 186, 189, 200, 260–61n96
terminology: "Black" vs. "African American," xii; capitalization of "B" in "Black," 213, 217n5; courtesy titles, 96, 235n17; "N" capitalized in "Negro," 68–69, 87, 235n16, 237–38nn38–39; "Negro" designation in press, 3; "rioting," 147; Shoemaker on "segregation" and "desegregation," 2; "white," xii, 217n5; white supremacy, 266n15
*Texarkana Gazette* (Texas), and racial identification, 88
"The Courts and Racial Integration in Education" (Howard University conference), 95, 115, 119–20, 125, 246n90
*The Negro and Race Relations* (textbook), 62
"The Negro Family: The Case for National Action" ("Moynihan Report," U.S. Department of Labor), and dysfunctional-family stereotype, 235n11
Theoharis, Jeanne, 16, 222n48
Thomas, Rex, 152, 153
Thompson, Charles, 115–16, 118–19, 162, 196–97
Thurmond, Strom, 210
Till, Emmett: AP and racial identification, 88, 89; hoax claim about death of, 139–40, 142; and journalistic objectivity of murder, overview, 8, 209; murder and trial, North-South press divide on coverage of, 126, 133, 135, 138–46, 250n34; Pegler on murderers of, 41; "wolf-whistling" allegation, 144, 205, 265n9
Till, Louis (father of Emmett Till), 143–45, 251n49

Till-Mobley, Mamie Bradley (mother of Emmett Till), 144
*Time*: and Black press as indicted/othered, 39; and racial gradualism, 104; and SERS, 183
Tindall, George, 6
Tobias, Channing, 53
*Toledo Blade*, and racial identification, 85, 86
Topeka School Board (Kansas), x. *See also Brown v. Board of Education of Topeka* (1954)
*To Secure These Rights* (Truman administration), 104
"Triplets Born, Dad Is 'Stork'" *(Baltimore Sun)*, 67, 235n12
Truman, Harry, 64; on civil rights, 105, 244n54; and FEPC, 104, 243n43; military integration by, 10, 64; and racial gradualism, 104–6, 110; second term declined by, 244n51
Tucher, Andie, 212
Tuchman Gaye, 17
*Tulsa Tribune*, and racial identification, 80
Tuskegee University, 200

*Uncle Tom's Cabin*, 134
United Press (UP)/United Press International (UPI): on Ashmore's statements, 107–9; and North-South press divide, 131; and racial identifier issue, 75–76
University of Arkansas, 106
University of Chicago, 121–22
U.S. Department of Labor, 235n11
*U.S. News and World Report*, "When Negroes Move North: Many Problems of the South-and Others, Too-Come with Them," 133
U.S. State Department, 95, 115, 119–20, 125, 246n90
U.S. Supreme Court: Ashmore's letter to Warren, 100; early integration cases, 234n2; *Loving v. Virginia* (1967), xii. *See also Brown v. Board of Education of Topeka* (1954); *Plessy v. Ferguson* (1896)

Valentine, Harold, 250n34
Valien, Bonita: and Black press as indicted/othered, 59, 63; Gilpin on, 255n9; SERS and Boston speech by, 182–87; SERS and firing of, 27, 170, 180–92, 201–3, 206, 260n89, 260n92, 261–62n109, 261n103; SERS role of, 162, 164, 172–80
Valien, Preston, 255n9
Veil of Ignorance, Rawls on, 224n69
Vos, Tim P., 17
Voting Rights Act (1965), 210
Vultee, Fred, 238n39

W. W. Norton, 122
Ward, Jason Morgan, 15
Ward, Stephen J. A., 17–18
Waring, Thomas R.: AP and racial identification, 74, 87, 92; and Committee of 52, 259n70; on communism, 226n78; and journalistic objectivity, 8–9, 13, 14, 19, 22; and North-South press divide, 134, 138, 144, 154–55, 253n85; on "paper curtain," 221n28; and racial gradualism, 123; and SERS, 27, 162, 164, 172–77, 178–79, 182–84, 186–87, 197, 199–202; "The Southern Case against Segregation," 258n43
Warren, Earl, 100
Washburn, Patrick S., 35
Washington, Booker T., 191
*Washington Evening Star*, and racial gradualism, 118
*Washington Post: Collision of Power: Trump, Bezos, and the Washington Post* (Baron), 268n34; and racial gradualism, 117, 120; and SERS, 165
*Washington Star*, and racial gradualism, 104
*Washington Times-Herald*, and Black press as indicted/othered, 43
Wechsler, James, 139–43, 145, 209, 251n41
Wendell Wilkie Awards for Distinguished Writing by Negro Journalists, 262n115
Whalen, John, 67–68, 71
"When Negroes Move North: Many Problems of the South-and Others,

INDEX                                                              283

Too-Come with Them" *(U.S. News and World Report)*, 133
White, Walter, 94, 110, 115, 122, 231n83, 237n33
White, William Allen, x
White Citizens' Council (WCC), 1, 173, 178, 180, 198
Whitehead, Don, 104, 108, 112
whiteness, concept of, 219n9
white press. *See* North-South press divide; *individual names of publications*
white southern identity, significance of, 222n50
white supremacy, terminology for, 266n15. *See also* race, racism, and race relations
"white," terminology for, xii, 217n5. *See also* terminology
Wilkins, Roy, 196, 234n123
Willett, Henry, 260n88
Williams, Roger M., 258n43
Winant, Howard, 4, 167, 219n11
Wirephoto (AP), 64–67, 66, 76, 86, 89
*With All Deliberate Speed* (Shoemaker, ed.), 179
"wolf-whistling" allegation, against Till, 144, 205, 265n9

Woods, Jeff, 22
Woodward, C. Vann, 221n30
Workman, William, 113, 171, 179–80, 182–83, 186, 202
World War II: Charles Johnson on racism following, 51; Double V campaign, 6, 24, 31–36, 42, 44, 61, 227n16; newsprint rationing during, 57, 61, 62, 233n107. *See also* Black press, indicting and othering of
Wright, Fielding, 108–9, 113, 114
Wright, Mose, 141, 142, 143
Wright, Richard, 48

Young, P. B., Sr.: award nomination, 262n115; and Black press as indicted/othered, 41, 45, 63; marginalization of, 208; SERS resignation by, 191–99, 263n132; SERS role of, 27, 161, 162, 164, 168, 171–73, 179, 182–84, 186, 200–203, 260n88
Young, Thomas, 37, 195
Younge, Gary, 266n19
Ypsilanti (Michigan) triplets, 64–67, 66, 72, 75, 86, 89

GWYNETH MELLINGER is professor of Media Arts & Design at James Madison University, where she teaches courses on media ethics and the media's impact on society. Her first book, *Chasing Newsroom Diversity: From Jim Crow to Affirmative Action* (2013), won the Frank Luther Mott Kappa Tau Alpha book award. Her scholarship on civil rights-era media history has received various awards and funding support, including the 2019 Ronald T. and Gayla D. Farrar Award from the University of South Carolina. She is co-editor of *Journalism's Ethical Progression: A Twentieth-Century Journey* (2019).

www.ingramcontent.com/pod-product-compliance
Lightning Source LLC
Chambersburg PA
CBHW032050230426
43672CB00009B/1548